ISLANDS OF HERITAGE

A heritage not defined — might be purposeful

NATHALIE PEUTZ

ISLANDS OF

HERITAGE

CONSERVATION AND
TRANSFORMATION IN YEMEN

STANFORD UNIVERSITY PRESS • STANFORD, CALIFORNIA

STANFORD UNIVERSITY PRESS

Stanford, California

© 2018 by the Board of Trustees of the Leland Stanford Junior University. All rights reserved.

Printed in the United States of America on acid-free, archival-quality paper

Library of Congress Cataloging-in-Publication Data

Peutz, Nathalie, 1972– author.

Islands of heritage : conservation and transformation in Yemen / Nathalie Peutz.

Stanford, California : Stanford University Press, 2018. | Includes bibliographical references and index.

LCCN 2018004658 (print) | LCCN 2018005975 (ebook) | ISBN 9781503607156 (e-book) | ISBN 9781503606395 (cloth : alk. paper) | ISBN 9781503607149 (pbk. : alk. paper) | ISBN 9781503607156 (ebook)

Soqotra (Yemen)—Social life and customs. | Cultural property—Protection—Yemen (Republic)—Soqotra. | Nature conservation—Yemen (Republic)—Soqotra. | Soqotra (Yemen)—Politics and government.

Classification: LCC DS247.7.S63 (ebook) | LCC DS247.7.S63 P48 2018 (print) | DDC 363.6/9095335—dc23

LC record available at https://lccn.loc.gov/2018004658

COVER DESIGN: Angela Moody

COVER PHOTOGRAPH: Meeting of the Association for the Conservation and Development of Homhil

Typeset by Bruce Lundquist in 10/15 Minion Pro

For Mataio, Anahita, Clio, and Makeda

CONTENTS

PREFACE

The first time I set foot in Abu Dhabi, the city where I now live, teach, and write this book, was to meet a Soqotran woman who had been exiled from her island in the early 1960s. Baqalhen (a pseudonym) had been accused of witchcraft after her wounded brother consulted a local medicine man (*mekoli*) to discover the cause of his affliction. When the *mekoli* identified the recently widowed Baqalhen as the culprit, she left Soqotra immediately. In this way, Baqalhen was able to escape the conventional trial by ordeal that the scores of Soqotran women accused of witchcraft had endured. Moreover, her "voluntary" departure allowed her to keep custody of her young daughter, whom she took first to Sur (Oman), where Baqalhen found work as a housekeeper, and later to Abu Dhabi, where she became the recipient of government housing and allowances. Although Baqalhen never remarried, her daughter eventually married an Emirati citizen with whom she bore six children. Neither Baqalhen nor her daughter ever returned to Soqotra. Nevertheless, Baqalhen sent money to her natal family repeatedly so that they could afford to dig a well and build a mosque. With her donations, they built their village's first mosque in the 1980s and a new, larger mosque in the year that I met her. Over tea in her spacious villa in a suburb of Abu Dhabi, we talked about my reception and research in Soqotra. "Why don't you stay?" she asked me. "I will build a house for you in Qayher, and you and your husband can live there forever and open a small little store or something—but only if you become Muslim." I was struck by her commanding personality. Some of her adult grandchildren appeared unaware of the reason behind her departure; however, her island relatives who had benefited unexpectedly from her newfound wealth in exile talked about it candidly. "Some blows are a blessing," one told me. *the mehra ppl.*

Until 1967, when the sovereign Sultanate of Qishn and Soqotra was absorbed into the newly independent state of South Yemen, it had not been uncommon for Soqotran women accused of witchcraft to be subjected to a trial by drowning by being thrown from a log boat into the sea with stones tied around their waists. If found guilty, by virtue of floating, they would be banished from the island via the first passing dhow. (Those who sank to the seafloor were considered innocent and hauled back to the surface before it was too late.) During the 1940s and 1950s, at what appears to have been the peak of these accusations, as many as fifteen to twenty women may have been tried and deported each year.[1] Many of these alleged witches ended up in Oman or in the United Arab Emirates (UAE), where they married into and helped establish Soqotran communities across the sea. This was a time when the British had considered developing large-scale agriculture in Soqotra, while the island of Abu Dhabi could barely source potable water. Yet, with time, before the state of South Yemen restricted travel to and from Soqotra, more and more Soqotrans left the island, settling near or among these diasporic communities born of trial. And, with time, as the humble desert ports to which these women had been "deported" were transformed into oil-rich nations, these women and their children became comparatively wealthy rent-receiving citizens on whose gifts and donations their increasingly isolated island relatives grew to depend. If banishment aimed to restore the social body during the sultanate period, it also contributed to maintaining the social—and religious—community in the years to follow as these "witches" financed the building of mosques throughout their native land.

What I find remarkable about Baqalhen's life story is less her brush with alleged sorcery than this strange twist of fate that turned a banished Soqotran pastoralist into an affluent Emirati citizen and patron. For all its arresting particularities, this is a story that is also emblematic of Yemen and its Soqotra Archipelago. It was, after all, a similar ironic twist that turned what was once deemed "Arabia Deserta," the relatively desolate part of the Arabian Peninsula, into what is now home to the region's booming cities. And what turned "Arabia Felix," the once flourishing and felicitous southern flank of the Arabian Peninsula, into today's ailing Yemen, an impoverished cousin to its northern neighbors. A severe punishment in the time of Baqalhen's youth, expatriation from Soqotra to the Arabian Gulf littoral is now the dream of many young Soqotrans for whom Abu Dhabi and other Gulf cities represent the pinnacle of progress.

This is a book about the transformations that simultaneously connect and distinguish Yemen's Soqotra Archipelago to and from the Arab Gulf States

and the Western Indian Ocean region. It begins during the period of the archipelago's postsocialist ascendance from being one of the most impoverished and
neglected regions in the Republic of Yemen to becoming, in the words of a Soqotran poet, its globally recognized crown jewel. This metamorphosis occurred
through the (re)discovery of a newly commodifiable natural resource—the
archipelago's biologically diverse flora and fauna—and the subsequent arrival
of an internationally managed environmental regime. Consequently, at the beginning of the twenty-first century, and as more and more people woke up to
the stark realities of the Anthropocene, international scientists and Gulf-based
immigrants began flocking to Soqotra again. The following story focuses on
these heady years just before and after the United Nations Educational, Scientific and Cultural Organization (UNESCO) inscribed the Soqotra Archipelago
as a World Heritage Site—at a time when Soqotrans began insisting that this
heritage belonged to them, too. It ends with Soqotrans achieving a heritage-
inspired revolution culminating in the uprisings in 2011–2012. The book's
main argument is that, despite the conservative and insular nature of heritage
making in the Arab world today, heritage can have transformative, even revolutionary, effects. Yet six years later, as I write this, the Yemeni—and Soqotran—
Revolution has ground to a halt. Moreover, after more than three years of civil
war, proxy wars, naval blockades, and air embargoes, Yemen is suffering the
severest famine and cholera outbreak of the twenty-first century. The Soqotra
Archipelago, which has become once again isolated from the Yemeni mainland, is one of the few regions of Yemen that has remained relatively unscathed.
In part, this is due to the islanders' connections with the Arab Gulf; indeed,
as if through another kind of conjuring, the UAE's interests and influence
in the island appear to be stronger than ever. But the future of the Soqotra
Archipelago—with all its biocultural diversity—is ever more uncertain. Will it
remain part of Yemen? What will become of its protected status? Will the blows
of the current war come to be considered a blessing?

ACKNOWLEDGMENTS

Moved as ever by the profound generosity and courage of the people of Yemen, I am deeply beholden to the many Yemenis, and particularly Soqotrans, who hosted, guided, and assisted me over the course of this project. My greatest debt goes to the people of the village I call Qayher. I will always be grateful to them for having enfolded me into their lives with such kindness, magnanimity, and trust. I thank the rest of the families of Homhil for their warm hospitality. I also thank the families of Rashid Ali, Shukri Nuh, and Ahmad Saʻd for opening their homes to me in Hadibo and abroad. Special thanks are owed to Fahmi Ali, Ahmad al-Anbali, Abdulrahman al-Eryani, Muhammad Di-Girigoti, Abdullah Isa, Taha Muhammad, Ali al-Rigdihi, Fahd Saleem, Ismail Salim, Tanuf Salim, Abdulraqib Shamsan, Hamad Di-min-Sirihan, Salih Umar, Muhammad Uthman, Maʻd Duʻahen, and the late Ahmad Saʻd and Muhammad Showhir for graciously sharing their wisdom, poetry, history, and genealogies and for helping me with everything from translation to transportation.

The field research and initial training for this project were made possible by generous funding from Princeton University, the Social Science Research Council (International Predissertation Fellowship Program), the Center for Arabic Studies Abroad, the American Institute for Yemeni Studies (AIYS), the Fulbright-Hays Program (Doctoral Dissertation Research Abroad Research Fellowship), Wayne State University, and New York University Abu Dhabi. The Soqotra Conservation and Development Programme aided and supported my work in numerous ways. Permission to conduct research in Yemen was granted by the Yemen Center for Studies and Research and facilitated by Dr. Chris Edens, resident director of the AIYS. In Yemen, I benefited greatly from conversations with David Buchman, Steve Caton, Carolyn Han, Matthew Hopper, Lamya Khalidi, Michele Lamprakos, Samuel Liebhaber, Miranda Morris, Maurice

Pomerantz, Marina de Regt, Nancy Um, Daniel Varisco, and other scholars passing through the AIYS's charming home away from home. The Friends of Soqotra
Association has been a godsend for researchers working in Soqotra; a special
thanks to Hugh Morris, Miranda Morris, and Kay Van Damme for their assistance. Haifa Abdulhalim and Khalifa al Khalifa from the Arab World Regional
Centre for World Heritage and Tarek Abulhawa working on behalf of the IUCN
kindly allowed me to join them during a mission to Soqotra and a workshop in
Bahrain; my debt to Tarek Abulhawa extends more than a decade.

I began this project at Princeton University, where I received exemplary
guidance from James Boon, Carol Greenhouse, Lawrence Rosen, and Carolyn
Rouse. Carolyn Rouse, the most intrepid and encouraging of mentors, took
time out of her own research to visit me in Sanaa and has continued to brighten
my home through her visits in Vermont. I started writing these chapters during a fellowship at the Council on Middle East Studies at Yale University. I am
grateful to Ellen Lust and Greta Scharnweber for their support. The Department of Anthropology at Wayne State University provided a most welcoming
and stimulating environment from which to continue this project. I thank all
of its faculty members for making my time there so enjoyable. Thanks also to
the Department of Anthropology at New York University for serving as my
academic home and for hosting me so warmly during my fellowship year in
New York. Michael Gilsenan, Bruce Grant, and, again, Greta Scharnweber provided valuable assistance; Bruce Grant and Irina Levin continue to inspire me.
I completed this manuscript as an assistant professor at New York University
Abu Dhabi during its exhilarating, inaugural years. In such a small and invigo-
rating community, there are few people to whom I am not indebted. Neverthe-
less, I thank especially Marzia Balzani, Al Bloom, Carol Brandt, Saba Brelvi,
Martin Klimke, Pascal Menoret, Judith Miller, John O'Brien, Cyrus Patell, Erin
Pettigrew, Fabio Piano, Ron Robin, Matthew Silverstein, Justin Stearns, Kate
Stimpson, Roberta Wertman, Deborah Williams, Robert Young, Shamoon
Zamir, and the late Hilary Ballon for their exceptional support during challenging periods and over the years. It has been my great fortune and honor to
be a part of this venture.

Colleagues and students from various institutions have provided useful comments on portions of this book in one form or another. Among these were the
participants at conferences and workshops at NYU Abu Dhabi, NYU Florence,

NYU New York, Brown University, Princeton University, the Smithsonian Institution, the American University of Sharjah, the Paris Sorbonne University Abu Dhabi, the French Institute in Cairo, the University of Malaysia, and AAA and MESA meetings. I thank Vladimir Agafonov, Andrew Bush, Steve Caton, Nicholas De Genova, Michael Herzfeld, Ismail Salim, Don Scott, Werner Sollers, and Tony Souter for their insightful suggestions on individual chapters. I am especially grateful to Miranda Morris, John Tallmadge, Justin Stearns, and two anonymous reviewers for reading the manuscript in its entirety and providing valuable feedback. Of course, any errors remain mine. NYUAD students Zahida Rahemtulla, Hongjun Byun, and Norbert Monti located and organized archival documents; Fadhl al-Eryani conducted first-rate research in Soqotra. I thank Kate Wahl at Stanford University Press for her enthusiasm for this project and Leah Pennywark and Anne Fuzellier for guiding the manuscript through the revision and production process. I also thank Nadia Benchallal for editing my photographs, Bill Nelson for drawing the illustrations, Cynthia Lindlof for copy-editing work, and Mary Mortensen for compiling the index.

My deepest gratitude is reserved for my family—for so many things, including their faith in my abilities and their patient endurance of this long-lived project. I thank my sisters, Tammy and Jessica, and my in-laws, Beverly and Stephen Stearns, for helping care for my children so that I could carve out time to write; Beverly especially helped us during the bleary-eyed transition to life with triplets. I also thank Apsara Perera and her family for becoming family and for taking care of my children as if they were her own. The completion of this book owes much to her own labor. My parents, Pieter Peutz and Beverly Peutz-Betz, always encouraged me to write. My father believed long before I did that I would achieve a project like this; I so wish he had lived to see the outcome, and so much more. My mother, my role-model, has always been my most enthusiastic supporter and dearest friend. My extraordinary children, Mataio, Anahita, Clio, and Makeda, grew up alongside this book as if it were yet another sibling. I thank them all. Finally, there is one person whom I cannot thank enough—Justin Stearns, my partner in all things, who accompanied me to Soqotra; assisted me at every stage of this project; and anchored our family as I traveled and worked. Without him none of this would have come to fruition; *des solt dû gewis sîn.*

NOTE ON LANGUAGE, TRANSLITERATION, AND CONFIDENTIALITY

In Soqotra, speakers shift regularly between Soqotri, Arabic dialects (Southern Yemeni Arabic or Gulf Arabic), and standard Arabic, depending on the context. Soqotri, with its six dialects,[2] is one of six unwritten Eastern South Semitic languages spoken by minority populations on the southern borders of Yemen and Oman. Each of these Proto-Semitic languages is endangered. (Mehri and Soqotri, with some 100,000–180,000 and 50,000–75,000 speakers, respectively, are the most widely spoken, but even they are threatened by the dominant influence of Arabic.) In my research, I relied primarily on Arabic but was also immersed in a Soqotri-language environment. While many assisted me in translating Soqotri poems and phrases as well as certain Arabic terms, unless otherwise noted, all translations are my own. Because the majority of these come from Arabic, I distinguish the fewer Soqotri terms (which are predominantly from the rural dialect of the eastern region) with the following notation: [Soq.].

Despite recent efforts by linguists and several Soqotrans to develop a writing system for Soqotri using a modified Arabic alphabet, no singular orthography has been adopted for common use.[3] For this reason, and for the sake of readability, I have minimized my inclusion of both Soqotri and Arabic transliterations in the text. Where possible, I transliterate Soqotri terms following the systems used by Morris (2002) or Naumkin and Kogan (2015). Elsewhere, I transliterate Soqotri terms and names using the same the system recommended by the *International Journal of Middle East Studies* for the transliteration of Arabic. Although this system does not accommodate all of Soqotri's ejective consonants and other unique phonemes without the introduction of special characters, I rely on it for simplification. Similarly, in my transliterations of Arabic, I do not use diacritics or long vowel markers, with the exception of the glottal stop *hamza* (') and the pharyngeal *ayn* ('): *ta marbuta* is transliterated as "a" (with the exception of some place-names). Likewise, I use anglicized plurals in place of broken plurals (e.g., fatwas, not *fatawa*; Soq. *mekolis*, not *mekilhitin*), but retain plurals with regular endings (e.g., *shamali/shamaliyin*). For common names of people and places, I use the conventional English spelling: for example, Ali Abdullah Saleh (for ʿAlī ʿAbdullāh Ṣāliḥ) and Sanaa (for Ṣanʿāʾ). I do, however, preserve the definite article "al" when part of Arabic place-names, as this helps distinguish al-Mahra (the place) and the Mahra (the people). Most scholars prefer the transliteration Soqotra (with a "q") over the commonly used Socotra (with a "c"); I follow this convention but retain the spelling used in project titles or in publications (e.g., the Socotra Conservation and Development Programme).

To maintain my interlocutors' anonymity, I have used pseudonyms and altered the place-names of smaller villages. I continue to use teknonyms for elders or close acquaintances, as I did when referring to them in person: for example, Bu Yaqub (father of Yaqub) and Umm Yaqub (mother of Yaqub). Public figures (e.g., politicians, scholars, prominent poets) are identified by their real names. Those whose work or position makes it impossible to obscure their identities are identified by name or nickname, with their permission.

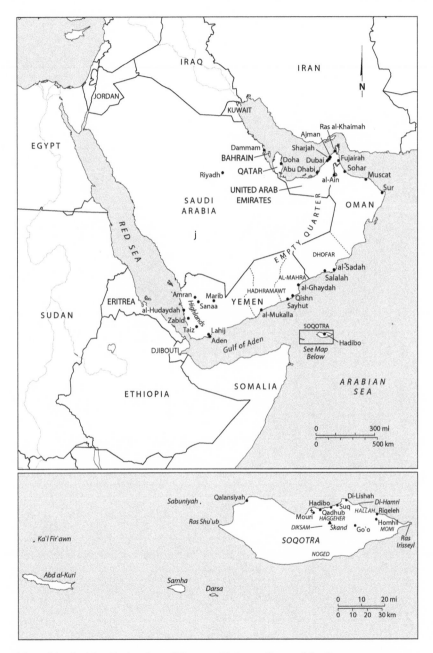

Map of the Arabian Peninsula and Yemen with inset of map of the Soqotra Archipelago showing archipelago in relation to the Arabian Peninsula and broader region.

ISLANDS OF HERITAGE

FIGURE 1. Demonstration against Yemenia airlines, Hadibo, Soqotra, 2011.

INTRODUCTION

The poets were waiting. It was a morning in late 2011—nearly a year into Yemen's revolution—and nine Soqotran poet contestants from across the island had gathered in a derelict courtyard to prepare for the opening night of the annual Festival of Soqotri Poetry. Up to that point, poetry had been a valued register through which to express local cultural ideals and political frustrations. But this was to be a turning point: emboldened by the Arab uprisings, the recitations would for the first time openly challenge the history of intrusive governance "from [across] the sea" (Soq.: *min rinhem*). I sat with the nervous poets, many of them semiliterate pastoralists, as they awaited the arrival of local teacher and activist Fahd Saleem, one of the competition's key organizers.

Meanwhile, Fahd was at the other end of town leading a protest against the national airline, Yemenia, which had relinquished its Soqotra routes to a more expensive competitor. Earlier that morning I had driven past the demonstration outside Yemenia's local office, parked my car, and got out to observe the crowd of self-proclaimed revolutionaries assembled: dozens of men and several women who were demonstrating regularly against the Saleh regime and for revolution in Yemen. Fahd was delivering an impassioned speech, bullhorn in hand, arguing that Yemenia's presumably pragmatic financial decision was a grave atrocity—all the more so because it was government sanctioned. On a distant island lacking even basic medical equipment, he declared, the absence of regular, price-controlled flights to the mainland had added a high premium to the cost of Soqotran life.

When Fahd arrived at the courtyard of poets, he gave another rousing speech, this time about the significance of the festival. Fahd described having lived through a period in which "the system" convinced Soqotrans that the use of their own language was shameful. He applauded the poets for their role in preserving Soqotran cultural heritage—especially the Soqotri language, which had been losing ground to the hegemonic spread of Arabic on the island. He decried the partisan divisions that had recently emerged among Soqotrans as they debated Yemen's uncertain future. And through concern that the competition itself would become another site of tension, he pronounced the festival a unifying event of which "the ultimate winner is Soqotra." After the address, I commended him for having organized the protest in the morning and a poetry festival that same day. "It's all part of the same work," he replied.

What is this "work" that connects a poetry festival in the name of heritage (*turath*) to a demonstration against a national airline in the name of revolution (*thawra*)? And how can we reconcile the seeming incongruity between heritage cultivation to *reduce* the effects of change by preserving cultural artifacts and traditions, and popular revolution to *achieve* significant change in political and socioeconomic conditions? Heritage, after all, is widely regarded as inherently conservative (conservationist) and nostalgic. Moreover, scholarship on the heritage industry in Arab-majority societies has focused primarily on the exclusionary and violent effects of top-down heritage projects or on their nationalist displays of political and cultural unity. This is especially the case in the Arabian Peninsula, where the engineering of heritage functions foremost as a form of nation branding by governments to kindle nationalism and cultivate tourism and, crucially, where heritage is principally a state-funded and expert-curated endeavor. In light of these conventional critiques and presentations of heritage, what can this example of grassroots mobilization at the margins of Arabia tell us about the power of heritage in the context of the Arab uprisings—and at a time when heritage sites in Yemen and other Arab-majority nations are being destroyed by dynamite and dropped bombs?

.   .   .

The Republic of Yemen is one of the poorest, hungriest, and least-developed countries in the world. Even prior to the start of the war in March 2015, Yemen was struggling. Over half of its population lived below the poverty line, surviving on less than two dollars per day. More than 40 percent of its population was malnourished, and more than 60 percent required humanitarian assistance to meet their daily basic needs.[1] In 2018, as this book goes to press, Yemen's civilians are suffering critical shortages of food, water, fuel, and medicines; a recurrent cholera epidemic; and large-scale internal displacement—in addition to the untold deaths and injuries from three years of warfare.

Yemen is also one of the world's driest countries.[2] If not for its protracted war and spreading famine, Yemen's pressing environmental problems could in themselves constitute a humanitarian crisis. The most acute of these challenges include the country's extraordinary rates of land degradation, deforestation, pollution, and, above all, groundwater depletion. Hydrologists have long predicted that Sanaa will run out of economically viable water supplies by 2020. Another way of saying this is that Sanaa, one of the oldest continuously inhabited cities in the world, may be the world's first capital to become uninhabitable for lack of water. When this happens, Yemen's environmentally displaced persons (environmental refugees) may eclipse its already unprecedented number of persons displaced by conflict.

In addition to this human suffering, Yemen's rich cultural heritage has been *war →* hit hard. Since the start of the war, some twenty-five archaeological sites and *destruction* monuments have been damaged or destroyed by aerial bombardments, includ- *of* ing the ancient dam of Marib, a museum holding more than ten thousand ar- *heritage* tifacts, mountaintop citadels, and a historic neighborhood in the Old City of *sites* Sanaa.[3] In July 2015, UNESCO placed two of Yemen's three "cultural" World Heritage Sites—the Old City of Sanaa and the Old Walled City of Shibam— onto its List of World Heritage in Danger. (Yemen's third "cultural" site, the Historic Town of Zabid, had been moved to this list a decade and half earlier due to its deterioration.) Yemen has a fourth, "natural" World Heritage Site that is not officially endangered: its biologically diverse Soqotra Archipelago. Protected as much as imperiled by its distance from the Arabian Peninsula, the archipelago is the one governorate of Yemen that has not seen armed conflict. Nevertheless, Soqotra's natural and cultural environments have been profoundly affected by Yemen's 2011 revolution and its current war.

This book examines the impact of development, conservation, and heritage projects in prewar Yemen by tracing the intersections of these projects in Soqotra, the largest island of the eponymous archipelago. Soqotra has long

been imagined by outsiders as a "protected" island, a natural enclosure for safeguarding plants and peoples. Situated at the maritime crossroads between the
Arabian Peninsula and the Horn of Africa yet inaccessible by sea during
the southwest monsoon season, it has a history of being conceived as both central to foreign interests and isolated from external events. But over the span
of a decade, this relatively remote Western Indian Ocean island—one of the
most marginalized places in Yemen—was transformed into an internationally
recognized protected area, a UNESCO World Heritage Site, and (until recently)
a prime destination for ecotourism. During this period, Soqotra's rural pastoralists accommodated and sustained a series of integrated conservation and
development projects (ICDPs) as a de facto state. They also responded to the
UNESCO World Heritage Convention's problematic nature-culture divide—
and what had effectively become the commandeering of their environment as
a global commons—by appropriating the language of heritage to claim a place
for themselves that could withstand hegemonic cultural influences. Despite its
recognition as a natural World Heritage Site—one of only a handful of such
natural sites in the Arab world—Soqotra stands out not only for its unique
biotic species but also for its indigenous inhabitants' endangered language
(Soqotri) and distinctive culture. This book investigates how the archipelago's
recent ascendance has motivated everyday Soqotrans to actively create, curate,
and mobilize their cultural heritage in a period of political upheaval to negotiate increased autonomy from the embattled Yemeni state.

WHY STUDY HERITAGE?

First-time European and American visitors to the UAE, where I live, are often
surprised by the prevalence of heritage villages, heritage festivals, and heritage
sports in the otherwise hypermodern Abu Dhabi and Dubai. "Heritage" in the
Arab Gulf, as elsewhere in the Middle East, is a central and growing industry,
attracting the attention of scholars as well as investors and tourists. At the same
time, much of the region's invaluable cultural heritage has been and continues
to be obliterated by insurgents and governments alike. Spectacular assaults on
historical sites, cultural institutions, and symbols of cultural-religious diversity
in Afghanistan, Egypt, Iraq, Libya, Mali, Saudi Arabia, Tunisia, and, more recently, Yemen suggest that the "new wars" of the twenty-first century are being

fought on the terrain of cultural heritage as much as they are over other pre-
cious resources.[4]

Yet anthropology, my discipline, continues to have an uneasy relationship with the vast assemblages of objects, places, practices, and phenomena
that are presently deemed heritage. On the one hand, many anthropologists—
archaeologists especially—have devoted their careers to discovering, researching, preserving, and protecting parts of the world's cultural legacies and
treasures. On the other hand, today's booming, global heritage industry profits
from the homogenization, fossilization, and commodification of "culture"—the
very concept that once buttressed North American (cultural) anthropology. Not
only have anthropologists yielded one of their foundational concepts to self-
critique, only to see it embraced and deployed by forces like the US military.[5]
They are also witnessing a worldwide surge in the objectification and revaluation
of "intangible heritage" by governments and other corporate entities eager to demarcate (and market) their national, cultural, or ethnic distinction while eliding
internal differences and inequalities. If historians debunk heritage as a shoddy
or sanitized form of history, anthropologists may dismiss heritage as an ossi-
fied or oppressive form of culture—another concept to critique or circumlocute
were it not that heritage has become more, not less, meaningful in the past few
decades to peoples the world over. And because UNESCO's influential World
Heritage program encompasses yet maintains as separate the realms of culture
and nature—a dualistic conception that has long plagued Western thought, as
well as anthropology[6]—we can see why heritage might make anthropologists
so uncomfortable, despite (if not due to) its common reception as a universal
good. Indeed, scholars are right to remain "deeply suspicious of heritage," notes
archaeologist Rodney Harrison, for "heritage is rarely deployed innocently, in
the absence of some form of claim toward a self-evident truth that is often divisive or exclusionary, defining the difference it specifies as a function of the past."[7]

But, as many scholars in the growing, interdisciplinary field of critical heritage studies also argue, heritage as it concerns us today is less about the preserved
past than it is about the emergent future.[8] Heritage draws on ostensibly past materials, expressions, and entanglements to assemble and mobilize a more sustainable present in anticipation of growing resource scarcity and other uncertainties.
In this sense, heritage making (and unmaking) makes the future. It is a form of
political engagement—discursive, material, and affective—with the world's most

critical and imminent concerns: identity, indigeneity, democracy, human rights, justice, reconciliation, globalization, neoliberalism, neoimperialism, sovereignty, religion, language endangerment, sustainability, resource extraction, anthropogenic climate change, and extinction. Nowhere is this more apparent than in the attacks on, over, and *by means of* cultural heritage in the Arab world today.[9]

HERITAGE, CONFLICT, AND POSSIBILITY

Cultural heritage in the Middle East and North Africa (MENA) region has long been a site of struggle against foreign domination and for political and cultural sovereignty.[10] In the early nineteenth through early twentieth centuries, European powers used the modern, scientific language of protection and conservation to justify their imperial interventions across the region. Following the breakup of the Ottoman Empire after the First World War, the fledgling governments of the emerging Arab nation-states struggled to wrest control of their museums, archaeological sites, antiquities, and other patrimony from European "protection." At the same time, in several countries, Arab nationalists debated which one of their legacies—Pharaonic, Mesopotamian, Phoenician, Islamic, Arab, Andalusi—they should draw on to consolidate their national identity. After achieving political independence in the 1940s through 1970s, many Arab states invested in cultural institutions and production as a pathway toward modernization. The professionalized, nationalized, and largely state-controlled practice of protecting cultural heritage and promoting popular folklore (*al-turath al-sha'bi*) was part of this. But the strong influence of pan-Arabism during these decades left little room for the recognition of cultural, linguistic, or religious diversity. Most newly drafted constitutions—including the 1978 constitution of the secular Marxist People's Democratic Republic of Yemen (PDRY)—designated the nation as Arab, its official language as Arabic, and its religion as Islam. This was a clear shift away from colonial policies that had suppressed Arabic language and Islam and, in places like Morocco and Algeria, had favored the indigenous (Berber) populations. Instead, the new Arab states promoted a folkloric heritage as a national unifier or relegated it to the museum, where culture difference could be contained.

Nevertheless, by the early 1970s heritage had become a central concern among Arab intellectuals who debated whether their Arab-Islamic heritage was the source of or solution to the perceived Arab stagnation.[11] In contrast to the conservative "traditionalists" who advocated a return to what they considered to be a sacred and incontrovertible Islamic *turath*, "progressive" intellectuals (both religious and secular) called for a reevaluation of inherited values and traditions to better adapt their Arab-Islamic heritage to the needs of the present. Whereas many scholars involved in these debates embarked on a critical study of *turath* with the aim of revitalizing it, several idealized the transformative power of heritage to the extent of "wanting to draw a line from *turath* to revolution."[12] The Syrian Marxist scholar Tayyib Tizini even called for a "heritagial revolution" (*al-thawra al-turathiyya*)—"meaning not only a revolution in the cognitive understanding of heritage but also a revolution grounded in the progressive elements of heritage"—as one piece of a greater cultural and socialist revolution.[13] Having surfaced in the aftermath of the 1967 Arab defeat, these debates gathered steam in the wake of the 1979 Iranian Revolution and in the context of the Islamic revival.

Around the same time, the now-global heritage industry characterized by the manufacture and marketing of heritage for economic development began to flourish in the Arab world, too. In many nations, the commodification of heritage commenced with the economic liberalization of the 1980s. It then proliferated in the 1990s and 2000s because of, among other factors, the end of the Cold War and the corresponding decrease in foreign funding to the region, an increase in US military and cultural power in the region following the 1990 Gulf War, the end of civil wars in Lebanon and Algeria and the reemergence of the Arab-Israeli peace process, and the promotion of cultural tourism. During the past two decades, nearly all the MENA-region governments have extended their cultural policies, introduced legislation to protect cultural and natural heritage, created new bodies responsible for heritage, increased their number of heritage sites, and funded historical restoration projects.[14] In the Gulf, the "heritage revival" has manifested itself in the state-funded restoration of old forts; the establishment of heritage villages and festivals; the development of "heritage sports," such as camel racing and falconry; televised competitions of colloquial poetry; and the proliferation of landmark national museums.[15]

While this global heritage boom could reflect a deepening, collective sense of cultural, economic, and environmental endangerment, it emerged out of the post–World War II faith in technical progress and international collaboration.[16]

Indeed, during the very decades that the modernizing Arab regimes were endorsing a nationalist pan-Arab and popular heritage, the concept of a universal "world heritage" was born. It was midwifed, in fact, in the Arab world where in 1959 UNESCO mounted the world's first collaborative international campaign, to save the ancient Nubian monuments of Egypt and Sudan from being flooded by the Aswan High Dam development. This unprecedented action resulted in the relocation and reconstruction of twenty-three monuments, the displacement of thousands of Nubians, and ultimately UNESCO's 1972 adoption of the Convention Concerning the Protection of the World Cultural and Natural Heritage, which gave rise to the World Heritage Site and brand.

As initially formulated, World Heritage was embedded in places (monuments, buildings, or sites) classified as "cultural" or "natural" properties of "outstanding universal value."[17] It did not take long, however, for its critics to recognize that this natural/cultural distinction was problematically Eurocentric. Yet, despite the World Heritage Committee's efforts to accommodate more diverse notions of heritage, this fundamental divide between culture and nature was maintained.[18] Similarly, UNESCO's 2003 adoption of the Convention for the Safeguarding of Intangible Cultural Heritage—one of the outcomes of the committee's "global strategy" to create a more representative and balanced list—underscored yet another divide: "tangible" versus "intangible" heritage.[19] Notably, this second major UNESCO instrument also has its genesis in the MENA region in a proposal to protect the oral (storytelling) traditions found in Jemaa el Fna Square in Marrakech, Morocco.[20] Where UNESCO's 2003 convention departs from the 1972 convention and the short-lived Masterpieces of the Oral and Intangible Heritage of Humanity program (2001–2005) that preceded it is in its aim for the *representativeness* of its list as a whole rather than the "outstanding universal value" of any one property (a key concept of the 1972 convention) or its designation as a "masterpiece."[21]

This broadening of World Heritage from tangible and outstanding sites to intangible and representative elements (cultural traditions and practices) benefits many nations, such as the Arab Gulf States, marked more by their oral traditions than by their built monuments. This shift could even open the door to a renewed interest in a pan-Arab heritage. For instance, in 2015, the governments of the UAE, Saudi Arabia, Qatar, and Oman jointly nominated "Arabic coffee, symbol of hospitality" for inscription on UNESCO's Representative List of the Intangible Cultural Heritage of Humanity. (Notably absent as a nominating party is Yemen, the birthplace of Arabian coffee.) Even more significant in light of the current rate of language extinction would be if this new valorization of intangible cultural heritage were to galvanize additional state support for cultural and linguistic diversity. Within the Arab world, Algeria—the world's first member state to ratify the 2003 convention and the host of the Islamic Educational, Scientific and Cultural Organization's (ISESCO) 2004 session where the Islamic Declaration on Cultural Diversity was adopted—has made strides in recognizing and promoting its country's Berber heritage. In 2001, the Algerian government constitutionally recognized Amazigh (Berber) as an official state language, alongside Arabic; in 2014, Algeria established the Regional Center for the Safeguarding of Intangible Cultural Heritage in Africa under the auspices of UNESCO.

Although these and other states' measures are encouraging, the most significant shifts toward the recognition of long-marginalized peoples, languages, and cultures in the Arab world have occurred as a result of political activism and popular mobilization. Whereas Tunisia and Morocco also took steps toward recognizing Amazigh identity in the 2000s, it was only in response to the "Arab Spring" and the reemergence of Berber activism in 2011—thirty years after the "Berber Spring" in Algeria—that Amazigh was constitutionally recognized as an official language of Morocco (in July 2011). In Yemen, too, the Arab uprisings in 2011 paved the way to the National Dialogue Conference (2013–2014) and a draft constitution giving official recognition to Yemen's South Semitic languages: Soqotri and Mehri. Despite the prospects for this constitution becoming increasingly unlikely, this draft represented a remarkable step toward the recognition of cultural diversity and minority heritage in a state long defined as "Arab." One of conference members who fought for this recognition was Fahd Saleem, the Soqotran activist who had rallied the protesters and poets during the revolution. But how did Fahd and other Soqotrans come to view their cultural heritage as a powerful mode of political discourse and action?

Many scholars have been critical (and suspicious) of UNESCO's still largely Eurocentric notions of intrinsic "universal" value, its Cartesian (natural/cultural and tangible/intangible) taxonomies, and its cultural imperialism.[22] Others, influenced by theories of the French philosopher Michel Foucault, have

shown how heritage at any level (local, national, world) is a means by which a
state exercises control over its population.[23] This control can be exerted directly
by authoritarian regimes. But it can also be exerted indirectly in advanced liberal democracies through "neoliberal" strategies that "create a distance between
the decisions of formal political institutions and other social actors, conceive
of these actors in new ways as subjects of responsibility, autonomy and choice,
and seek to act upon them through shaping and utilizing their freedom."[24] Heritage is one such way of what Nikolas Rose calls "governing at a distance"—a
way of encouraging social actors to become "experts of themselves" and of their
pasts.[25] Heritage is a particularly effective form of government, for its authority is grounded in liberal notions of expertise, ethical self-understanding, and
consumption-based identification. But Rose also draws his readers' attention to
"the 'reversibility' of relations of authority" in that "what starts off as a norm to
be implanted into citizens can be repossessed as a demand which citizens can
make of authorities."[26] In such instances, heritage as a technology of government and subjectification may be redeployed as a platform for self-governance
in a political community. For example, anthropologist Chiara de Cesari ana-
lyzes how a creative, artistic heritage movement in Palestine "embodies an activist project of resistance to the occupation" while, at the same time, engaging
in national institution building in the shadow of the Palestinian "quasi-state."[27]
De Cesari's work offers a provocative example of heritage as a *creative* form of
governance—creative not only in its reliance on art and material culture but
also in its capacity to produce new forms of governance and new relations of
and demands on authority—in an area long subject to occupation. Still, even
in such an embattled site, the heritage nongovernmental organizations (NGOs)
that she observes are well-established organizations staffed by "cosmopolitan"
Palestinian heritage practitioners and financed by international donors.

In contrast, *Islands of Heritage* examines the emergence of what may also
be designated a creative, activist heritage in a context of extreme immisera-
tion and unexpected upheaval. This context, in itself, is neither more nor less
worthy of study, but it does demand inquiry into why seemingly conservative
concepts like heritage took hold among presumably inexpert individuals and
self-proclaimed revolutionaries. In the case of Soqotra, this means considering
how heritage has become entangled with other imperatives of preservation and
improvement. It means analyzing the current (primarily external) emphasis on

the protection of nature in light of the historical nature of outsiders' concerns with Soqotra's protection. And it means exploring how heritage has come to matter—both discursively and materially—as a generative force that is being created, curated, and mobilized from below toward new forms of political empowerment.[28] Although I, too, regard heritage as a form of external and internal governance (and often refer to the workings of UNESCO as the world heritage "regime"), this book is less interested in the "reversibility of relations of authority" than it is in their potential unraveling. Drawing on Tayyib Tizini's notion of a heritagial revolution described previously, it argues that—albeit for a limited period before the war intervened—Soqotrans succeeded in articulating and animating "a revolution grounded in the progressive elements of heritage." Indeed, far from being a conservative endeavor or merely a governmental technology, their work demonstrates how the mobilization of nature-culture heritage can have profoundly transformative, even revolutionary, effects.

A "PROTECTED" ISLAND

Located 150 miles east of the Horn of Africa and 240 miles south of the Arabian Peninsula, Yemen's Soqotra Island is the second-largest island in the Western Indian Ocean. Along with its neighboring islands, Abd al-Kuri, Samha, and Darsa, it forms the Soqotra Archipelago, one of the most botanically diverse island groups in the world.[29] More than one-third of its 825 plant species are endemic, meaning that they cannot be found anywhere else on earth. These include plants like the dragon's blood tree (*Dracaena cinnabari*), with its ruby red resin (cinnabar) and umbrella-shaped crown; the tubby cucumber tree (*Dendrosicyos socotranus*), the only gourd species to grow in tree form; and the Soqotran frankincense tree (*Boswellia socotrana*), whose aromatic resin, prized in ancient times, now sells online for USD 20 an ounce. In addition, the archipelago with its soaring Haggeher Mountains (up to five thousand feet above sea level) is home to seven endemic bird species and at least twenty-two species of reptiles, nineteen of them endemic. There is good reason that conservationists have branded it "the Galápagos of the Indian Ocean."

Despite the archipelago's recent ascendance, Soqotra is still characterized by outsiders as one of the most enigmatic and "forgotten" places in the region. This has less to do with its ostensibly remote location—for many empires, past

and present, Soqotra's geographic position at the entrance to the Red Sea has
been its prime value—than with its continuing inaccessibility and seasonal
isolation. Lacking natural harbors and directly impacted by the gale-force
winds of the southwest monsoon that "close" (*tughliq*) its surrounding seas,
the islands of the Soqotra Archipelago were effectively cut off from the outside
world, and one another, every May through September. This seasonal isolation
ended only in 1999 with the opening of an all-weather, commercial airport
that has enabled travel and transport to and from the mainland year-round.
More than simply opening Soqotra Island to foreign researchers and tourists,
this and other recent developments consolidated Yemen's grasp over the island
while also invigorating the islanders' historical and present-day links to the Soqotran diaspora in the Arab Gulf States.

Monsoon winds and rough seas notwithstanding, Soqotra has attracted
sailors, settlers, and soldiers since early antiquity.[30] Historical accounts suggest
that, by the second century BCE, colonies of Arabs, Greeks, and Indians had
settled the island, alongside its autochthonous population. Around the mid-
fourth century, Soqotra was Christianized and brought under the influence of
the Nestorian church of Sassanid Persia. Until the end of the fifteenth century,
Soqotra was intermittently ruled or held under tributary subjection by various
Omani and South Arabian dynasties. Yet it remained a nominal Christian settlement—in the midst of what had become a predominantly Muslim sea—until
well into the sixteenth century. Finally, in approximately 1480 CE, Soqotra
became subject to the chieftains of Qishn, a coastal enclave of al-Mahra: the
vast, desert territory wedged between the Hadhramawt (Yemen) and Dhofar
(Oman). Despite several challenges to its rule, the 'Afrar family of Qishn established itself as a hereditary and titular dynasty that would rule the Sultanate of
Qishn and Soqotra until 1967 (see Appendix).

Throughout much of this period, Soqotra was renowned for its natural
bounty: frankincense, myrrh, cinnabar, aloes, ambergris, tortoise shell, pearls,
and pearl shell. It also attracted merchants, missionaries, and explorers on account of its notorious inhabitants: its "St. Thomas Christians" (the descendants
of those who had ostensibly been converted by the apostle himself); its powerful sorcerers; and its marauding pirates. However, by the time the fleets of
the English East India Company began anchoring off its shores, Soqotra's "natives" were described by their captains as comprising two groups: the coastal-

dwelling Arab Muslims and the mountain-dwelling aborigines. Sir Thomas Roe, visiting in 1615, described the latter as "a savage people, poore, leane, naked, with long hayer, eating nothing but rootes, hidinge in bushes, conversing with none, afrayd of all, without howses, and almost as savadge as beasts; and by conjecture the true ancient naturalls of this island."[31] Notwithstanding continued evidence of the island's diverse population, this stark typology prevailed for centuries; as late as the 1960s, British explorers drew sharp contrasts between the "mixed" Arabs and Africans along the coast and the presumably autochthonous Bedouin, "untouched by the progress of civilization."[32] Soqotrans, too, distinguish between highland, indigenous populations (the so-called real Saqatri) and coastal communities of "Arab" or "African" descent. In recent decades, these distinctions have lost ground as more and more pastoralist families have descended to the coastal towns and new migrants from mainland (and especially northern) Yemen moved to the capital. (In this book, I use the term *Soqotran* to refer to anyone who originates from the island, differentiating only between the Saqatri and Arab- or Afro-Soqotrans when relevant. In keeping with my interlocutors' habit, I do distinguish between Soqotrans and mainlander Yemenis—even though Soqotrans are, by way of citizenship, Yemeni as well.)

Soqotra has also long been imbued with a sacred quality—sacred, in the sense of being intentionally *set apart*. Time and again, the island's natural resources and population were placed under varying forms of artificial isolation or "protection." For example, as early as the first century CE, Soqotra was said to be "subject" to the "king of the frankincense-bearing lands"—a region that covered eastern Yemen and western Oman—who had "leased out the island" to an unnamed sovereign and placed it "under guard."[33] Centuries later, when Oman's first Ibadi imam seized the island as a strategic base for Oman's East African slave trade (ca. 750 CE), Soqotra's Christians were given protected (*dhimmi*) status in exchange for submitting to a per capita tax.[34] When the thirteenth-century traveler Ibn al-Mujawir visited Soqotra, he noted that its Christian sorcerers could make "the protected island" invisible to foreign invaders.[35] In 1507, some twenty-five years after the Mahra had taken Soqotra (as a refuge from their neighboring rivals), the Portuguese king Manuel I (r. 1495–1521) dispatched a fleet to "Çocotora" to establish it as a base from which to occupy the Red Sea and, ostensibly, to "guard and protect" its celebrated Chris-

protected island

tians."[36] This four-year occupation failed miserably. But the allure of Soqotra as a military base and protected site endured.

Thus, in 1834, the Government of British India tried unsuccessfully to first purchase and then occupy Soqotra to use it as a coaling station for British steamships plying their way between Suez and Bombay. Although the British no longer needed Soqotra following their capture of Aden in 1839, they were loath to have any other power acquire this strategically located island, especially following the 1869 opening of the Suez Canal. Therefore, they negotiated a series of treaties with the 'Afrar sultans in Qishn (in al-Mahra) in 1876, 1886, and 1888, resulting in the Mahra Sultanate of Qishn and Soqotra becoming the first British protectorate in southwestern Arabia. Later, in the wake of its second (this time, successful) occupation of Soqotra during World War II, the British government wavered between seeking to strengthen the island's connections to the mainland and separating it altogether—a schizophrenic engagement that made Soqotra pivotal to their policies while keeping it artificially remote. Indeed, for years, British ministers debated whether to retain the island as a sovereign military base following Britain's impending withdrawal from South Arabia.

In November 1967, the People's Republic of South Yemen (later called the PDRY) was established. The formation of this independent Marxist state in South Yemen brought to an end the various sultanates that the British had propped up, including the Sultanate of Qishn and Soqotra. Annexed by South Yemen, Soqotra was governed as a restricted-access military zone. This is the period during which Soqotrans today describe their island as having been most closed off from outside contact, for they needed permission to leave the island and their migrant relatives were prevented from returning. Finally, the unification of North and South Yemen into the Republic of Yemen in 1990 led to Soqotra being "discovered" once again. While the embargo it had suffered was lifted, this former *state* of exception was soon replaced by the swift transformation of the archipelago into a *place* of exception: a place whose exceptional nature, literally, required yet another protection regime.

And its protection has been noteworthy: within years of Yemen's 1990 unification and 1994 civil war, the Government of Yemen declared the Soqotra Archipelago a national protected area (in 1996) and adopted a legislative framework (in 2000) to identify and manage the several categories of protected areas within the archipelago. By the time I began my fieldwork there in 2004, the Soqotra Archipelago had been recognized by BirdLife International as an Endemic Bird Area, by the World Wildlife Fund as a Global 200 ecoregion, by Conservation International as a crucial center of biodiversity within the Horn of Africa biodiversity hotspot, by the Regional Organization for the Conservation of the Environment of the Red Sea and Gulf of Aden (PERSGA) as a Marine Protected Area, and by UNESCO's Man and the Biosphere Programme (MAB) as an integrated biosphere reserve. And in 2008, this ostensibly "Hidden Land" was added to the world map of nationally protected, globally recognized, and universally valued World Heritage Sites—to this new "archipelago of enclaves."[37] Far from being obscured, Soqotra was transformed into a tourist site attracting (primarily) European visitors—mainly, for its white sandy beaches but also for the very narratives that have attracted visitors since Thomas Roe's time: Soqotra's "weird" flora; its "mysterious" Christian history; its "legendary" Portuguese connections; its "strange" sorcery; and its "forgotten" nature.[38]

A quick review of these imperial engagements demonstrates that the fluctuations in the island's connections and closures are as regular as the monsoon gales that close the sea around it and as its transitions between protected area and military zone. In the past decade, it has been rumored repeatedly (but falsely) that the United States or Saudi Arabia had occupied Soqotra or garrisoned a top-secret military base there. When I returned in 2013, my friends informed me that the United States was in negotiation with the Government of Yemen to relocate the remaining Yemeni prisoners from Guantanamo Bay to Soqotra. In February 2016, rumors circulated that Yemen's President Hadi had leased out Soqotra to the UAE for ninety-nine years in return for its military support.[39] Since then, Emirati forces have used Soqotra (closed to tourists since March 2015) as a military training ground. In other words, if Soqotra has been cut off seasonally, it has also been cut off cyclically, from one period and century to another. Although it is this "interplay between isolation and interconnectedness that characterizes the life of every island,"[40] in Soqotra this isolation has been more or less imposed by sovereigns seeking to protect the island or to be protected by it. The contours of this protection, from sacred to protectorate to protected area to defense zone, have changed, as has the cast of empires drawn to its shores. But the impulse is familiar. How have Soqotrans responded to the unsolicited arrival of one imperial project after another? And how do they perform their ostensible "remoteness" to each wave of strangers?[41]

ETHNOGRAPHIC (IM)POSSIBILITIES

This book is the product of longitudinal and multisited fieldwork in Soqotra
and my ongoing friendship with several Soqotrans I met through this research.
Given Soqotra's cyclical closures, it is worth noting that it was, in part, the island's imputed apartness that both drew and steered me there initially. When I
first visited and traveled through much of Yemen in 1999, Soqotra still seemed
virtually out of reach: "the last great sidetrack," as Tim Mackintosh-Smith was
to depict it in his erudite travel narrative.[42] Yemeni friends in Sanaa had never
heard of the place or did not know its location. (Soqotran friends recall a visiting mainlander asking for directions to al-Mukalla in a stolen car; having flown
to Soqotra, he did not realize it was an island from which he could not drive
away.)[43] However, just five years later, the archipelago was minted, quite literally, into the national consciousness: In 2004, a new twenty-riyal (YER) coin
with Soqotra's metonymic dragon's blood tree emblazoned on its face was released into circulation. Images of these iconic trees began sprouting up on the
painted metal doors and signs of apothecaries and honey shops along Zubairy
and other crowded streets in Sanaa. And documentaries extoling Soqotra's
biodiversity aired frequently on national television. In the interim, during the
buildup to the US invasion of Iraq in March 2003, foreigners were prohibited
from traveling outside Sanaa—with the exception of the supposedly secluded
Soqotra, to where I then flew. At the time, I had limited knowledge of the island
and, as a graduate student, limited funds. Finding its "capital," Hadibo, oppres-
sively hot and expensive, my partner and I spent much of those two weeks seeking respite in our poorly air-conditioned hotel room, watching Operation Iraqi
Freedom unfold. One day, we splurged on a half-day car rental and asked our
driver to take us to the mountains. He took us to the arborous Homhil plateau,
a newly established nature sanctuary. Unbeknown to me then was that I would
eventually end up living among its Saqatri pastoralist community for more than
a year and thinking and writing about Homhil for over a decade to come.[44]

During my field research in Soqotra, I relied on conventional anthropological methods, such as carrying out participant observation, conducting unstructured interviews, and eliciting life histories. I also studied the conservation and
development project documents, collected Soqotri poetry and oral histories,
and (later) researched colonial archives. I conducted these interviews and conversations primarily in Arabic and English but also learned and used some

basic Soqotri. I had not intended to study or even collect Soqotri-language
poetry, until I realized the extent to which people's concerns were expressed
primarily through this medium.[45] In the following chapters, I provide a sense

[handwritten margin note: NK(e in the other reading)]

of daily life in a pastoralist community at the margins of the Arab world—not
because this was the subject of my research but because livelihoods like these
are increasingly marginalized even as they, too, are affected by the uprisings,
revolutions, and armed conflicts that have rocked this region. However, because I refrain there from describing my own activities in the protected area,
here I briefly summarize what this entailed.

In Hadibo, where I had also rented a house, I spent most mornings inter-
acting with project staff of the Socotra Conservation and Development Programme (SCDP) and the Environment Protection Authority and attending
their meetings whenever possible. My partner, who accompanied me during
this period, worked part-time for the SCDP drafting the initial nomination
document for Soqotra's World Heritage recognition; he, too, spent his mornings at the SCDP headquarters. In the afternoons and evenings, I tried to meet,
socialize with, and interview persons of varying backgrounds and occupations,
such as the Hadibo-based rural-urban migrants; Afro-Soqotran fishermen and
state employees; mainland Yemeni shopkeepers, teachers, and government
representatives; visiting Soqotrans from the Gulf; and European researchers,
NGO administrators, and tourists. I also spent considerable time with persons
from Homhil who frequented the capital to obtain day labor, pick up welfare
monies or state salaries, purchase food staples, sell livestock, petition the court,
visit the hospital, and catch up on recent events. (In most cases, it was the men
performing these tasks; women traveled to Hadibo, too, but mainly for medical
treatment or to visit relatives.) Usually, we teamed up to find transportation
between Hadibo and Homhil—a four- to five-hour drive during the rainy season; a mere two hours by the end of 2005, when a good stretch of roads had
been paved—until I finally purchased a used car, after which the residents of
Homhil would seek me out for rides. If I was not moving physically between
the local center (Hadibo) and its hinterland (Homhil) with my rural neighbors,
or following in their paths as they circulated back and forth, then I was party to
their engagements, both physical and imaginary, with communities and goods
located farther afield. Truly—if this still needs repeating—even ethnography at
the "margins" is necessarily multisited and transnational.

In Homhil, I resided in one of the hamlets I will call Qayher ("houses" in Soqotri), where I rented a one-room house. There, I spent less time interviewing and more time observing, while struggling to participate in some productive way. For part of the school year, I taught English to seventh-graders; I also helped organize and run the newly functioning campground at a time when the very concept of tourism was unfamiliar to the pastoralists whose job it had just become. Whenever my partner visited from Hadibo, he participated in the men's daily activities and communal labor, such as hauling stones to build a house. Such communal labor is customarily recompensed through a meat-rich meal, but we considered it, as we did my volunteer efforts, one small (symbolic) way to return my hosts' generosity. For although I lived alone, each of the Qayher households—all of them patrilineal kin—took turns inviting me to every meal. One household in particular became my Qayher home. Umm Yaqub, my next-door neighbor who was only a few years older than I, enfolded me into her family with a brusqueness I found endearing. When my partner returned to the United States and Umm Yaqub's eldest daughter's husband returned to the mainland for work, she recited mournful poetry in dedication to her "daughters" whose husbands' absence they "pined."

In Middle Eastern anthropology, it has been common for anthropologists to talk about their social incorporation as fictive kin. A book, after all, is testament to the anthropologist's ability to gain entry (often through privilege) to a different social universe and to have convinced other people to confide in her. How better to measure and demonstrate one's success than by articulating one's forged or bestowed kinship with one's interlocutors? Indeed, despite longstanding critiques of the theoretical naïveté and material asymmetries that undergird not just the classic fiction of rapport but even its later (re)imaginings as "collaboration" or "engagement," and despite disputes over the advantages of being a relative insider or outsider, many ethnographies give the impression that a genuine relationship, no matter how tenuous its beginnings, has been achieved.[46]

This was not my experience; or rather, mine was not a linear experience from distant outsider to increasingly kindred relative. Rather, my relationships with various Soqotrans were alternately close and estranged—as many relationships are. Moreover, they were often strained due to the already hostile political climate. The following examples merit mentioning as they illustrate some of challenges of conducting fieldwork in a place and time dominated by US military interventions and rising global economic inequality. My arrival in what anthropologists call "the field" was more or less typical: My hosts were exceptional hosts and I was an eager, if unusual, guest. However, during the first six weeks, a life-threatening medical condition necessitated an operation on Umm Yaqub's infant granddaughter in Sanaa, which my partner and I felt compelled to facilitate. When I returned to Qayher after the successful operation, Umm Yaqub and others pronounced that we should live there forever; that they would give us a house and some livestock with which to settle down. For months, similar exhortations followed. Meanwhile, people in Homhil began referring to me as the infant's milk-mother (Soq.: *méme*), a form of fostered kinship that in Soqotra still carries much of the same implications (such as marriage prohibitions, obviation of veiling, and socioeconomic obligations) as do affinal and consanguineal relationships.[47] The women of Qayher even entreated me to return someday while lactating so that I could literally nurse my "milk-daughter" (or her new siblings) and her biological mother might nurse my infant in return, transforming our fictive milk-relationship into actual kinship.

But all of this mutual goodwill could not transcend the local, regional, and global politics in which I was or was thought to be complicit, however unwittingly or abstractly. Over time, I came to learn that some people from Homhil distrusted my reasons for being there. On the one hand, my presence and (limited) advocacy were viewed as external resources that had been unequally distributed: my naïve desire to "give back" to my hosts in Qayher came across to others as biased or discriminatory. On the other hand, I was accused of meddling in the protected area's affairs and threatened with removal from Homhil, and even Soqotra. Underlying much of these misgivings was the suspicion that I was a spy. I have mentioned that my first visit to Soqotra—and, consequently, my research there—was sparked by the difficulties of traveling elsewhere in Yemen during the US invasion of Iraq in 2003. Prior to this, in the wake of the USS *Cole* bombing in Aden in 2000 and the attacks on US soil a year later, FBI agents had been dispatched to Aden; in 2002, a CIA-operated drone had killed six alleged al-Qaeda operatives in Marib; and Yemen was attracting increasing media coverage as the reported ancestral home of Osama bin Laden.[48] As a result, Soqotrans were already worried that the United States would command their island as a military base for its regional counterterrorism operations. Even after the US Marine Corps established its base in Djibouti in 2003, rumors of US military interests in Soqotra continued to circulate and were fueled by, among other things, dubious media reports to this effect that continue to emerge every few years; Senator John McCain's visit to Yemen and, according to a trusted friend, to the island in 2009; and my own uncertain presence there. Thus, when the British ambassador sat next to me during a dinner in Hadibo; when other foreign diplomats peeked curiously into my house in Qayher; and when my page proofs for an article were discovered on a hotel computer (one of the few places in Hadibo that had a dial-up Internet connection in the mid-2000s), these incidents were seen as evidence of my government ties. For example, the northern Yemeni hotel employee who found my article informed me that he had turned it over to local intelligence officers for containing "everything there is to know about Soqotra." Even one of my closest friends suspected that my funded academic research must have been directed by US intelligence until I was prohibited from embarking on my scheduled flight to New York due to my lack of exit visa. "Now I know you are not a VIP person," he jested, but only in part.

If any of these accounts seems amusing now, this may be because the distress they caused me, and my interlocutors, has long subsided. The Soqotrans I came to know were neither narrow-minded nor misinformed. On the contrary, they were and remain aware of just how much influence a temporary visitor could have on their abilities to access external resources. I would like to believe that the bonds between my former hosts and I have grown despite these many challenges; indeed, my return to the island with my son in 2007 and in 2012 (and with photographs of my daughters in 2013) seems to have quelled any lingering suspicions about me. Moreover, my unexpected relocation to Abu Dhabi in 2011 deepened my relationships with my former hosts, many of whom have relatives living in the Arab Gulf. In fact, my new location and locatability in the UAE has made me more intelligible to my former hosts than I ever was during my actual fieldwork. It has also, I believe, changed our mutual expectations. But this does not make us kin. When I did return to Soqotra with my six-month-old son—when the possibility for *real* kinship had become more than a fictive trope—my friends in Qayher, clearly remembering their former "longing" to nurse and foster my future children, proffered excuses instead. "I am sorry—I have no milk," Umm Yaqub's daughter said, moments before turning to nurse her second child. Nor did I insist on nursing my supposed milk-child's new sibling. Whether fictive or real, kinship comes with real and interminable responsibilities. Sometimes, even an "engaged" anthropology is not up to the task.

IN DEFENSE OF ISLANDS

Beyond its focus on the entanglements of development, conservation, and heritage projects in Soqotra, this book can be read as an ethnography of the unification and unraveling of the Republic of Yemen as seen through the eyes of a marginalized population. Whereas the bulk of its material draws on events that occurred between 2000 and 2011, many of the conversations I participated in and followed revolved around the radical changes Soqotrans experienced starting in the early 1990s and, again, as a result of the 2015–present war. Moreover, my interlocutors seemed more comfortable speaking about the past than they did about the political present—until the 2011 uprisings bestowed them with the confidence to voice their dissent. Despite Soqotrans' eagerness to delve into their history, the heritage projects that permeate the island—and the Arabian Peninsula as a whole—tend to elide historical events, conflicts, confrontations, and analyses in favor of an empty, homogeneous past: a time before oil, before statehood, or before unity.[49] My consideration of the British colonial interventions in Soqotra (1876–1967) and my attentiveness to historical transformations more broadly come from an attempt to speak to my interlocutors' interests while documenting the history of their heritage.

Although each of the following chapters forwards an independent argument, they have been conceived as three interlocking pairs, each bound by a common theme. The first two chapters interrogate Soqotra's ostensible remoteness in light of the islanders' long history of hosting foreign visitors and regimes. Chapter 1 describes how the unprecedented "opening" of the island gave rise to a crisis of hospitality (*karam*), a long-held cultural value. Soqotrans' discourse of hospitality in crisis reveals significant mutations in the island's political economy and social structures, precipitated by its 1990 absorption into the newly unified Yemeni state and its transformation from a militarized enclave to a national protected area. Chapter 2 demonstrates how, the 1990–opening notwithstanding, Soqotrans have "hosted" various states, each of which has governed the island through fear and food. I argue that Soqotrans' experiences of these visiting (and "eating") states determined their expectations when they were called on to host another (de facto) state: the ICDPs.

The middle two chapters examine the arrival of the ICDPs at the turn of the twenty-first century and, with them, the very concepts of "the environment," "conservation," and "heritage." Chapter 3 reviews how these projects were preceded by the decades-long arrivals of foreign researchers and the continued dissemination of their ideas about Soqotra's environmental exceptionality. Soqotrans habitually refer to these ICDPs as "the Environment," betraying the ways in which they have constructed the environment as an abstraction and its conservation as the Soqotrans' (pastoral) heritage and (development) future. Chapter 4 considers the material, social, and political effects of several conservation and development initiatives in a pilot protected area (Homhil) during the height of its economic development. Although these projects were meant to improve the pastoralists' material well-being, they wound up pitting tribes, villages, and men and women within the community against one another. Together, these chapters illustrate why, in my interlocutors' view, "the Environment" failed—despite its strong influence in and on the island.

The final chapters explore the ways in which, as a response to "the Environment," Soqotrans appropriated and mobilized the language of heritage to claim a place for their language and culture that could withstand external control. Chapter 5 focuses on the influence of the Soqotran diaspora in island politics in the decade preceding the revolution. It shows how the diaspora sought to denature and reorient Soqotran heritage by shifting the focus from nature to culture, from Soqotran autochthony to Arab descent, from Indian Ocean hybridity to genealogical purity, and from the Yemeni nation to the transnational Gulf. Chapter 6 discusses how the islanders mobilized heritage in the years bracketing the Yemeni revolution, when several positioned themselves as "para-experts" alongside foreigners working for the environmental projects. It maintains that Soqotrans' preoccupation with their cultural heritage was not a provincial, insular, or even conservative concern. Rather, their turn to heritage reflects a distinctly twenty-first-century realization that vernacular languages and endemic species are on the verge of extinction and require concerted care.

Collectively, these chapters make evident that heritage is not an isolated enterprise. One of this book's central claims is that because heritage discourses, examples, and practices circulate globally (through institutions like UNESCO), regionally (through, in this case, diasporic networks), and through time (for instance, through evolving notions of protection), we cannot fully understand their impacts without evaluating them in context of other development, conservation, and tutelary projects that have come before and alongside them. Yet what this case study also illustrates is the persistent—and, in some cases, productive—nature of heritage *distinctions* on the ground. In this spirit, this book takes its title from anthropologist Marshall Sahlins's renowned *Islands of History*, a series of essays that argue against the notional (and largely Western) oppositions between structure and event, history and culture, past and present.[50] Sahlins's islands—Hawaii, Fiji, and New Zealand—are neither insular nor historyless. Rather, in his view, it is the insularity of Western thought that has created and maintains an archipelago of antitheses between stability and change.[51] Building on Sahlins's primary assertions, this book is, prima facie, an ethnography of the diverse and dichotomous notions of heritage that buoy its regime: global and local, universal and particular, natural and cultural, incarceral and revolutionary. But it is not just divergent visions of heritage that are in contention here. As the following chapters show, the various producers of Soqotra's heritage(s)—international experts, state bureaucrats, Soqotran para-experts, Soqotran emigrants, Bedouin Soqotrans, and Afro-Soqotrans—remained isolated in their efforts by their own circumscribed notions of what heritage is and does. Despite scholars' critical efforts, heritage as it is constituted in practice continues to separate nature from culture, tangible from intangible, and expert from inexpert. Moreover, these same scholarly commitments to bridge the nature-culture and human-animal-thing divides may, in fact, isolate scholars from the work of heritage(s) in practice. For while the academic impulse to transcend the nature-culture dualism is compelling, it could undermine Soqotrans' and other indigenous actors' desire to maintain such divisions—these conceptual "islands"—as a bulwark against the neogreen imperialism of the global environmental movement. This explains why Fahd was less interested in overcoming the UNESCO distinction between nature and culture than he was in drawing a line from cultural heritage to revolution. And why we should continue to interrogate our own work and conceits from the vantage of other "islands," geopolitical, conceptual, and cultural.

FIGURE 2. Hospitality in the countryside, Soqotra, 2013. Broth and bone marrow (Soq.: *karhem*) are traditional appetizers.

CHAPTER 1

HOSPITALITY IN UNSETTLING TIMES

A CHALLENGE

"Ah, he's a poor fellow [*miskin*],"[1] my neighbor, friend, and fictive aunt Umm Yaqub said of one of the new teachers, scrunching her nose in pity. "He can't bear the sight of women."

It was December 2005, nearly midway through the school year, when three additional teachers were assigned to the primary school in Homhil. The men, two from Hadibo and one from Lahij, a governorate in southern Yemen, were to be housed with the other male teachers in a one-room house in Qayher, the hamlet in which Umm Yaqub lived and where I was residing that year. Although Homhil's inhabitants were eager to receive these government-employed teachers, the presence of the Arabic instructor from Lahij, a self-described Salafi I will call Sayf, posed a number of challenges to his village hosts and his increasingly irritated roommates.[2] For Sayf's determination to follow the example of the Prophet Muhammad demanded an architecture of gender segregation that was not only new to but also unfeasible within this close-knit community. Yet, within a day of his arrival, the men of Qayher erected a feeble plastic screen between the teachers' house and its external kitchen, where the women of Homhil took turns cooking the teachers' meals from the community-provided staples.

"He can't bear the sight of women," one of the men reiterated, as I watched them construct this outdoor partition from emptied rice sacks and other plastics.

The women must have been advised to lower their voices while cooking in the compound, for the banter that used to dart between them and the visiting teachers had come to a halt. Moreover, they all made sure to cover not only their hair but also their faces when walking between houses or when fetching water from the communal tank. Even within their homes, the teenage girls suspended their favorite pastime of dancing to cassette recordings of Faysal Alawi, a Yemeni oud player. And the other teachers retreated to their neighbors' homes where they could smoke cigarettes or listen to (muted) radio broadcasts without offending their pious new roommate.[3]

"He's *miskin*," everyone agreed, generously dispelling any signs of encumbrance brought on by these special accommodations.

Weeks later, my departure from the field offered my hosts a more promising solution. Sayf moved into "my" house—a former widow's home that had fallen into disrepair and was used as a cattle stall prior to my arrival—where he could live alone without bothering or being bothered by the other guest teachers or their compliant hosts. This seems to have worked out well enough until my unexpected return in February 2006 placed my hosts in a difficult situation. I felt the tension as soon as I returned. Whereas just months earlier, I had walked throughout Homhil freely, visiting friends in this hamlet or that, this time all my movements were monitored. Not only was I shepherded in and out of homes, but I was gently discouraged from spending any time outside. When I encountered Hamdan, one of the senior teachers, near the dry riverbed (wadi) one afternoon, I discovered why.

"Sayf says this is sinful, that is sinful [*haram*]," Hamdan said as we rested on the spongy trunk of a fallen dragon's blood tree. Hamdan recounted a series of injunctions expressed by Sayf during my absence: that it was *haram* for the girls to engage in physical exercises at the school; that it was *haram* to raise Yemen's flag above the school building; that it was *haram* to serve food to "the Jews" (Sayf's description of the Western tourists) patronizing the nearby campground, a campground "gifted" by the Japanese embassy in Yemen to the inhabitants of Homhil as a means of income generation; and that it was *haram* for the area's children to accept small trinkets, such as pens, from foreign visitors.[4] Sayf had even criticized the esteemed local judge (*qadi*) for mixing with Europeans (*ifrang*) by accepting rides to Hadibo in their vehicles. "But what's the problem?" Hamdan asked rhetorically. "The foreigner sits in front and you sit in back. There's nothing wrong with that. You don't need to talk. And the Prophet, peace be upon him, was kind even to unbelievers [*kuffar*]. If you were to invite an unbeliever into your house, he might take note of your generosity and see that your religion is the correct one and convert."

In light of Sayf's denunciations of my hosts' "unconditional" hospitality, it began to make sense that they would work so carefully to keep Sayf and me apart and that the other teachers, like Hamdan, conversed with me only in places where Sayf could not see them. What surprised me was the extent to which my former neighbors, both male and female, seemed anxious about their *karam* during my weeklong return. *Karam* is an Arabic term used by Soqotrans to signify generosity and hospitality, especially in the form of livestock slaughtered and eaten in one's honor. It appeared as if all of Homhil was concerned that I receive *karam* (specifically, goat meat), but no one felt able to offer it themselves. (Yet my former neighbors had insisted that I stay in their home instead of at the campground and made sure that I was fed abundantly at every meal.) "We would like to give you a feast [*karama*], but we don't have any goats right now," Umm Yaqub apologized, as we walked down to the coast one morning. The next day, as I returned from lunch in a nearby hamlet, two girls from Qayher ran up to greet me. "What did you eat? Did you eat meat? Did you?" they demanded, embarrassing me in front of my lunchtime host.

This conjoined discourse of regret (we'd like to give you *karam*, but) and remorse (did *they* offer you *karam*?) continued until my final day in Homhil when Sayf's temporary absence was even more conspicuous than had been his, to me, invisible presence. It was a Friday, and Sayf had walked to Hadibo to attend the weekly sermon. In Qayher, Hamdan turned up his radio, dialing for news. The women allowed their scarves to slip below their chins. And outside, on a hilltop overlooking the Arabian Sea, my female friends presented me their ideal version of *karam* through a feast of mutton that the men had boiled in large tin pots in the valley below.[5]

Later, reassured by the afternoon's congeniality, I made a point of asking the elderly *qadi* his thoughts on Sayf's pronouncements. "The teacher is correct," the *qadi* said, despite his family having shared their meals with me on several occasions. "Men and women shouldn't sit together. Muslims shouldn't share food with unbelievers. And unbelievers mustn't enter the village." I searched for a response. "You are here now," he conceded, "and we have given you *karam*, but we won't permit another foreigner to live in our village again."

The judge's resolution put an end to our conversation that day, but not to the entrance of foreigners in Homhil. Three months later, at the end of the school year, Sayf was transferred to the mainland and the people of Qayher must have turned to new challenges, such as the monsoon winds that were about to sweep through the valley. When I returned in June 2007, there was not a single shred of the plastic screen that had been erected between the teachers' house and their kitchen—the gales would have destroyed it in days—and the women's movements were, once again, less circumscribed. I had worried about my return to the village but was received, along with my husband and infant son, with exemplary acts of *karam* and kindness. My generous and pragmatic hosts, I learned, had not retreated from catering to tourists in the nearby camp-ground, nor had they constructed further barriers, physical or ideological, as their former guest-teacher had proposed. Although the people of Homhil had been eager to accommodate their visitor, whose learning and profession they respected, and were probably quite moved by his pietist principles and prac-tices, Sayf's teachings had not visibly reversed their reception of foreign visitors or aid. But that is not to say that they did not leave a trace.

. . .

I start with this challenge—to my generous hosts; to my unconventional pres-ence; to interfaith commensality; and to anthropological fieldwork, more gen-erally—because it encapsulates a predicament faced by rural Soqotrans living in newly designated protected areas in a globally recognized World Heritage Site who are increasingly called on to host—to *give place and time to*—a di-verse spectrum of foreign bodies, discourses, and regimes.[6] This may be one of many predicaments shared by marginalized communities the world over: how to engage and even benefit from the unexpected arrival of transnational reg-ulatory regimes without being inundated by their neoliberal and moralizing agendas. In Soqotra, these new bodies and ideas arrived in the persons of na-tional and foreign dignitaries, conservationists, development workers, donors, entrepreneurs, tourists, anthropologists, and missionaries, both Muslim and Christian. What interests me here, then, is not the all-too-easy juxtaposition of the Salafi male Arabic teacher and the non-Muslim female English "teacher."

Clearly, we both presented significant challenges to our agreeable hosts, who just a few years prior to our coincident arrivals would have not have encountered, much less housed, Yemeni proselytizers (representing one form of heritage) or American anthropologists (representing, through my association with the SCDP, another form of heritage) in their midst. Yet the fact that our hosts could abide us simultaneously speaks to the virtuosity of their *karam*. It illustrates, moreover, the ways in which "hospitality does not mark the acceptance of the stranger so much as the moral superiority of the host," especially over "strangers who may represent offices and countries of much greater political power."[7] Indeed, our hosts called each of us *miskin*: poor, but in a pitiable sort of way, like helpless but endearing dependents in need of their nourishment and nurture.

The actual challenge to the inhabitants of Homhil, I propose, was posed less by our awkward copresence than it was by the underlying crisis of hospitality engendered by the unprecedented opening (*al-infitah*) of the island to such a diverse range of foreign persons and practices. Far from being an archaic or insular concern, a similar crisis is afflicting many postindustrial countries: a crisis that in recent years has been made all too visible by the European states' failure to welcome the refugees stranded at their borders; by the US administration's attempts to implement a refugee ban; and by populists' anxieties that their governments have been too hospitable already.[8] Yet, in Soqotra, the "crisis of hospitality" was exacerbated not nearly as much by my acquaintances' fears of being too hospitable as by their concern that they were no longer hospitable enough. Rumors about hostile guests were eclipsed by many Soqotrans' anxieties about having become *inhospitable* hosts: hosts who have more but give less than their forefathers did. One might read this perception of a past mediated by an unconditional hospitality as a form of structural nostalgia: the "collective representation of an Edenic order—a time before time—in which the balanced perfection of social relations has not yet suffered the decay that affects everything human."[9] Certainly, nostalgia for a (past) time and (faraway) place of unconditional *karam* is expressed throughout the Arab world. It also drives the region's hospitality-as-heritage industry.[10] But an emphasis on these similarities would draw our focus to the sentiment of nostalgia and away from the specific message being communicated in a particular place and time. These messages are inherently critical and political.[11]

THE HOMHIL PROTECTED AREA

Heading east from Hadibo, one proceeds past Soqotra's erstwhile capital called Suq [Soq.: *Shiq*], its shallow-water port, and a rusted Soviet radar antenna; by-passes Di-Lishah's soaring dunes spilling into the azure Arabian Sea; traverses date palm plantations and several small villages nestled among date groves; crosses the Qaryah Lagoon, home to pink flamingoes and the endemic Socotra cisticola; winds through open scrubland strewn with croton trees; ascends a dried wadi obstructed by giant boulders; and climbs up a nearly vertical escarpment by way of a precariously steep and ungraded road. This last segment—which the apprehensive, like me, prefer to walk—takes one into Homhil, a hanging valley, in Soqotra's northern plateau. This valley, five square miles wide and thirteen hundred feet in elevation, contains a running wadi, several springs, pastures and date groves, and more than eighty plant species endemic to Soqotra. Of these species, seven are native to Homhil alone.[12] The valley is home also to some four hundred persons from four tribes spread across nine small settlements.

Homhil's pastoralist population has long considered their valley exceptional—and not just due to its diverse flora. One of its "citizens"—Soqotrans refer to themselves less by their tribe than by their domicile; inhabitants of Homhil refer to themselves as *Hamiliho* or as "citizens of Homhil" (*muwatinin humhil*)—told me that the valley was formed by the impact of a meteorite sent by God to channel rainwater to the coastal inhabitants below. He illustrated his claim with a story of a "Bedouin" who had once found a piece of this kohl-black rock while digging among his date palms; unfortunately, no sooner had the Bedouin placed it in a cave for safekeeping than a genie (jinn) came along and stole it. ("Poor man! If he still had it, it would be like gold," he said as we walked down a narrow footpath descending along this depression.) Others value Homhil as a center of Islamic knowledge and practice, for it was said to be the first place in Soqotra, outside Hadibo, to host a communal mosque—built seven generations ago. One neighbor told me proudly that Soqotrans used to walk to Homhil from afar for the Friday prayer and that "knowledge of Islam" was disseminated from there. Another showed me a prized "Soqotri text" that had belonged to his father. This had intrigued me because Soqotri is not a written language—and, in fact, the pages turned out to contain Muslim devotional literature, in Arabic, describing the prophets preceding Prophet Muhammad (*qisas al-anbiya'*). But what mattered to him was that it had been a "citizen of

Homhil" who had diligently copied this text, decades ago. Beneath the Arabic lettering, faded ink revealed that these were pages from a German shipping log, likely having belonged to the SS *Gdor* wrecked off Soqotra in 1887.[13] What had been used to inventory the steamer's library and the crew's rations—for instance, I could read that on 12 December 1886, they had consumed six *Stangenspargel*, two *Himbeer Saft*, and one *Fass Sauerkohl*—was now a record of the Hamiliho's early literacy.

More recently, Homhil was rendered exceptional anew when its rich biological diversity came to light. In 2000, Homhil was demarcated—by law, not by a physical boundary or fence—as one of the archipelago's twelve terrestrial "nature sanctuaries" and an area of "special botanical interest." Additionally, Homhil was identified as one of Soqotra's two pilot protected areas (*mahmiyat*) to be supported through community-based natural resource management. As envisioned by the consultants running the ICDP, the newly established Association for the Conservation and Development of Homhil, comprising the male adults living in Homhil, would manage the protected area with their earnings from ecotourism. The Bedouin pastoralists, who as recently as a generation ago had been living with their sheep and goats in modified caves high up in the surrounding limestone cliffs, were to become the environmentally conscious custodians of a nature sanctuary now flooded with Latin names: *Boswellia socotrana, Commiphora ornifolia, Dorstenia gigas, Aloe perryi, Dendrosicyos socotrana, Croton socotranus, Jatropha unicostata, Euphorbia arbuscula, Adenium obesum socotranum, Dracaena cinnabari*—the list continues. As researchers and tourists flocked to Homhil, its inhabitants became fluent in this scientific nomenclature.[14] Again, it could be said that people were coming from afar and that knowledge was being disseminated from there.

Today, the increasingly settled transhumant (seasonal) pastoralists who live in the valley continue to depend on animal husbandry and date cultivation for their daily sustenance. In theory, and in general practice, they maintain a traditional division of labor. Typically, men herd goats and pack animals; milk livestock; transhume with cows when necessary; slaughter the livestock; plant, pollinate, and harvest the date palms; trample and pack the dates for storage; construct fencing and pens; repair and build houses; and go to market in Hadibo. One of the four tribes in Homhil owns land both in the valley and along the coast below; its men fish, too. Women manage their own sheep (but also look after goats and cattle), water livestock, process milk products, collect firewood and water, prepare food, and care for the children. Additionally, they may keep home gardens, make pottery, plait palm-frond mats, weave sheep's-wool rugs, and harvest aloes or tree resins for their own use or for sale. However, with some exceptions (women do not slaughter animals or climb date palms), these tasks are often shared. It is not unusual, for example, for a young father to stay home with his children while his wife socializes with her neighbors or visits relatives outside the valley.

In addition to its communal mosque, Homhil now boasts an elementary school for grades one through seven. In contrast to the situation in the 1970s and 1980s, when many pastoralists were suspicious of the government efforts to educate their children, parents today send all their children to school, male and female.[15] Many view education as a potential pathway to salaried employment in Hadibo. Indeed, before the introduction of tourism in 2004, salaries and wages were available only to those who left the valley. A handful of men migrated seasonally to mainland Yemen to work in fishing, agriculture (including the construction of *karif* water catchment systems), or retail. Others sold livestock or sought day labor in Hadibo. Apart from these sporadic earnings, only five adults from Homhil received regular paychecks or pensions. For a few years, the ICDP gave three men a monthly "incentive" for environmental monitoring or their help in the campground. To cover the shortage of teachers in Homhil, the ICDP also paid three volunteer teachers from the area monthly supplements of YER 5,000 (USD 25), which were matched by the Homhil Association—when they had funds. Otherwise, the only regular income the majority of households could rely on was the assistance they received from the government's Social Welfare Fund: YER 6,000 (USD 30) every three months or USD 10 per month.

Aside from the mosque and school—and, more recently, cell phone reception—there are no institutions, services, or facilities in the valley. None of the houses have plumbing, latrines, or electricity. To reach the nearest health clinic or shop one must walk down a steep and narrow mountain path to the coastal plain. In the mid-2000s, one of my neighbors stocked a few basic commodities in his home for nonprofit resale: tea, sugar, flour, flip-flops, plastic mats, batteries, pens, canned tuna, and tomato paste. His ability to purchase these items was contingent on the remittances from his eldest son working on the mainland in al-Mahra.

FIGURE 3. Palimpsest, Homhil, 2004.

But food (in)security—the greatest challenge—was and remains as much determined by weather events as by income. In years of abundant rains, grasses sprout; livestock fatten; calves, lambs, and kids are born; milk is produced; and buttermilk, ghee, and meat are plentiful. In drought years, pastoralists may spend as much buying grains to feed their herds as they do to feed their families. When torrential rains follow drought, animals weakened from starvation are caught by flash floods and washed out to sea. Herds are decimated. This was brought home to me, to the extent that it ever could be, during my first week in the protected area in November 2004.

Serb (Winter) 2004

Bu Yaqub and his family were elated to wake up to the sight of full riverbeds and the signs of imminent pasture. I was staying with them while the clay plaster used to resurface the interior of my house dried. But the heavy rains that had battered Qayher in the night had left rivulets of mud running down everyone's walls. Throughout the morning, neighbors I had yet to meet stopped by to report on the damage to their homes: this wall had collapsed; that roof was leaking; this room was "like a sea" inside. But their complaints rang joyous; the monsoon season (Soq.: *horf*) had been long, hot, and dry, and the animals were starving. Their relief was palpable.

The following night brought more rain, and the following morning, more reportage. A man from a nearby hamlet stopped by with news of a shipwreck off the northeastern coast: five Indian sailors died; nine were rescued and brought to shore. A shaykh from the coastal plain below reported that his house had also caved in a little, but "thank God, no one died." Except for the goats. "Thank God for the rain, but the goats were washed out to sea," he said. According to him, six Indians had drowned. Some Soqotrans saw the boat sinking and went out to save them: "a dhow traveling from the Emirates to Somalia, perhaps."

"Even cows were washed out to sea," Umm Yaqub told me as I watched her sew dresses for her daughters for the Eid. "First, there was no food and we were feeding our goats from our own supplies, bringing them flour and wheat. Then the rains came, and they were out in the riverbeds and were washed out to sea," she explained.

"These were the worst rains in ten years," said the shaykh, whom I accompanied to the campground to assess its damage. Sixty goats had drowned. A schoolteacher walking up from the coast stopped at the campground and informed us that two Indian boats had been affected by the storm: the one rescued by Soqotrans and another that sank at sea. That evening, as more rain began to fall, Umm Yaqub's youngest daughter, Bilqis, peered outside the doorway to notice a single star emerging in the darkness. "Thank God, there's a star! Thank God, there's a star!" she shouted, relieved that storm clouds were moving away.

The next day, Bu Yaqub's brother Bu Jum'an returned from Hadibo, where he had gone to purchase sugar, tea, and rice for the Eid al-Fitr, celebrating the end of Ramadan. The rains had washed out the two access roads to Homhil, forcing him to walk up the mountain footpath carrying the fifty-kilo sacks on his back. Bu Jum'an told us that nine Indian sailors had drowned and only six were saved. As he was talking, a shout from the nearby field caught our attention. A gaunt, sickly cow had fallen down and was too weak to stand up. Yaqub, a gangly teen, was pulling it by the horns, but the cow's body would not budge. (I later found out that this cow—one of the cows that had been kicked out of its stall to make a home for me—had been slaughtered and left in the wadi to be washed out to sea, in the trail of the goats.) The cow's passive gaze was disquieting, for it resembled the gaze of Umm Yaqub's granddaughter, an infant who, due to what would be diagnosed as a case of pyloric stenosis, had for months vomited all the breast milk that her mother had fed her. Her eyes, too, looked eerily large and calm, as if accepting of her own slow starvation. (She survived.)

Remarkably, these challenges did not deter the people of Qayher from "hosting" me in their village. (Maybe they felt that they had no choice—I had been unwittingly introduced to them as an employee of the ICDP project.) Not wanting to burden anyone, and anxious about my diet, I had come prepared with my own stock of food: two large metal trunks filled with canned beans, fruits, and vegetables. At first, I cooked myself single meals on a camp stove in my courtyard. The children found it hilarious. Soon enough, Umm Yaqub took it upon herself to coordinate my every meal: lunch at her house, dinner with Umm Jum'an, breakfast with Bu Tariq. One of her daughters entered my house each dawn, while I slept, to leave me a full thermos of tea. I was never certain where I would end up for any given meal, but it was clear that I would never again cook for myself for as long as I stayed in Qayher.

THE NATURE OF *KARAM*

It is well known that hospitality is considered—and increasingly commoditized as—a defining feature of Arab sociability, cultural identity, and politico-moral economy. Indeed, *karam*, which also can refer to nobility, honor, dignity, respect, and esteem, is widely celebrated as an essential virtue: a "sacred duty" inherited from nomadic or Bedouin traditions of solidarity, honor, and protection.[16] Among Soqotran pastoralists who identify themselves as Bedouin, as among the Balgawi Bedouin of Jordan discussed by the anthropologist Andrew Shryock, *karam* is "a virtue whose best forms are located away from present space and time."[17] In Soqotra, these best forms are located in the rural countryside (*badiya*)—or, for those living there already, then in a *badiya* more distant than one's own—and in Soqotra's past, principally in the "days of the sultanate" (*ayyam al-sultan*), which ended in 1967.

"*Karam* is above everything—especially for the people of the *badiya*," Sownhin said following a long discussion about the various stages of government on Soqotra. Sownhin, Umm Yaqub's brother, is Homhil's self-appointed keeper of tradition and local cauterizer, the person to whom elders turned to dull the pain of their aching backs or pulsing gums. We had just finished dinner as guests of a family in a neighboring hamlet, and I had pressed him on whether *karam* in Homhil had changed over time. I grabbed my tape recorder.

"So, I asked you about *karam* in the time of the Party [*waqt al-hizb*]—" I repeated. "The [Socialist] Party" is a term Soqotrans use metonymously to describe the government of the People's Democratic Republic of Yemen and the era during which Soqotra was part of South Yemen, 1967–1990.

"And not in the time of the Party, alone!" Sownhin interjected. "I will tell you about the time of the sultan and until today, the stages that we've heard about. First, in the time of the sultan, when the sultan came from Hadibo or from his area to here, he'd come and visit a few different places, either Qayher or [other hamlets], and all the people of Homhil would make dinner for him, not just the people of [hamlet name] or Qayher. They'd send people around Homhil, from place to place, and say, 'The sultan is here; we need your help.' Every tribe or neighbor would give a head or two [of livestock] and we'd make dinner."

"Two heads?"

"One head, or two! If we had it, God willing. And they would make dinner for the sultan and his servants [*akhdam*]—he had servants who would ride with him—and they'd make everything."

"How many servants usually accompanied him?" I asked.

"Maybe twelve or fifteen . . . ten, twenty . . . fewer or more," Sownhin said. "And people would walk with him; they'd walk with him for food because in that time there wasn't much food. And when the sultan came, they'd have to make a lot of food. And all the people would be satisfied. And they'd come and eat, and when the sultan left, they left. This is *karam*. This custom of providing hospitality comes from generosity and sincerity. That is *karam*: a feast for the sultan. And it was like this in the time of the Party. When the government officials [*ashab al-hukuma*] came and went anywhere in the *badiya*, or anywhere—but outside of Hadibo—the people would make lunch and dinner for them. If there was an issue, they'd talk about it over dinner and address it. If they couldn't do something about it, they'd go back to Hadibo. And that's it; that's how it worked. And it's like this during the Unity [*al-wahda*] now [from 1990 onward]. Rural hospitality never ceases. What does God decree? That people must have *karam*. Even now, foreigners come. Foreigners come to us from far away and we don't know them. The people of the Party are from the government [*ashab al-hukuma*], and the people of the Unity are from the government, and the sultan is also the government [*al-hukuma*]. The foreigners are distant from us and we don't know them, but even when they come, we give them generosity—the same thing. *Karam* is above everything—especially for the people of the *badiya*. They give to others *karam* that they don't give to themselves. It's like this."

Karam, as Sownhin describes it, is a virtue and responsibility located specifically in the *badiya*, where pastoralists pool their meager resources to regale their guests and assuage their own hunger. In Soqotra, as elsewhere, hospitality is a political act. But in Soqotra, this idealized *karam* is an assertion not only of the domestic sovereignty of the host—the host who offers up his place, time, and property to the visiting guest—but also of the political sovereignty of the guest. For *karam* is associated in particular with the feasts offered to the itinerant sultan: "This is *karam*." Indeed, the memory of the hospitality granted to the sultans in the *badiya* has become something of a template on which all subsequent forms of *karam* are modeled and measured. So unwavering is this narrative of rural Soqotrans hosting "the state" that it elides the extreme differences between the sultan, the Party, and the unity governments and eras. Rural hospitality is the thread of continuity in the face of change. "Even when [the foreigners] come, we give them generosity," Sownhin asserts, giving way to a distinction that tests this ideal. For the distinction Sownhin emphasizes is not one between the disparate regimes that have governed Soqotra but rather between the people of the government(s) and the newly arrived foreigners, whose distance from Soqotrans renders the relationships between the Bedouin and their governments all the more intimate. *Karam* may be above everything, but as Sownhin's narrative hints, something in the tapestry has changed.

The most dramatic example of rural hospitality in this era—the one that most evokes the communal feasts offered to the visiting sultan—is the banquet (*'uzuma*) mounted in honor of the emigrant Soqotrans visiting from Oman, the UAE, and Saudi Arabia. Many young men migrated to the Arabian Peninsula during the sultanate in search of wages; many more left Soqotra, together with their families, during the early 1970s to escape the socialist regime. Having acquired citizenship in the petroleum-rich states of the Gulf, these relatively wealthy Soqotrans have long provided material and financial support to their family members remaining behind. But few had visited Soqotra prior to the definitive downfall of the socialist government in 1994; a decade later, I was still meeting emigrants returning for the first time since their departure and Gulf-born Soqotri youth who had never been to the island before. Those who did visit in the 1990s and 2000s were treated regally. Evening after evening, their island-based family members, extended relatives, and even former neighbors took turns slaughtering goats, sheep, cows, and camels for a communal feast. (Families living in "urban" Hadibo returned to their natal villages in the *badiya* to stage the *'uzuma* there.) Large tin platters heaped with buttermilk- and ghee-topped rice and circular palm-frond mats holding the boiled meat, fat, organs, and intestines were distributed among the guests. Following the meal, men often drummed and chanted hymns in praise of the Prophet (performing a *mawlid* celebration) or recited poetry; women danced inside their homes, listened to the drumming circle from the periphery, or joined the poets engaging in call and response. These were spectacular events in which everyone ate their fill and spent the next day recalling how many "heads" had been slaughtered in the guests' honor. Not unlike wedding celebrations (*diyafa*) or religious festivals in their substance (with the exception that people buy or sew new attire for these events), or even the smaller feasts offered to the community in exchange for their labor (Soq.: *girif*), what set the *'uzuma* apart was the sheer scale and number of the parties hosted for each emigrant. Indeed, the *'uzuma* was the primary venue through which the islanders expressed their gratitude to, and cemented their relationships with, their relatives abroad. In this sense, and similar to the function of the *'uzuma* in the Balga region in Jordan, the *'uzuma* in Soqotra "continue[d] to serve as an elaborate, multi-dimensional index of real political power."[18] The difference now was that the real locus of Soqotran power and wealth, as indexed by the *'uzuma*, was situated abroad.

At the other end of the spectrum, individual and quotidian examples of *karam* abound. These include the requisite two to three cups of tea offered to any visitor; the gift of a poem to a friend or to a researcher in need; and the circulation of a female host's cosmetics among other married women who stop by. Nearly daily, the women of Homhil spent their afternoons or evenings engaged in serial visits, drinking tea and applying makeup in each of the village homes. (I realized, after a while, that this was why I was brought a thermos each morning—so that I too could offer tea at a moment's notice.) However, unlike the competitive hosting and guesting found in the Red Sea town of Zabid (in northern Yemen), these habitual acts of *karam* among neighbors are less rituals of distinction—"tournaments of value"—than they are assurances of equilibrium.[19] It was not unusual, for example, for women to drink tea and apply cosmetics at Umm Yaqub's house, only to move on to Umm Jum'an's house, where Umm Yaqub would be encouraged to (re)apply the same products. On the one hand, these daily visits to every village home—by men, too—were simply a way to pass time in a place with little structured entertainment while also showing respect for one's neighboring relatives. On the other hand, they fostered an environment in which hosts and guests were always and immediately trading places and roles; with each reciprocal and commensurate makeover, every woman's generosity and equal standing were confirmed. Yet their anxieties concerning *karam* were ever present. Despite Sownhin's assured claim that rural *karam* will never disappear, its perceived departure from the *badiya* is precisely what animated both mundane conversations and crowd-pleasing poetry.

One December evening, I was sitting around with some female friends in Qayher. After having offered us tea, Umm Jum'an pulled out her wedding trunk containing her gold jewelry, cash, and cosmetics: candy-apple-red lipstick, black kohl, cologne, and skin-lightening cream. We had just drunk tea and applied the identical products at Amira's house—Hadibo did not have much of a selection then—and at Selimah's house before that. My face was already sallow from the turmeric paste (Soq.: *kerkam*) I had been encouraged to apply earlier as a skin "whitener," but Umm Jum'an began to mix another batch for me.[20] Eager for change, I fetched my laptop so that we could watch part of a French documentary series, *En terre inconnue,* starring the renowned French actress Emmanuelle Béart. In this episode, Béart is chauffeured to Paris's Orly airport, where she is blindfolded and taken on a surprise journey to . . . Soqotra. French viewers are invited to travel to this "mysterious" location with Béart, to observe her as she visits a honey project, dives in the Indian Ocean, and spends an evening with cave-dwelling goat herders who serve her boiled goat after first performing "ancient" incantations for health and rain. I had looked forward to watching this documentary filmed in Soqotra only a few months prior and to seeing my friends' reactions to this celebrity appearance on their island, despite none of them knowing who she was. But as we watched Béart delicately gnaw on a goat rib, politely accept tea, and smile warmly at her elderly hosts, I realized that what intrigued my friends most was not the disjuncture between these worlds—Béart's and the pastoralists'—but rather the disjuncture between hospitality gifted and, quite literally, staged.

"Did they pay for the goat, or did the people of Diksam offer it?" Amira asked slyly, nudging my side. Diksam is the upper region of Soqotra's central high plateau: mist covered, drizzly, and dappled with dragon's blood trees, the quintessential *badiya* (second, in this regard, only to the island's western plateau). Diksam is where one would expect to find genuine *karam*.

"Look, the woman is serving the tea red [black]!" Selimah noted, implicitly answering Amira's question. A generous host would serve a highly sweetened milky tea, going as far as substituting fresh milk with purchased powdered milk if her herd's supply was low. Thus, even if this meal had been gifted, the "red tea" betrayed a subtle stinginess on the part of the host.

Significantly, the majority of my women friends in Homhil had never entered a complete stranger's home, Soqotran or foreign. This film, then—unlike the plethora of satellite-beamed images that provide the visual and acoustic background in many of the Hadibo homes they may visit on occasion—presented them with an image that was both familiar and curious: a domestic environment that was clearly Soqotran yet outside their network and realm of experience. Therefore, the signs of miserliness or animosity that they were sensitive to in their immediate social interactions were underscored. The camera closed in on Emmanuelle's face—blue eyes and blond hair tied loosely behind her head—framed by the headshot of a young Soqotran girl whose tightly wrapped black face veil (burqa) revealed only her dark eyes.

"Oh, she is beautiful!" exclaimed young, impressionable Bilqis, referring not to the celebrity but to the Soqotran in her shadow.

CHILDREN OF NESTLÉ

"In the past, when Soqotrans used to talk to each other about their goats and who owns the largest number, someone would always bring up the example of Ma'laha," Ismail mused. I had met Ismail in the rainy "winter" season of 2004 when he worked as a driver for the ICDP project and I would catch rides with him from Hadibo to Homhil and back. Ismail would pass the time playing scratchy recordings of Soqotran poetry he had collected in the *badiya* while telling me stories of his youthful exploits and transgressions. Over the years, we became close friends and I began to rely on him more and more for his candid insights regarding the problems of the ICDP project and the overall changes in

Soqotra. One "summer" evening in February 2006, we were guests of a mutual friend in a small hamlet in the even remoter western plateau, where the pastoralists are said to better maintain their traditions and language. We had just finished the customary first course: goat bone marrow—which, in Soqotran fashion, we got at by cracking the bones and ribs between two large stones—and broth (Soq.: *riho d-te*; literally, water of meat). The next course would be rice covered with ghee and piled high with goat organs, fat, and meat.

"I remember when once, in my village, someone was talking about a man who owned lots of goats and another person said, 'Yes, he has many goats, but not like Ma'laha,'" Ismail continued. As in many hospitality-oriented societies, Ma'laha is remembered less for what he owned than for what he gave away. At Soqotran weddings, for example, it is customary for each family of the groom's neighboring tribes to contribute one goat to the wedding feast. Once, Ismail said, when Ma'laha's tribe was to supply goats to a neighboring groom, Ma'laha contributed one handsome goat for each of the families in his tribe—but everyone knew that they had really come from Ma'laha.

Ma'laha's name may be used by Soqotrans to evoke memories of exceptional *karam*, but he was far from being the only person commended for his generosity. Ismail told me that one of his neighbors was also known to have slaughtered nearly all his goats for visitors—to his father's increasing frustration. One day, the man's father slaughtered three of his own goats in supplication, begging God to make his son "less generous" so that he would not give away his entire herd and worth. (When the son discovered this, he became so angry that he disappeared for a while farther "into the *badiya*.") Although Ismail had not meant for these two stories to be compared, they read side by side as an illustration of the "impossibility" of unconditional hospitality that has animated Jacques Derrida's and other scholars' writings on this topic. Whereas the tacit "law" (or ethics) of hospitality demands that true hospitality be unconditional, the "laws" (or politics) of hospitality are discriminating and contingent.[21] Moreover, the "mastery" of hospitality requires the possession of place and property that one can offer—even relinquish—to one's guest. As Tracy McNulty explains it, "The best host is the one who has given the most, even to the point of giving away that which defines him as master and host. This tension identifies an aporetic limit at which identity is established at the very moment of its dissolution, through contact with the nonidentical, the other."[22] Ma'laha had so many goats that he could afford to be selective and, in a sense, was merely giving "conditionally" according to the politics (laws) of hospitality. Ismail's neighbor, on the other hand, gave unconditionally to the point at which his ability to host and, with it, his very identity, were threatened.

These stories of exemplary (past) hospitality are narrated by Soqotrans as an indictment of their material and political present. Once beset by famine, the island in more recent years has been plagued by a hunger of a different kind: a hunger for landownership, riches, and power that, in hindsight, makes the days of (actual) hunger (*ayyam al-ju'*) seem like days of plenty. Indeed, despite the acute hunger experienced by most elders at various times in their lives, many remember God's blessing (*baraka*)—the yields from their livestock, honeybees, date palms, and even the sea—as having been greater in generations past. They thus attribute the attenuation in God's *baraka* over the past forty years to the weakening of their body, spirit, and *karam*.

This sense of Soqotrans having strayed from the ways of their ancestors is a common theme in contemporary Soqotri poetry. If poets—as tongue-wagging guests—are feared for their ability to tarnish their host's reputation,[23] Soqotra's poets have taken the entire population to task for its dwindling *karam*. Just before setting out with Ismail to the western plateau, I had met up with one of the island's most respected poets, Ali Abdullah al-Rigdihi, who shared with us his own assessment of Soqotra's present state:

> The people of Soqotra have embarked on a difficult and dangerous path
> A way of life that is not the one they inherited from their forefathers,
> God have mercy on them, the most beloved!
> They used to bring back their herds evening and morning to the one home, and in the morning they would say farewell to one another.
> And the next day, at first light, they would discuss together in which direction each would go.
> In the morning a long line of the most blessed goats would be brought in to the two folds of Di-Rowkeb to be milked.
> And another long line would go to the fold of Di-Sebereni: that clan would gather there.
> Some of them would be milked and some slaughtered for food; all was warm and friendly in those days and those who gave and those who took did so gladly.

The butter-making skin would be filled to the top from the milk of only ten goats, and
    even the most beloved and precious of the goats would be killed to feed others.

In a hole in a rock or tree trunk, two bees would make enough honey to fill a clay
    milking pot.

The Soqotri people were content: from the plateaus of the east and the center
    overlooking the Noged plain right to the Ma'alah plateau of the Di-'Esoni
    peoples in the west.

And they were just as happy in the two Hantiyo areas [in eastern Soqotra], and as
    far as the grazing reserves of the people of Seberho [in western Soqotra].

[The face of] anyone you met with would light up [with a warm and open smile], a
    sweet and lovely sight.

For [in those days] people did not spend the midday hours arguing about land and
    disputing over who owned the ground so irrationally and ludicrously.

Nor did they spend their evenings in desperation, trapped [by such worries]. What
    more must be taken from them [in bribes] before they will finally come to
    realize [how futile and destructive all this is]?

For today goats in their hundreds are gathered into the fold, and the ground of the
    milking areas is darkened by their great number.

But only half a small coffee-cup of milk is to be got from them, just enough for the
    Thermos to offer to the visitor [i.e., not enough for the household].

And the tribes are dipped in and out of boiling water, and are only still half-raw,
    like someone newly released from prison.[24]

In this and in similar poems, al-Rigdihi chastises his fellow islanders for having abandoned their inherited way of life for a new lifestyle filled with contention. We could read this literally: Soqotrans are relinquishing their pastoral past for an urban modernity, where they become ensnared in land disputes and other arguments. Or we could read this metaphorically: Soqotrans have surrendered their charitableness and generosity for individual gain. Either way, Soqotrans are faulted for having abandoned a blessed life of plenty, as evidenced by the relative productivity of the goats and the bees. In the present, in contrast, despite the plains being "darkened" by livestock, Soqotrans can barely extract enough milk to serve to a guest—and when added to tea, no less. It is due to their greed and lack of concern for each other's well-being, al-Rigdihi intimates, that God's *baraka* has disappeared.

Ismail, too, talks a lot about the loss of God's *baraka*, which he attributes to the various forms of development that have made Soqotrans insatiable and weak. Over dinner, he linked what he considers to be his own generation's moral and physical lassitude to a "change of heart." "People used to have pure hearts," he asserted, "even if they were weak in religion back then." Ismail has been an outspoken critic of the piety movement that has swept across the island. This is a dilemma for many Soqotrans: how to parse what they believe to have been a period of *baraka* with one now repudiated for its religious ignorance (*al-jahiliya*). I asked him what caused these changes.

> Before, there were no cars like Layla 'Alwi and Munika and mobile phones and all these kinds of things. [Layla 'Alwi, the name of a famous Egyptian actress, and Munika, a reference to Monica Lewinski, are nicknames for different models of large, "buxom" Land Cruisers in Yemen.] If Soqotrans had goats and were satiated—the most important thing was that these goats had enough food, water and grasses—then, okay, they were comfortable. This was their desire—that their goats were healthy, and their children. But now, no. Now, I want a car—how do I get it? I need a job. And to get a job I need to lie or to get ahead by saying, for example: 'That person working for you is a liar. He doesn't know anything, but I know this and that.' And to get a telephone I will need to get another job. Our desires are changing and increasing. This is due to development.

I reminded Ismail of all the stories he had been telling me of how hungry his people had been. "It's true, there wasn't enough food," he replied, "but they were stronger and more powerful than we are now." For Ismail, and many of the Soqotrans who share his anxieties, the purportedly insatiable desires of his generation are precisely the result of their new, urbane diet. "In the past, Soqotrans grew up on fresh milk, honey, dates, and everything one hundred percent natural. But we are the children of bottles [*marda'a*] and Dano and Nestlé. Ten individuals now can't do the work of one person from back then." Dano and Nestlé are the company names written across the tins of powdered milk sold in Hadibo, which even pastoralists try to keep on hand in case their livestock's milk runs low.

And it is precisely for this reason that Ismail had brought up Ma'laha in the first place. "About a year ago," he continued before the main course appeared, "I was in the area where Ma'laha had lived and saw his granddaughter. The family still had a good number of goats—enough that if she milked them all at once, she should get sixty to eighty liters of milk. A lot of goats. But I saw her walk across the plain carrying just one yellow gallon [an empty vegetable-oil container]. She knew her goats wouldn't yield more than two liters of milk. And I stopped to talk to people and asked, 'How is it possible that the granddaughter of Ma'laha does not get more than two liters of milk in these days?' This is evidence to us Soqotrans that *baraka* has ended. *Baraka* has left our property."

SUGHAYR'S DILEMMA

Another summer evening in late February, during the beginning of the date-pollination season (Soq.: *qeyat*), I walked across the now-verdant plateau to visit Sughayr, Homhil's most reputable poet. I had wanted to ask Sughayr about the *mekolis*, the male "healers" (or sorcerers) whom the islanders had depended on in the days of the sultan. Sughayr had once intimated to me that he had been "like a *mekoli*"; others told me that both he and the *qadi* had worked as assistants to a *mekoli* during their youth. By the time I reached his village, it was nearly dark and his family was just sitting down to dinner. I joined them for what was a standard meal at this time of year—rice covered with fresh butter-milk—and we made awkward small talk as I tried to broach the subject of *mekolis*. When this did not work, I asked Sughayr if he would recite one of his poems.

"What's the use? To me? To you? Why should I recite a poem for you?" he asked in Arabic, implying that I would not understand the Soqotri poetry any-way. As I was trying to convince Sughayr otherwise, Hamdan and two other teachers appeared at the door. Earlier, I had asked the teachers if they would accompany me on this visit—the teachers were always looking for something to do, and I wanted to avoid making my way home through the darkness alone—but they had demurred. It was during the period that Sayf was living in the vil-lage, and our hosts were trying their very best to keep us from crossing paths. Hamdan had made excuses about not wanting to leave Sayf alone. Then, under the cover of darkness, they hurried over, hoping that Sughayr had slaughtered a goat for me and that they, too, would enjoy meat that night. Joining us, the teachers also tried to cajole Sughayr into reciting his poetry. Finally, he complied.

"These are from my generosity [*min karamati*]," he said, before reciting two poems about his experiences working as a seasonal migrant laborer in an agricultural farm in al-Mahra for the past two decades. Significantly, the two poems that Sughayr "gifted" us—with maybe a twinge of embarrassment over not having served us meat—were precisely about *karam* and its ostensible demise. The first begins with Sughayr's description of his hospitalization in mainland Yemen and his gratitude toward his three Soqotran friends for bringing him food, prescription drugs, and intravenous fluids while he was bedridden. Then, as if his illness had been a sign of foreboding, he decides to return to Soqotra and contemplates the timing of his arrival:

> It is better that you retire now, O you old-timer Sughayr.
> Refrain from traveling in the period right before the monsoon begins
>   [Soq.: *sudhayten*][25]
> For then the southwind [Soq.: *medeh*] will block you, closing all doors.
> And your letters will not reach there nor will your telephone calls.
> We do not have any means to know about your state, the conditions in the
>   countryside [al-Mahra] are poor.
> When will you leave for Soqotra? God alone knows the date.
> Perhaps I shall stay in April and March, and at the end of August I shall depart.
> Perhaps I shall wait until January and go at the New Year.
> At that time, it will be the height of winter [Soq.: *sereb*] and Soqotra will be
>   verdant.
> Or perhaps I shall wait until the pre-monsoon season [Soq.: *doti*] and arrive when
>   the dates begin to yellow.
> For no one is welcomed at the end of winter,
> And no one will heed me when they are pollinating dates.
> I am not an emigrant [Ar.: *muhajir*]; they will not slaughter six goats for me.
> I would be fortunate to be offered some tea; this would satisfy me.
> And if people asked as a mere courtesy, "How are you?"
> This would be suffice as recognition of my migration.

Whereas Sughayr details his Soqotran friends' tireless care while he is hospitalized in al-Mahra, he is less convinced about the reception he will receive when he returns home. The poet cannot travel to Soqotra during the southwest monsoon season because of the strong winds that close the sea. Nor can he contact his family to inquire how they are doing or to inform them of his plans. Should he return at the end of the monsoon (Soq.: *horf*), once the sea opens up? Should he wait until the end of winter when the pastures have greened and milk will be plenty, but the men will be busy? Or should he wait until the pre-monsoon season (Soq.: *doti*) just prior to the following monsoon, when the date harvest begins to ripen? Despite his years working abroad, Sughayr is not counted among the emigrants whose visits occasion a spectacular *'uzuma*. He may be lucky enough to be recognized when he arrives home after his Odyssean migration, but no one will celebrate his return, not even as a guest.

Later, as I transcribed the poems with the help of the teachers, I expressed my confusion regarding Sughayr's migrant status. What did he mean, he wasn't an emigrant? Hadn't Sughayr's second poem detailed his constant travel overseas—his exhaustive toil in the sun: "I have heard of cars being unregistered if they have no plates. / This is how it is with our nationality and identity cards. / When the sun rises high and the morning shadows vanish these cannot move us into the shade." The teachers chuckled at the very thought.

"Emigrants are those who go to the United Arab Emirates!" one said. "Not to Yemen, which is poor [*miskin*]." Sughayr may work overseas, another explained, but he still depends on gifts and money from the Soqotran emigrants who live in the Gulf. As he himself states in the last lines of the first poem: "Before I was proud of being supported by a few emigrants. / They would give me a cigarette or some prayer beads. / But now they arrive empty-handed, without a shawl [*radi*] or a [Kuwaiti] cord [*'iqal*]."[26] As a pastoralist with no paid labor except seasonal employment in poverty-stricken Yemen, Sughayr used to be reliant on the Soqotran emigrants in the Gulf, as are many of the islanders today. These are the emigrants whose visits are celebrated with the slaughter of "up to six" animals at a time. Yet, as Sughayr wryly notes, these emigrants have started to return empty-handed; they barely even *appear* Kuwaiti or Emirati. Have they become miserly, or have they, too, become *miskin*?

Sughayr's and al-Rigdihi's poems, like Ismail's musings, depict a common sentiment that something in Soqotra is off-kilter. Whereas their nostalgia for the kind of lifestyle that connotes a communal, pastoral care—of flocks and people—may be particular to the autochthonous Saqatri of the *badiya*, I heard similar concerns expressed by members of both the Arab and Afro-Soqotran populations living along the coast. "In the past, people loved each other," a young, Afro-Soqotran shaykh from Suq once told me. "If I went with a group of people to Hallah [the northeastern coast], the people there would slaughter a goat for us, even if they didn't know us—like I am one of them. Now, if we go somewhere where we don't know the people, it's difficult for us to enter their houses. Fear has arisen in them."

Even men who had been enslaved by or had worked as servants to the former sultans spoke of the sultans' generosity and of the subsequent PDRY government's care for its people. Talk of dwindling *karam*—often over generous meals, no less—was as much a critique of the late-capitalist "unity" regime as it was a critique of the modern, individuated self. But it also bespeaks, as Mandana Limbert has shown in the context of Oman, the material and social effects of the developments in infrastructure that have thoroughly transformed Soqotra's landscape in the course of two decades.[27] In this sense, the discourse of *karam* in crisis is not merely a walk down memory lane. Rather, it indexes contemporary predicaments and dilemmas arising from new roadways, both metaphorical and concrete. One of these is the predicament voiced by Ismail and the poet al-Rigdihi that development generates dissatisfaction. Another is the dilemma expressed by Sughayr: Where is my place in the island in relation to the Gulf-based emigrants returning in this era? For it is precisely the island's new developments and infrastructure—airport, roads, parks, and telecommunications—that has been the conduit for an upsurge in guests and strangers.

NEW INFRASTRUCTURE, UNFAMILIAR GUESTS, AND NEFARIOUS STRANGERS

Following the unification of North and South Yemen in 1990—and especially the northern regime's victory in the 1994 civil war—many of the former socialist government's political, economic, and religious restrictions were lifted. Soqotrans often refer to the introduction of multiparty elections, economic liberalization, and public piety during the early to mid-1990s as *al-infitah* (the opening)—a term that carries the same mixture of approval and opprobrium as it does in Egypt, where it signifies the capitalist reforms and political "normalization" with Israel inaugurated in the 1970s by President Anwar al-Sadat. In Soqotra, however, the term *al-infitah* is used also to refer to the "opening" of the sea after the annual monsoon. These two openings came together with the all-weatherization and commercialization of the Hadibo airport in 1999, which resulted in, well, a sea change for the islanders who had suffered this annual isolation.[28] Now connected to the mainland year-round, Soqotra was opened to mainland Yemeni entrepreneurs looking for new markets; European ecotourists chasing pristine beaches and landscapes; and scores of foreign scientists, researchers, and developers searching out new projects. Nevertheless, even into the mid-2000s, air travel remained exceptional enough to draw Soqotrans to the airport on Fridays to watch the weekly plane arrive. By the end of the decade, the weekly flights from Sanaa and from Aden had turned into daily flights operated by the national airline, Yemenia, and its competitor, Air Felix. The now "international" airport also serviced biweekly flights between Soqotra and Sharjah, in the UAE. This new connectivity to the mainland enabled Soqotrans to travel more regularly in search of employment, higher education, and medical care. At the same time, it resulted in a tremendous influx of guests and strangers to the island.

The Soqotran diaspora, many of whom had been in self-exile for nearly two decades, returned to the island in droves. One effect of the government's investments in the island's infrastructure in the early to mid-2000s was a marked increase in the emigrants' affective and financial investments in the island's social and religious welfare, economic development, and politics. Even prior to Yemen's unification, Soqotran emigrants in the Gulf had been sending money to their island relatives to pay for wells, water pipes, generators, and mosques in their natal villages. Although several of these emigrants returned to Soqotra as early as 1990 and 1991, they remained fearful of the socialist system (*nizam al-hizb*) that prevailed until 1994. However, once Arab state socialism (and secularism) was dismantled, emigrant-funded mosques sprouted up in nearly every village. For the Gulf-based Soqotrans, this was a relatively prudent form of charity that would benefit the impoverished islanders, reinscribe Islam into the island's postsocialist landscape, and bring the charitable (*muhsin*) closer to God. (More cynical Soqotrans pointed out that this trend led to a rather impious form of competition among the emigrants, all vying to build the loftiest mosques.)[29] Then, with the increase in air travel between Soqotra and the Gulf and the introduction of international tourism to the island in the mid-2000s, emigrants supplemented their spiritual investments with commercial ones, like hotels and restaurants. Their increasing involvement in the island's day-to-day business was facilitated by the government's construction of hundreds of kilometers of paved roads (in 2001–2008) and the introduction of nearly islandwide cell-phone coverage (in 2005), which allowed Soqotrans in places like Homhil and Ajman to speak with one another regularly. Soqotran emigrants—and for-eign anthropologists—can now be apprised immediately of any exigencies, such as the need for airfare to seek medical treatment on the mainland. This kind of connectivity has also engendered the marriage of young Soqotran girls to their Gulf-based cousins or even to elderly Gulf-based Soqotrans, Emiratis, or Oma-nis in search of inexpensive first or second wives.

Although the initial return of these emigrants to their families was, and remains, occasion for a grand 'uzuma in the *badiya*, the increasing frequency of their visits has also posed new burdens on their less fortunate hosts. In addition to rural Soqotrans being expected to regularly yet generously host their visiting relatives and their Gulf-born children—as well as their own emigrant daugh-ters, who have traded life in the *badiya* for a more comfortable urban existence with air conditioning, abundant foods, and housemaids—the introduction of new commodities and the influences of Gulf (*khaliji*) culture means that the very expectations among islanders of what constitutes proper hospitality have grown. "Life has become more complicated," Ismail said when I visited Soqotra in 2013. Whereas it used to be considered generous to offer one's guests a meal of goat meat and rice, Soqotrans have come to expect sugared drinks and fruits and vegetables, too. (As an example, Ismail said that he had recently hosted three hundred people for an 'uzuma in honor of his parents' Gulf-based friends for which he had purchased a camel, a cow, and ten goats. But the women in his village were horrified when they discovered that Ismail had not purchased drink mix. Immediately, they sent someone to the next village to buy cans of powdered orange drink, which ended up being thoroughly diluted, yet this fla-vorless, orange-in-color-only water was a vital component to the meal.) As a result of such traffic, rural Soqotrans are being called on to host more people more often with more cost to them—it is no wonder that Sughayr was cynical about whether his return from the mainland would be celebrated.

Alongside the emigrants, a new kind of guest arrived in the mid-1990s. Fol-lowing Yemen's "reunification" in 1994, Tablighi (and in later years, Salafi) pros-elytizers from mainland Yemen—referred to as *mutatawwi'in*—began visiting what must have struck them as an ideal site for Islamic missionary or proselyte activities (*da'wa*).[30] Not only had the island become more accessible after its enforced isolation under socialist rule, but also its inhabitants were considered underdeveloped and undereducated—and thus in particular need of religious instruction and guidance. These *mutatawwi'in,* often joined and emulated by pious islanders, traveled the countryside—staying regularly in the newly built mosques, where the rural women cooked for them—to instruct the Bedouin in proper Islamic practice, prayer, deportment, and dress. For instance, they pressed Soqotran women to replace their traditional knee-length and short-sleeved dresses with more modest attire. They discouraged men from drumming, engaging in religious supplication, and participating in mixed-sex poetry recitations. And they encouraged a more vigilant separation of the sexes.

This shift toward religious conservatism in Soqotra reflected broader shifts in mainland Yemen that had occurred during its transitional period (1990–1994), when the socialist, secular, and gender-egalitarian elements of South Yemen's constitution and progressive Family Law of 1974 were replaced by the less progressive laws and customs from the north, the declaration of Islamic jurisprudence (sharia) as *"the* source of all legislation," and the enactment of a new, gender discriminatory Personal Status Law in 1992.[31] A good majority of Soqotrans, male and female, perceived this not as a regression but rather as an enabling form of spiritual and material development. Still, the effects of the *mutatawwi'in* were not lost on the islanders, many of whom worried about losing their cultural practices, including their conventions of hospitality. The challenges posed by the Salafi teacher in Homhil were, in this regard, not at all unusual.

If the emigrants and the *mutatawwi'in* were welcomed guests, the mid-1990s also ushered in platoons of newcomers whom Soqotrans generally resented. First among these were the "northerners" (*shamaliyin*) who moved to Soqotra in search of economic opportunities. Some of these young Yemeni men had never heard of Soqotra before being deployed there by the national army or before meeting other internal migrants lured to the island by the news of its opening to international companies and NGOs. For example, Usama, a young high school graduate from Taiz, enlisted in the army to help support his widowed mother and his siblings. In 1999, the army deployed him to Soqotra, where he fulfilled his duties in the mornings and spent his afternoons working casual jobs and taking advantage of the low-priced English and computer lessons offered by an Australian-run school. When I met him five years later, Usama had opened a little computer printing shop, in which he slept the few nightly hours when he was not hard at work. In 2010, having worked his way up to becoming a manager of a local hotel, Usama married his cousin and resettled her and their newborn child on Soqotra. Another young man, from Ibb, was lugging cement for a construction company in Aden in 2003 when he heard about a place called Soqotra that his fellow worker described as "heavenly" (*janna*). Too poor to afford the airfare, the twenty-eight-year old journeyed by boat, making his way to Hadibo, where he worked menial jobs and slept in a YER 50 (USD 0.25) per night flophouse (*lukanda*). After several months, he landed employment as a driver for the ICDP project, which provided him English classes and additional forms of continuing education. For these and many other hardworking young men, Soqotra was an El Dorado: a semimythical place where mainland Yemen's undereducated and underemployed young adults might find opportunities foreclosed to them at home.[32] Indeed, tour operators, hotel managers, merchants, and shopkeepers from Taiz, Ibb, Aden, and Sanaa soon monopolized Hadibo's budding private and service sectors. Not all mainlanders were successful, however, and not all of them stayed. Even Usama, who had fared well, struggled to make a home for himself and his family in a harsh climate made harsher by rampant inflation.

Although my Soqotran acquaintances respected people like Usama and the individual migrants whom they knew, Soqotrans as a whole—much like other Yemeni southerners—have been quick to scapegoat the northerners for their own perceived misfortune. Whether accused of having stolen and slaughtered Soqotrans' goats (having assumed they were feral), or of collaborating to increase the prices of commodities on the island, or of receiving scholarships and advancement ahead of their Soqotran counterparts, or of buying up all the available land and thus contributing to the soaring inflation, the northerners were often criticized for "eating" at the Soqotrans' expense. "The Yemenis have eaten our livelihoods [*al-yamaniyin akalu rizqina*]," was a common refrain. Moreover, the northern Yemenis were perceived not only as an economic threat but also as a cultural one. Referred to disparagingly by Soqotrans as *dahabisha* after a particularly uncouth Yemeni television character, the northerners—the Sanaani tribesmen, in particular—were also considered alien in their ways, having brought with them habits widely perceived to be negative, such as chewing qat.[33] The longer I lived in Soqotra, the more I became privy to jokes about the *dahabisha* and to Soqotrans' implicit distrust of them. For example, when I related an incident about some merchant overcharging me, my neighbor immediately assumed I was speaking of a northerner: "A northerner? What devils!" he harrumphed.

My gracious hosts and friends were certainly not mean-spirited. Rather, we might view their mockery as creating "an illusion of doing battle in an inti- mate setting and on a level playing field" amid rising imbalances in wealth and power.[34] Yet the islanders' frequent mention of the northerners' deviant slaugh- tering practices demonstrates their awareness that the playing field was not at all level. Not only had some northerners slaughtered Soqotrans' goats—the underlying cause, according to the Afro-Soqotran shaykh quoted earlier, for why "fear has arisen" in Soqotra—but also, as he went on to tell me, "Once, in a restaurant, they slaughtered a cat! Really! . . . The owner made a soup of cats and sold it for twenty riyal. Everyone thought it was chicken. Until they found the skin of a cat—behind the restaurant." (This is true; when, in the mid-1990s, the cat was let out of the bag, so to speak, the restaurateur was imprisoned and committed suicide.) One could say that the northern townsmen were viewed not only as rapacious strangers but also as degenerate hosts.

The other major types of newcomers to arrive in Soqotra at the turn of the millennium were the foreign nationals (non-Yemeni Arabs and Europe- ans) employed by the ICDP project and its affiliated NGOs, the majority of whom moved into makeshift guesthouses in Hadibo, and the foreign tourists (primarily European), who moved about the island from one ICDP-funded campground to another. Whereas the foreign administrators, researchers, vol- unteers, and health professionals were a relatively small and stable fixture in Hadibo, the numbers of tourists visiting Soqotra increased exponentially dur- ing the course of the decade.[35] In the mid-2000s, the residents of Homhil and other protected areas were still trying to wrap their heads around the very con- cept of tourism. During the training sessions I attended in 2004, residents of the Homhil Protected Area were enthusiastically informed about an archipel- ago called "al-ghalabaghus" that captured a hundred million dollars from tour- ism each year; that tourists would visit Soqotra to see its biodiversity; and that this income would help build schools and roads. This information intrigued my neighbors, who were nevertheless confused about why people would travel so far and pay so much to see trees or were shocked when German women appeared in Homhil baring their upper thighs. By the late 2000s, however, the tourists' ingressions (and transgressions) were widely anticipated. Soqotrans reported on the presence or absence of tourists as they did of rain; young men from the *badiya*, like Yaqub, had picked up a fair bit of English, Italian, Czech, and Japanese; and the suavest among the tour operators and drivers from Hadibo had secured themselves seasonal European girlfriends.

Yet, even at its peak in 2010–2011—before tourism to Yemen succumbed to the Arab uprisings and Yemen's own unresolved revolution—Soqotrans questioned the true benefits of this seasonal economy. The holiday activity along Soqotra's coasts did not extend with near-equal vigor into the island's interior. Few tourists passed through Homhil during the holiday season; even fewer stopped to spend the night, even though its campground was operational, albeit bedraggled. Inhabitants of Homhil remembered the conversations about Soqotra being "the Galápagos of the Indian Ocean" and wondered where the money was. "We haven't tasted anything from the tourists," one of my elderly neighbors declared when I returned from the campground with some of the tourists' discarded food items one day. Even the coastal lodges, their New Year's windfall notwithstanding, were doing poorly. One site's "community-based" management team has been paying the local shaykh YER 600,000 per year (about USD 3,000) to "lease" the campground located on the shaykh's tribal land—despite the ICDP having financed its construction. Moreover, even though the managers struggled in the wake of the Yemeni revolution to attract the six hundred tourists annually needed to break even, the shaykh would not reduce the rent because of the many Soqotrans he had to compensate to keep them satisfied. The tourism season in Soqotra was simply too short and too impacted by events in mainland Yemen to be truly sustainable. Given these pressures, it is not so surprising that some Soqotrans who were said to be "from the *badiya*" (i.e., "Bedouin" and thus, ostensibly, unworldly) had a group of researchers arrested in 2008 for having allegedly enhanced the toxicity of the endemic scorpions' venom. While my Soqotran friends made light of and were even embarrassed by this manifestation of their compatriots' credulity, it is not incredible that the turn to tourism had increased the islanders' vulnerability to hazardous encounters.

Although the commercialization of the airport opened Soqotra to these new guests and nefarious strangers, the construction of the island's asphalt "ring road" has most impacted Soqotrans' physical and socioeconomic mobility. While biologists have detailed the destructive effects of this road network on the environment, few have noted, as Soqotrans have, its destructive effects on their cultural practices, including forms of *karam*. Despite the many direct and indirect benefits of paved roads, those living alongside them were suddenly more likely to receive visitors multiple times per day. "Before, whenever a guest came, I wouldn't let him enter the house," Dhetiyan explained to Ismail and me as we drank tea in his yard overlooking the Diksam plateau. " 'Come, you *must* come with me to the goat's pen,' I would say. That was so that we could milk the goats and give the guest fresh milk—a pot of it—right there." Dhetiyan's reflections turned, as do so many Soqotrans' poems, back to the memory of the full, large goatskins that dwarf the half-liter plastic bottles used to milk livestock today. "Now we say, 'Come in, sit down. I'll go see if I can find some milk. If not, then we'll drink tea.' " Whereas our host attributed these changes most directly to the loss of *baraka*, he also noted, with some reluctance, the impact of the increased transportation on his level of generosity. "If someone were to visit me for the first time, of course, I would slaughter for him," Dhetiyan asserted. "There must be blood. But for someone like Ismail, who comes two or three times a month: maybe I'll slaughter for him, but maybe not." What Dhetiyan did not want to say, what Ismail told me later, is that already that morning a Soqotran driver had stopped by with his tourists for some "local" bread and tea. Then we had arrived. And in the afternoon, another group would stop by.

"The poets who complain about the loss of *karam*," Ismail said, "don't think about such things, like the problems of the road or the changes in people's diets."

SOUP OF LIES

Once, there was a brave man named Rehabhen who lived with his wife, son, and servant in a cave in Di-Kishin, in the western part of Soqotra. When the "Franks" (*ifrang*) arrived from across the sea, they slaughtered and ate many of the islanders' livestock. The Soqotrans were upset and afraid, so Rehabhen devised a plan to scare the Franks (Europeans) away. One day, Rehabhen's son and servant captured two European men and a girl who had wandered away from the group. They tied the two men together and covered the girl with a rug, underneath which they had also concealed a goat. They took the girl to Rehabhen, who, pretending to slaughter her, shed the goat's blood instead. Rehabhen cooked the goat's flesh over a fire and offered some of this meat to the men, who thought they were being served their companion. Then the horrified men were allowed to escape so that they could rejoin their group and report on the Soqotrans' apparent cannibalism. As a result, the Europeans fled Soqotra. Rehabhen eventually married the girl, who bore him another seven sons. Their offspring became known as the tribe of il-Kishin, which grew to be the largest tribe in Soqotra. Today, when one encounters Soqotrans with green eyes and light skin, there is a good chance that they inherited these from their (kidnapped) European female ancestor.

There are many ways to interpret this well-known Soqotran story, which I was first told the day that I moved into the Homhil Protected Area with my two trunks of canned foods and my flimsy camping stove. Although related to me in the context of other kidnapping narratives—the kidnapping of Bedouin children by the socialist state to send them to school; the kidnapping of a Soqotran woman by a Russian officer who married her and took her back to the Soviet Union—the Rehabhen story is, at its core, a story of a Soqotran safeguarding his livestock and people from hostile strangers. It is at the same time an etiological tale explaining the allegedly half-European origin of Soqotra's largest tribal group: il-Kishin. Over the years, I have heard and read several versions of the Rehabhen story, which differ in their particulars but not in their central plot.[36] Although the story does not appear to have been recorded in European histories—or even prior to the 1970s and 1980s, when the Russian anthropologist Vitaly Naumkin first conducted fieldwork on the island—it resonates with nineteenth- and early twentieth-century British beliefs that Soqotrans were or had recently been anthropophagic. Tellingly, when the British Royal Air Force decided to construct an emergency landing ground on Soqotra in 1939—the island's first airstrip—the code word that the British chose for their signal station there was "CANNIBAL ISLAND."[37] Indeed, Soqotrans themselves relate freak stories of their ancestors having eaten human flesh during periods of great famine. Despite the common narratives of Soqotrans' past and present hunger, hunger is not what this story is about.

As I see it, the Rehabhen story—and its circulation at the turn of the millennium—serves as a parable about how to fend off foreign incursion. Most significant in this regard is its reverberations in contemporary stories of the arrival of the northerners and their indiscriminate slaughtering of livestock. (Or perhaps it is the recent memories of the northerners' animal thievery that has made its way into the Rehabhen narrative today.)[38] Whereas the northerners slaughtered Soqotran-owned livestock, served Soqotrans taboo (cat) flesh, married Soqotran women and stayed, the Franks slaughtered Soqotran-owned livestock, were duped into thinking *they* were being served taboo (human) flesh, lost one of *their* women to an exogamous marriage, and *left*. This more desirable outcome was achieved through the actions of one unarmed man: a cunning host who had literally imprisoned his guests and through an act of perverse hospitality—perverse, not because of *what* he offered them but because of what he *pretended* to offer them; the inverse, again, of the restaurateur's deceit—was able to maintain or at least prolong some form of sovereignty over his tribal lands. Although Rehabhen ultimately "ingests" and thus symbolically conquers his foreign opponents—not through cannibalism but through marriage—it is the sacrificial feast that remains at the center of this narrative and of il-Kishin "independence."

As anyone who has ever felt the constraints of unbridled hospitality undoubtedly knows, hospitality can be deployed as a measure of one's self-mastery; a gesture of domestic sovereignty; a form of symbolic control over one's guests; and a demonstration of one's moral, if not political and economic, superiority.[39] Rehabhen exhibits all of these qualities: self-possession, domestic sovereignty, the ability to turn a foreign threat into political opportunity, and moral superiority. He did not, after all, kill or eat any of the Franks—nor did he eat their property, as they did his. In a similar but less dramatic fashion, Soqotrans transform the quotidian act of *karam* into a form of sovereign (if symbolic) control over the platoon of guests and strangers that come to them from beyond the sea—even if it means ultimately accommodating, incorporating, and becoming indelibly marked by their presence. Yet, at the time of the island's opening, Soqotran poets and their audiences no longer saw in themselves or their compatriots a Rehabhen or even a Maʿlaha. This is not to say that Soqotrans no longer valued *karam* or that their generosity toward guests and strangers was compromised; as these various anecdotes should demonstrate, quite the opposite was (and remains) true. Rather, Soqotrans' oft-expressed concern about their supposed diminishing hospitality masked (and simultaneously revealed) an underlying anxiety about their perceived loss of self-possession and self-mastery in the wake of the island's opening to new governments, new visitors, and new desires. For, if Rehabhen ingested his enemies and Maʿlaha provided for the entire tribe, it was now the Yemeni state

ingesting the island, the northerners eating more than their share, and the Soqotrans hungering for actual sustenance while barely tasting the scraps of tourism.

This new form of hunger—not so much physical as metaphysical—became
more apparent to me during my second winter in Soqotra, a year after the citizens of Homhil had lost more than sixty goats to flash floods. This year, my female neighbors walked two hours daily to bring water, flour, and dates to their
emaciated and dehydrated cows seeking to graze at higher altitudes—this, during Ramadan, when they were fasting, too. Throughout Ramadan and into the
winter, before the pastures greened and the herds reproduced, my gaunt friend
Selimah complained frequently about her "lying sauce" (*maraq kadhdhab*). "I
can't stomach this false sauce," she decried, pointing to the watered-down tomato paste that flavored the platter of (meatless) rice she served to her family
and to me. Like other hosts who often apologized for serving me meals "from
the *badiya*," Selimah's comments communicated an acute awareness of the material and social inequities that defined our relationship. And not only our relationship: Selimah's comments spoke equally to the emigrant Soqotrans who
proclaimed their inability to "bear life" in the countryside. Although Selimah
must tolerate this life, by asserting that she too could not stomach it, she was
professing herself to be worldly and worthy, like them.

Yet the posturing here hinges not only on what can be borne and by whom;
it pivots, crucially, on the lie. Comments like Selimah's expressed a hunger for
real food, like the meat afforded to and by tourists, and for a real state that sus-
tains its citizens—like the socialist state that had introduced food subsidies to
Soqotra or like the rentier states that support the Soqotrans living in the Gulf.
In their absence, it was through tourism that Soqotrans were supposed to taste
sustainable development. But until this would happen, many of the men from
Homhil worked at the campground merely to eat of the real food left over by
tourists—scraps that rarely made it back to the villages from where they had
come. There, in villages such as Qayher, women, children, and the elderly simply made do on, what was to them, a semblance of a meal: a pacifier. (Soqotran
women refer to a child's pacifier as a *kidhdhaba*, a term drawn from the same
Arabic trilateral root *k-dh-b*, to lie, as the term Selimah used to qualify her
"lying" sauce.) In this sense, much as babies are appeased regularly through
pacifiers, and just as the Soqotran livestock must often be pacified with wa-
tery gruel, Soqotran pastoralists have been reduced to satiating their own

want through a soup of lies—albeit with the full awareness that their life in the *badiya*, now without *baraka*, has rendered them infantilized. To put it another way, not only were Soqotrans served a "soup of lies" by the northerners, the state, and the conservation-and-development regime, they were now also engaging in self-deception.

This explains why seemingly minor complaints—al-Rigdihi's charge that the tribes are "only still half-raw"; Sughayr's claim that "no one will heed me"; Selimah's aversion to her own *maraq kadhdhab*; or the slippage from goat meat to bread and from fresh milk to tea—are meaningful indexes of the degree to which Soqotrans considered themselves to be "at home" in their self-identity, in their place (particularly in the *badiya*), and in their place in the world. If, as Tracy McNulty argues, the "host is the perfect embodiment of identity, the one who is 'eminently identical' to himself," Soqotrans' "crisis of hospitality" suggests that they no longer recognized themselves and their desires.[40] As my hosts' reflections, my friends' ruminations, and the poets' rebukes reveal, it was not so much through their dispossession—through radical acts of hospitality—that their identity was challenged. Rather, it was through the *increase* in their material possessions and desires that these "children of Nestlé" had lost their way.

A RIPOSTE, OF SORTS

At the turn of the millennium, Yemen's Soqotra Island was inundated with alien envoys, experts, and regimes eager to impart their wisdom, visions, and values on the people living there. This was not the first time in history that Soqotrans were called on to give place and time to strangers' efforts to assist and develop them. But it was quite possibly the first time that Soqotrans received so many and such diverse strangers, so many of whom were driven by "the will to improve" them.[41] Soqotrans responded to this incursion of foreign visitors and visions less through resistance—as has been noted in the protests of rural residents against park creation in places as diverse as Papua New Guinea, Tanzania, and Sardinia[42]—than through *accommodation*, both literal and metaphorical. This accommodation has taken the form of rural communities hosting the various emigrants, volunteers, state extension officers, protected area managers, teachers, dignitaries, foreign ambassadors, and tourists in their village homes: including improbable guests like Sayf and me. It has also taken the form of

individuals and communities accommodating the various modernizing, conservationist, development, and religious discourses that ebb and flow with their
envoys from "across the sea." In both forms, rural Soqotrans have been called
on to "give place to" these strangers, foreigners, and guests—be it through an
invitation into one's home; a home, itself; a terrain given over to "home" gardening projects fenced off and managed by foreign NGOs; or a terrain set apart for
tourists. Likewise, they have been called on to "give time" to these extrinsic projects whose funding prospects rely on how many Soqotrans they have "reached."
As further chapters show, although the Soqotrans I knew did not always want to
engage in this disposal of their place and time, their lack of outward resistance
was not a sign of total acquiescence. Rather, it is precisely through their role as
hosts that geographically and structurally vulnerable Soqotrans have been able
to "highlight and invert structural relations of exploitation"; reassert their moral
superiority; and provide "proof and practice of [their domestic] sovereignty."[43]

Still, as a deeply political practice, *karam* can be hazardous to both guest
and host.[44] It is not only the guest who may be made "prisoner of" the host
for as long as he remains within the host's terrain.[45] The host, too, is always in
danger of being challenged, violated, usurped, or held hostage by his guest: a
guest who may turn out to be an enemy, a parasite, or simply a nonreciprocator.
Thus, when the citizens of a rural protected area in Soqotra welcomed a handful of strangers into their village, they were risking the very kind of challenge—
a challenge to their identity—with which I began this chapter. Certainly, it was
not at all clear whether an American volunteer like myself would be hostile,
or even could be socialized into being a proper and reciprocating guest. After
all, when I arrived, the United States was already launching drone strikes in
mainland Yemen. And in the eyes of my hosts, I did not pray. (I later learned
that the residents of Qayher had considered placing me in a semi-abandoned
house—abandoned by humans but not jinn—on the very outskirts of the village but decided not to after feeling "sorry" for me.) Treated as a *miskin* dependent, I was schooled in the practices of hospitality. It must have been all the
more unnerving, then, when I began to ask my hosts about how *karam* had
changed. On a more recent visit to Homhil, when Yaqub—now the head of his
own growing household—had slaughtered a goat to honor my visit, his sister
grabbed me and brought me outside to witness its preparation. "This is your
karama," she said, pointing to the carcass, the gesture—as if trying to ensure

that it would not be lost on me. The educated Arabic schoolteacher who started leading Friday prayers in the place of the *qadi* presented a challenge of an entirely different sort. He did not disdain his hosts by refusing to enter into dialogue with them, as he did with me; rather, he challenged them directly to stop extending hospitality to "strangers."[46] The inhabitants of Homhil responded by doing exactly what Sayf preached—at least, in his presence. Their actual riposte was to assert their moral superiority as exemplary hosts by accommodating us both separately and simultaneously.

To the extent that *karam* invites risk, it is also a risky topic for ethnographers to engage. On the one hand, hospitality as an object of study has been considered "quaint" or "timid."[47] Perhaps the practice of hospitality evokes intimate relationships in small-scale settings, even though hospitality as metaphor (and politics) is invoked regularly by powerful states and multinational corporate entities. Or we believe we understand what there is to know about hospitality already; hospitality is, after all, the very practice that enables and conditions anthropological fieldwork.[48] On the other hand, to say or write anything about the politics and practices of hospitality elsewhere—other than to lavish one's host with praise—can itself be a form of trespass. Revealing the "conditions" that structure the allegedly "unconditional" nature of hospitality in specific settings exposes exactly that which all good hosts labor so very hard to keep concealed. Does this mean we should not take up this challenge?

My riposte to those who would challenge my decision to write about this quaint but contentious topic in this way is to say that the "crisis of hospitality" spreading into rural protected areas and into the metropolitan cities alike may well become one of the most significant crises of the twenty-first century. What we learn from Soqotran anxieties at the turn of the millennium expressed in the idiom of hospitality is not that Soqotrans are good hosts (although they are that, too). Rather—at a time when images of Muslim migrants and refugees washing up on European beaches or being detained at airports due to hastily executed bans have rekindled debates in the media and elsewhere about the duties and dangers of state hospitality toward displaced, abject strangers—we are reminded that one can lose one's mastery over environment, home, and self not only by being too hospitable but also by not being hospitable enough. In the next chapter, I take up this connection between hospitality and sovereignty more directly by turning to the Soqotrans' history of hosting the state.

FIGURE 4. Remnants of Sultan Isa's palace, Hadibo, 2013.

CHAPTER 2

HUNGERING FOR THE STATE

HORF 2005

The road up the escarpment ('*aqaba*) had been dry and passable for months, but with the onset of the monsoon the arrival of a vehicle was a notable event. It was midmorning, and having finished their daybreak chores, the men and women of Qayher were resting under the palm-frond arbor ('*arish*) set within their courtyards or against the thick-walled interiors of their stone houses, themselves nestled up against the outer edges of the plateau. I was lying around with Umm Yaqub, her daughters, and her infant granddaughter under their family's '*arish*. We had already sipped several cups of tea and were playing a game of "fivestones" with stray pebbles from the courtyard. Because of the gusting winds, we could no longer hear the distant humming of the motor as we would have just days earlier. Instead, a passing child alerted us to the billowing dust rising above the plain.

"Car!" yelled the child.

"*Salon!*" confirmed his cousin. (*Salon* is one of several English loanwords used to describe large, four-wheel-drive vehicles in Yemen).

We sat up, straining to see whether the vehicle would turn eastward toward Momi or head into the Homhil Protected Area, to one of the villages or the ecotourism campground. As soon as the vehicle had passed the final turnoff, we all sprang to our feet. Women straightened their vibrant satin dresses and adjusted their headscarves. A teenage girl rinsed and stacked the scattered tea glasses. The sitting area was quickly swept; children were shooed off to play. Men exited their houses and began walking toward the village entrance. Many of us spent the next minutes guessing whom the vehicle would bring: tourists? "the Environment"? the development NGO? pest exterminators? the Ministry of Health? my husband?

.   .   .

In Homhil, as in other rural areas in Soqotra that lie at the far margins of the weak Yemeni state, "the state" appears much as anthropologists James Ferguson and Akhil Gupta have described it. "Mediated by the semiotic of dust," vehicles containing state and NGO employees "swoop" suddenly and sporadically into the geographic space of the citizens of Homhil.[1] What marks these governmental encounters is not only their element of surprise but also sameness, regardless of who the visitors may be. These encounters are marked also by the expectation that rural Soqotrans *host* these officials—providing drinks, food, lodging, and hospitality—whenever they do arrive. This may not seem all that remarkable in a small island where the boundaries between public servants and private citizens (and family members) are often blurred.[2] Nor perhaps can it be otherwise in an underdeveloped hinterland devoid until recently of any stores, restaurants, or lodging. Nevertheless, what Soqotrans and other observers naturalize as a cultural practice—*karam*—allows them, as periodic *hosts of the state*, to deemphasize their dependence on the sojourning state and to articulate their role in sustaining it. It also feeds into their hope that the state will return their generosity with sporadic gifts or through feeding them in turn. This "political economy of hospitality" is neither exclusive nor conclusive.[3] Yet my own hosts' acute sense that they must host the state to gain any material returns was pervasive in daily discourse regarding the Saleh regime and in their reflections on past states of very different natures.

This particular positioning vis-à-vis the state is all the more significant when we consider that each *dawla*—each (turn of) state—experienced by Soqotrans in the past fifty years appeared not only as a guest in places like Homhil but also as a stranger to Soqotra. Indeed, the checkered history of state formation in the Middle East is acutely reflected in Soqotra's own recent political history during which the islanders endured four distinctive regimes before the war beginning in 2015: the British-"protected" Mahra Sultanate of

Qishn and Soqotra (1876–1967); the Soviet-backed People's Democratic Republic of Yemen (1967–1990); the "unified" Republic of Yemen (1990–2014);
and the UN-supported environmental regime (1997–2013). Each of these regimes was externally imposed and geographically distant—with the exception
of the sixty-year period from 1907 to 1967, during which the seat of the Sultanate of Qishn and Soqotra was based on the island. Even then, the sultanate
was divided across the noncontiguous territories of al-Mahra and the Soqotra
Archipelago. The political history of Soqotra is therefore a history of foreign
interventions and, from a state-centered perspective, of the archipelago's increasing political incorporation by outside regimes.

However, whenever I asked Soqotrans to tell me about their collective
past, their conventional narrative was one of ingress, if not incursion: arrivals
that began with the sultans and continued long after the "entry" (Ar.: *dukhul*;
Soq.: *aykub*) of the unity regime. "First, there were the sultans, but they were
poor [*miskin*], like us. Then the British entered, and then the [Socialist] Party
[*hizb*], and then the Unity [*al-wahda*]," I was commonly informed. It is not only
these political entries that are counted as foundational junctures. Religious, social, and development regimes are said to have entered Soqotra as well: "When
the *mutatawwi'in* [missionaries] entered, we learned more about our religion."
"When the environmental projects entered, we learned more about our environment." Like the succession of states that entered Soqotra "from the sea" (Soq.: *min
rinhem*)—as the flotsam and jetsam washed up on its shores, as it were[4]—these
tutelary projects and their followers were now making their own incursions into
the island's hinterland. But these various regimes shared more than their visitant
nature and their washed-up development schemes. Because of the archipelago's
monsoon isolation in addition to its variable rainfall, Soqotrans have not been
strangers to food scarcity and famine. Accordingly, their interaction with each
state was mediated by food: its taxation, prestation, allocation, subsidization, and
commodification. It was not only the administration of food *by the state* that governed Soqotrans' interactions with each regime. In addition, Soqotrans have a
long history of feeding—and simultaneously hungering for—the state in return.

The metaphor of a state that eats underscores the corruption, decadence,
corpulence, and nepotism of the accumulating postcolonial state in Africa or
in places like Yemen where food shortages are still very much—in fact, a growing—part of daily life. What Cameroonians refer to as "the politics of the belly"

operates similarly in Soqotra, where those in power are often criticized for having "tasted" or "eaten [up]" money; where the *miskin* have not tasted anything of
sustenance; where witches are said to eat people, especially children; and where
sexually promiscuous women are rumored to eat many men. In Soqotra, as in
Africa, where "not everybody 'eats' equally" and where, in fact, "'to eat' is a matter of life and death," eating is not only a way "to nourish oneself, it is also to
accumulate, exploit, defeat, attack, or kill with witchcraft."[5] In Soqotra, however,
the eating state is more than a metaphor. Rural Soqotrans literally *feed* the state's
representatives whenever they extend into the hinterlands. Moreover, because
many Soqotrans can afford only to "taste" meat during the feasts occasioned by
celebrations or esteemed visitors or by the periodic visits of the peripatetic state,
it is only then that the *miskin* can count on eating "real" food. By hosting—and
sustaining—the state, rural Soqotrans were and are also sustaining themselves.

Food and roads are central to the story of the intermittent arrival of various
state representatives into Soqotra as "guests." Both elucidate how each of the
diverse political regimes governed Soqotra. But they also show how Soqotrans
viewed and experienced the itinerant state(s) through the lens of a host-guest
relationship (defined by the politics of the reception), which has the ability to
invert the locus of power.

IN THE TIME OF HUNGER

If a common theme in modern Soqotri poetry is that Soqotrans are losing
their sense of selfhood, another is that the sultan was the defining essence of
Soqotran society, culture, and history: the island's "foundation stone." However,
this nostalgic vision of the scaffolding of the sultanate sits in tension with the
perception that the sultans were outsiders, having come "from the sea." Despite the last five sultans having resided solely on the island, having married
Soqotran women, and having spoken Soqotri, the 'Afrar were not considered
a Soqotran tribe. This is remarkable given that it was as far back as the mid-
sixteenth century that the 'Afrar family of Qishn (in al-Mahra) established itself
as the hereditary and titular rulers of Soqotra.[6] Nevertheless, for most of this
period, the sultan of Qishn ruled Soqotra through his heir apparent, who governed the island until becoming the next ruler of Qishn. Thus, when in 1834 the
Government of British India sought to acquire Soqotra, it sent the commander

of the Indian navy to Qishn to negotiate the purchase. (Vehemently, the Mahri sultan refused.)⁷ Forty years later, in an effort to prevent other foreign powers from acquiring the island, the British government concluded the first of a series of treaties with Sultan Ali bin Abdullah bin Salim bin Saʿd bin Tawari al-ʿAfrar, "the Sultan of Socotra"—in Qishn.⁸ These included a pledge by the sultan and his heirs "never to cede, to sell, to mortgage, or otherwise give for occupation, save to the British Government" Soqotra or its neighboring islands in exchange for a payment of 3,000 MT (Maria Theresa) dollars and an annual subsidy of 360 MT dollars in 1876; a treaty establishing a British protectorate over Soqotra and its dependencies in 1886; and a treaty establishing a British protectorate over Qishn and its dependencies in 1888.⁹

But when Sultan Ali bin Abdullah died in the early twentieth century, his heir remained on Soqotra—as did the seat of the sultanate during his and his successors' rule. Five generations of Soqotra-based sultans were to rule the island directly: Salim (r. 1880s–ca.1910), Abdullah (r. 1910–1932), Ali (r. 1932–1938), Hamad [Ahmad] (r. 1938–1952), and Isa (r. 1952–1967).¹⁰ It was during this period that the geographic distance between the two disjoined territories of the Mahra Sultanate of Qishn and Soqotra widened into a political divide as the Qishn-based relatives of the Soqotra-based "treaty sultans" struggled to assert their own authority vis-à-vis the mainland tribes and to be recognized as the sovereign rulers of al-Mahra. Meanwhile, the Soqotra-based sultans rarely if ever visited their mainland territories, a fact that frustrated the various British governors of Aden to no end. Instead, they appear to have been quite content shepherding their flocks and subjects (raʿaya) while collecting subsidies from the British government and taxes from the Soqotran tribes.

The British colonial administrators' customary disparagement of the island's ostensibly reclusive sultans notwithstanding, the archipelago was far from isolated during their rule. Even after Soqotra stopped attracting European and Gujarati merchants following the collapse of the aloe market in the eighteenth century, Soqotrans remained as dependent on maritime trade for certain foodstuffs, textiles, and other provisions as they were on their livestock, date palms, and the surrounding sea. In fact, the islanders were to become increasingly dependent in the nineteenth and early to mid-twentieth centuries on Western Indian Ocean trade. Soqotrans who came of age prior to the 1970s remember trading their ghee, woolen rugs, and dried fish for maize from East

Africa, small amounts of rice and cotton cloth from India, and dates from
Oman. Usually, it was Omani merchants stopping on their way to and from
Zanzibar and Mombasa who exported and imported these goods. Dhow owners from Dubai, Ajman, and Sharjah also frequented Soqotra to dive for pearls
and nacre. On Soqotra, the few Arab merchants who owned dhows—the sultan
among them—imported grain, some cloth, and a smattering of luxury goods
for themselves and the small population of wealthier Arabs, Mahra, and the
Hadhrami religious aristocracy (*sayyids*) inhabiting the coastal towns. Meanwhile, the majority of the island's indigenous population—estimated to be
roughly seventy-two hundred persons in 1966[11]—had to survive on the milk,
fat (ghee), and meat of their livestock; dates; small quantities of homegrown
finger millet; wild plants and animals (such as birds); fish and shellfish, if they
were near the coast; and, on average, one bag of imported maize per household
per year. Still, it was Soqotra's very embeddedness in a "regional food network"
spanning from Karachi to Dar es Salaam that made its entire population more
vulnerable to famine and other crises.[12]

One aspect of the sultans' rule most surprising to its foreign observers—especially to the British administrators struggling to "pacify" the tribes in Hadhramawt and al-Mahra in the 1930s through 1960s—was their (seemingly)
undisputed control over the island despite its lack of infrastructure and their
lack of a modern administrative establishment or military. Prior to the second
British occupation of Soqotra (1942–1946), it had no roads—let alone primary
schools or health centers. Soqotrans navigated the coasts using wooden dug-
outs. They traversed the interior with pack animals lumbering along camel
tracks. In the three major northern coastal towns—Hadibo, Qadhub, and
Qalansiyah—the coral rag houses of the wealthy were neatly whitewashed
with limestone. In the interior, many families, including Umm Yaqub's, lived
in modified caves set high into the limestone cliffs. To the various British visitors who set foot on the island in the 1940s through 1960s, it was precisely
this absence of internal infrastructure that obscured the island's external connections. Thus, for example, the leader of an Oxford University expedition to
Soqotra in 1956 could write of one of the Bedouin "troglodytes" living in the
Haggeher Mountains: "He had always been there, he would always be there,
he knew of no other world, he was interested in no other world."[13] (Yet during
the 1950s and 1960s, some hundred young men left the island to seek their

livelihoods [*rizq*].) In similar fashion, the expedition leader declared that Sultan Isa's administration "was practically invisible" and that "a police force of only a dozen or so Africans armed with old rifles [wa]s sufficient to police the whole island."[14] It is true that the sultans' affairs were handled primarily by their ministers and by a sparse administrative system of local, regional, and district-level supervisors (*muqaddamin*) responsible for keeping order, settling disputes, and collecting taxes within their respective localities. And it is true that the sultans' meager guard force did not require sophisticated arms to subdue a population that was itself unarmed. Nonetheless, the sultans were able to extract through taxation (Soq.: *'asher wa-geri*) roughly 10 percent of the pastoralists' dates, ghee, and livestock on an annual basis. The Hadhrami *sayyids*, Mahra (and other) elites, and Arab merchants were exempt from paying taxes but were charged custom duties on imported goods and rents for the right to certain trade monopolies: pearling, grain import, ghee export, and transport.[15] The sultans' ultimate control—shored up by the British colonial administration—came through their monopoly over the "papers" (later, passports) that permitted Soqotrans to travel. At the mercy of the sultans' documents, all the island's inhabitants were a captive population and tax base.

In January 2010, as Ismail was driving me to visit some of his friends in Diksam, we stopped to pick up an elderly man on the side of the road. I had just asked Ismail about the sultans' taxation and the power they derived from this. As usual, Ismail's scratchy cassette recordings of Soqotri-language poetry pealed forth from his jeep's speakers. "The sultan didn't need weapons," Ismail had said; "he ruled through food. The regime [*al-hukm*] was [one of] food and fear." As the hitchhiker climbed into the back seat, our conversation was interrupted by the customary exchange of greetings:

"Al gu'urken?" (Is anyone ill?)

"Al di gu'ur bayn wa al di hubur." (None of us are ill or misfortunate.)

"Inam leha mereśhe?" (How are the people over there?)

"Hamdulillah, bekhayr. Difol mesa shaken?" (Thanks be to God, they are fine. How much rain have you had?)

"Hamdulillah, leesuh." (Thanks be to God, it's been raining.)

"Difol dhadhiyow?" (How grassy is it?)

"Hamdulillah, fitar hadeb." (Thanks be to God, the soil is cracking open [with grass].)

This back and forth about illness and rains—as idiomatic as the English-language "How are you?"—continued for a good few minutes until Ismail signaled his desire to shift from greetings to conversation.

"I want to ask you a question," Ismail said.

"Ask!" the hitchhiker said, yelling over the poetry.

"How did the sultan rule over the island?" Ismail asked.

"Because you asked me, listen to the answer—I am going to tell you," the old man said. "The sultan ruled by his staff and his slaves [hukm bil-'asa wa bil-akhdam]. If you disobeyed him, he'd order his slaves to tie you up."

Neither Ismail's nor the hitchhiker's response surprised me. I had learned from one of the teachers in Homhil that the sultans used to come to Qayher and stay in the same rocky outcrop where, during the mid-2000s, the teachers were housed and fed. But when I asked one of my neighbors if he remembered these visits, he said that he had never actually met Sultan Isa because, whenever he heard the sultan was coming, he would flee into the nearby hills—afraid of being beaten. For at the times when the sultan's regime did make itself visible, it did so spectacularly. If the sultans maintained their position through monopolies and taxation, they demonstrated their sovereignty—and, indeed, the extent of their rule—through their royal progressions throughout their territory and their ban of undesirable subjects from their realm. The first of these, the msilhim—a Soqotri term for both the meetings with the sultans and the sites in which they took place—occurred usually when a regional muqaddam, unable to settle a local dispute, required the sultan to step in as the final arbitrator or to mete out a punishment. Arriving on his camel by way of the tracks leading into the interior, the sultan was always accompanied by a small but imposing retinue of his minister, heir, or councilors, slaves, and armed guards. Like the nineteenth-century Moroccan royal progress, or the twentieth-century Omani royal progressions, the sultan's peregrinations around the island, from msilhim to msilhim, reaffirmed his dominion over his territory and over a population unified by "a restless searching-out of contact."[16] The Soqotran historian Ahmad Said al-Anbali goes as far as to argue that the msilhim constituted the sultan's subjects as much as it embodied his rule for "whoever was summoned and did not come, was considered an outlaw [kharij 'ala al-dawla]."[17]

Those who were summoned would stand judgment and, if found guilty, were often punished immediately by the sultan's accompanying slaves. Punishments consisted of lashings, amputation, "imprisonment" (forced labor) in Hadibo, or banishment. The prevalence of amputations during times of drought—when starving men stole goats to feed their families—has been widely chronicled in Soqotri poetry. Di-'Abudihel bin Shaloulhe, an elderly man from the west of the island, recalled these amputations clearly: "And the one who was found stealing goats would lose his right hand. They would cut it and hang it on a Ziziphus tree in Hajra to serve as an example—to scare people from stealing from one another." His reminiscence was peppered with verses, like the following: "You have many amputees, o Homhir [a place in the West] / Who gather on the rooftops of Ili'i / They are unable to taste the foam / of the Friday butterfat with their right hands." Upon losing their hands, the amputees' bleeding stumps were cauterized by being forcibly submerged in boiling shark's-liver oil. Nevertheless, they often died of complications.[18] It is hard to imagine a more draconian punishment. But the "sovereign ban" through which the sultans suspended the juridical order of the *msilhim* and abandoned accused Soqotrans to the fates of the sea—first, through a trial by drowning; then, through their deportation by way of any passing dhow going any which way—was brutal, too.[19]

During this period, when the islanders did not have access to universal education—or, as the previous example illustrates, modern medicine—many attributed most if not all illness and misfortune to witchcraft. They also believed in the power of the male diviners (Soq.: *mekolis*) to identify witches and cure physical affliction. Both witches and *mekolis* were thought to be allied with jinn who aided them in attacking their victims and defeating their adversaries, respectively. Accordingly, witches and *mekolis* were engaged in a "gladiatorial contest" exerted offstage between their respective jinn but expressed visibly in the human body.[20] Not only did the *mekolis* receive compensation for their work (usually in the form of scarce food), but their diagnoses were recognized and even solicited by the sultans, who relied on them for the protection of their subjects and themselves. Women accused of witchcraft by a *mekoli* were usually "tried": laden down with stones and heaved into the sea to see whether they would float (guilty) or sink (innocent). Guilty women (or good swimmers) were subsequently exiled from Soqotra for life. Most of these women settled down in the first port towns they reached—Sur, Ajman, Sharjah, and Dubai—where, having become citizens of the newly emerging nation-states of the Arab Gulf, they grew wealthy enough to support their family back home, but only after having suffered this violent separation.[21]

It is not surprising, then, that the majority of Soqotrans feared their sultans and that the sultans were able to exploit these and related fears. Many islanders recall this period as a "time of ignorance" (*waqt al-jahl*) marked by illiteracy and unorthodox beliefs. For most Muslims, *al-jahiliya* refers to the pre-Islamic period during which the pagan Arabs were ignorant of Islam. In Soqotra, *al-jahiliya* maps onto the sultanate period and is widely considered to have lasted until 1967 due to the perceived poverty of religious knowledge that, from today's perspective, marred the sultanate and was only partially improved with the entry of the socialist state. Prior to this, only a few children were taught to read the Qur'an, and fewer still were sent to boarding schools in al-Mukalla or Kuwait.[22] Even mosques were few and far between; thus, the inhabitants of Homhil consider their area to have been a center of religious knowledge. Still, some Soqotrans reject the common notion that, prior to the arrival of the Islamic missionaries (*ahl al-da'wa*) in the 1990s, they were Muslim in name only. As a rejoinder to this, they hold up the example of Sa'd bin Elfin, a man whose unflinching faith protected him from the sultan's wrath. One day, it is said, in response to Sa'd bin Elfin having renounced the *mekolis* and refused to kiss the sultan's hand, Sultan Isa set out with his retinue to punish him. But when the party neared Sa'd bin Elfin's village and heard him calling his neighbors to worship, Sultan Isa's men stopped in their tracks. "We're not strong enough to punish a man calling the *adhan*," they insisted, and returned to Hadibo.

However, as much as Soqotrans feared the sultan's staff, they had more to fear from seasonal starvation. During the southwest monsoon severe gales blowing in from Africa impede human and vehicular movement, uproot trees, and cause structural damage to concrete buildings. Desiccating and salt-laden winds dry up pasturage and water holes, causing hunger and excessive thirst among the livestock.[23] Moreover, from June to September, the "angry" (*za'lan*) white-capped sea prohibits local sea traffic and fishing. At the time of the sultanate, all dhow-based trade was suspended during this season and emergency food supplies were hard to obtain. Soqotrans relied on their dates and finger millet, shellfish and dried fish (if they lived near the sea), stored ghee, and livestock. Traditionally, pastoralists managed this five-month dry season through transhumance and through their reciprocal relationships with families in other regions. Under what Miranda Morris calls the "*mahrif* system," a pastoral family of the interior might move in with and help out their *mahrif* family on the coast to have access to fish and other sea products; in winter months, when milk and meat were once again abundant, the pastoralists of the interior would host the coastal family. These relationships between pastoralists of the interior and fishermen or townsmen of the coasts included reciprocal gifting of ghee, buttermilk, livestock, and woolen rugs from the interior in exchange for dates, cereals, clothing, and sea salt from the coast.[24]

The real trial ensued when this annual dry season extended into full-blown drought and famine because of the failure of winter post-monsoon rains followed by weak or absent summer pre-monsoon rains. When this happens, as it still does, livestock begin to die and Soqotrans resort to stockpiled and imported foods. During the "days of hunger" (*ayyam al-ju'*) the islanders survived on wild food or food substitutes to stave off hunger. Older men and women remember periods during which they foraged tubers, ate the interior fibers of date palms, or ate boiled strips of the sodden goat skins that had been used to store milk or butter.[25] Most elderly Soqotrans have lived through several famines in their lifetime. These famine-inducing drought years, named for their particularities, index Soqotra's modern history as much its regime changes do. To name only a few: *'enoh di-tifheriten* (the Year of Fingernails), when the island was so dry that the wind rustling through tree branches sounded like nails scratching the ground (around World War I); *'enoh di-misibli* (the Year of Red Millet), when the only grain available was the imported grain Soqotrans least enjoyed (around 1956); *'enoh di-kerkam* (the Year of Turmeric), when the malnourished colored their rice with turmeric to give it the semblance of a meal (in the mid-1990s). Severe rainstorms, as devastating as droughts, are similarly named and recalled. Most memorable among these—prior to the two back-to-back cyclones that battered Soqotra and flattened several houses in Homhil in 2015—is *'enoh di-rubu'* (the Year of Wednesday), when a weeklong deluge that washed numbers of livestock out to sea ended on a Wednesday (in 1972).

At times like these, impoverished Bedouin indentured themselves to the sultans for food. An elderly man from Suq told me that he had been orphaned as a young boy and taken in by the penultimate sultan, Sultan Hamad, who provided him with work, food, clothing, and even money for his wedding. About fifty men and women were "under his care"—as servants (*akhdam*)—during his time. The sultans and the wealthier Arab notables and merchants kept both servants and slaves; technically, these servants were free men bound only by necessity, while the slaves, fewer in number, could be manumitted only by their owners (until slavery was declared illegal by the socialist regime). I interviewed a man in Hadibo said to have been one of Sultan Isa's slaves and asked him whether he had been free to leave.

"Yes, without a problem," he said. "If you wanted to go, [you would] go. If you wanted to stay, [you would] stay."

"And would people leave?" A younger man sitting with us asked rhetorically. "Where would they go? There was hunger!"

"No," affirmed the man. "There was hunger. No one would leave. We didn't have rice—only if we were at the sultan's house and there were other guests. [Otherwise], we ate only maize and finger millet. This was the food we had at first, before there was rice—maize, millet, and dates. And meat, of course."

If the sultans' servants were trapped essentially by their want of food, their slaves (as well as other Soqotrans of East African descent) had been entrapped initially through the prospect of food. Afro-Soqotrans relay vivid stories of their grandparents having been lured as young children in Zanzibar and Mombasa onto Omani dhows with the promise of sweet dates. Some were then sold into slavery on Soqotra; even more may have jumped ship there when the dhows stopped for water en route to Oman. But even the Soqotrans who never worked for the sultans were bound to them through food. The sultans controlled much of the food imports to the island, which they purchased with the taxes—the "tenth" ('asher) of all dates, ghee, and livestock—they had collected from the pastoralists. In addition, every interaction with the sultan was mediated by food. Communities hosted the itinerant sultans whenever and for however long they came through. Of course, the ethos of hospitality and generosity obliged each community to slaughter their livestock for the sultan and to offer him and his men the best of whatever food they had available—even when he came to mete out punishment.

A story told to me by a Hadibo resident now in her mid-fifties illustrates precisely how such acts of punishment and hospitality were often intertwined:

> My grandfather, a merchant, had a number of servants living in Qadhub, one of whom stole a few goats. ["He didn't really steal," interjected her son who was sitting with us; "it was the time of hunger and people were hungry and *miskin*."] So, the people of Qadhub were having problems ["They still do," interjected her

mother, who was also present], and they claimed that one of his servants had stolen goats and went to tell the sultan, Sultan Abdullah. The sultan said that he would come on such and such day for lunch and it was expected that he would chop off the thief's hand ["This is what happens to thieves in Islam," explained her mother]. So, one Friday, the sultan got on his camel—there were no cars then—and with all of his servants, he traveled to Qadhub. He had told the complainants that he would chop off the thief's hand, but he only told my grandfather that he was coming for lunch. My grandfather told his servants to prepare the rice and goats and everything the sultan has asked for in an area at the base of the mountains, away from the village. He himself stayed away. Sultan Abdullah came and asked for my grandfather. My grandfather's other servant said that he was out in the countryside and hadn't known that the sultan was coming. So the sultan ate of the large lunch provided him—meanwhile, the thief had been tied to a tree—but when he finished the lunch and was preparing to cut off the thief's hand, he saw a figure near the mountainside and realized it was my grandfather. "You said he was in the countryside," Sultan Abdullah said to my grandfather's servant. My grandfather approached the sultan and sat down next to him. Seeing his own servant tied up, my grandfather asked the sultan what was happening. "This man is a thief," said Sultan Abdullah. My grandfather asked him if he had any proof. "All the people together cannot be lying," said Sultan Abdullah. He demanded his pipe and smoked some tobacco, then placed his pipe by his side. "If there's tobacco left over, let me have it. If not, shame on you!" said my grandfather—he was trying to provoke a fight. The sultan stood up to hit him, but my grandfather stood up and grabbed his arms. "No, we will not fight. Let *them* hit each other," my grandfather said, and he pulled the sultan down next to him. Then Sultan Abdullah's servants fought my grandfather's servants and, during the commotion, the thief was untied and ran off. My grandfather told the sultan, "Don't come here to chop off the hand of my servant, my son, without proof." [He was like a son to him, her mother stressed.] And so, the sultan realized that he'd been wrong, and he took a boat back to Hadibo, while his retinue returned along the mountain path with his camels.

This family history, which the merchant's granddaughter told me after I had asked her about slavery and servitude on the island, was likely meant to serve as an example of a good master, one who stood up to Sultan Abdullah in defense of his dependent. But it also illustrates the centrality of food and food scarcity in interactions between the sultans and their subjects: *their rule through food*, as Ismail had stressed. Sultan Abdullah's visit was centered on a sumptuous lunch precipitated by the lack of food that had caused the alleged thief to steal livestock in the first place. Nevertheless, for the chronically food-insecure pastoralists of the interior, the *msilhim* provided an occasion to eat meat—much as it offered an opportunity for the sultans to collect their tenth of all their produce. If, as the Soqotran historian Ahmad al-Anbali writes, "everyone would hope to invite the sultan with all glory and pride," this may have been because the sultans' visits satisfied the Soqotrans' physical hunger as much as it satisfied their hunger for "access to their sultan."[26]

And at times the sultan would become host to his hosts. "When there was a ruling [to be made] in disputes and in issues between the citizens in the ruler's court [*diwan*], everyone stayed at the house of the sultan, especially the peoples of the countryside, eating and drinking and sleeping until their problems were solved," recalls al-Anbali.[27] Of course, the food the sultan used for hosting his subjects came directly from the people's "tenth." I heard that this had been denounced once by a Soqotran from Chiseb who visited the sultan's house but refused to eat his dates: "'*Haram*, these dates come from other people, from '*asher*,' the man said. Sultan Isa remained silent until he had finished his breakfast [*iftar*]. It was during Ramadan. Then he said, 'I have property. I'll feed myself. But then stop sending orphans and poor people to me, and when you come here for judgment, bring your own food.'" By collecting the subsistence goods from an underfed population, the sultans commanded a food surplus through which they could host their subjects and attract and retain indentured labor, as well as—through the redistribution and gifting of food in times of famine—the nominal support of their populace. In this sense, by satiating their sultans, Soqotrans were also feeding themselves.

INROADS

Most histories of Soqotra reduce the British imperial interventions to the Royal Air Force (RAF) having established an airbase and transmitter station on the island during World War II and to the scientific expeditions that followed. Although it is true that the majority of British schemes for the archipelago floundered or failed, it is indisputable that the British helped the sultans consolidate their rule over Soqotra through the monopolization of labor, means of transport, and, most dramatically, food. Moreover, the inroads made under British occupation were to set the path for subsequent state incursions—and, of course, future road projects.

Even prior to the war, it was the British Empire's desire for control over sea and air routes in the Western Indian Ocean and the Arabian Peninsula, respectively, that motivated its involvement in Soqotra. Despite the sultan's refusal to sell Soqotra to the British, the governor-general of India dispatched a detachment of British and Indian troops to take possession of the island as a coal depot for the East India Company's new steamships. This first British occupation of Soqotra (December 1834 to November 1835) proved disastrous; those who did not drown during the landing succumbed to malaria.[28] (Then, three years later, the Bombay government captured Aden instead.) Eventually, the same advancements in steam navigation that had drawn the British to Soqotra in the 1830s precipitated a surge in shipwrecks off its rocky shores. In 1912 the government sent Aden's political resident (PR) James Bell to investigate the wreck and plundering of two British steamships, the SS *Aden* in 1897 and the SS *Kuala* in 1911. Bell's visit piqued his interest in "developing" the island's resources, and he spent a few years advocating a survey expedition "to test the productive capabilities of the island," to no avail.[29] Despite his belief that "there must be some lucrative asset in the island," Bell never realized his project.[30] Nor was there any other significant British involvement there for the next twenty years. However, Bell's proposals to send experts to explore the land and its resources reflected and initiated a growing British interest in developing Soqotra into an enclave of some kind.

The 1930s ushered in a new phase of Britain's imperialist expansion into the Aden Protectorate and its hinterlands facilitated by its development of air routes and roads. Remarkably, the ostensibly remote island of Soqotra was quickly implicated. For the British responded to the tribal opposition to their air and land incursions into al-Mahra with trade embargoes and population bans that threatened not only the Mahra's livelihood but also the food security of Soqotra. When in 1932–1933 the local notables opposed the RAF's efforts to establish a landing ground at Qishn, Aden's chief commissioner Bernard Reilly responded by announcing an embargo on all Mahra and Soqotran trade in the ports of al-Mukalla, Dhofar, Muscat, and Bahrain. It worked. Worried that his dhows would return to Soqotra empty just before the onset of the monsoon, the newly incumbent sultan Ali managed to convince the Qishn notables to withdraw their opposition.[31] Similarly, in response to the extortion of Qu'ayti tribes (in the Hadhramawt) by the Zuwaydi (a Mahri tribe) in the late 1930s, the British resident adviser Harold Ingrams advised the Qu'ayti sultan in al-Mukalla to impose a general boycott on all the Mahra—despite the Mahra and the 'Afrar family also having been taxed and terrorized by the Zuwaydi. And when, again, the new incumbent sultan Hamad condemned the Mahra ban, Ingrams offered to extend it to Soqotra. It may well have been this ban that impelled Sultan Hamad to consent to the British development of a Soqotra landing ground in 1939.[32] Regardless, the British began asserting their influence over Soqotra—primarily through their ability to control access to the imported foods on which Soqotrans had grown to depend—well before they actually (re)occupied the island.

Still, the British wartime occupation of Soqotra was hardly straightforward. In October 1939, just weeks after the United Kingdom declared war on Germany, the commander in chief, East Indies, proposed the construction of aircraft bases at Soqotra and Salalah (Oman) to facilitate their defenses against enemy warships in the Western Indian Ocean.[33] The first two runways and bomb and petrol stores on Soqotra were built near Hadibo that December but were blown up by the British six months later out of fear that the Italians might use them.[34] In May 1941, in the wake of a series of British successes against the Italian forces in East Africa, the British forces in Aden decided to reopen their landing ground in Hadibo and sent a small party to clear it. Near the end of this short visit, B. J. Hartley, the agricultural officer who supervised the work, reflected on the absurdity of their expectation that Sultan Hamad protect the British arsenal while being denied the arms and ammunition he had requested: "Looking around the heated Court Yard, with its lines of slaves and few armed Arabs, perhaps 40 men in all, I felt rather ashamed in having to tell this Ruler of Sokotra to defend the Royal Air Force Stores at Hadibo."[35] And then, having paid Sultan Hamad a partial stipend, the officers left Soqotra to its own defense.

Whereas the British were worried about their enemies circling the archipelago, the young sultan was preoccupied by domestic challenges to his authority, both locally and from al-Mahra. On the one hand, a Somali merchant who had refused to pay taxes had recently instigated an armed rebellion against him, resulting in Sultan Hamad expelling him and all Somalis from Soqotra.[36] On the other hand, Sultan Hamad's Qishn-based relatives had challenged his nominal election as treaty sultan.[37] Thus, when the British Air Ministry Works Directorate (AMWD) dispatched engineers and equipment to Soqotra in February 1942 to upgrade the landing ground, the sultan was none too pleased. For the voluminous offloading of five hundred–pound bombs and fuel stocks also gave ammunition to the sultan's local opponents. Not only did the elders in Hadibo protest the extension of the landing ground so close to their homes, but the RAF had decided that it needed a new landing ground near the village of Qadhub: the very home of the sultan's local opposition. The officer accompanying the AMWD team tried to assure Sultan Hamad that his sovereignty would not be challenged and that "occupation of the island was not intended."[38] By March, however, in view of ongoing military deliberations over turning Soqotra into an advanced air base, the Air Headquarters in Aden decided to deploy a company of Aden Protectorate Levies to the island to guard their growing stores—or, as the governor of Aden informed Sultan Hamad, "so that you and your people may feel secure in these troubled times."[39] The first one hundred soldiers arrived in May 1942. And by November 1942, the resident political officer was referring to their presence as the "British occupation."[40]

If the original motivation for Britain's Soqotra base had been largely defensive, the island soon developed into a launch pad for strikes against German and Japanese submarines. Between 1942 and 1944, Axis submarines sank at least ten Allied ships and Omani or Mahra-owned dhows in the vicinity of the island.[41] Meanwhile, the garrison had grown to house British, Canadian, South African, and Dutch squadrons flying antisubmarine patrols in addition to the companies of Aden Protectorate Levies, Aden Labour Corps, Indian Pioneer Corps, and French West African troops for guarding, works projects, and other duties.[42] And much as the construction of the runways and stores required local corvée labor, the maintenance of this garrison depended on local food provisions. At a minimum, the occupation of Soqotra had a direct impact on Soqotra's labor market and food security.

Indeed, the base was an economic windfall for the sultan and his agents, who controlled conscripted labor and monopolized the local means of transport. In 1939, the British commanding officers had paid Sultan Hamad's "gang of slaves" a substantial wage of 1 MT dollar per laborer per day, knowing full well that their wages went directly into Sultan Hamad's coffers.[43] But when the British returned in February 1942 to upgrade the airstrip at the reduced, Aden rates for labor (.75 MT dollars/day), Sultan Hamad ordered his "coolies" to strike. At issue was nothing less than the sultan's fear of appearing weak to his local opposition. Eventually, the political officer in charge strong-armed Sultan Hamad into accepting their deployment but agreed to pay him 1 MT dollar per laborer per day—plus 3 MT dollars per day for each agent (*muqaddam*) standing by. This amounted to a substantial works project "employing" more than 10 percent of the island's estimated six thousand inhabitants.[44] Nevertheless, then and over the course of the occupation, Sultan Hamad and his henchmen kept demanding higher wages and transport rates. The problem was that the British had introduced a glut of cash into a predominantly barter economy where few goods were available for purchase. On an island with only two principal merchants, whatever wages the laborers managed to retain lost value so quickly that even the most impoverished Soqotrans melted down this coinage for jewelry.[45] Yet the expectation of "extortionate" wages had been set. As Harold Ingrams presciently noted, "[The officers] are going to make Socotra a very expensive place if we continue to do anything there after the present emergency arrangements."[46]

Despite, if not due to, this racketeering bonanza, tensions continued to escalate. While the residents of Hadibo and Qadhub competed for labor at the same time that their respective headmen impeded their work to demand higher wages, the residents of Mouri (the site of the new landing ground) objected to the airstrip cutting through their grazing lands. Then, as the workmen complained of being beaten by the RAF supervisors, various acts of alleged sabotage were carried out against the British camp.[47] Even more troublesome to the British was the growing power struggle between the sultan's primary advisers: his *qadi*, whom the British considered the "de facto ruler" on the island responsible for stirring up the opposition to their presence, and his vizier (*wazir*), who sought to curry favor with the British.[48] When the British tried to mollify Sultan Hamad by paying him rent for the landing ground, the *muqaddam* of Qadhub and his brothers wrote to the governor of Aden claiming that the property belonged to them.[49] Sultan Hamad responded by having the Qadhub men—including his *qadi*, whom he accused of having written the letter—imprisoned: a perfectly "satisfactory" outcome according to the British stationed there.[50] The British responded by working to prop up Sultan Hamad's regime even further. They began paying his vizier a wartime stipend of 40 MT dollars per month and increased the sultan's stipend by the same amount in "recognition of his special assistance in present circumstances."[51] At the same time, the Aden government prohibited the AMWD supervisors from contracting labor through any agents not directly sanctioned by the sultan. By holding Sultan Hamad "responsible for the difficulties and delinquencies encountered in dealing with local labor," Aden ceded him full control over the laborers and their wages: endowed him, in effect, with full and uncontested sovereignty.[52] Thus, having fanned the flames of the sultan's Qadhub opposition, the British occupiers found a way of extinguishing them—at least, for a while.

These gains notwithstanding, Sultan Hamad was said to have remained "disappointed with the pecuniary results of the British occupation"; he had expected and bargained for more.[53] Moreover, his "cooperation" with the British did not win him favor at home. Yet Sultan Hamad accommodated the RAF in the spring of 1942, a year and a half after the Mahra ban had been lifted. Although Sultan Hamad's reasons were undoubtedly complex, there is one decisive factor that seems to have driven much of the sultans' periodic collaboration with the British: Soqotra's ceaseless need for food. Already, Sultan Hamad had experienced firsthand the effects of the British embargo on his Mahra subjects and their threat of embargo on Soqotra: an island that depended on the import of about twenty thousand bags of maize per annum.[54] Then, during World War II, worldwide food shortages and the restrictions placed on the export of maize from East Africa made Soqotra's food security all the more contingent. In light of these circumstances, Sultan Hamad seems to have capitulated to the benefits of British protection; for example, in response to the governor's letter apprising him of the garrison, Sultan Hamad confirmed that he would welcome the troops and requested immediate food relief.[55] In fact, one of the main lessons learned by the sultan and the British during this wartime occupation was that Soqotra needed to improve its food security. Contrary to depictions of Soqotrans having been self-sufficient pastoralists and fishermen until recently, the pastoralist economy of the interior sufficed for only one-fifth of the island's inhabitants.[56]

Indeed, one of the earliest and most severe famines in living memory occurred under British watch. In May 1943, the dhows that had set sail for Zan-

zibar and Dar es Salaam in search of maize returned empty. In response to
Sultan Hamad's plea for help, the Aden government sent five hundred bags of
sorghum (*jowari*) for their resident political officer to sell. By mid-June, when
the monsoon had wrapped itself around the island, nearly all these stocks were
exhausted—in a drought year, no less.[57] By August, all the grain was consumed.
Emaciated Soqotrans sat just outside the RAF camp, waiting for scraps. Officers
noted "evidence of considerable and appalling infant mortality."[58] At least one
person died of starvation in the direct vicinity of the garrison.[59] In the interior,
the drought—and famine—was even worse. This is the year remembered as
"the Year of the Pecking [Vultures]" ('*enoh di-mindo*'). It is remembered for
the preponderance of theft among herders driven to steal one another's livestock for survival. And it is remembered for how the sultan dealt with such
"petty lawlessness"—by cutting off the offender's right hand and stringing it
from a tree or around his neck. According to the resident political officer, "one
such gruesome relic was brought into camp recently followed by a request that
the Doctor be asked to treat it with preservatives as it was to be worn for one
month. The request was refused."[60] Although the islanders experienced some
relief by October—the Aden government had shipped another fifteen hundred
bags of grain following the opening of the sea; grazing in the central and eastern plains had started to improve; and dhows carrying dates from Muscat and
Sohar arrived in large numbers—hunger and starvation continued to afflict Soqotrans into the winter.[61] "We still occasionally find and bury dead Bedouin,"
the political officer noted, "mostly old women and young boys who are apparently outcast from their tribes. There have been nine of these corpses in the last
seven weeks."[62] It was during this period of disorder and dismemberment—of
vultures and carrion—that the secretary of state for India suggested (for a second time) that the British establish an "overflow" Jewish colony on Soqotra,
evincing just how great the imperial disconnect could be.[63]

Although it appears that the garrison itself was well supplied during the
famine, it too depended on local food production. Not to be isolated and
starved off the island as were the Portuguese in the early sixteenth century, the
British garrison insinuated itself in the island economy, as buyer and supplier.
After all, the officers desired meat, vegetables, dates, and ghee for themselves
and their troops. Thus, on the eve of the 1943 famine, the acting political officer negotiated the purchase of all available ghee.[64] Then, in the aftermath of

the famine, the Aden government started sending regular shipments of grain to
Soqotra. By January 1944, the garrison had set up a weekly market where this
grain was exchanged for the Bedouin's livestock and fish.[65] But the longer Aden
supplied Soqotra with grain, the more time each successive political officer had
to spend devising and supervising new grain distribution schemes: a task so
onerous that one officer asked to be relieved from his post just a month into his
appointment.[66] In October 1944, when this increasingly frustrated officer met
with Sultan Hamad to negotiate yet another grain agreement, he made the sultan solely responsible for all grain distribution on the island, including the "free
issue" grain held aside for the destitute.[67] In return, Sultan Hamad attempted to
pay for the grain shipment with the two hundred tins of ghee he had collected.
This seemingly innocuous transaction turned the tables on the sultan's former
creditors. Whereas the chief secretary in Aden refused to purchase this much
ghee at the previously agreed-on but now above-market rates, Sultan Hamad
argued, correctly, that the former political officer had promised to purchase all
the ghee on the island.[68]

   This "ghee question," as it was called, would plague the British for the remainder of their occupation. Sultan Hamad now controlled what both the British officers and his Soqotran subjects needed most—labor conscription and
grain distribution, respectively—and did not shy from ordering his subjects
to strike or from setting "extortionate" rates for the dhows and dugout canoes
(*huris*) needed to transport, among other things, the free grain around the island.[69] Subsequent political officers found themselves trying to clear the garrison's ghee debt by selling the sultan more grain. Meanwhile, Sultan Hamad
retained the upper hand, demanding payment for the pastoralists' ghee but
refusing to reduce his labor and transport rates.[70] In October 1945, the British
forces declared that they would disband and evacuate the RAF unit on Soqotra
shortly, saddling the incoming political officer with a new problem: the sale
and disposal of over 230,000 pounds of old, weevil-ridden grain to a population that was by then well supplied with Indian grain imported directly by their
sultan.[71] Weevily grain, venereal disease, crashed aircraft, gutted vehicles, oil
drums, scrap metal, the wives and children of Arab and French Sudanese soldiers—perhaps also of a British officer or two—these are just a few of the many
things, and persons, left behind following the disbandment of the garrison in
January 1946.[72]

But the British left their imprint on the territory, too. One of the reasons that the RAF required as much "coolie" labor as it did was not only to maintain the landing grounds but also to construct and maintain roads between Hadibo, Qadhub, and Qalansiyah and from the airfield to their defense outposts scattered along the coast. From the time of their arrival, the AMWD supervisor put its labor corps and Soqotrans to work turning camel paths and goat tracks into serviceable roads. Between February 1942 and January 1943, the Auxiliary Indian Pioneer Corps dug out a mountain pass (ʿaqaba) between Hadibo and Qadhub.[73] Between June and October 1943, the dirt road between Qadhub and Qalansiyah was completed, and the Levies began working on other roads to and from the Mouri airfield.[74] The British even toyed with the idea of developing a road system throughout the entire island and, in March 1944, considered building a motor road to the southern coast.[75] But in August 1944, after reassessing Soqotra's liability to land and air attack, the British forces decided to vacate the coastal outposts and reduce the size of the garrison. Consequently, headquarters ordered the remaining Aden Labour Corps to concentrate strictly on the maintenance of the landing ground at the expense of "road construction and . . . other developmental works."[76] Although their roads project was thus discontinued, the British had turned "goat tracks" into dirt tracks, preparing the grounds, literally, for the more extensive road system that was introduced by the socialist state in the 1970s and upgraded by the unity government in the 2000s.

The impact of this road construction, embryonic as it was, left a lasting impression on the Soqotrans who experienced it. In 2005, an elder from Suq was telling me how powerful Sultan Hamad had been. To illustrate this point, he recounted an oft-cited example of a British supervisor who had hassled and hit the Soqotran laborers building the landing ground at Mouri. When Sultan Hamad discovered this, he rode his camel to Mouri, struck the supervisor himself, and ordered his removal from the island. Indeed, the meticulous reports produced by the political officers stationed on Soqotra document several instances of physical violence—in addition to examples of charity. Probably the most dramatic impact of the road construction occurred when a Soqotran man was knocked over by an AMWD lorry and died.[77] Not surprisingly, the roads constructed on the back of corvée labor led to other frictions. For example, to construct the road to the jetty, the AMWD cut down twenty date palms owned by residents of Qadhub. This caused enough outrage for Aden to replace the AMWD overseers and to order that the trees' owners be compensated five rupees for every palm destroyed.[78] If this association of the island's first roads with physical violence and dispossession is seared into the memories of the elder generations, the more mundane forms of verbal aggression are captured in the list of "Socotrian phrases" the officers recorded. "Karrimah al tatahar ogik na'ah" (If you do not go, I shall strike you now) is the first phrase on the list.[79]

Despite Soqotra having been central to the British war efforts in the Western Indian Ocean, when the Aden government disbanded its garrison, it essentially abandoned the island, too. This disengagement was bred in part by Soqotra's renewed (seasonal) isolation from the mainland. As long as the British garrison was stationed on Soqotra, the Aden government maintained nearly daily contact with the island through the RAF's transmitter station, weekly flights, and the rapid succession of resident political officers (as many as twelve in three years). Following their evacuation, the government's contact with Sultan Hamad and his successor was limited, for a long time, to the connections available through seasonal dhow traffic and the occasional navy ship. The British adviser continued to send famine relief; he also helped institute a rudimentary health unit in Hadibo in 1955 and persuaded Sultan Isa to send several youths to the Bedouin Boys School in al-Mukalla. But the roads deteriorated, as did the landing grounds. So much so that during his trip to Mecca in 1956, Sultan Isa declined King Faisal's gift of a Cadillac due to the lack of motorable roads in Soqotra.[80] And by 1961, the Aden government was relying on its RAF pilots to once again airdrop letters (as well as arms) onto Hadibo—even directly into Sultan Isa's courtyard—to alert him to developments in al-Mahra.[81]

At the same time, this disengagement reflected a shift in British interests from maintaining a military base on Soqotra to establishing a colonial administration in al-Mahra, where the prospects of oil discovery had then seemed likely. In the 1950s, in an effort to secure this territory for oil exploration, the Aden government attempted unsuccessfully to establish roads between al-Mahra's coastal towns and the Northern Deserts Area (where it had garrisoned military posts to protect the operations of the Iraq Petroleum Company) and drafted several al-Mahra "penetration" plans. Eventually, in 1962, the Pan American Oil Company entered into an oil exploration agreement with Sultan Isa, who in turn received annual rents totaling 105,000 British pounds (more than two million pounds in today's value based on the retail price index alone). Spurred on by the promise of oil, the Aden government launched Operation Gunboat in October 1963 to occupy the coastal town of al-Ghaydah by force. It then set up a Mahra Tribal Council in al-Ghaydah, which by early 1967 had established "several emblems of statehood" funded, in part, by the oil rents: a small army, a post office, stamps, a weekly air route between al-Ghaydah and al-Mukalla, its own passports, and its own flag.[82]

Despite having been the region of southwestern Arabia most neglected by the British, on the eve of independence this embryonic Mahra state was the one that represented both the greatest challenge to the decolonizing govern-ment and its only hope.[83] But in February 1966, Whitehall issued a Defense white paper announcing its intention to abandon its military base in Aden and to revoke its former commitment to provide military defense for the new Fed-eration of South Arabia and the Protectorate of South Arabia following their independence (then scheduled for January 1968). For the federal ministers and the rulers of the protectorate "states" (including al-Mahra), this retraction of military support sounded the death knell to their "traditional" rule. Moreover, in May 1966—during the very week that the British government rejected a pe-tition from the Mahra Tribal Council for a "crash development programme" to fund hospitals, doctors, schools, and roads prior to its departure—Pan Ameri-can Oil announced its decision to surrender its oil concessions in the Eastern Protectorate states.[84] Not only was Sultan Isa to lose his military support, but the nascent Mahra state would no longer receive any development funds be-yond what had already been allocated: funds for one primary school and health unit in both al-Ghaydah and Hadibo, which never came to fruition.[85] These developments sent the Mahra Tribal Council, and its opposition (regularly backed by Sultan Isa, who had not appreciated the devolution of his power to the council), scrambling for alternatives. While the council looked to the rulers of Kuwait, Saudi Arabia, and Muscat for aid that would allow them to sustain their administration,[86] a Mahra "Congress" held in Qishn in February 1967 called for the dissolution of the British-backed council, the disbandment of the British-formed Mahra Armed Constabulary, and the expulsion of all British government staff from the area.[87] Having reached these resolutions, the twenty-eight-member armed group traveled to Soqotra to enlist Sultan Isa's support and to exhort him to declare a Republic of Soqotra and al-Mahra.

But the Aden government intervened. In March 1967, under Operation Snaffle, the Middle East Command dispatched two platoons of the Hadhrami Bedouin Legion and the entire Mahra Armed Constabulary to Soqotra to arrest this "subversive band."[88] Most of the men "snaffled" were brought to al-Ghaydah, where the Mahra Tribal Council detained them until they swore their allegiance. The group's alleged ringleaders were imprisoned and interrogated in Aden, where they were accused of having received funding from the increasingly powerful National Liberation Front (NLF) leading the insurgency in Aden; having recruited other Mahra to join the NLF; and having provided support to the Dhofar Liberation Front, which was seeking to establish a separatist state in Oman. As Soqotrans tell it, the group's leader, Muhammad bin Bukhayt al-Jidhi of Qishn, had come with "his army" to prevent Sultan Isa, his maternal uncle, from giving Soqotra to the British.[89] After all, Soqotrans were well aware that London had considered separating Soqotra from the mainland to retain it as a military base. Archival records show that only the Conservative ministers supported the separation plan, but Soqotrans remember the British having offered to extend their formal protection of the archipelago in 1967. Many, in fact, regret that this never materialized: "We would have been so much more developed today," one man told me wistfully. "We would have studied physics, not just Marxism and Leninism!" a former leading member of the Yemeni Socialist Party said. These same Soqotrans exonerate Sultan Isa, who they claim would have negotiated a new treaty with the British if not for his vizier's improper counsel.[90] Some of my friends even ventured that it was the "illiterate" and "humble" (*miskin*) sultan rather than the educated vizier who understood that Soqotrans would have fared better under a British regime than under whatever federal or unified state was to follow.

Following the Snaffle arrests, the British adviser wrote to Sultan Isa: "The plans of these people for the future of your state leave no place for Sultans; but I do not think you will see them in Soqotra again."[91] The British adviser's first prediction proved correct: there was to be no place for sultans in the People's Democratic Republic of Yemen declared on 30 November 1967. But he was wrong about the second. Within weeks of South Yemen's independence, the NLF sent a squadron of three hundred to Soqotra to claim the island for the PDRY. The leader of this operation was, again, none other than Muhammad bin Bukhayt, who had been released from prison in late March.[92]

FIGURE 5. *Min rinhem*: a view "from [across] the sea." Photograph of Hadibo and the Haggeher Mountains taken by Muhammad bin Bukhayt or his "snaffled" colleagues on film developed by the Aden Intelligence Centre when the group was arrested. © The British Library Board (IOR R.20.C.1953–345). Reprinted with permission.

After overthrowing his uncle, whom he had imprisoned in Aden, Muhammad bin Bukhayt became Soqotra's first governing commissioner (*ma'mur*) under the socialist regime.

THE ROAD TO HAYBAK

In the 2000s, many Soqotrans looked back on the "time of the Party" (*waqt al-hizb*) as a time of peace and stability (*amn wa istiqrar*): a period of law and order (*nizam*) distinct from the days of ignorance and hunger that preceded it and from the days of northern hegemony that followed. On the face of it, the entry of a centralized, socialist state in Soqotra could not have been more antithetical to the patrimonial rule of the itinerant sultan. Yet the pastoralists living at a remove from the administration in Hadibo experienced as much continuity in their encounters with the state as they did change, for they continued to host and give *karam* to a visitant state, one that leveraged itself through food. And they continued to fear the state despite its efforts to eradicate the underdevelopment it attributed to the British and to tribalism (which it outlawed) and to implement social policies that advanced the welfare of underprivileged groups, including the Bedouin.[93] As a middle-aged man in Homhil put it, "We used to have the sultan and his family, and he was *miskin* like we were. Then the state [*dawla*] came from overseas [*min al-bahr*], and we didn't know what the state was or what it would do. Maybe they would slaughter us!" Hundreds fled the island altogether. For many, the totalitarianism of the Marxist regime (1967–1990) was simply an extension of the sultan's authoritarian regime—an extension duly personified through Soqotra's first commissioner, Sultan Isa's nephew.

As on the mainland, the party leadership in Soqotra tried to implement a nationalization policy, agrarian reform, the collectivization of production, and centralized development planning to restructure and revitalize the stagnant, rural economy.[94] Administratively, Soqotra was separated from al-Mahra and placed under the jurisdiction of Aden. It was henceforth governed by a series of Aden-appointed commissioners from mainland Yemen who also headed the District Committee of the Socialist Party.[95] The party replaced the sultans' regional and clan-based headmen with five-member village committees (*lajnat*), which were incorporated hierarchically into the centralized administration. However, in Homhil, as in many other regions, it was the former *muqaddam* who was elected chairman (*ra'is*) of the region's committee. Though Soqotrans possessed little in the way of institutions to be nationalized, the government claimed all tribally owned lands as state property. Plots, houses, and even date palms belonging to the sultan, his advisers, the *sayyids*, and the island's few merchants were confiscated and redistributed to the formerly dispossessed groups, such as the Soqotrans of African descent. In an effort to boost economic growth, the PDRY established state farms and fisheries and fostered several types of rural cooperatives. In Soqotra, the experiment in large-scale agriculture succeeded poorly—three pilot horticultural farms and a sheep farm were started in the mid-1970s but terminated soon thereafter, and home gardens were introduced instead.[96] However, Soqotra's first cooperative, a fishing cooperative established in 1969 that sold its catch to the government for export, succeeded well enough to be held up as a model for the variety of new cooperatives and civil society organizations that were formed following unification,

including the Association for the Conservation and Development of Homhil. Increasingly, rural Soqotrans began to leave the highlands for the denser,
coastal settlements, where some became fishermen and others gained employment through the army or police or as day laborers.

Of the many state-making projects implemented by the PDRY government,
four stand out in Soqotrans' narratives of the period: the establishment of basic
health services, the institution of primary education, the provision and stockpiling of subsidized goods, and the construction of roads. Various public health
measures, like mass inoculation and malaria eradication programs, made their
way to Soqotra and into its hinterlands. Moreover, the right to medical care, as
enshrined in the 1970 constitution, allowed Soqotrans—the majority of whom
had relied until then on the costly and somewhat dubious services of the sooth-
sayers (mekolis)—to access free health care in local clinics or to be flown to Aden
for treatment. (The mekolis' practice was banned and forced underground.) As
an elder in Suq put it in 2005, "If you were sick, you'd go to the hospital and the
government would pay for it. Even on the plane! It would be on the account
of the government—your medicine and your travel. But now—God help you!"

Free education, too, was a constitutional right, and basic schooling was
made compulsory. One of the first secular, primary schools in Soqotra was the
coeducational Salimin School for Nomadic Bedouin established in the mid-
1970s at Mouri (west of Hadibo). As its name suggests, this residential school
was part of a larger state effort "to assimilate the bedouins into the mainstream
of Yemeni life."[97] But party officials in Hadibo had great difficulty convincing
rural Bedouin to send their children to a boarding school so foreign in concept and so far from home. Consequently, they had to round up—Soqotrans
say "kidnap" (khatifa)—the Bedouin children who fled into the mountains
whenever a party vehicle approached. Five students from Homhil attended
this school, including two boys who were to become the consecutive heads
of the Association for the Conservation and Development of Homhil. A man
from Momi (the plateau above Homhil), fearful that he would be recruited to
join the army at eleven years of age, fled with his friend and his goats into the
mountains, where eventually the police director and other party officials found
them. He was then forcibly enrolled in the boarding school, from where he
visited home just twice per year. In addition to receiving free basic schooling
in Hadibo, several Soqotrans were sent to Aden for secondary education and

to other socialist countries for tertiary education. What made the residential school so distinct, though, was as much its provision of free board to its pastoralist students as its curriculum.

To feed its malnourished population, the PDRY government introduced several measures to improve its food supply and distribution, including the price stabilization of "essential foodstuffs" in 1974.[98] The introduction of these commodities to Soqotra had a tremendous impact on the islanders' diet, while also accelerating the shift from a barter to a (state-regulated) market economy. Eventually, Soqotrans abandoned the export of ghee, the import of African maize, and the local horticulture of finger millet for the convenience of these state-subsidized imports: rice, sugar, wheat, flour, tea, milk powder, cooking oil, and tomato paste. No longer reliant on the climate-susceptible productivity of their herds and the seasonal availability of fresh milk and dates, rural Soqotrans adopted a staple diet that was seasonally invariable: sweetened tea for breakfast, rice for lunch, and fried bread for dinner. However, the price for this food security was the pastoralists' growing dependence on irregular wage labor in Soqotra and on the mainland, on other livelihoods, and on the state.

The state also made its imprint visible through the construction of dirt roads to replace the sultan's camel tracks and the overgrown British military roads that traversed parts of the island. As during the British occupation, Soqotrans were paid in food—now, flour and cooking oil—to cut the roads. The development of a relatively extensive road network changed the interaction of rural Soqotrans with the state and its representatives. In place of the infrequent, spectacular arrivals of the sultan, whose visits had been solicited and expected, the new bureaucrats, security forces, and distinguished party representatives were able to enter into rural spaces with nothing but rising dust clouds to announce their arrival. (During the early 1970s, it was the dust kicked up by a military truck—for a time, one of the few motor vehicles on the island—that would send frightened Bedouin running into the hills.) In contrast to the feasts associated with the sultans' visits, these visits are remembered for their governmental nature: the "abduction" of children, the administration of vaccinations, and road planning. As one of my neighbors in Homhil recalled, "Ba Haqiba [the former secretary general of the Soqotra branch of the Yemeni Socialist Party] came here once and stayed in my father's house. He came to talk about the road." Despite the reduction in travel time and distance between Hadibo and places like Homhil made possible by the road, rural Soqotrans continued, as my neighbor indicated, to host these visitant representatives of the state. As another so-called citizen of Homhil put it, "We kept slaughtering our goats for them."

Rural Soqotrans encountered a range of benefits and restrictions that continue to divide popular opinion on the legacy of socialism, the future of southern Yemen, and the viability of secession. Depending on whom one asks, the "time of the Party" was an anomalous period of progressive policies and welfare provisions sandwiched between two equally backward and exploitative regimes, or it was anathema to Soqotran culture, patriarchal traditions, and Islamic faith.

"When we talk about the socialists, that period, Thank God, [we say] knowledge began," one of the elders of Suq told me during the same conversation cited previously. "They opened schools, increased the students. Before that, there weren't any schools. There were no hospitals—"

"People were afraid of schools," his friend interrupted.

"And there were about fifty or sixty deaths per day, maybe seventy, young and old, from malaria. And so, when the [social] democrats entered, Thank God, we began to get knowledge ['ilm]. The food was better. We got rice. Before we didn't have sugar for tea. We didn't have drinks: [canned] mango juice, Pepsi. And we didn't know about these things. Everything is from God!"

In contrast, a Soqotran residing in Oman decried the "force of ignorance" (quwat al-jahiliya) that would allow the Party to proclaim: "There is no word above ours." Like other émigré Soqotrans originating from pastoralist families, this man was most critical of the Party's totalitarianism and the restrictions it had placed on political expression, religious practice, travel, and even communications with non-Yemenis.[99]

Such restrictions, implemented across South Yemen, must have seemed all the more confining in an island demarcated as a strategic military zone and closed to nonessential travel. As the PDRY government established closer relations with the Soviet Union, Soviet interests extended to Soqotra.[100] Although the Soviet Union did not establish a base on Soqotra, it anchored ships offshore and used the island for military maneuvers.[101] Some Soqotrans attended parties on the ship; others interacted with the Russians when they landed on the island to purchase goods. Ismail remembers encountering the Russians only once: on the anniversary of the 14th of October Revolution (commemorating the beginning of the armed uprising in Aden in 1963), Russian service members who came ashore to join the celebration projected a version of *King Kong* on the whitewashed walls of the Socialist Party headquarters.

Nevertheless, whatever peace and stability the island may have experienced, this period has been forever tainted by the 1974 execution of ten men by Soqotrans affiliated with the NLF. The "martyrs," as they are now called, were shot at Haybak, a mountain pass midway between Hadibo and the airport that was under construction. This was the same cliff from which the sultans used to execute alleged witches by having them thrown into the sea (prior to turning to their exile as punishment). An anonymous poem from these years advised the émigrés in the Gulf to stay away from Soqotra, where life had become difficult due to the turbulent "winds" that had entered from abroad. After imparting the news of the recent upheaval, the poet addressed the perpetrators directly through a reference to the new airport road:

> While the road you constructed near the sheer cliff was not cheap
> And you cleared a path for cars passing downhill and uphill
> The people, indigent, could not return your exemplary generosity.
> Poor and oppressed, they were unable to respond.
> Why did you act like this, when all of you grew up together?

The poet implies that the road construction was planned, or at least utilized, to obscure and mitigate the killing of the old regime. It did so by creating a seemingly innocuous excavation site that could be cordoned off for digging (the mass grave) and by producing a gift that would indebt—and thus silence—Soqotra's citizens, poor and weak.

THE OPENING

The 1990 unification of North and South Yemen introduced yet another political import to Soqotra: a "neopatrimonial" regime sustained by patronage networks, the revitalization of tribal politics, and the emergence of an "Islamist" coalition.[102] It also rendered Soqotrans and their environment vulnerable in an entirely new way. For if the PDRY government had inherited a grossly underdeveloped economy from the British in 1967, the newly unified Republic of

Yemen inherited staggering debt in addition to two underdeveloped economies, two currencies, and two disparate sets of political and civil institutions,
including two militaries, which it struggled to integrate.[103] Moreover, at this
pivotal moment, Saudi Arabia and Kuwait withdrew their financial aid and expelled nearly one million Yemeni laborers in retribution for the government's
lack of support for the US-Saudi coalition during the 1990–1991 Gulf War.
Not only did Yemen lose the expatriate remittances on which its economy depended, but it struggled to reintegrate the hundreds of thousands of returnees,
many of whom had lived most of their adult lives abroad.[104]

To sustain its ailing economy, the Government of Yemen relied on foreign investments, loans, and food aid from international financial institutions
and multilateral donors, who subsequently pushed for structural adjustments and stringent economic reforms. When the government tried to reduce its deficit in 1998 and, again, in 2005—largely by cutting its costly fuel
subsidies—the resultant near doubling of the prices of fuel, food, and water
sparked deadly riots across Yemen. (Yet both times, following the government's inability to implement these reforms, its donors suspended or reduced
their funding to Yemen.)[105] These cuts were especially exacting in places like
Soqotra, where the secondary import of fuels and staples (into Yemen and
then to the island) had already increased the prices. Because the government
had expected these adjustments to disproportionally burden the poor, it had
established the Social Fund for Development in 1996, responsible for aiding
community-development programs and for creating employment opportunities.[106] These social safety net programs were supplemented by the Social Welfare Fund, which allocated cash transfers to the most vulnerable, including to
the people of Homhil. Nevertheless, even these direct cash transfers "to allevi-
ate *poverty now*" were unable to bridge the rise in consumer prices.[107] Although
these programs succeeded in reducing poverty in some urban areas,[108] the state
of development in rural and remote areas remained dire.

Meanwhile, the Saleh regime encouraged the growth of tribalism (formerly outlawed in the PDRY) to fragment its opposition and co-opt the local
elites.[109] Novel to Soqotra was the government's attempt to aggregate the island's
"clans"—essentially, extended families —into "tribal formations within their territorial domains and to organize their relationship vis-à-vis the State according
to a patron-client model."[110] Receiving a monthly stipend from the government's

Department of Tribal Affairs in Sanaa, these new stamp-carrying tribal leaders worked (officially) to settle disputes and (unofficially) to mobilize voters on behalf of the ruling General People's Congress (GPC). Because this imposed shaykh system was so obviously associated with the GPC, opposition parties like al-Islah began issuing their own list of shaykhs.[111] Aspiring individuals could even purchase their own "official" stamps, used to assert their political authority on written documents.[112] Soon enough, official and unofficial shaykhs were vying for power as the number of shaykhs exceeded the number of subregions dividing the island.

Despite the entrenchment of this neopatrimonial system, the Republic of Yemen was still described as an "emerging democracy."[113] It was, after all, the first state on the Arabian Peninsula to hold multiparty elections that fielded women candidates.[114] In addition, the government passed a Local Authority Law in 2000 to promote financial and administrative decentralization, democratization, and transparency. Yemen's (then) twenty governorates were divided into 333 districts, each with its own elected local council. Under this new administrative system, Soqotra was separated into two districts (Hadibo and Qalansiyah) and transferred jurisdictionally from Aden to the Governorate of Hadhramawt. Subsequently, all government funds for Soqotra filtered through the Hadhramawt, where spending had to be negotiated among its thirty district representatives, only two of which represented Soqotra. In Soqotra, the thirty-six local council members (eighteen for each district) were to be the elected counterparts to the growing numbers of shaykhs with jurisdiction over Soqotra's forty-five subregions: a discrepancy that often stymied local governance.[115] Moreover, the local councils each reported to their respective director general of the district (*al-mudir al-'amm*), who, by law, was appointed by the governor of Hadhramawt, with the approval of the Ministry of Local Administration. Thus, for Soqotrans, similar to the government's experiment in neoliberal reform, which doubled the prices of their imported staples, this experiment in decentralization inserted additional layers of intermediaries, beneficiaries, and bureaucracy between themselves and the central government. It was thus experienced as a form of political and geographic distancing from the nation-state's center.

At the same time, the Saleh regime made itself ever more visible in Soqotra through its conspicuous construction of a new jetty (1997), the airport (1999), a presidential mosque (2005), and the paved road network (2001–2008)—all of which imprinted the island with the signature of the modern state.[116] These

infrastructural investments, as well as unrealized plans for a new seaport to
accommodate large cargo ships and cruise liners, clearly exceeded the needs
of the island's (then) forty-five thousand residents.[117] Conservationists, ecolo-
gists, and even tourists criticized the new 275-kilometer asphalt ring road
project in particular for the roads' unwarranted width, poor construction,
unsuitable locations (within nature sanctuaries or far from people's villages
and existing tracks), and contribution to large-scale environmental damage,
such as soil erosion, obstruction of water courses, habitat fragmentation, and
the extinction of flora and fauna.[118] Indeed, the road construction was, by all
accounts, haphazard and seems to have been carried out more with an eye
toward financial gain than toward the exigencies of the island and its people.
In an island already designated as a "special protected area" by the government, roads were cut without environmental impact assessments having been
conducted, without reference to the road master plan, and in contravention
of the island's Conservation Zoning Plan (ratified in 2000).[119] It is telling that
one of the ICDPs' greatest successes during this decade (1997–2008) was its
eleventh-hour prevention of road construction within a coastal lagoon in
2002.[120]

For most Soqotrans, however, the introduction of paved roads—which
had lengthened to more than nine hundred kilometers by 2010—was a most
welcome and vital development. These roads halved or even quartered the
travel time between the island's distant settlements and its hospital in Hadibo,
thereby decreasing the risk of infant mortality and maternal death. They facilitated the transport of foods and goods to and from these settlements; they increased traffic, enabling Soqotrans without transportation to hitch rides more
frequently to the hospital, pharmacies, market, juice shops, and courthouse
in Hadibo; they spawned privately owned bus services, making it possible
for women to travel to markets; they enabled some villagers to open roadside
stores for the no-longer-so-weary, but ever-more-consuming traveler; and
they brought tourists and their pocketbooks to previously distant areas (even
as they negatively affected practices of *karam*). They also increased the geographic reach of the state, making it possible for its representatives (and the
representatives of transnational NGOs) to enter rural areas more frequently.
The roads did for Soqotra's hinterlands what the airport did for Hadibo: they
made seemingly remote areas less remote.

In addition to this road network having facilitated Soqotrans' physical and economic mobility, it was credited by Soqotrans and others with having contributed to their social mobility. In this view, Soqotra's new infrastructure reduced the sociocultural distance between the islanders and their mainland compatriots, and between Soqotrans and the outside world. The project director of GATCO, the Sanaa-based civil engineering company that was building the roads—almost exclusively through Yemeni migrant labor—certainly thought so. Describing them as "the mainline to the prosperity and to the development" of Soqotra, he applauded how they had "changed everything" by increasing Soqotrans' mobility. Yet what he emphasized most during our conversation in 2006 was not the significance of the roads as conduits but the *mission civilisatrice* of his company: "We observed when we started working in Diksam that people did not know anything about the world, about this modern world." When the people of Diksam began to visit the GATCO camp, he asserted, they learned about bathing, toilets, different foods, and television: "They saw many strange things—many modern things—and they really changed. We found them within a month wearing shades and watches and combing their hair and wearing shoes—really, this is a fact I have seen with my own eyes."

Although Soqotrans may take issue with this characterization, my interlocutors attributed their own advancements to these roads. This became clearer to me one day as I was driving Basmah, a young Afro-Soqotran woman, from Hadibo to another coastal village. On our return, upon reaching the newly laid asphalt after what had been hours of rattling over the rugged paths that traversed most of the island in 2005, Basmah breathed a sigh of relief. "We've Arabized!" she exclaimed. This expression, in itself, was not that unusual. In a place where "Arabness" was (and still is) less a marker of ethnicity than of caste or status, Soqotrans could become "Arab" by attaining a certain level of material development.[121] Thus, during the sultanate, the so-called Bedouins could Arabize by buying date palms or a donkey. More recently, my self-identified Bedouin friends in Homhil aspired to Arabize by constructing *'Arabi* (cement) houses, eating *'Arabi* (imported) foods, or seeking out *'Arabi* (Prophetic) medicine in place of their *Soqotri* stone houses, limited diet, and rudimentary medical practices. However, the paved road system enabled an entire population to Arabize: to be regarded, and to regard themselves, as urbane and civilized. This development needs to be understood, then, not just as an exemplar of modern infrastructure, an avenue to economic and social development, or a threat to Soqotra's natural environment and cultural heritage but as the physical manifestation of Soqotrans' view of their social standing in the world.[122]

Accordingly—and not unlike the dirt roads cut during the socialist period— these new acquisitions were conceived by Soqotrans as a gift granted to them by the state. This view was only reinforced by President Saleh's high-profile gifts of paved roads in excess of the original government plan during each of his two island visits in the mid-2000s. During his first visit, President Saleh purportedly encountered an elderly Bedouin woman in the highlands who complained that the new road bypassed her village. Without consultation, he ordered GATCO to extend the pavement to her village—which turned out to be a single home. Additionally, President Saleh created twenty new, highly coveted government jobs for the pastoralists of Diksam to guard his Diksam "camp"—itself a gift from GATCO to the president. During his second visit, President Saleh expressed his desire to visit Hoq, a cave in which speleologists had recently discovered significant archaeological artifacts (including a third-century wooden tablet in Palmyrene script). When he heard that he would have to walk up the escarpment to reach the cave, Saleh ordered GATCO to construct a paved road to its entrance. Again, he gifted twenty government jobs to its prospective guards. These presidential gifts were the talk of the town—and of the *badiya*. Rarely did I hear anyone criticize these spontaneous performances of power. Instead, my interlocutors clung to these examples as testament to the president's generosity and as evidence of the island's development from a hungry sultanate to a stable socialist administration to the unity regime of "goodness" (*khayr*).

"Never in our lives did we expect to see so many changes in Soqotra," an Afro-Soqotran fisherman in Hadibo exclaimed in 2005 after we had been discussing the island's political transformations: "We never expected to see an asphalt road in Soqotra. We never expected this! We are thankful, *alhamdulillah*. The president of ours, he presented this. This is the best change! We never expected this!"

"How can you expect something if you're asleep?" his friend joked, echoing Ismail's view that the island's opening had awakened Soqotrans to new expectations and desires that are symptomatic of their development—of their Arabness, even.

Many observers of Saleh's Yemen would identify these gifts as manifestations of his reliance on patronage networks and distributions to consolidate his regime.[123] But in rural areas, such as Homhil, the gift was nevertheless contingent on the irregular presidential, ministerial, or ambassadorial visit and, thus, on the political economy of hospitality. Rural Soqotrans may visit state offices and representatives in the capital and on the mainland, and they may have close friends, relatives, and neighbors who work for the state, but "their presence doesn't exactly bring the state into the town" or into the community.[124] For this to happen, Soqotra's Bedouin had to attract and host the visitant state to capture its attention and services.

Consider Homhil, one of Soqotra's first protected areas. In 2000, Homhil's designation as protected area introduced a host of environmental regulations that nominally legislated the pastoralists' use of their traditional grazing grounds. Homhil's first public school was built in 2003, through charitable funds and local labor. This manifestation of Homhil's mundane inclusion within the Republic of Yemen—of "the state infusing the everydayness of life"[125]—was signaled through the school uniforms of its children who, through their daily movements across the plateau, mark both the dispersion and centrality of the state even in its margins. The boys dress in black trousers and a white shirt; the girls, in a black overcoat and white headscarf, which in the mid-2000s was embossed with one of two endorsements: "Alkuds Lena" (Jerusalem Is Ours) or "Christian Dior"—both illegible to their wearers due to their Latin script. One can say also that the state was embodied in the handful of salaried government employees who lived in Homhil; however, with the exception of the teachers, none worked on behalf of the state locally. It remains the case that to access any type of administrative or social services apart from primary education, the citizens of Homhil must descend to Hadibo.

Periodically, this "visibly absent state" did present itself through the unexpected arrivals of the mobile clinic, census enumerators, vaccination teams, or pest extermination crews.[126] Rural Soqotrans accommodate this visitant state by providing its representatives meals and lodging but also by legitimizing it through their participation in these performances of stateness. On a moment's notice, houses are numbered and chalked; homes are turned inside out; medical symptoms are publicly disclosed; vaccinated children are marked; and every act is photographed as evidence that the government is, in fact, "acting like a state."[127] My neighbors seemed to appreciate these visits, if for nothing else than their providing diversion from an otherwise uneventful day. But they often questioned their efficacy or benefit; some blamed the extermination process for increasing the fleas in their homes, while others criticized the mobile clinic for administering tests and collecting data with little if any benefit to the rural patients who would wait another year for the clinic to return. From where we sat under the 'arish that morning, wondering which manifestation of the state would be dropping by for project legitimization, it was not so much Homhil that appeared marginal to the Yemeni state as that the state was viewed and experienced "as some kind of margin to the body of the citizens."[128]

Nevertheless, as extraneous and piecemeal as these visitors and their services may have been, the Soqotrans I came to know generally expressed their desire for more state presence, not less. In an area like Homhil, it was clear that infrastructural developments would occur only as a result of such attention. For example, the steep and gravelly ascent to the plateau with its multiple hairpin turns had been constructed largely by the Hamiliho (as they tell it). At one point, a foreign NGO donated funds, cement, and expertise toward its improvement, but the Hamiliho claim that this only worsened the road. Moreover, during the annual winter rains, which coincide with the start of the tourism season, the road suffers substantial erosion and becomes impassable for days. In several community meetings I attended, the people of Homhil prioritized their desire for a safer access road over any school expansion or the establishment of a local health clinic. Yet their only hope of fixing the road lay in their ability to attract high-profile visitors. This conclusion was only confirmed when, in December 2004, the SCDP hired a bulldozer to grade the road prior to a visit by the head of UNDP's Sanaa office, its main donor. Consequently, my neighbors fantasized about a presidential visit to Homhil—as did I. If only Saleh would visit Homhil, we imagined, then surely he would order the asphalt to extend to this road, too. So infectious was this desire to attract and host the state that I found myself contemplating sending an invitation to the president of Yemen himself.

However, if the presence of the state brought with it the promise of roads, the new roads also delivered rural Soqotrans to the exigencies of the market. The new road system enabled rural Soqotrans to sell their livestock, produce, and labor more easily, but in doing so, it made pastoralists more dependent on Hadibo and more desirous of imported goods. It also lured the youth into town, where they fell prey, the poets claimed, to the baneful grip of qat and other vices. And if Hadibo's market was not harmful enough, the opening of Soqotra as epitomized by these asphalt roads also made Soqotrans more vulnerable to global capitalism. The renowned Soqotran poet Uthman Abdullah Uthman Baidobah captured this vulnerability in a poem he composed during the early years of road construction. Drawing on the entrenched dichotomy between Soqotra's ostensibly ignorant mountain dwellers (Bedouin) and those who live on the coast, his poem is framed as a dialogue between two goats: a provincial mountain goat named Gahabon and a worldly coastal goat named Gelaom.[129] During a visit to the coast, Gahabon encounters his friend, Gelaom, with whom he discusses his bewildered first sighting of an automobile and the relative lack of development in the mountainous hinterlands in comparison to the coast. Later, Gelaom visits Gahabon in the mountains to inform him of the dramatic bush clearing happening below. But whereas Gelaom naïvely believes the road crew who claim to be working in his interest, it is Gahabon, the mountain goat, who understands that roads lead to markets—and, therefore, to their eventual slaughter. In this sense, the "gift" of the road is ultimately, as it was under the socialist regime, a betrayal.

"THERE IS NO GOVERNMENT NOW"

In February 2006, Basmah visited my Hadibo residence shortly after my return to Soqotra. Early into our conversation, Basmah began listing the latest prices of staple foods. Since I had been gone for nearly two months, it is possible that she simply wanted to apprise me of recent changes in Soqotra: "Everything is expensive now," she lamented. But her complaint about the rapid inflation expanded into a comparison between the Saleh regime and "the days of the Party":

> There is no equity [hukm] on the island today. Some are very rich; others are poor and have nothing. Now the merchants can raise their prices as they want and people pay. There is no government [hukuma] now. Before, there was a government—in the days of the Party, they took care of people. Now, we've left the days of government [kharajna min ayyam al-hukuma]. Before, they would think about the people.

Basmah, who was in her early twenties then, would have been a child at the time of Yemen's unification, so I was surprised to hear her speak with such authority about the socialist past. It was clear that she had been influenced by her elder relatives who, like many of my interlocutors, spoke of the absence of government. For as much as the unity regime's incursions into rural Soqotra had been concretized by the asphalted roads, its retreat from welfare policies was palpable, too.

Following the July 2005 riots, the government tried to cushion these reforms. But the 42 percent of Yemen's population that lived on USD 2 per day still suffered the effects of these marginally reduced cuts. Moreover, additional price hikes in 2007–2008 and 2010–2011 due to the world's food price crises doubled the percentage of Yemen's food-insecure population: from 22 percent in 2003 to nearly 45 percent in 2011.[130] In Soqotra, the 2007 hikes coincided with a severe monsoon-season drought, during which hundreds of animals died. To address the country's food crisis, the government developed a comprehensive National Food Security Strategy in December 2010, which included subsidies reform as only one of its seven action plans.[131] However, it delayed its implementation because of the Arab uprisings and the political upheaval that followed. Then, in August 2014, just when Yemen's overall level of food insecurity had started to decline (from 45 to 41 percent), the government once again slashed fuel subsidies in return for an International Monetary Fund (IMF) loan, resulting in yet another cycle of price hikes, protests, and increasing poverty.[132] Remarkably, the Soqotra Archipelago—which became an independent governorate of Yemen in 2013—is no longer even one of most food-insecure regions of Yemen. In this sense, Soqotra's relative isolation from the conflict-ridden mainland and its modest domestic food production—but also its historical and ongoing direct links to the Arab Gulf States from where the Soqotran diaspora continues to ship tons of foodstuffs annually—may have actually protected the archipelago as much as if not more than any of the previous protections imposed on it.

Yet, as Basmah's comments suggest, the absence of a functioning government—or, alternatively, the presence of a gluttonous government—was felt by many Soqotrans at least a decade before the Saleh regime's tumultuous fall. As a case in point, the famines that had been relegated in people's memories to the days of hunger were reexperienced in the mid-1990s and even more dramatically in 1999 as a result of the failure of the unity government to stockpile food supplies prior to the monsoon, as had the socialist regime before it.[133] In 1999, by the time of the monsoon, nearly all of the island's grasslands had been grazed out and herders had turned to gathering and cutting foliage for their livestock; when the foliage was gone, they fed them imported dates and cereals.[134] It was in the midst of this "worst drought in living memory" that Soqotra's commercial airport opened[135]—a development that hailed the end of the island's seasonal isolation. But even then, it was too late to save the thousands of sickly animals: "What was most noticeable all over the island that year," Miranda Morris recalls, "were the busy vultures and the smell of diseased, dead and dying livestock."[136] Soqotrans did not need to suffer the cuts in government subsidies in 2005 to feel that their government was no longer caring for them. Nor were all their experiences of the state's withdrawal related to food: in December 2004, for example, the island's coastal communities suffered one fatality and lost at least 16 fishing boats, 36 outboard engines, 174 nets, and 486 traps to the Indian Ocean tsunami, but government assistance was not forthcoming.[137] Yet the widely shared narrative of state-sponsored development under the socialists followed by a lamentable retreat of the state after Yemen's unification—shared even by those who praised the unity government for bringing a different form of development and, above all, religion to Soqotra—was often voiced through critiques of the satiated, "eating" state.

A little more than a year after my conversation with Basmah, I happened to revisit Soqotra during the 2007 drought that coincided with the worldwide rise in food prices.[138] As usual, my friends complained bitterly about the eating-while-retreating regime. One morning, my husband and I spent an hour or so driving Bu Ilham, a father of seven from Homhil, through the streets of Hadibo as he searched for the least expensive provisions. Bu Ilham complained repeatedly about the northerners' control of the market: two days earlier, a tin of milk powder had cost YER 1,000; a day later, it was YER 1,050; and on this day, it was YER 1,100 in every shop—a YER 50 daily increase that Bu Ilham took as evidence of price gouging. "If there was a government, the merchants would all be put in jail," he asserted. Later, as my husband sat with Bu Ilham and his male relatives, the men spoke about a group of alleged northerners and Soqotrans from Hadibo who had been caught stealing goats. More scandalous than the theft itself was the rumor that these men had stolen these goats not out of destitution but to feast on them prior to their afternoon qat chew. (The Soqotrans involved were young men who, it was implied, had succumbed to the negative influences of the town, the northerners, and their vices.) In the eyes of my Bedouin neighbors, the northern merchants, shopkeepers, and service providers ate from their metaphorical table but did not feed them in turn. Likewise, the state and its representatives were said to eat from the provisions allotted to Soqotra. Nevertheless, the majority of the Soqotrans I came to know hungered for the state that would feed its poor and return "integrity" (*amana*) to the entire social body. In the meantime, the closest they could get to a caring state was by hosting and accommodating its itinerant representatives, with the hope that their *karam* would ultimately engender a substantive return.

This is where the eating state exceeds the metaphor. *Karam* is equated not only with the slaughtering of livestock; it is also associated with the feasts, the *'uzuma*, once offered to the iterant sultan. So unwavering is this narrative of rural Soqotrans hosting the state that it elides the extreme differences between the sultans, the party, and the unity government. Nevertheless, unlike the sultans and the socialists who also hosted or (re)distributed food to the Soqotrans in times of need, the unity regime came across as a gluttonous guest that ate and ate. Following Sownhin's depiction of the various government officials they had hosted, I remarked that they were often hosting the environmental regime (ICDPs), too. After all, in the mid-2000s, the SCDP managers ferried nearly all visiting dignitaries and donors to feasts staged in Homhil's campground to showcase their own interventions. Even though these potential donors were seeking funding opportunities, the Hamiliho perceived the extent of the donors' gifts to be contingent on their own hospitality. (They were not misguided to think so: in 2005, a USAID representative berated a Soqotran SCDP employee for having declined to shake his wife's hand and threatened to withhold USAID's donation if the men did not do so.) Sownhin concurred:

> For six years, we've been giving hospitality [*karam*] to the Environmental Project [*al-bi'a*]. We've been asking for a better road, but nothing happens. We've given our demands to the government for years . . . six years for the mountain pass [*'aqaba*], and nothing happens—*karama* or not—because our government is weak. The Environmental Project sometimes does something, but usually not. The only one who does something is [Abdul Karim] al-Eryani, May God Protect Him.

Dr. Abdul Karim al-Eryani (d. 2015), President Saleh's one-time close adviser and Yemen's former prime minister (1998–2001), had accompanied President Saleh during one of his visits to Soqotra. Bu Yaqub had told me about this encounter, too. As before, the Hamiliho had heard that President Saleh had landed on Soqotra but assumed that he and his entourage would visit only Diksam, reputed to be the president's favorite site. But this time was to be an exception. Bu Yaqub recalled seeing a vehicle enter the plateau and watching as it moved across the common grazing area in the direction of the new campground. Curious, Bu Yaqub and a few others walked toward the campground to see who had arrived. Approaching the parking space, Bu Yaqub met "a northerner" who pointed to a frail man sitting under the canopy of a nearby dragon's blood tree. "That's Abdul Karim al-Eryani, adviser to the president," the northerner said. Astounded, Bu Yaqub and his neighbors approached the tree and greeted al-Eryani, who then asked, "What do you need? What can I give you?" Later that evening, after what was most certainly a lavish (for Soqotra) *'uzuma* in the campground—Homhil's new venue (*msilhim*) for receiving its visitors of stature—Dr. al-Eryani collected the names of each head of household so that they, too, would receive monthly financial assistance from the nation's Social Welfare Fund.

In Bu Yaqub's telling recollection of this event, this was "the first time" that the state (*dawla*) had ascended to Homhil. What I think he meant to say, given the long history of state visits to Homhil, is that this was the first time that the unity government is considered to have granted something significant to its hosts in return. It was as if the esteemed Dr. al-Eryani—the guest standing in for the state—had become "the host of the host."[139]

TRANSFORMATIONS AND CONTINUITIES

Contemporary accounts of Soqotra depict a remote, isolated island that was cut off from the modern world until the beginning of the twenty-first century, when its modern infrastructure was developed. This narrative excites conservationists, development workers, and tourists alike, who see in Soqotra an island that time forgot or an island hit by a tsunami of change, as manifested by its "road to ruin."[140] In either view, the emphasis is on the perceived chasm between the otherworldly island and the outer world; between Soqotra's near past and developing present; and between the putatively asynchronic, unworldly Soqotrans and their contemporary, cosmopolitan observers.[141]

Many Soqotrans have experienced tremendous changes in their lifetimes, but these changes have not arisen in the past fifteen years alone. Moreover, adult Soqotrans have been witness—and host—to several distinctive political regimes under which the subjects of the sultan of Qishn and Soqotra became citizens of Yemen and other Arabian Peninsula countries. However, rather than represent epochal ruptures, these political transformations share continuities in the ways in which Soqotrans' relationship with each entering state was mediated by food, fear, and roads, which come together in rural areas like Homhil where the state is received (and perceived) as an unfamiliar guest; where politics is intimately related to *karam*; and where hosts and guests are expected to exchange roles. The Bedouin were expected to host the itinerant sultan whom they fed in taxes on their dates and ghee, and, on occasion, the sultan would feed his subjects in turn. The British imported and gifted nominally free grain, at no cost to them, and began to develop roads for their own military incursions. The socialist government introduced subsidized staples, thereby effecting a fundamental transformation in Soqotrans' alimentary habits and encouraging a greater dependence on imported goods. They also presented dirt roads, but in doing so made Soqotrans more dependent on the state. The unity government gifted roads but took away food subsidies—both of which made Soqotrans more vulnerable to the global market.

My focus on these continuities does not amount to saying that Soqotrans are unchanging or that they do not draw clear distinctions between "the days of hunger," "the time of the Party," and "the opening." Rather, I argue that "in the eyes of the villagers, continuities were often more important than the structural and ideological distinctions."[142] Examining the continuities that bridge rural Soqotrans' encounter with these various states reveals the flaws in the narratives of the island's timeless isolation and the hubris in the view that Soqotra's development is new. It reveals that Soqotra's infrastructure has a violent history. There is a vast difference of course between the perceived extraneity and marginality of the state and the desire to host a state that would feed Soqotrans in return. Today, when rural Soqotrans cannot take their grievances and their stomachs to the very home of the executive, as they did under the sultans, it is even more important that the state come to them.

Seen through the lens of these continuities, Soqotrans may have experienced physical hunger in the past, but in the 2000s, they hungered for a state that would provide real and lasting sustenance. Instead, they were to play host to another guest (and de facto) state: the Socotra Conservation and Development Programme.

FIGURE 6. Meeting of the Association for the Conservation and Development of Homhil, Homhil Protected Area, 2004.

CHAPTER 3

WHEN THE ENVIRONMENT ARRIVED

It is undoubtedly a providential thing for the Socotran that his island is harbourless, that his mountains are not auriferous, and that the modern world is not so keen about dragon's blood, frankincense and myrrh as the ancients were.   —*Theodore J. Bent*

And the Rhinoceros upset the oil-stove with his nose, and the cake rolled on the sand, and he spiked that cake on the horn of his nose, and he ate it, and he went away, waving his tail, to the desolate and Exclusively Uninhabited Interior which abuts on the islands of Mazanderan, Socotra, and the Promontories of the Larger Equinox.

—*Rudyard Kipling*

When the rains let up following my move to Homhil, the women of Qayher slapped another layer of mud plaster onto the interior walls of my stable-turned-house. As they rejected my attempts to assist them, I spent much time with their children—perhaps one of the most common but least-commented-on pastimes of immersive fieldwork. One afternoon, while sitting in Bu Yaqub's courtyard with some school-age boys, I asked them for the Soqotri names of some nearby items. A few names in, the boys consulted among themselves in Soqotri.

"Wait!" one said. Then each boy ran off separately and returned some minutes later with handfuls of leaves and twigs.

"Tirimo!" said one, handing me a cluster of waxy, green leaves.

"Sebira!" said another, waving a different bunch. Dutifully, I traced each specimen in my notebook and recorded its Soqotri name: *'ikshih, tayf, mitrer, 'imtihe, a'arhiyib*. The boys took off again only to come back carrying more: *qamhin, rihini, zama'ano*.[1] I was surprised: this was not the vocabulary I had considered essential—at least not for daily communication. Was this an example of the "high level of environmental awareness" or "strong ethic of environmental stewardship" commonly attributed to Soqotrans—especially the herders—by the managerial "global ecocrats" deployed to promote biodiversity conservation on the island?[2] Or were the boys simply gathering the objects that had most interested foreign researchers and experts before?

As I observed in the following months, there was no shortage of researchers alighting on Homhil or in any of the designated "areas of special botanical interest" on the island. Indeed, my interlocutors often spoke of their island being overresearched and even showed signs of research fatigue—in their steadfast refusal to answer economists' household surveys, in their learned critiques of other ethnographers' practices and writings, and in their assured instructions for how I should conduct my fieldwork. Most of these researchers, myself included, were in some way connected to the successive integrated conservation and development projects that operated in the archipelago between 1997 and 2013. Despite these projects' shifting objectives, varying donors, and changing directors, Soqotrans referred to each and all of them indiscriminately as "the Environment" (al-bi'a), an abbreviation for "the environmental project" (mashru' al-bi'a)—itself a striking synecdoche for the range of biodiversity conservation and rural development interventions introduced during this period.

Much like Soqotrans spoke about the emergence of the various political regimes, they also described the turn-of-the-millennium arrival of the Environment as a foundational juncture. "When the Environment arrived," a neighbor explained, "Homhil became a protected area." "When the Environment arrived," one of the shaykhs in Homhil told me, "we stopped cutting down trees." "When the Environment arrived, we learned about conservation," was a common refrain. So I was surprised, six months into my fieldwork, to hear Sownhin suggest otherwise. "We knew how to protect our trees even before the Environment arrived!" he proclaimed. Whether or not the ICDP interventions impacted their environmental practices, Soqotrans generally regard them as having inaugurated a significant transformation in their relationship to their surroundings and to the outer world. Essentially, these ICDPs introduced the *concept* of "the environment" as a distinct object to be governed, managed, abstracted, commoditized, and consumed for the purpose of saving it. Tellingly, the Soqotri language has no term for "the environment" as a single entity, despite Soqotrans' long-standing traditions of resource conservation and regulation. Additionally, these projects introduced the neoliberal assumption shared by many ICDPs—what the anthropologist Paige West calls "conservation-as-development" projects—that conservation could be a source of economic growth.[3] The ICDPs, working in tandem with the government, had determined that environmental tourism would become one of the main avenues for generating sustainable development on Soqotra.

The influx of foreign botanists, zoologists, marine biologists, geologists, archaeologists, linguists, and ethnographers during this period was unprecedented. Nevertheless, the far-reaching allure of Soqotra's natural resources dates back at least two millennia, if not earlier. Likewise, the advent of scientific expeditions to Soqotra dates back to, and developed hand in glove with, the beginning of Britain's colonial protectorate over the Sultanate of Qishn and Soqotra. Armed with depictions of Soqotra and its inhabitants found in classical Greek and Roman histories, medieval Arabic and Persian geographies, early-modern travelogues, missionaries' letters, and merchants' journals, these nineteenth-century European scientists arrived with a preformed notion of what kind of environment they would find and how it could be cultivated through imperial interventions. Just as these explorers' "environmental imaginaries" were shaped by those of their predecessors (many of whom had never been to Soqotra),[4] their own representations continue to influence the technocratic interventions of the transnational ICDPs today. In this sense, the arrival of the Environment on Soqotra at the turn of the twenty-first century, however novel, was preceded and prefigured by the centuries-long arrivals of foreigners and the continued, reiterated dissemination of their ideas about Soqotra's environmental exceptionality.

Historians have shown that Anglo-European colonial powers relied specifically on their environmental imaginaries of the Middle East and North Africa to justify their colonization of the region and to frame their ensuing modernization projects. These imaginaries were often influenced by Western clichés of exotic (feminized) Nature and degenerate (overly sexual, overpopulating) nonwhites; that is, non-Western environments were also (and continue to be) viewed through an "orientalist" lens.[5] Believing the region's arid environments to have been degraded by their inhabitants' land-use practices (over-irrigation or deforestation), their goats (overgrazing), or Islam, colonial and imperial powers sought to "improve" or even "restore" them to their former mythical productivity.[6] As elsewhere in the region, contrasting imaginaries of Soqotra's barrenness and verdure gave rise to Soqotran pastoralists being alternately blamed for their island's alleged environmental degradation and upheld as seasoned environmental stewards.[7] From the early-modern period onward, Anglo-European visitors to Soqotra depicted its environment as a degraded or neglected version of its mythical, fertile past. Describing Soqotra as a barren island inhabited by a debased, ignorant, and idle population, nineteenth-century colonial officers blamed its "natives" for failing to cultivate the island's rich soil. A century later, colonial administrators and scientists faulted them for overgrazing their pastures. What makes these colonial-era representations of Soqotra particularly noteworthy are the ways in which they portrayed its landscape(s) as both utterly extraterrestrial and positively domestic. Soqotra's environment stood out for being exotic and for *not* resembling the arid and ostensibly wasted landscapes of southwestern Arabia and the Horn of Africa. Conceived as a place apart in space and time, as well as a landscape of "self,"[8] Soqotra's imagined decline was both environmental and social.

Thus, as mercantile interests in Soqotra's natural products were supplanted by imperial and neoliberal efforts to exploit and monetize Soqotra's environmental resources, rural Soqotrans were deemed in recurrent need of agricultural and environmental tutelage. With the arrival of the ICDPs, Soqotrans were taught to view their natural heritage as their financial future. As Soqotrans would also learn, however, the greater the economic value attributed to their island's material and symbolic nature, the less control they would retain over this increasingly privatized and alienated commodity.

NATURE'S EMPORIUM

In late 1965, the British Colonial Office in London demanded to know why there was no political officer stationed on Soqotra to prepare its sultan—"the most difficult of all [the high commissioner's] parishioners"[9]—for the impending withdrawal of the British from southwestern Arabia. (The last officer based there had left in January 1946.) The high commissioner of Aden, who would go on to advocate (albeit fruitlessly) for the continuation of development aid to Soqotra, tried to explain why their postwar engagements on the island had been so limited:

> Soqotra has been admittedly neglected. The reason for our not having posted an Assistant Advisor there permanently is primarily one of money. . . . *The island is*

rich neither in natural resources nor in skilled men, and most of what was needed
both in materiel and personnel would have to be imported by sea or, in emergency, by air charter; and there is no economy, and no prospect of the development of an economy, capable of sustaining even a hundredth part of the recurrent costs that would be needed to keep even this small development exercise
in being.[10]

The high commissioner's evaluation of Soqotra's paucity of natural resources
is striking—not only in light of the (re)"discovery" just three decades later of
the island's biological richness but also in view of its historic significance as
an Indian Ocean entrepôt renowned for its natural bounty. It was not that the
colonial government was unaware of Soqotra's exceptional and endemic biodiversity; this find had been made as early—or as late, if we consider the early
nineteenth-century studies of the endemic flora on St. Helena, for example[11]—
as 1880. But the market for its particular products had long collapsed. So, after
years of failing to discover nonrenewable resources (metals and oil) or to productively cultivate its land, the British presumed that there was little in Soqotra
that they could exploit into the next century.

Since antiquity, Soqotra has attracted scores of sailors, settlers, soldiers,
and scholars captivated by its famed flora, its enchanting nature, and its strategic location. During the Hellenistic period, Soqotra was widely known for
its frankincense, a gum resin prized in the ancient world for its aromatic and
medicinal properties, burnt in temples and at funerals, and consumed ra-
paciously by the Greco-Roman elite as "the classical equivalent of wine and
cigarettes, the indispensable luxuries of everyday life."[12] Graffiti discovered in
the cathedralesque Hoq cave above Soqotra's northeastern coast attest to the
continuous visits of seafarers and merchants from India, Ethiopia, Egypt, and
even Palmyra between the second century BCE and the sixth century CE.[13]
Yet by the end of the third century CE, the market for Arabian frankincense
had collapsed.[14] As a result, Soqotra suffered social and economic stagnation. It appears to have been precisely during this period, around the mid-
fourth century, that Soqotra was Christianized.[15] Cosmas Indicopleustes, a
sixth-century Alexandrine merchant who met Greek-speaking Soqotrans in
Ethiopia, reported that Soqotra was home to Greek colonists sent there by the
Ptolemaic pharaohs (r. 305–30 BCE), "a multitude of Christians," and a "clergy

who receive their ordination in Persia."[16] Significantly, Cosmas discusses the export of Ethiopian frankincense to South Arabia, India, and Persia but does not mention Soqotran gum resins at all.[17]

During late antiquity and into the Middle Ages, Soqotra became as famous for its salutary aloes has it once had been for it aromatic frankincense. Muslim geographers such as al-Mas'udi (d. 956), al-Sirafi (d. 979), al-Idrisi (d. 1165), and Yaqut (d. 1229) showed particular interest in the island's aloes, which they claim to have been the catalyst for the Greeks' "protection" of the island over a millennium earlier. For instance, in his tenth-century *Accounts of China and India*, the Persian seafarer al-Sirafi described Aristotle's advising Alexander the Great (r. 336–323 BCE) to "seek out" Soqotra "where aloes grow," to expel its inhabitants, "to resettle it with Greeks who could keep guard over it," and to export its aloes. Accordingly, Alexander dispatched a "force" who settled the island and later converted to Christianity.[18] Although now widely discredited, this Alexander legend was repeated and expanded on by later geographers, indicating perhaps the growing import(ance) of Socotrine aloes—their cultivation ordained, as it were, by Aristotle himself.[19] From the thirteenth through sixteenth centuries, Soqotra's aloes (and other natural products) continued to attract Arab, Persian, and European merchants, missionaries, and explorers, whose writings gave rise to and further propagated Soqotra's growing reputation as a Christian outpost, a pirates' den, and a haven for sorcerers.[20]

Throughout most of this period, Soqotra had been generally portrayed as a lush and fertile island. The anonymous author of the first-century CE seafaring manual *Periplus of the Erythraean Sea* described Dioscuridês, the Greek name for Soqotra, as a large island: "barren and also damp, with rivers, crocodiles, a great many vipers, and huge lizards."[21] Ibn al-Mujawir, the thirteenth-century Damascene merchant who either visited or sailed right past Soqotra in 1221, regaled his readers with stories of Soqotrans' sorcery and debauchment, while providing a fairly realistic account of Soqotra's arable interior:

> [Soqotra] has date palms, cultivated areas [*basatin*] and fields of sorghum and
> wheat. There are camels and cattle and thousands upon thousands of sheep.
> Water flows on the surface of the ground, sweet and fresh. It is a large river,
> which gushes out, long and wide, from the mountains. More often than not [this

river] provides the excess of fish for the sea. The aloes tree and dragon's blood grow, watered by it. On the shores [of the island] there is much ambergris.[22]

Ahmad Ibn Majid, the late fifteenth-century Arab navigator famed for having allegedly guided Vasco de Gama from Malindi to India, wrote circa 1490 that in Soqotra "there is water everywhere."[23]

It is following the failed occupation by the Portuguese in 1507–1511 that we see a shift in Europeans' depictions of Soqotra's natives and its environment. Although the Portuguese continued to take in water at Soqotra—and were even permitted by their eventual Mahra allies to send Catholic missionaries there from time to time[24]—the island would come to be known more for its geographic and spiritual "barrenness." For example, the venerated Jesuit missionary St. Francis Xavier (d. 1552) described his 1542 stopover en route to Goa as an "altogether sterile and arid" island where he found the Soqotrans to be "Christian in name rather than in reality."[25] Despairing of the debased state of Christianity on the island and the persecution the Christians suffered under their despotic "Mussulman lord," Xavier perceived even the environment to be degraded. "The island is very poor in crops and provisions; a rough place enough and full of troubles," he wrote to St. Ignatius Loyola, his mentor.[26] Yet it was Xavier's promulgation of the St. Thomas legend that provided the justification for Portugal's ongoing engagement with Soqotra's oppressive Muslim rulers while further whetting the European imagination of this "wretched" place.[27]

This narrative of Soqotra's barrenness—of all but its aloes—persisted until the time of the first British occupation of the island three centuries later. By the early seventeenth century, with Dutch and English merchant fleets venturing to the Indian Ocean to compete with the Portuguese spice trade, the number of European visitors to Soqotra had increased substantially. Captains and merchants in service of the newly established English East India Company (EIC) stopped there regularly on their way to Aden and Surat between 1608 and 1615 to procure water and fresh victuals (cattle, goats, dates) and to purchase Socotrine aloes. These captains commended Soqotra as a place for obtaining information on other passing ships, a repository for letters to their successors, and a secure site in which to weather the monsoon. They were also introduced to "coho" there, suggesting that the first English sip of coffee may have occurred on Soqotra's shores.[28] However, most of the EIC ships anchored off coastal towns for only a week or two, during which their captains ventured ashore but no farther.[29] Accordingly, many regarded Soqotra as a "very barren countrye," offering little but aloes, dragon's blood, dates, and livestock; "what else this Iland may yeeld, I am yet to be informed of, but of rockes and stones, drie and bare, it seems the whole Iland is composed."[30] Of course, Soqotra's barren nature and appearance were as much determined by its seasonal monsoon as it was by when and where these visitors landed. In 1608, the EIC merchants found aloes "in great abundance," claiming that Soqotra "could make yearely more [aloes] then Christendome can spend."[31] In 1610, after a two-year drought, even the aloes were scarce.[32] Following the establishment of an English factory at Surat in 1613 and a trading factory in Mocha in 1618, the island "ceased to be a regular port of call" for EIC fleets on their way to India.[33] Nevertheless, the EIC continued to dispatch vessels from Surat to Soqotra to purchase its aloes throughout much of the seventeenth century.[34] Dutch, French, Portuguese, Danish, and Gujarati ships called on Soqotra, too—as did the Omanis who plundered the island in 1669 and 1674.[35]

During the eighteenth century, the regional trade in aloes decreased and shifted from Soqotra to Sohar.[36] As in the third century, Soqotra's economy declined following the collapse of its near monoculture. Consequently, there are fewer records of European visitors to Soqotra during this century, although Soqotra's trade with the Swahili Coast (and presumably also Gujarat) remained substantial.[37] With Soqotra's dwindling aloe production being paid as tribute to the sultans of Qishn and "the modern world" no longer being "so keen about dragon's blood, frankincense and myrrh as the ancients were,"[38] Soqotra might have fallen into greater obscurity were it not for the advent of steam navigation in the early nineteenth century and the subsequent resurgence of European interest in the Red Sea route to the East. In 1830–1834, the Government of British India sent several scouts to Soqotra to assess its suitability as a coaling depot.[39] One scout, the young naval lieutenant J. R. Wellsted, traversed Soqotra's interior—allegedly becoming the first European to have done so. It was based on Wellsted's report, in particular—which challenged the narrative of Soqotra's barrenness—that the government attempted to purchase and then occupy the island in 1834–1835, failing at both.

Whereas the government was interested initially in the island for its own energy needs as well as its geostrategic location, the mythic narratives surrounding Soqotra played a significant role in shaping subsequent interventions. These imaginaries—that Soqotra had been a prized Greek-settler plantation; that it had been home to one of the earliest (and longest-lasting) Christian communities in the region; that the land and its people had "lapsed" from a state of greater productivity and civilization;[40] and that its endemic plants and aboriginal inhabitants represented remnant populations of antediluvian flora and of ancient Greek (or even ancient South Arabian) civilizations—combined to make Soqotra especially alluring. Although speleothem records suggest that Soqotra used to be wetter during the early classical period than it is today,[41] climate change itself may not account for the abrupt shift from Ibn Majid's depiction of a very wet island circa 1490 to St. Xavier's depiction of a desert island fifty years later. This perceived degradation was as much linked to Europeans' perceptions of Soqotrans' Christian degeneracy as it was to their propensity for not advancing beyond Soqotra's arid shores. Travelers' letters and journal entries popularized through the compilations of the English cleric Samuel Purchas (d. 1626) certainly contributed to the prevailing portrayal of Soqotra's degenerate environment and natives. It is likely that these same depictions influenced Rudyard Kipling's "just so" story of how the rhinoceros got his skin in Soqotra's "desolate and Exclusively Uninhabited Interior."[42]

Accordingly, late nineteenth- and early twentieth-century botanists, ethnographers, archaeologists, missionaries, and colonial officers were eager to discover Soqotra's unique flora and fauna, uncover Soqotrans' mysterious origins, recover the island's European influences, revive the "latent germs" of Christianity,[43] and restore the island's agriculture productivity and commercial prospects. As a result, the near century of Soqotra's British protection (1876–1967) ushered in a new array of European explorers, surveyors, and natural scientists drawn to the island's Christian past, Portuguese ruins, preliterate language, unique flora, and productive potential—but now for collection as well as commerce.

"SOME LUCRATIVE ASSET"

Histories of scientific research in Soqotra tell the same basic story: Although the island's flora had long attracted foreign merchants, the first scientific expedition to Soqotra occurred in 1880, nearly fifty years after Wellsted's initial exploration.

Led by the Scottish botanist Isaac Bayley Balfour under the auspices of the British Association for the Advancement of Science, this team spent forty-eight days on Soqotra collecting hundreds of botanical, zoological, and geological specimens. Balfour's expedition was followed by five other expeditions—variously botanical, zoological, archaeological, ethnographic, and linguistic—between 1881 and 1899.[44] However, after this late nineteenth-century flurry, scientists once again neglected Soqotra for another fifty years, until the British launched several expeditions there in the 1950s and 1960s. Then, following Soqotra's annexation by South Yemen, the archipelago was effectively closed to research until 1990, with the exception of several missions in the 1980s by the University of Aden and a Soviet-Yemeni team. Yemen's unification "opened" the island, therefore, not only to economic liberalization, religious conservatism, and global tourism; it heralded also, through several scientific and fact-finding missions to Soqotra in the early to mid-1990s, the (re)discovery of the archipelago's extraordinary biodiversity.[45]

Yet, like many of their peers, these scientists were interested not only in studying, collecting, and preserving Soqotra's natural vegetation but also in actively cultivating and exploiting it.[46] Indeed, nearly all of these protectorate-era expeditions were motivated and facilitated by imperial goals, which themselves were driven by and advanced an "environmental orientalism."[47] Further, these expeditions were products of and enabled by the world's changing energy regimes. That is, scientific interest in Soqotra, imbricated as it was with imperial desires, waxed and waned in concert with the transition from the age of solar energy (pre-1800) to the age of coal (1800–1914) to the age of petroleum and natural gas (1880–present).[48] In this sense, the twenty-first-century (re)discovery of Soqotra's unique environment was less a discovery of its rich natural resources than of a new market for their commodification and exploitation.

Despite prevailing perceptions of Soqotra's religious and environmental degradation, one of the first things that the nineteenth-century explorers noted—when they actually ventured inland—was Soqotra's distinctively temperate climate, fertile soil, and "exuberant vegetation."[49] In contrast to the barren shores observed from the decks of passing ships, the island's elevated interior appeared both pastoral and preternatural. Wellsted described and collected several plant specimens but focused on those with exchange or use value.[50] He also drew Europeans' attention to Soqotra's bucolic, if not English, nature: "Its valleys and plains afford luxuriant grass, herds of cattle are numerous, *and the scenery in many places is equal to that of our own country.*"[51] In his view, it was Soqotra's familiar environment, within an "inhospitable" setting, that rendered it exceptional:

> I know not of a more singular spot on the whole surface of the globe than the island of Socotra. It stands forth, a verdant isle, in a sea girt by two most inhospitable shores; yet its wooded mountains, its glens, its sparkling streams, differ not more from their parched and burning deserts, their bleak and wasted hills, than do its mild and inoffensive inhabitants from the savage and ferocious hordes by which they are traversed.[52]

Wellsted was not a botanist. (Nor was he innocent of the bigotry of his day.) And Soqotra's malarial environment was certainly not hospitable to the British and Indian troops dispatched there nine months later. Still, Wellsted's published memoirs of Soqotra's singular nature and indigenous inhabitants would guide Balfour and other nineteenth-century European naturalists, who were nevertheless astonished by what they found.

"The island surpasses my expectations in the interesting nature of its fauna and flora as well as it geology and I expect to make a very large and valuable collection," wrote Balfour in a letter to Aden in February 1880, a few weeks into his stay.[53] What surprised Balfour was less Soqotra's glens and streams than its significant proportion of endemic (to him, exotic) flora. To Balfour and subsequent botanists and collectors, this vegetation appeared otherworldly and allochronic. Its "gouty" *Adenium* "looks like one of the first efforts of Dame nature in tree-making, happily abandoned by her for more graceful shapes and forms . . . as if it belonged to a different epoch of creation to our own trees at home."[54] Its *Dracaena* were "like trees made for a child's Noah's ark" or "a strange freak of Nature."[55] To some, the trees seemed almost bestial. Both Bent and Forbes described the *Adenium* as if afflicted with elephantiasis.[56] Charles Moser, the US consul-general to Aden, likened his 1913 expedition to find a frankincense tree to a hunt for wild game.[57] Eventually, Moser's Soqotran guides spotted a large frankincense tree—"an enormous sea-serpent in the act of shedding its skin, so awkwardly contorted and alive it seemed"—and uprooted two others. Years later, Moser wrote, these trees were thriving in Arizona.[58]

Motivated as these collectors were by discovery, they were also excited by the island's commercial prospects. Many advised the government how to cultivate profitable crops and develop the island's natural resources. Wellsted, who had been employed for this reason, commented on the soil's fertility and noted that parts of the island were particularly "susceptible of cultivation." He thus blamed the Soqotrans for the island's limited production: "[The hills] might be tilled and cultivated in the same manner as is customary in Syria and Palestine. In a word, were it not for the prevailing ignorance and sloth among its inhabitants, Socotra, in a few seasons, might be rendered as celebrated for the extent and variety of its productions, as it is now perhaps remarkable for their small number and little comparative value."[59] Similarly, Balfour observed that "large tracts of country" could be terraced to produce "a large crop of cereals, fruits, and vegetables" for "the adjacent continents and for passing ships." He further suggested exporting the island's aloes, dragon's blood, boxwood, and lichens as "articles of commerce."[60] George Schweinfurth, a German botanist who visited Soqotra a year later, suggested harvesting its trees for charcoal for export to the neighboring coasts.[61] Ernest Bennett, an arthropod-collecting British war correspondent, recommended the island be used as a sanatorium; a cotton, indigo, or tea plantation; a cattle ranch; and even a penal settlement.[62] Although these researchers may simply have been trying to be helpful, it was precisely such observations that influenced colonial administrators and metropolitan politicians bent on exploiting the island for their own political or economic gain.

The conclusion of these fin de siècle expeditions did not halt specimen collection or commercial speculation. Soqotra's plants continued to be exported throughout the twentieth century and even into the twenty-first. In the early decades of the twentieth century, prior to Britain's second occupation of Soqotra, several private parties attempted to harvest, extract, or cultivate the island's natural resources, but were stymied by the Government of British India.[63] However, in the early 1930s, Britain's expansion into the Aden Protectorate and its hinterlands began to envelop and embroil the archipelago. When Aden's chief commissioner Bernard Reilly visited Soqotra in 1933 to resolve the Mahra opposition to the establishment of a Royal Air Force landing ground in Qishn, he was delighted by its "thickly wooded hills" and its "small, neat houses surrounded by plantations of date trees, patches of water melons, and pasture for sheep and goats and the straight-backed breed of cattle peculiar to Socotra." Reilly became convinced not only of the need for "more direct contact with the outlying parts of the Protectorate" (thus instigating more visits to Soqotra, among other places) but also of the need to modify their preconceptions of the Socotrans.[64] "It is high time," reflected the ship's commander, "that the legend that Socotra is populated by a savage and truculent race was finally dispelled, at any rate as regards the neighborhood of Hadibo."[65]

This rediscovery of Soqotra's pastoral nature and tame population came at the time of Aden's reconfiguration as a Crown Colony, which itself generated interest in Soqotra's specimens and products. For example, in March 1937, just days prior to Aden's administrative separation from British India, a Mr. Hughes wrote to soon-to-be-governor Reilly seeking a prospecting concession for Soqotra. In the months that followed, the governor received letters from a Thomas Sharp requesting a *Vitis subaphylla* cutting from the island; from a Danish missionary itching to collect insects, and evangelize; from a late acting consul of Harar eager to hunt butterflies; and from a Frank Howard of Florida aiming to import aloes.[66] During this time, it appears that Governor Reilly even attempted to help someone export trees *to* Soqotra, prompting the sultan to respond, "Our land does not have the capacity to accept trees whose growth is contrary to what is customary"—that is, alien species.[67]

Governor Reilly drew the line, however, at the Colonial Office's proposal in March 1939 to resettle up to five thousand European Jews from Palestine on Soqotra. From the distant perspective of planners in London—people such as Leopold Amery, secretary of state for India and Burma (1940–1945), who was alerted to this possibility by the same Ernest Bennett, now MP, who had collected arthropods there in 1896–1897—Soqotra presented a more palatable solution to the problem of large-scale Jewish immigration to Palestine than did other sites under consideration.[68] On this "large and thinly populated" island, they reasoned, Jewish settlers could make their living growing cotton, dates, and tobacco; marketing the island's dragon's blood, frankincense, and myrrh; engaging in maritime commerce; and even exporting the guano accumulated on its neighboring islands.[69] Whereas al-Mukalla's resident adviser Harold Ingrams conceded that non-European settlers might cultivate Soqotra's underdeveloped resources, he maintained that "European Jews could never survive on the island as settlers"—despite the bandied-about example of "Alexander's

Greeks."[70] Worried, however, that such a scheme would damage his own plans for the "pacification and development" of the Aden Protectorate, Governor Reilly insisted that "any idea of settling Jews either in Socotra or in any other part of the Protectorate should be completely ruled out." Moreover, he pointed out, if they were to investigate the "economic possibilities of Socotra," they should do so "in the interests of the inhabitants, and not in those of foreign colonists."[71] (These and other objections did not stop Amery from resuscitating his proposal four years later.)

It was during this period—marked by the Allied forces' wartime occupation of Soqotra—that the British finally gained the chance to act on their century-long desire to cultivate the island. At first, the resident political officers simply tried to grow vegetables for their own consumption.[72] But by the summer of 1943, the entire island suffered from the war-induced food shortages. Thus, in addition to importing grains to prevent famine, the political officers encouraged the sultan to improve the island's crop production.[73] When Aden's agricultural officer B. J. Hartley revisited Soqotra in late 1943 (in May 1941, he had overseen the rebuilding of the British-bombed landing ground), he proposed developing a "new rural economy" based on terraced farming in the highlands and floodwater irrigation in lowlands. To initiate this, Hartley suggested importing "Arabian settlers" to Soqotra—about 120 Yemeni farmers and their families—on the model of what the Italian government had done in Massawa. Their first obstacle was that the sultan did not own the lands—neither in the Haggeher Mountains nor in the Hadibo plain—selected for this "collective farm."[74] Their second obstacle was what the resident officer C. Tudor-Pole called "the human factor." Although Tudor-Pole had noted the date palm groves and tobacco patches cultivated in the island's riverbeds, observed the coastal women tending their vegetable gardens for household use, and recognized the *absence* of a viable market for produce (aside from the garrison), he still blamed the Soqotrans for their horticultural lack. "It will be realized," Tudor-Pole wrote to Hartley in May 1944, "that one is dealing in the main with an extraordinarily low type of humanity, for the most part ill-favoured for either spirit or intelligence. If it is demonstrated that cereals and various starchy and sugar vegetables can be grown in certain conditions imitation will be slow, and will require a guiding and encouraging hand."[75] This guiding hand came via the agricultural instructors dispatched between spring

1944 and summer 1945 to cultivate vegetable gardens for the troops. Among their successes was the delivery to the garrison of nearly three hundred pounds of tomatoes in one month—before grasshoppers consumed their seedlings.[76] But the agricultural scheme envisioned by Hartley never germinated: funding was not made available, and the agricultural instructors were recalled at the war's end, together with the rest of the garrison.

The narrative of Soqotra's paucity of natural resources notwithstanding, it was precisely Soqotra's verdant nature that motivated several nineteenth- to mid-twentieth-century interventions there. Certainly, the British sought control over Soqotra because of its advantageous location. But it was Soqotra's arable environment that made it (seem) viable for British occupation and Jewish settlement. Underlying these failed or aborted projects was the belief that Soqotra had been successfully settled and cultivated by Greeks once before. If Soqotra's natural resources were now underdeveloped, or if colonial agriculture projects failed, this narrative implied, the reason was that Soqotra's native inhabitants were ignorant and lazy, themselves having fallen from their once "advanced position." The scientific expeditions that coalesced in the late nineteenth century and extended in an imperial-developmentalist vein throughout the first half of the twentieth century underscored these declensionist narratives—and, to certain extent, continue to do so to this day.

"THRESHOLD OF THE WORLD"

The 1950s–1960s flurry of scientific expeditions in Soqotra were as much launched by the colonial government and shaped by imperial policies as had been the expeditions of the nineteenth century—if not more so. However, whereas the nineteenth-century expeditions precipitated and were facilitated by Britain's colonization of southwestern Arabia, these mid-twentieth-century expeditions were instigated by Britain's impending withdrawal from southwestern Arabia and its attempt to retain Soqotra as a military base. Moreover, whereas the first British surveys of Soqotra were motivated by the British Empire's need for coaling depots along its Red Sea route from London to Bombay, many of these latter expeditions were conducted in the service of petroleum—whether in search of oil and gas in Soqotra or in connection with the sultan's mainland territory (al-Mahra), where sustained oil exploration was under way. What distinguishes this set of explorations from those a century earlier is that now the environmental and oriental imaginaries of al-Mahra were drawn into and contrasted with the environmental imaginary of Soqotra. As the territory of al-Mahra became increasingly implicated in the British plans for withdrawal, Soqotra was reimagined once again as an isolated, archaic, and denuded place.

The first postwar surveys of Soqotra reflected these shifts. As the Aden government continued to field requests from the sultan for agricultural assistance and famine relief, it dispatched an entomologist, George Popov, to the island in early 1953 to investigate a reported locust infestation. During his three-month visit, Popov conducted the first general ecological survey of the island, while also collecting various plant and Orthoptera specimens. At the same time, the petroleum geologist Zaid Beydoun conducted a one-month geological survey of Soqotra on behalf of Petroleum Concessions Ltd (PCL), which had been granted a concession to the Eastern Protectorates in 1938.[77] These surveys occurred during the tense interval between Sultan Ahmad's death in early 1952 and the Crown's delayed recognition of Sultan Isa as the "treaty" sultan of Qishn and Soqotra in late 1953—against the aspirations of his distant Qishn-based cousin, Sultan Khalifa, who had declared himself the sovereign ruler of al-Mahra back in 1949.[78] Moreover, it was during this period that the colonial government finally realized that its own claim to the potentially oil-bearing regions of al-Mahra depended on the Mahra tribes' recognition of the sultan of Soqotra who, in reality, had "no authority or leadership whatsoever over the mainland."[79] Consequently, the colonial government pressured Sultan Isa to sign an advisory treaty with them (which he did in April 1954); to establish control over "his" mainland territories by appointing a deputy there (which he effectuated only in 1965); and to agree to divide any would-be oil profits from his territories among the protectorate states as a whole (which he never did).[80] To this end, the assistant adviser at al-Mukalla, Major Ian Snell, traveled repeatedly to Soqotra in the 1950s and lived in Hadibo for nearly five months in 1955–1956—longer than any other researchers had. When not working on the sultan to sign the agreements, Snell occupied himself treating tuberculosis patients and observing witch trials.[81]

For years, the Aden government had rejected the requests of various non-British researchers, journalists, and merchants to visit Soqotra on the grounds of the island's inaccessibility and lack of facilities, but in reality to protect its interests and conceal its failings.[82] Then, in 1956—within months of Snell's futile mission and the governor's subsequent efforts, ultimately aborted, to depose Sultan Isa for refusing to sign the oil agreements[83]—the government permitted and even facilitated a "general scientific reconnaissance" led by a twenty-two-year-old undergraduate student. Douglas Botting, the organizer of this Oxford University expedition, depicted it as the first expedition of its kind since those of the late nineteenth century.[84] Flown to Soqotra by the Royal Air Force, Botting and his party spent two months surveying and excavating archaeological sites; collecting plants, reptiles, crickets, and soil samples; drawing blood samples from unwitting Bedouin; and excavating "Christian" tombs. This expedition is known less for its findings than for Botting's memoir about their excursions—the first detailed narrative about Soqotra's environment and people since Wellsted's memoir. But if Wellsted sought to make the island appear habitable and its "savages" noble, Botting emphasized, on the eve of Britain's ultimate withdrawal, Soqotra's primordial nature:

> I do not think I shall ever forget the strange sensation I had, silent among the bushes, of living in a past and depopulated world. . . . In the presence of these incredible ancient rocks and the primeval dragon's blood trees and the screaming birds and the wind roaring and nothing else anywhere, I felt I was treading on the threshold of the world. Humanity had no place in these terrifying, watching, silent and animated mountains. The mountains were alive, watching me.[85]

Not just barren, the landscape as he saw it was also surreal: "Dali-esque," "Disney-esque," and generally uncanny.[86] And the Bedouin, in his view, were cloistered, childish, animal-like, and primitive: "culturally . . . in the Stone Age."[87]

As Botting was writing his recollections, Conservative British cabinet members were debating the political separation of the Soqotra Archipelago from the Arabian mainland.[88] The spread of Arab nationalism throughout the region had already threatened Britain's ability to maintain its hold on southwestern Arabia. While the Aden government worked toward the creation of an independent (but presumably pro-British) Arabian state, Conservative ministers in London insisted that Britain could maintain its influence in the Middle East only if it were to maintain a sovereign base in Aden or on an island enclave, such as Soqotra.[89] The proposal to separate—and thus retain—Soqotra was endorsed in particular by the parliamentary undersecretary at the Colonial Office, Julian Amery.[90] (Julian Amery was the son of Leo Amery, the undersecretary who had proposed resettling Jews on Soqotra some twenty years earlier.) It is conceivable that Botting's depiction of a "depopulated" island had also influenced Julian Amery. Nevertheless, the governor of Aden rejected this proposal, pointing out that Sultan Isa would never agree to a military base on Soqotra were the British to deprive him of his oil profits in al-Mahra.[91] Although the proposal for separation was thereafter suspended, it was not yet put to rest.

On the face of it, the next exploration of Soqotra occurred as late as 1964, when the British ornithologist Alec Forbes-Watson spent more than three months collecting bird specimens for the Smithsonian Institution. However, just a few weeks earlier, Pan American Oil—which had purchased the exploration rights to the Eastern Protectorate States (including al-Mahra) after PCL relinquished its concession in 1960—sent a geology team to Soqotra to search again for potential oil fields.[92] It was precisely during this period of state building in al-Mahra, guided by the promise of oil revenues, that the British Ministry of Defense resuscitated its plan to separate Soqotra from the mainland.[93] Yet Forbes-Watson, who was in Soqotra collecting birds while these debates were playing out in London—and on Radio Cairo, which Sultan Isa listened to—could see Soqotrans, as had Botting, only as being geographically isolated, culturally archaic, and living out an "Old Testament way of life." But not so insular, apparently, that they were unaware of these maneuvers.[94]

From this point onward, the scientific expeditions to Soqotra cannot be separated from Britain's decolonization strategies. By the summer of 1964, the date for Britain's withdrawal from southwestern Arabia had been set. One of the main dilemmas for both the Conservative government and the newly elected Labour government was how to retain a sovereign base in Aden—and, failing that, in Soqotra. In December 1964, Captain Peter Boxhall of the Intelligence Corps led the two-month Royal Air Force and Army Scientific Expedition to Soqotra to survey the island, collect flora and freshwater snails, record graffiti markings, study the Soqotri language, provide medical assistance to the local population, and convince Sultan Isa to allow the British to train paratroopers there. Despite Boxhall having been stationed there before, members of the RAF-Army party spent weeks searching for Soqotra's "elusive" dragon's blood tree—a striking indicator of how poorly the army knew the island beyond its coastal posts.[95] Meanwhile, in London, the ministers continued to debate whether to "separate" Soqotra from al-Mahra to retain it as an "option for future development."[96]

It is in light of these circumstances that we may understand the high commissioner's frustrated response to the Colonial Office in late 1965 when he emphasized the island's paucity of natural resources. Here was a land that the British had tried to cultivate for years—as a market for exotic products, a plantation, a farmland, and a settlement—but the resources it lacked, the ones that mattered, were minerals and oil. Nevertheless, in what amounted to a last-ditch effort to consider the development of Soqotra, the Mukalla Residency dispatched its assistant adviser G. H. Brown there in the spring of 1966 to assess the island's socioeconomic conditions and possibilities. Three months later, Brown returned with a three-point plan that bears a striking resemblance to the aims of the various development projects of the 2000s: (1) to generate employment through outside funds (in the 2000s, tourism); (2) to increase exportable products (in the 2000s, fish and honey); and (3) to develop food crops through increased cultivation (in the 2000s, home gardens). Notably, Brown advised against "open[ing] up the roads and introduc[ing] motor transport to the island," on account of the harm it would do to Soqotra's camel owners while benefiting only the wealthy.[97] In fact, his own plan notwithstanding, Brown remained skeptical of the viability of development in Soqotra for two reasons. First, there was the problem of the island's monopolistic and exploitative regime, which, in a scathing "confidential addendum" to his report, Brown likened to "Vampires."[98] Second, there was the expectation among Soqotrans that a foreign company or government would finance their labor:

> At present, one belief that is rife is that a Company [like Pan American Oil] proposes to take over the land at a large rent, paying magnificent wages to everyone, and develop it. . . . A variation is that the British Government will develop the land, instal [sic] the pumps, and according to some, even pay the islanders for working in the fields while nevertheless giving them all the produce. . . . It may take a little while and some hearburning [sic] before they realise that whatever else may happen, neither of these will, and that any assistance given will be to enable them to get ahead by their own efforts.[99]

This expectation, which may well have been rooted in the Soqotrans' experience of the British occupation during World War II, was not as ill founded as Brown had made it out to be. It is pretty much what happened when the ICDPs arrived thirty years later. But Brown's acerbic assessment of Soqotra's rulers and subjects must have tempered any enthusiasm the Aden government could muster for advocating economic assistance to it on the eve of their impending departure—especially on the heels of Pan American Oil's surrender of its oil concessions to the Eastern Protectorate a month earlier, which brought a crashing end to any hope for the further development of the embryonic state in al-Mahra.

Finally, in the spring of 1967, the colonial government deployed one last scientific expedition to the island: a thirty-four-member joint services and civilian expedition mounted by the Middle East Command (led again by Captain Boxhall) and various British academics. This expedition produced a wealth of material in terms of archaeological findings, new collections of plants and other specimens, and hydrographic and ground surveys.[100] Despite the island having been surveyed for more than a century, a member of this team was still compelled to describe it as "Socotra Incognita."[101] The same person mocked his Soqotran guide for studiously memorizing the Latin names of all of the plants documented by the team's botanist—as if Soqotrans knowing this terminology was so incongruous as to be a laughing matter. But the most damaging characterization to emerge from this expedition was the belief that Soqotra's vegetation had been all but ruined by the pastoralists' activities. Already, G. H. Brown had noted that the island's pasture had been "seriously damaged by over-grazing," essentially blaming its pastoralists for the alleged environmental degradation and misuse.[102] (Notably, ten years earlier, George Popov had emphasized that, despite Soqotra's predominantly pastoral population, overgrazing was not a problem.)[103] But "pessimistic reports" authored by the 1967 expedition team—a team that visited in the March–June dry season, as had Brown a year earlier—resulted in the belief that Soqotra's vegetation had been "decimated by the unrestrained cutting of trees and the vast, uncontrolled flocks of goats which were being allowed to roam freely over the island."[104] These characterizations found their way into the IUCN Red Data book and other publications on endangered plant species, which indicated that nearly half of Soqotra's endemic plant species were "on the verge of extinction" due to the Soqotrans' "poor husbandry."[105]

In the years following South Yemen's independence, the PDRY government nationalized landholdings and established several pilot agricultural farms, co-operatives, and a boarding school for nomadic Bedouin in Soqotra—all part of its nationwide efforts to restructure South Yemen's rural economy and to settle its Bedouin populations. As in other newly independent Arab states, the government operated on the assumption that rangelands had been degraded as a result of the Bedouin's traditional land management practices.[106] At the same time, it limited foreign researchers' access to Soqotra. This restriction was nothing new—except that now it also extended to British scientists and explorers. Research expeditions continued but were predominantly anthro-pological in nature.[107] In 1982, the University of Aden launched an expedi-tion under the leadership of the German zoologist Wolfgang Wranik (who returned several times thereafter) to study Soqotra's flora and fauna. But this did little to dispel the environmental imaginary that Soqotra's endemic veg-etation was critically endangered, if not already destroyed, due to pastoral overgrazing.[108]

Given this narrative of Soqotra's increasing isolation and defoliation, it is not surprising that the island's opening in 1990 was heralded as a period of rediscovery of the archipelago's extraordinary biodiversity. A burst of botani-cal and other scientific explorations of Soqotra between 1989 and 1996 led to a "reappraisal of the conservation status of [Soqotra's] flora and confirmed its international importance."[109] Whereas in the 1880s Balfour and Schweinfurth had jointly discovered 565 species of flora, 206 (36 percent) of them endemic, in the 1990s, botanists counted 825 species, 307 (37 percent) of them endemic. This level of botanical diversity and endemism—a measure of Soqotra's plants' *intrinsic* value—placed Soqotra among "the world's most botanically important island groups."[110] Significantly, Soqotra's allegedly unskilled men were rehabili-tated, too. No longer blamed for overgrazing, Soqotrans were now praised for having "lived with and used biological resources in a sustainable manner . . . for hundreds if not thousands of years."[111] Or when it became increasingly evident that habitat degradation due to overbreeding and overgrazing was a significant environmental problem, the blame was not attributed to the pastoral ecosystem itself but to the changes in and *loss* of the Soqotrans' traditional land manage-ment practices: a different kind of lapse.[112] This was the new environmental imaginary that was to fuel Soqotra's conservation.

THE NATURE OF PROTECTION IN SOQOTRA

Yemen has a long tradition of ecosystem protections drawn from customary and religious principles. These include traditional water-management practices (through spate irrigation, elaborate terracing, and other rainwater-harvesting structures); communal forms of rangeland management; local tribal interdictions against forest felling or unauthorized entry; indigenous plant-protection methods; the Islamic injunction against grazing or excessive resource use in protected or inviolate territories (*hima*); and Islamic trust law, which transforms privately owned properties into inalienable preserves (*waqf*).[113] Variants of these protections continue to be employed in Soqotra where pastoralists collectively share and safeguard their rangeland, distinguish between areas open for communal grazing (Soq.: *mibdihil*) and tribally owned reserves or enclosures (Ar./Soq.: *zeribah*), control livestock breeding through the use of contraceptive aprons, practice soil conservation, and levy fines to prevent unsustainable and unauthorized tree cutting or harvesting.[114] Similarly, Soqotran fishermen impose their own bans on taking small pelagic species, using nets during a full moon and using fish traps in certain areas.[115] Nevertheless, many of these customary protections depend on strong community-level enforcement. In Soqotra, as elsewhere, the shift to centralized resource management enfeebled the local shaykhs' jurisdiction over their communities' natural resources. Additionally, the growth of the public and private sectors devitalized the pastoral economy and, with it, the indigenous impetus for and expertise in these traditional management systems.

In contrast to these and other forms of resource use and conservation, environmental management through Yemen's state institutions and legislation is quite recent. By the 1980s, both North and South Yemen had established an environmental protection council and had ratified a number of international environmental conventions, including the 1972 Convention Concerning the Protection of the World Cultural and Natural Heritage. In 1990, shortly following the unification of North and South Yemen, the Republic of Yemen created an interministerial Environment Protection Council (EPC) to replace the formerly separate institutions, which it expanded in 1992 and again in 1995, when it developed its first comprehensive national legislation concerning the environment. But Yemen's watershed moment for statewide environmental management was its 1995 ratification of the Environmental

Protection Law. This law defined the scope of the EPC; outlined objectives for the protection and management of national environmental resources, including calling for the establishment of national protected areas; and stipulated the establishment of an Environment Protection Fund. In the following year, the government established a National Water Resources Authority and ratified the three Earth Summit (Rio) Conventions on Biological Diversity, Climate Change, and Desertification, making it eligible for Global Environment Facility funding. Yemen also developed its first environmental planning document, the National Environmental Action Plan (NEAP) for 1996–2000.[116] Among the NEAP's priorities were the constitution of an ecotourism department within the General Tourism Authority and the establishment of Soqotra as a national protected area.[117]

At the turn of the millennium, the government redoubled its commitment to environmental resource management. In 2001, a constitutional amendment declared the protection of the environment a "religious and national duty" of each citizen.[118] At the same time, the EPC was transformed from an interministerial agency to a full-fledged authority, the Environment Protection Authority (EPA). In the years that followed, new laws were enacted, ministries created, and plans drawn up to support water-resource management and biodiversity.[119] In 2004, the newly established Ministry of Water and Environment released a five-year National Biodiversity Strategy and Action Plan (NBSAP; 2004–2008) "to achieve a better quality of life for all Yemeni people through the conservation and sustainable use of biological resources."[120] Significantly, the NBSAP counted as its "sustainable development principles" not only the by-now-global faith in community responsibility, nature heritage, and ecotechnology but also the relevant "Islamic values" enshrined in the Qur'an and numerous hadith.

It was during these two decades that one of the least developed and most neglected areas in Yemen emerged as one of its most valuable resources. In 1996, following an international symposium on Soqotra, the government decreed the archipelago a "special, natural area in urgent need of protection."[121] Shortly thereafter, the Global Environment Facility provided funding for a large-scale ICDP on Soqotra. Through this project, the EPC developed a legislative framework to identify and manage several categories of protected areas within the archipelago. In 2000, the president of Yemen ratified this zoning

plan, establishing the Soqotra Archipelago as a national protected area. International recognition of and foreign aid to Soqotra blossomed. Moreover, with
Soqotra having been thrust to the forefront of the government's environmental
initiatives, Yemen made its own entry onto the global environmental stage. In
July 2008, UNESCO recognized the Soqotra Archipelago as a World Heritage
Site. At the time of its inscription, Soqotra was one of only five natural sites
located within the Arab world. In contrast to other regions, such as Africa,
natural heritage within the Arab world has not been privileged over cultural
heritage.[122] The rarified nature of these natural sites is illustrated by the fact
that they constitute only 10 percent of the total properties listed by Arab states,
in comparison to the 22 percent of all properties worldwide that are natural
or mixed sites.[123] Thus, through this particular kind of universalist lens, the
"peripheral vision" of Yemen's ailing state appears to have placed it among the
emergent environmental protectors in the Arab world.[124]

Between 1997 and 2013, the Government of Yemen implemented four
large-scale ICDPs in Soqotra: the Socotra Biodiversity Project (SBP; 1997–
2001), the Socotra Conservation and Development Programme (SCDP-1;
2001–2003), SCDP-2 (2004–2008), and the Socotra Governance and Biodiversity Project (SGBP; 2009–2013). As I write, another large-scale intervention
has been launched. Funded at different stages by multilateral organizations
such as the Global Environment Facility (GEF) and the United Nations Development Program (UNDP); bilateral donors such as the governments of Yemen,
Italy, the Netherlands, Poland, and Germany; and by small grants from other
donors and transnational NGOs, these and affiliated projects injected nearly
USD 25 million into Soqotra during this fifteen-year period. This may seem
paltry, but given Soqotra's small population and its socioeconomic marginalization in relation to the mainland, this funding has appeared—to Soqotrans,
at least—quite prodigious. Moreover, given the anemic state and limited resources of Soqotra's local government, it was in many cases the consecutive
ICDPs (and EPA) that served as its "proxy local governance structure."[125] However, while every project sought to integrate conservation with development,
each had a particular emphasis. Thus, despite the diverse range of activities
undertaken by all, each project epitomizes a distinctive phase in Soqotra's
environmentalization.

Just one year after the Government of Yemen ratified the Rio Conventions, it received GEF funding for the SBP, which aimed to "integrate biodiversity conservation, environmental management and development objectives in an holistic manner."[126] In practice, this phase focused on information collection and dissemination, with only marginal development. Consequently, the project management would later depict this as the research-and-conservation—as opposed to the conservation-and-development—phase of the projects. However, according to the anthropologist Serge Elie, who was present during this period, the SBP barely managed to integrate even its scientific research with its conservation planning and policies.[127] Notably, scientists I met during the subsequent phases complained about their inability to analyze the reams of data collected by the island's local environmental extension officers because there was no viable data base and the data amassed were not useful. What the SBP did accomplish was the preparation of two major planning documents, which laid the groundwork for future developments.

The first document, the Conservation Zoning Plan of Socotra Islands, demarcated the archipelago's terrestrial and marine territories into five tiers of resource management and conservation: resource use reserve, general use reserve, national park, area of special botanical interest, and nature sanctuary.[128] Each region was defined by its increasing or decreasing development potential. Initially, the SBP management celebrated the "participatory" nature and extensive "consultation process" through which the zoning plan came into being. An early indicator of the plan's (and their) success was its apparent sanctioning by the "local community": when the draft plan was "explained to" approximately five hundred Soqotran community leaders at meetings held throughout the island in 1999, these leaders called for *more* protected areas and "less infrastructural development."[129] Nevertheless, the plan soon became the object of considerable critique by international experts and Soqotrans. The plan's comprehensive nature was particularly problematic in the nature sanctuaries, which were now legally required to be "preserved . . . in as undisturbed state as possible."[130] Yet these were precisely the areas targeted for ecotourism development. Community-managed protected areas, as they had been presented to Soqotrans, were tapped to become community-bounded zones of profit for the Soqotrans and the SBP. But when revenues fizzled, Soqotrans were left with zoning-induced limitations. Moreover, because this far-reaching zoning plan was largely unfeasible—and thus unenforceable, despite having been ratified into law—it has not stopped foreign investors from snatching up the entire beachfront of this national protected area.

The second document, the Socotra Archipelago Master Plan, was a ten-year strategic vision (2000–2010) for the economic and social development of the islands in tandem with the Conservation Zoning Plan. Like the zoning plan, this development master plan was completed in 2000 and "effectively shelved" two years later; unlike the zoning plan, the master plan is not legally binding.[131] The plan identified sixty-nine large-scale interventions in addition to sixty-two "immediate impact projects" to address the islanders' urgent basic needs. With neither the government nor the SBP able to finance this vision (estimated to cost two hundred million euros), the British consultancy firm that devised the master plan singled out the projects that helped Soqotrans most directly.[132] However, because the minister of planning and development never approved their final proposal, the funds earmarked for these projects were reallocated to other projects in Yemen, and the master plan was set aside—leaving a "development vacuum" on Soqotra.[133] Nevertheless, the master plan articulated a development model based on Soqotra's two "engines of economic growth"—sustainable fisheries and nature-based tourism development—that would guide external investments in the archipelago for the following decade.[134] There is one other plan worth mentioning, despite its also having been shelved on arrival. Tourism expert Hector Ceballos-Lascuráin, who has been credited with coining the term "ecotourism,"[135] visited Soqotra twice in 1999, during which time he helped the SBP team identify sites with "high ecotourism potential," drafted the Ecotourism Development Plan for the Socotra Archipelago, and sketched attractive drawings of rustic ecolodges nestled into a "natural rock" edifice.[136] Although his designs were deemed "too ambitious," his vision of a natural terrain landscaped to accommodate ecotourists remained an integral principle of Soqotra's conservation-as-development regime.[137]

The SBP was supposed to operate for five years. When its funds ran out in mid-2001, the renamed Socotra Conservation and Development Programme SCPD aimed to direct more of its efforts toward community development while still accomplishing the SBP's initial goals.[138] The SCDP-1 established two locally based NGOs: the Socotra Conservation Fund, which supported small-scale conservation and development initiatives through solicited donations; and the

Socotra Ecotourism Society, which trained Soqotran guides and drivers, developed tourism plans, and dispensed tourist information. For about two years, the Ecotourism Society employed dozens of young men eager to enter this new industry but then lost its mandate (and SCDP funding) to continue as the only Soqotran-operated tour agency at that time. This phase also witnessed the establishment of two pilot protected areas—Homhil and Di-Hamri—together with the civil society organizations (CSOs) required to manage and operate them. In addition, the SCDP-1 continued to invest in research and initiatives related to conservation. Some of its most widely touted accomplishments during this period include environmental awareness campaigns, the diversion of road construction that would have destroyed a natural lagoon, and draft legislation to regulate biodiversity prospecting. Whereas the awareness campaigns aimed to teach Soqotrans to value their environment qua environment (and for the income it could generate), these legislative efforts were aimed at protecting this asset from external biopiracy, in accordance with the Convention on Biological Diversity's Cartagena Protocol. Thus in 2003, the SCDP required me to sign an agreement pledging that I would not remove any species, living or dead, from the island. At the time, it seemed that the SCDP-1 was the institutional gateway to all scientific and commercial research on Soqotra. Yet, when I began my fieldwork on Soqotra a year later, this document was no longer required. Like the zoning, master, and ecotourism plans formulated before it, it too had been suspended.

Despite the noted shortcomings of these initial project phases, it was the SCDP's legislative muscle with regard to the road development and other environmental threats that contributed to its de facto governance over the archipelago—at least in these early years. This was helped, of course, by the combined projects' copious funding relative to the monies available to Soqotra's EPA office and its two local councils. With a 180-person staff, the SCDP was also the island's second-largest employer, after the army. Nevertheless, Soqotrans were less than thrilled with these projects. This was as much due to the lack of apparent benefits to most Soqotrans relative to the money spent on research and staff salaries as it was to the projects' regulatory power. For instance, although a concurrent USD 1 million Health and Water Project (HWP) supported a mobile health clinic, improvements to the Hadibo hospital, and several water interventions, nearly half of its funding went to data collection and modeling, which did little to help poor communities directly.[139] Given the Soqotrans' overall dis-satisfaction with the Environment, the authors of the terminal evaluation of these three projects (SPB, SCDP-1, and HWP) advised that the "SCDP interventions should be 're-branded' as development . . . with less emphasis placed on conservation."[140]

The third project phase, consciously renamed the Sustainable Development and Biodiversity Conservation for the People of Socotra, aimed to embody this shift.[141] (Its renaming had little impact on the ground, where the project continued to be called "the SCDP"—or, in Arabic, *saun wa tanmiya* [conservation and development]—after the coordination unit that ran it.) For the most part, the SCDP-2 aimed to continue the work initiated earlier: to bring about sustainable fisheries and ecotourism; aid community mobilization and development; and enhance local governance capacities and resource mobilization. To this end, the SCDP-2 allotted USD 60,000 annually in 2003–2008 to each of the two district councils for local development expenditures.[142] Still, these sums were a far cry from the SCDP's approximately USD 1 million per annum budget, which rendered it the true fiscal power in Soqotra. Like the research and conservation phases before it, this development phase had modest successes and mixed results. It ended with the Soqotra Archipelago being inscribed as a World Heritage Site, but this achievement meant more to the project management and international community than it did to most Soqotrans. However, there were some tangible successes. Campgrounds to facilitate nature-based tourism and thus provide income for vulnerable communities were erected in five of the eleven protected areas.[143] And the numbers of tourists skyrocketed.

Nevertheless, by the mid-2000s, many Soqotrans were demonstrably frustrated by the limitations the zoning plan and the SCDP management were placing on their own activities. One could sense this in the act of villagers attempting to downgrade their area from a "sanctuary" to a "general use area" (by replacing official signs with their own hand-drawn placards) to prevent the paved road from circumventing their village; in the reluctance of an environment extension officer to censure his neighbors, friends, and relatives for cutting down trees for new roofing when the only alternative, imported timber, was unaffordable; in the insistence of a protected area "director" that there be a law *forcing* every tourist to visit the protected areas so that their inhabitants would actually benefit from tourism. Moreover, those who did not benefit directly from SCDP employment complained frequently that the Environment "ate up" all the money intended for the islanders. From the perspective of the target communities living in and around the protected areas, the SCDP continued to spend huge sums on expert and employee salaries, while their own economic development was dependent on the goodwill of seasonal tourists and individual donors. In their view, the project's initial goals of biodiversity conservation, community-based natural resource management, and development had been effectively reduced to a programmatic faith in the invisible hand of market ecotourism. Even SCDP employees complained of the project's entrenched nepotism, debilitating inertia, and political surrender. Aware that the third phase, along with its funding, would terminate in 2008, these employees had little to no confidence that an "emergency extension" would be granted again, despite the project document's assertion that "the present 5-year initiative represents the outset of a 25 year programme."[144] It was time for a new intervention.

In July 2008, UNESCO listed the Soqotra Archipelago as a World Heritage Site under natural criterion X (biological diversity and threatened species). In February 2008, as a precondition for its inscription, the Government of Yemen passed five cabinet decrees mandating its increased protection. The fifth decree endorsed the establishment of a national administrative structure for the management of Soqotra as a World Heritage Site. Efforts to establish a coordinating body were not new, just ineffective.[145] This special, independent Soqotra Authority was to uphold the government's administrative and financial decentralization policies promulgated through the Local Authority Law of 2000. It would also assume the role of coordinating foreign aid; indeed, its declaration was met with assurances of continued and new funding from the UNDP and the Agence française de développement. Most important, the Soqotra Authority was to operate hand in glove with the new Socotra Governance and Biodiversity Project, constituted to mainstream biodiversity management into the decentralizing governance process.[146] The SGBP aimed to strengthen and integrate both the conservation and governance of the archipelago by providing "local governance support"; improving the zoning plan; increasing the number of local NGOs and CSOs; expanding the "benefits of biodiversity conservation" through the sale of local natural products and more effective tourism; and supporting the fisheries sector.[147] Beyond this, the SGBP's primary task was to support the development and implementation of the islandwide Soqotra Authority.

Although the SGBP was approved in June 2008 and officially commenced work a year later, it had virtually no presence on the island until the spring of 2010. Even then, its activities began slowly, such that by January 2011, it had yet to run workshops to solicit community involvement and support. A former SBGP employee recalled her arrival at a compound without electricity, generators, Internet, or even toilets. Nevertheless, when the SBGP's new managers appeared, hundreds of Soqotrans showed up at their offices seeking jobs. But this was not to be another 180-person-strong project; this was an institution-building project staffed by four employees in Soqotra, three in Sanaa, and a few international consultants. "If our project disappeared tomorrow," she told me that January, "no one would notice, because it has had no effect on the local community." Three months later, it did in fact disappear; in April 2011, following the Arab uprisings, the UNDP suspended this along with its pending programs in Yemen, Bahrain, and Syria. By then, its expatriate staff and the employees of all international NGOs in Soqotra had vacated the island, leaving another development vacuum in their place.

FIGURE 7. Environmental awareness training for students, Wadi Ayhaft, 2005.

CULTIVATING (NEW) NATURE(S)

One pleasant afternoon, two vehicles crossed the Homhil plateau to park near the campground. Assuming they were transporting tourists, Yaqub left my yard to walk over and greet them. I had just begun teaching him and his cousin English-language phrases about the traditional uses of the dragon's blood tree—a lesson Yaqub requested after having been told by "the Environment" that, if he wanted to be a tour guide, he had to be able to explain his surroundings in English. The lesson interrupted, I got pulled back into other routine pastimes. As evening fell, nearly all the men in Qayher sauntered over to the local school where the SCDP's Environmental Awareness and Education Team, which had arrived earlier, was to conduct a training session for all the shaykhs and community-based extension officers of the eastern region. When one of the teachers headed toward the schoolyard after dinner, I joined him, stumbling my way across the rocky plain.

We arrived just as the Awareness Team had completed setting up a film screen and connecting a projector to their running car battery. A film was a novelty for rural Soqotrans without electricity—much less television—in their homes. At first, a small gathering (all men, except for me) watched the opening scenes of *The Lord of the Rings* while waiting for the others to return from the mosque. Then, the Awareness Team screened a locally produced video about the need for environmental conservation in Soqotra. Projecting well-known scenery and familiar talking heads, in addition to numerous references to the Qur'an, this film was well received. The men, who by now had wrapped themselves in blankets to ward off the evening's chill, were next shown a documentary on plant and animal life in the Egyptian desert and the Red Sea. Some men were nodding off, as was I, while a few seemed entranced by the underwater photography. As soon as this film ended, everyone returned to his village and home; it was late, and cold, and most would be waking in a few hours' time. On the way back across the moonlit plain, I asked my neighbor Bu Tariq if he had found the evening informative. "Yes, we benefited from it," he said. "Some of us have never seen these things before—have never watched television. But what we really want is to fix the steep road ['aqaba]. It's dangerous. All of us want a better road."

One way through which the majority of Soqotrans encountered the ICDPs most directly was in the form of their environmental awareness programs.

Much like the environmental regime was said to have arrived in Soqotra in the late 1990s, its employees arrived in rural areas, often unexpectedly, to cultivate among the islanders a certain way of understanding and seeing their environment. This was, by most official accounts, successful. For instance, in the years just prior to these films having been shown in Homhil, the SCDP's Environmental Awareness Campaign was reported to have "directly reached each inhabitant an estimated 3 times" through village gatherings as well as "approximately 4000 school children, and all teachers, of all 37 schools of Socotra" through environmental lectures.[148] Nevertheless, even eight years into the ICDPs, there remained a disconnect between how the projects framed the environment and how rural Soqotrans engaged their natural resources and surroundings. Similarly, there was significant tension between the ICDPs' tacit commitment to conservation-as-development and the Soqotrans' longing for development outright. We see this in the gap between what the Environment (the SCDP) brought to Homhil on this and similar visits and what my neighbors expected from a governing regime: food and roads. We see this also in the gap between the environmental imaginaries and expectations cultivated by the ICDPs during their visits and the actual outcomes of these interventions in a target protected area.

The following morning, the shaykhs and extension officers met at the campground for the second half of their event. Again, I was the only woman present, tolerated perhaps due to my foreignness and my official association with the SCDP. I was also the only one taking notes—until the facilitators suggested how much money Soqotrans could earn through ecotourism. This event is characteristic of the many meetings the SCDP held in Homhil in the early to mid-2000s, at the apex, it turns out, of Soqotra's environmental regime. Convened by the Soqotran director of the tourist police, this meeting was as much a lesson in civic responsibility as it was in environmental conservation. After a short introduction stating his desire for a police officer to be stationed in each of the protected areas—in regions that had never known a police presence—the director made the case for protection by reciting two verses from the Qur'an pertaining to natural resources, by stressing that states, like Yemen, are respected globally for their protection of the environment and by reviewing the national Environment Protection Law of 1995, which mandates the establishment of protected areas, among other things. "The law is written. Anyone can go and read it," he said, in Arabic, to the group consisting largely of semiliterate elders.

The next speaker was the SCDP's protected areas officer, a young man from northern Yemen. Trying to elicit environmental concerns from the attendees, the officer asked, "Why is the environment important, and why should we protect it?" No one replied. "Why do we have a Ministry of Water and the Environment?" he pressed on. Several men responded tentatively: to teach people; to live a better life; to protect plants and animals.

"We don't know what the ministry does!" one man called out.

After a few more such questions, the officer changed tactics. "Okay, I live in a city," he said. "So, I don't depend on the land. I buy everything from a store, so, go ahead, I say, cut down the trees!"

"You're crazy!" one elder said.

"See? That's because you depend on the land—see how this changes?" The officer launched into a rambling lecture on overgrazing, deforestation, pollution, disease, resource usage and protection, ecotourism, and Yemen's environmental legislation. I stopped taking notes. Finally, he slowed down and reverted to asking questions. "How many protected areas are there on the island?" he asked. No one knew how to respond. Neither did I. On the one hand, the entire archipelago is a national protected area; on the other hand, the zoning plan had identified twelve terrestrial nature sanctuaries and twenty-seven marine nature sanctuaries. But only four community-managed protected areas had been established at this time, and the SDCP managers were already admitting that the zoning plan was too ambitious. "People need to know," he prodded.

"You teach us; then we'll tell you," an elder replied.

The officer explained that, while the entire archipelago is a protected area, the zoning plan distinguishes between five different levels of resource use and conservation. The areas with the highest level of protection have been designated nature sanctuaries. "Like Skand [in the Haggeher Mountains]. This is the most important area," he said.

"More important than Homhil?" someone asked.

"Much more," he said, citing Skand's three hundred plant species.

"It's like a bank," Bu Qadir offered. As the SCDP-appointed local director of the Homhil Protected Area, Bu Qadir was particularly keen on securing more funding and frustrated by what the project failed to do. A month later, resolving to take Homhil's development into his own hands, he would draft a proposal to the embassy of Japan for funds to build a new school.

"The second most important place is Homhil," the officer continued, "with its 260 plants. Then Di-Hamri, Rosh, Galas, and Abd al-Kuri. As shaykhs, *you* are the representatives of the state, so it is your responsibility to know these things." He proceeded to describe the other zones before emphasizing, once again, that it was the shaykhs' responsibility to understand the law and to know what was permitted, and prohibited, in each zone. Following this, a member of the SCDP's Awareness Team turned the conversation to the topic of ecotourism.

"What is ecotourism?" the outreach facilitator—another young man from northern Yemen—queried.

"Seeing the environment," an elder said.

"What kinds of activities do ecotourists do?" the facilitator prompted.

Several men responded: "They look at birds! Take photographs! Contribute money! They research plants! Walk in the mountains! Visit important areas!"

"Try to distinguish between research and tourism," the facilitator implored, implying that the participants were confusing botanists for tourists. He asked the men to distinguish between general tourism and ecotourism but followed his question with a string of numbers: how many millions of dollars generated by tourism in 1993, in 1998, and in 2004; how many people employed in tourism, globally. At this point, the shaykhs sat up, attentive, and some began taking notes.

"In the Galápagos, for example, there are twenty-one islands," the facilitator continued. "The state cares about its environment a lot. They charge a hundred-dollar entrance fee for each tourist and earned five million dollars in one year, in 1998. So, what did Soqotra choose: general tourism or ecotourism?" Nearly everyone nodded. The comparison with the Galápagos was familiar. "If we had general tourism, everything would be ruined," he continued. "But *you* chose ecotourism. Soqotra has 307 endemic species—it's the island with the fourth-highest percentage of endemism in the world. And we have six endemic birds, and you know all of them."

"We don't know them. What are they?" replied an elder. Endemism, his answer suggested—the quality of not existing elsewhere—is an attribute always already evaluated from an external position. Undeterred, the facilitator listed the six birds by their scientific and English names.

After this speech, the director of the tourist police returned to the issue of security. Oddly, he brought up recent incidents of foreign kidnapping in Sanaa but assured the shaykhs that Soqotra enjoyed security—which, at this time, was one of the first things that Soqotrans would say about their island. As if they needed reassuring, however, he noted that the police recorded the "information" of every visitor. This prompted a longer conversation about the illicit felling of hundreds of dragon's blood trees by a Yemeni married to a Soqotran woman and the director urging the shaykhs to be the eyes and ears of the state in the countryside. The director underscored the growth of tourism on Soqotra by rattling off the numbers: in 2000, Soqotra received 193 foreign visitors; in 2001, 188; in 2002, 283; in 2003, 363; in 2004, 527.

"But how does this benefit us?" a shaykh asked.

"You can make things and sell them to the tourists," the director said.

"When I ask the tourists for support or if they want any service, they say that all their money has gone already to the [Ecotourism] Society," the shaykh said, belying the facilitator's implicit claim that ecotourism would yield jobs or profits for the populations who "chose" it.

Several elders began speaking among themselves in Soqotri, until the facilitator soon redirected the group's focus to conservation. Reminding them that some used to live in caves and that all had suffered poverty and hunger, the facilitator pointed out that they had been dependent on their land. Now, especially in the eastern region, he asserted, people were abandoning their traditional resource-management practices to the detriment of their livestock and their trees. "Don't say, about anything, this is not important," he told them. "Don't think that God put something on this earth without it being valuable. God created everything, and God made man His steward on earth. Angels said to God, 'If You put someone on Earth, he will damage it.' But God put man there. We need to conserve what we have, and we need a balance for the environment. Now we have five hundred tourists. This is nothing. What will happen when we have ten thousand?" He discussed the island's resources and how these needed to be developed sustainably. He also detailed the damages caused by unmitigated road construction, invasive species, infectious diseases, and rural-urban migration.

"We thank you for this," said Bu Qadir, indicating that the meeting was nearing a close. He then broached what was, in the view of the shaykhs, the crux of the issue: their desire for additional forms of income and more author-ity. "In the past," Bu Qadir explained, "no one lived in the west of the island, except for those who were underdeveloped [*mutakhallif*], because all the water and resources were here. But now, more of our goats die in the dry season be-cause we have more people and fewer animals, whereas in the west they have fewer people and more animals, so they can move around [with their herds] more easily. Also, the shaykhs here are not like the shaykhs on the mainland. We don't have the power to stop things. All of us stand ready to conserve things. We love our trees—they are our trees! They are our children! They are our wives! But if I love my wife and children, and yet, tell myself, 'Don't tire yourself, just sit and relax,' then we will die of hunger."

"We do conserve our resources," the region's extension officer added. "But when the Ecotourism Society comes to the village, they choose whomever they want to be their local guide. They don't go through our shaykh, who knows who is poor and needs the work." This opened the floor to several other de-mands: for more community-based extension officers; for more development, but with the input of the shaykhs; for English-language training for their chil-dren; for a better road; for beacons at sea.

Before the meeting adjourned, the facilitator announced that he had certifi-cates of achievement for each of the shaykhs present. This devolved into a tense discussion of who was recognized as a "shaykh" and by whom. As the facilitator distributed his preprinted certificates to the shaykhs who had been identified as such by the project's environmental extension officers, the two attendees left without certificates became increasingly annoyed. One—a shaykh by birth-right, but not in practice (it was his younger brother who had attended the boarding school for nomadic Bedouin)—left angrily after telling the facilitator that he should have presented a certificate to every attendee. Later that day, he approached me and said, "The people here are mad at me for saying that every-one should get a certificate. But we are all responsible for the environment—not just the shaykhs."

· · ·

It is evident that the Awareness Team tried to make this an enjoyable event for its conscripted audience. While the films were intended to be educational, the entertainment value of the rural screenings cannot be (and was not) overlooked. Although many of the men enjoyed this rare diversion, they also recognized it as a fleeting palliative for the protection *they* really needed: a safe road to the Homhil plateau.

Moreover, for a project that prided itself on the success of its extensive consultation process and its comprehensive awareness campaign, it was surprising just how little these shaykhs living in or near a protected area actually knew about Soqotra's zoning plan five years after its ratification. My intention is not to make these rural inhabitants appear environmentally and politically unaware; rather, as their responses demonstrate, they had yet to be taught or were still struggling to grasp what, according to the government and the SCDP, constituted this new environmental imaginary. "You *teach* us; then we'll tell you," one shaykh said—his statement a candid expression of what exactly consultation meant to the Soqotrans in practice. And it was not just a matter of educating the male herders (who ostensibly had protected their environment all along). The men were then meant to transmit this new awareness to their wives, children, and relatives *as well as* to the tourists who would come to view their surroundings. "Tourists have to feel that there is an interest here," the facilitator said. The interest to be cultivated—both in the environment and in the tourists—is a quality, much like endemism, that was framed extrinsically. Soqotrans were to cherish their plants not because they provided necessary food, fiber, firewood, or fodder but because these plants do not grow naturally anywhere else. Similarly, Soqotrans were taught that their island is valuable because it had been reimagined as the Galápagos of the Indian Ocean. Tourists would come to see this Galápagos even if they were no longer fascinated—as had been Purchas's readers—by "Soccotora" itself.

While the Awareness Team members tried to hold the shaykhs responsible for the actions of their community, the shaykhs expressed deep-seated frustration at their diminishing authority. Significantly, they attributed their powerlessness not only to climatic and political change but also and especially to the SCDP project: "When the Ecotourism Society comes to the village, they . . . don't go through our shaykh," and "we want development, but through the SCDP *and the shaykhs* and the citizens." The uncertainty over who counted as a shaykh had been exacerbated by the proliferation of shaykhs under the Saleh regime. But the SCDP had also played a role in concurrently elevating and undermining local authority structures. In concentrating much of their outreach on the shaykhs and the extension officers with the assumption that awareness trickles down—from the project to the shaykhs to their relatives, male and female—the SCDP had a strong hand in disseminating not only knowledge but also political legitimacy.

Of final note, here, is the effective pairing in this particular instance of the environment and Islam. While much of the meeting was devoted to generating Soqotrans' interest in the environment, in the zoning plan, and in ecotourism, and aligning this interest with external concerns—the concerned state, tourists, and the world at large—it was the scattered references to God and the Qur'an that seemed to resonate most among the attendees. Although some men expressed skepticism in the ICDPs' conservation-as-development logic, none voiced any doubts about man being God's steward on earth. Indeed, when the director of the tourist police convened the meeting with a recitation of relevant verses from the Qur'an followed by a review of the government's Environment Protection Law, he plainly underscored the correlation between the word of God and the law of the land, thus affirming the role not just of man but also, and especially, of the (Yemeni) state as God's custodian on earth. Yet, while members of the Awareness Team were certainly aware of the pedagogical value of the Qur'an—an Islam and environment campaign had been one of the key outputs of the government's National Biodiversity Strategic and Action Plan of 2004–2008—there was a noticeable reticence among the SCDP administration to employ or disseminate an Islamic environmentalism in any official capacity. Among other possible reasons for this, the two I noticed were a firm conviction by the majority of the Western project employees that, since this was a UN project, their mission and deportment should remain secular; and the belief by various Arab project employees that the explicit appeal to Islamic discourse would cast them (and the project) in an ostensibly backward light.

This became evident as I was searching the SCDP office one day for a copy of the Arabic-language video shown in Homhil that chilly evening. This video was the most explicit form of Islamic media produced on, or maybe even about, Soqotra to date. Yet, when I asked Hanif, a known Islah supporter and a leading member of the Awareness Team, for a copy, he regarded me suspiciously. "Well, you know," Hanif replied, "when we started talking about the environment, no one would have listened to us if we hadn't been able to point to what is said in the Qur'an—Bedouin, you know? So we had to use the Qur'an to make people listen and to be open to what we were saying. You think this isn't good?" Hanif's response surprised me. After trying to assure him that I considered religious references about stewardship important, I sought out the program manager and asked him, a secular Muslim from an Arab-majority country, for permission to borrow his copy. Instead, the manager gave me the English-language version, which had no references to Islam. When I pressed him for the Arabic version, he said, "This one is a little religious, so it's good for use on the island, but it's not so good for the outside." Some weeks later, I mentioned this incident to someone I knew to be a pious Muslim and a devout teacher. I voiced my surprise that the SCDP was not making greater use of Islamic teachings about the environment or even the Soqotrans' traditional resource-management practices. "There are three competing ways to conservation: Islam, the traditional ways, and SCDP or the West," he replied. "Now the island is going with the SCDP version, and they have left Islam and our traditional ways aside."

Not all outreach programs targeted adult men or their shaykhs. In fact, just as many if not more hours and resources went into educating pupils with the understanding that it would be this new job-seeking (postpastoral) generation that would have the greatest impact on the island's future development and conservation. (Women, too, were reached through gender-segregated programming, although the women's events I observed in Homhil were never quite as extensive as the men's.) In addition to conducting school visits to discuss environmental concerns, the Education and Awareness Team established the island's first Environmental Club in Hadibo and organized several class trips. After much coaxing, the SCDP team also agreed to take the seventh-graders of Homhil on a field trip. One Friday, we took the students to Hadibo's airport to see the weekly plane land and spent the afternoon in a scenic valley where we ate lunch, received a lesson about conservation, and played several games. The lesson, given by the same facilitator who had lectured their fathers a month before, started like this:

> It used to be that people didn't know about Soqotra, even just ten years ago. But now the whole world knows about us. Also, we did not know why our island is important. But after much study, we learned that it is important—because of what? Because of its biodiversity. Why else is Soqotra so important? Because

of its endemism. Three hundred out of nine hundred species are endemic to Soqotra. That means that they are not found anywhere else in the world. Soqotra has nine out of world's twenty-five frankincense species; in Homhil, alone, there are seven kinds of frankincense species. This is why it is a Protected Area.

Following the lesson, the team introduced a competitive quiz drawing on a set of questions they had compiled. Many of the questions pertained to Soqotra's natural environment; others were culled from the seventh-grade Ministry of Education textbooks for the purpose of increasing the trip's educational value. The resulting assemblage included the following questions: What is the purpose of man on earth (food and drink; worship; or rest and relaxation)? What is name of the place where people are born and live [the nation]? What are the names of the turtles in Soqotra? Name three Asian countries that are highly developed. What three things did the Prophet do in Medina? What did the people of Marib do that shows that Yemenis take care of the environment [they built a dam]? How do we get rid of malaria? What is the area of Yemen? How many endemic birds are there in Soqotra? What is the benefit of civilian planes? Which is older, the white or black vulture? When was Palestine divided?

In this manner, during the course of this afternoon, rural Soqotrans from pastoralist families—Yemen's young citizens—were being instilled with the sense of having "a religious and national duty to protect the environment."[149] At the same time, perhaps inadvertently, they were schooled in Soqotra's transition from being an "out-of-the-way-place" to becoming a "place-in-the-world."[150] Indeed, Soqotrans portrayed themselves as "awakening" to the (bio)diversity and endemism that surrounds them: "We did not know why our island is important." Were it not for this "new" environmental awareness, the ICDP narrative suggests, Soqotra would not have attained its special stature today. But what is just as illuminating here is the range of topics encompassed by the awareness quiz: Soqotra's geography, the environment, development, religion, politics, and the state. The making of "environmental subjects" is not limited in Yemen, if anywhere, to the development of solely environmental imaginaries. Rather, through an often uncoordinated and largely mismanaged regime of motley agents (state representatives, foreign experts, project employees, temporary visitors, local authorities, teachers and students, parents and children), environmental *citizens*—people who do not disassociate their environment from God, air travel, imperialism, historic greatness, the nation, and the state—are cultivated, too.

GROUNDHOG DAY

Each of the ICDPs and most of their donors recognized the needs of Soqotrans in their project designs. Nevertheless, the majority of this aid was tied to and invested in the island's environmental wealth and preservation rather than its human potential. The integration of conservation work, research activities, and development was, at best, fractured and tenuous. This is not to say that these projects were useless or that their planners, administrators, and employees were indifferent to Soqotrans' needs—quite the contrary. There may have been some people who took advantage of their positions and misused ("ate") the monies along the way. But the majority of the projects' managers and employees were nothing if not dedicated to the archipelago's people and their welfare. Some even lost their lives in their service.

Notably, it was not just the Soqotrans who ended up feeling that, a decade and some USD 20 million later, there was little to show for these investments—not even the conservation-focused ones. In the fall of 2012, the IUCN sent its first reactive monitoring mission to Soqotra to examine the status and integrity of this World Heritage property. This was, of course, a particularly uncertain time for Yemen and its transitional government, in power for less than a year after the forced resignation of President Saleh. Yet the mission noted that little had been achieved since the archipelago's inscription in 2008. Notwithstanding the cabinet decrees passed that same year, road construction had peaked between 2008 and 2010; "excessive grazing" had intensified; no concrete action had been undertaken with regard to invasive species or even the monitoring of present natural resources; and there was still no independent management structure in place.[151] And there were no indications locally that Soqotra had become a World Heritage Site. All this suggested that the so-called state party (Yemen) had treated Soqotra's inscription as the culmination of its conservation rather than its commencement. To be fair, this postinscription stagnation was due in part to the decrease in international support after 2008, the subsequent decline of the EPA's Soqotra office staff (by nearly 75 percent) and budget (to about USD 5,000 annually in 2012), and the post-2011 instability in Yemen.[152] Nevertheless, aside from the handful of Soqotrans employed by the EPA or working in tourism, few stakeholders even knew that the archipelago had been inscribed by UNESCO, or, if they did, they had little idea what this meant.

A year later, the same team conducted two follow-up missions to provide technical support to the EPA under the new "upstream processes" adopted by the IUCN.[153] During these missions, the team noted an even greater increase in environmental pressures and threats as a result of Yemen's political unraveling. Long stretches of asphalt, the construction of which had already led to erosion and habitat fragmentation, were now caving in and crumbling. More and more dead coral and charcoal were being harvested and collected for export to the Gulf States. Charcoal production had even increased during Soqotra's war-imposed isolation, as the islanders were forced to rely on wood fires instead of imported cooking gas. But this dramatic pace of development and change—so dramatic, in fact, that archipelago's "conservation outlook" fell from "uncertain" to "of significant concern"[154]—was rarely reflected in the design of these "integrated" interventions or in their conservation and development outcomes.

At one of the strategic planning workshops for the EPA held during the second mission (which I accompanied as an independent observer), its director talked about the various projects that had come to Soqotra for several years and then "died": "These projects come and go," he said, "and they keep repeating the same studies. The Italians come and study dragon's blood; the Czechs come and study dragon's blood; other groups come and study dragon's blood. We've had four groups come and study dragon's blood—they all do the same work, the same studies." Other participants concurred, recalling the string of foreign researchers who arrived, collected specimens or data, and left. Then, as the IUCN mission leader tried to encourage the EPA staff to strategize, he experienced his own sense of repetition. Stepping back from the whiteboard on which he had outlined the EPA's strengths and weaknesses, he said: "This is déjà vu all over again. If I took a picture of this whiteboard now, it would look just like a picture I might have taken twelve years ago." In February 2016, at an emergency planning meeting in Bahrain focused on the cyclones that had hit Soqotra in November 2015, biologists were surprised to hear that the SGBP project (which had recently returned to Soqotra) was training its (same) staff in terrestrial plant monitoring as they had already done ten or fifteen years ago. "It's like the movie *Groundhog Day*," one biologist said, referring to the 1993 film about a meteorologist who, stuck in a time loop, wakes up on the same day, again and again. Intervention after intervention, project after project, researcher after researcher: it was as if the arrival of the Environment was not just a moment in time but also an experience *of* time marked by endless repetition.

FIGURE 8. Mapping Homhil, Homhil campground, 2004.

CHAPTER 4

ARRESTED DEVELOPMENT

How lovely you are, Homhil Protected Area! And how lovely those who work for you
    and care for you!
How beautiful the trees and the earth, and the blossoms among the rich foliage!
How splendid the beautiful ground, cut off from the country of Yemen!
Westerners and tourists love you, and those who do not know you wonder at you and
    long to see you.
The Lord created you as the entrance through which lovely cool breezes blow.
If there were petrol at the foot of the escarpment and diesel at the settlement of
    Miharit'hitin
Why then Soqotra would live a life of ease and its owners would prosper and be devel-
    oped.
                                    —*Muhammad Di-Girigoti*[1]

The whole island is a protected area—even our women are protected.
                —*Our driver, eyeing my headscarf, after listening to tourists*
                              discuss the status of Homhil, 2005

We're used to talking about endemic corruption and endemic poverty—we talk about
this every day. So, I was surprised to come here and hear everyone talking about endemic as something good.
      —*US embassy employee during a weekend trip to Soqotra, Homhil, 2005*

It was near the end of the monsoon season and Qayher village seemed un-
usually deserted. I had just returned to Homhil after a month-long visit to
Soqotran families in Oman and the UAE, and it took me the better part of the
afternoon to discern what had changed: the men were missing.

"Where is Bu Qadir?" I asked his wife, Umm Qadir, during my social
rounds. I needed her husband's help to fix the clutch of my aging Toyota Land
Cruiser that had stalled just as I had reached the top of the escarpment.

"Possibly in jail," said Umm Jum'an, her sister-in-law.

"No, no," said Umm Qadir, clearly seeking to redirect the conversation.

"Really?" I asked Umm Jum'an. "Is he imprisoned?"

"No," she said, "I was only joking."

I was not sure what to make of this conversation or of the awkward silence that followed each set of greetings as I visited from house to house. At first, I attributed this disquiet to my prolonged absence. I, too, was feeling discomfort during my readjustment to Soqotran village life: unsettled. By the dank, diminutive kitchens in which women crouched over the cooking fires, the smoke piercing our eyes; by the cow nudging its drooling mouth through the palm-rib door of my one-room house as I lay sleeping; by the floor mats speckled with grains of rice and mouse droppings; by the gale-force winds that pushed me along, and sometimes to the ground, as I walked between the clustered homes; by the returning fears I had adopted while living in the village: the fear of driving off the escarpment, the fear of jinn in the middle of the night, the fear of my (imputed) infertility; unsettled, I felt by all of this. Later, as I gifted makeup sets to the women, their reserve dissipated, and by morning I felt more at ease. Relieved, I accompanied several women on their visit to a neighboring hamlet, where we called on each house and applied the skin-whitening turmeric powder (Soq.: *kerkam*) to our faces and arms. Still, several conversations quieted as I entered the room, and I could tell that something was amiss. I was told meanwhile that the men were in Hadibo due to a land dispute, but my hosts, clearly worried, were reticent to say more.

The next day, Tariq was making his rounds through the village. He had returned from Hadibo late in the evening by ascending the mountain footpath from the coastal plain below. It was clear that Tariq had brought news of Qayher's menfolk, even though these conversations remained hushed. After her other visitors left, Umm Jum'an explained to me what had become of the missing men. Her husband and two of his three brothers were imprisoned in Hadibo for having destroyed a small enclosure at the entrance of an empty cave. The men of Qayher asserted that the cave was theirs by use-right. Bu Faruq, a distant relative of theirs—from the same tribe but from Riged, a hamlet on the opposite end of the valley—argued that the cave belonged to his family, for they, too, used to live there seasonally. When Bu Faruq began to stake his claim by building up the enclosure, the Qayher brothers tore it down. In response, Bu

Faruq—who was known to chew qat with his friends in the police force—had his fellow tribesmen arrested. According to Umm Jum'an, the police were now looking for Tariq and the rest of the young men from Qayher. When I asked Umm Jum'an if she was worried about her husband, she laughed.

"Oh, no, jail is nothing [*basit*]" she said. "The jail is full of people from Qalansiyah and Momi, and they're not criminals—just people with problems. And in jail they receive food." This was true: as Soqotrans were already "imprisoned" by the sea (as my friend Ismail would often complain), local inmates were occasionally permitted to walk to the market to purchase meals and other necessities.

But when I prodded Umm Jum'an further, she admitted to being saddened that "the father of my children" was in jail. She noted that the women from a neighboring hamlet, who used to visit her daily after fetching water from the water tank (*birka*) near her home, now returned directly to their houses, rejecting her invitations on the pretext of being busy.

"The women of [hamlet] and [hamlet] want all our men in jail, even the boys," she said.

"Why?" I asked.

"So that we'll have only women here."

"What's the point of that?"

"To make our work difficult. To stop us from doing anything," Umm Jum'an said. In this fashion, the proverbial line on the ground had been drawn across and through the Homhil valley.

. . .

In the previous chapter, I discussed the arrival of what Soqotrans call "the Environment." My focus there on the politically and institutionally driven transformations of the archipelago reflects the scale and distance at which most decisions and policies regarding its management were made. Here, I turn from the development and implementation of the ICDPs in Soqotra more broadly to examine the effects of their particular interventions on the ground. Specifically, this chapter details the clash between the projects' imaginaries of community and its road to development, and the Hamiliho's experience of community and economic development agencies during the years that their surroundings were transformed into a protected area (*mahmiya*).

Although the reach of these ICDPs was islandwide, there is good reason to focus on the effects of their interventions in Homhil. Technically a nature sanctuary within a national park, the Homhil Protected Area was identified early on as one of the island's two "priority protected areas for development and conservation."[2] Accordingly, together with the Di-Hamri Marine Protected Area on Soqotra's northern coast, Homhil was one of the first protected areas *within* the archipelago—itself the first IUCN-recognized protected area in Yemen—to pilot a community-based natural resource management (CBNRM) program supported by nature-based (eco)tourism. Thus, it became one of the first managed and touristed protected areas in Yemen. The following "mapping" of the cave dispute in Homhil illustrates how a somewhat marginal population in one of the most disadvantaged regions in Yemen encountered this designation. This is worth reviewing not only because of the still *limited* terrestrial coverage of protected areas in Yemen (0.77 percent of its land area) but also because of the dramatic *proliferation* of protected areas globally over the past few decades (now covering 14.9 percent of the planet's land surface and 7.26 percent of the global ocean).[3]

"A NEW COSMOLOGY"

Given the material benefits and jobs provided by the ICDPs, it is not surprising that Soqotrans initially welcomed the idea of protected areas—requesting, in fact, that there be more of them. The SPB management interpreted their enthusiasm for conservation as a reflection of "the high level of environmental awareness of the local community," underscoring the new script that Soqotrans were natural environmental stewards after all.[4] Significantly, this script did not just redeem the rural Soqotrans, blamed earlier for environmental degradation. Through conscripting the Soqotrans as willing partners and supporters of the environmental project, it also legitimized and effectively depoliticized the "zoning technologies" deployed by the state to demarcate special enclaves within the national territory to profit from their specific characteristics and setting.[5] What this script does not reveal is the extent to which Soqotrans expected, and were led to believe by various ICDP employees, that they would benefit *materially* (and financially) from the establishment of state-legislated protected areas. This expectation was not just incidental but integral to the success of this project.

As critics point out, "Protected areas are spaces—virtual or real—that offer opportunities to the extension of capitalist and state interests as well as opportunities for resistance to this extension."[6] This integration of conservation and capitalism—what many call new conservation or neoliberal conservation[7]—has its roots in the neoliberal economic policies of the late 1980s and the post–Cold War optimism of the early 1990s. It was during this period of "global faith . . . in rapid and sustained economic growth" that the utilitarian notion of integrating conservation and development—specifically, through the community-based management of natural resources and protected areas—was embraced.[8] It has not always been this way.

Despite local and indigenous forms of resource management and protection having been practiced for millennia, scholars trace the history of protected areas to the royal forests, hunting preserves, and game reserves set aside for privileged use and enjoyment.[9] International conservation treaties, however, which emerged under the realm of colonial wildlife legislation, first came into being in 1900.[10] And it was only after World War II, when a number of international development institutions were established, that the world's first global environmental organization—the International Union for the Protection of Nature (IUPN; later, IUCN)—was founded.[11] Modeling its practices after these earlier genealogies of exclusionary preservationism, and mindful also of the devastation following World War II, the IUPN aimed to institute an international code for the protection of nature and to establish national parks and wildlife reserves worldwide. Notably, the IUPN advocated the protection of nature because of the prevailing belief in its *intrinsic value* rather than as a means to improve human well-being.[12] To this end, the first World Parks Congress convened in Seattle in 1962 with the aim of establishing more national parks based on the Yellowstone model: uninhabited.

Then, in 1970, UNESCO launched its Man and the Biosphere Programme, encouraging the establishment of a global network of "biosphere reserves" for conservation and research. This program exemplified a broader ideological shift from the protection of nature for its own sake to the merging of resource conservation with resource consumption and a stated concern for human "communities."[13] In 1972—the year of the second World Parks Congress, which continued to construe national parks as unmodified enclaves—the UN Conference on the Human Environment placed environmental issues related to humans on the international agenda.[14] The Declaration of the Human Environment, which explicitly linked environmental problems to underdevelopment, was not the only declaration to emerge from Stockholm that year. Independent proposals by the US White House and the IUCN, each calling for the conservation of the world's heritage, resulted in the UNESCO Convention Concerning the Protection of World Cultural and Natural Heritage. While the convention underscored the notion that both cultural and natural heritage must be preserved because of their intrinsic, "outstanding universal value," it also gave rise to heritage as a moralizing pretext for international intervention and new arenas of commodification.[15] Subsequently, the number of areas designated for conservation proliferated, prompting the IUCN to select "protected area" as an umbrella term for its (in 1978, ten; now six) different categories of management ranked from most restricted usage to multiple-use zones.[16] Protected areas were no longer just conservation units protected *from* human residence, use, or encroachment but now included areas explicitly designated *for* human settlement and even "human development" (consumption).

Although the 1980s is considered a "lost decade" for the theory and practice of development,[17] it was in fact a pivotal (and lucrative) decade for conservation, which gained increasing funding from international development agencies.[18] In 1980, the IUCN released its first World Conservation Strategy, which emphasized the need to integrate conservation and development through sustainability.[19] In 1982, the World Parks Congress adopted this new vision, focusing on the role of protected areas in balancing conservation and development needs.[20] In 1987, the UN-appointed World Commission on Environment and Development published *Our Common Future* (the Brundtland Report), which not only legitimized the conservation-development compromise reached earlier but also conceded that *sustainable* development actually means sustainable *development*: the "ensur[ance] that [humanity] meets the needs of the present without compromising the ability of future generations to meet their own needs."[21] In 1991, the IUCN published an updated version of its World Conservation Strategy ("Caring for the Earth"), which "revealed how dramatically the conservation tide had turned away from preservation and how strongly some conservationists now embraced the utilitarian approach advocated by the Brundtland Report."[22] Not only did the World Bank fund this report, but also it established its own pilot program that year—the Global Environment Facility—to promote sustainable development on a global scale. Thus, by the end of the 1980s, environmental conservation had become yoked to economic development,[23] as well as heritage.

While "Caring for the Earth" cemented the liaison between conservation and development put forward by the first World Conservation Strategy, it departed from the original's focus on state-based regulation and adopted a more decentralized approach relying on the conservationist activities of "communities and local groups." However, this turn to community-based conservation was "as much the result of a shortage of government money as the result of ideology."[24] Government programs that had failed or were financially stretched were to be replaced by resource privatization and community empowerment, an empowerment contrived from the neoliberal surrender of conservation and development to market demands. At both the 1992 United Nations Conference on Environment and Development (the Rio Summit) and the 1992 Fourth World Parks Congress, the relationship between local communities and their environment—especially in protected areas—was underscored. Indeed, the Convention on Biological Diversity, one of the five documents resulting from the Rio Summit, *requires* its signatories to establish a network of protected areas and to promote sustainable development in their surrounding regions for the conservation of biological diversity.[25] Consequently, between 1970 and 1997, the land designated as protected worldwide expanded more than tenfold, approximately two-thirds of which was located in so-called developing countries.[26] As a case in point, in 1992, when the Government of Yemen signed the CBD, Yemen could not boast one IUCN-recognized protected area. (In the MENA region, however, there were seventy-nine IUCN-recognized protected areas, making up 3.6 percent of the region's area.)[27] Today, there are six protected areas in Yemen, one which is further recognized as a World Heritage Site, a MAB Biosphere Reserve, and a Ramsar (wetland) Site : the Soqotra Archipelago.

This global devolution of conservation management to the local community was embraced by global conservation organizations and development agencies throughout the 1990s and into the 2000s. The epitome of this new conservation was the ICDP, often implemented in protected areas.[28] ICDPs, like other community-based natural resource–management programs, hinge on the assumptions that local communities are the bearers of "traditional ecological knowledge"; that they have greater incentive to use their resources in a sustainable fashion; and that they are always already natural conservationists.[29] Nevertheless, these communities' traditional practices were often deemed deficient and in need of external guidance. As the anthropologist Paige West writes, "These projects were at their base about *changing the actions and practices of local people* in order to meet the end goal of conservation. They were about the integration of local peoples into commodity-based systems of production as a strategy for the conservation of biological diversity."[30]

Critiques of this new conservation are wide ranging but derive from the following concerns. Many conservationists and scholars lament the utilization of "neoliberal economic models" that "move both the environment and social relationships into the realm of commodities."[31] They question whether this conservation-and (*as*)-development model is not just a more palatable form of economic globalization that privileges an integrated market while transforming both the spatiality and scale of environmental management.[32] Furthermore, they deplore the ways in which rural or indigenous peoples tend either to be blamed for environmental degradation or celebrated as innate conservationists, living in harmony with their environment. Despite this myth of the "ecologically noble savage" having been debunked, it continues to influence conservation policy while essentializing indigenous communities and their practices as static, temporally distant, and primordial.[33] Finally, they dispute whether community-based participation is actually participatory when, in some cases, participation can mean simply being the recipient of information about the project. For example, the anthropologist Dawn Chatty calls attention to the inadequate levels of community participation in Middle East conservation projects, especially among pastoralists, whose imputed overgrazing or overstocking is still considered a major obstacle to rangeland conservation—despite growing evidence to the contrary.[34]

In parallel, scholars have interrogated the very concept of *community* that has been driving both development and conservation projects since the end of the 1980s. This is not to say that community does not exist or should not be mobilized but rather that communities are rarely the "small spatial unit[s]" with "homogenous social structure" and "common interests and shared norms" that they are often imagined to be.[35] Indeed, Benedict Anderson's "imagined communities" exist not only in the imaginings of those who belong to the community in question;[36] they are also *imagined into existence* by external actors intent on developing said community's well-being. Crucially, it is the interactions and struggles between various stakeholders and the ongoing contest over group membership, political allegiance, and environmental entitlement that create "a practiced community"[37]—one that is often broader and simultaneously more limited than its purported spatial boundaries, group affinity, and shared norms suggest.

Protected areas, the loci of community-based conservation programs and their offshoot, the ICDP, are not immune from these critiques, despite their having becoming "a new cosmology of the natural—a way of seeing and being in the world that is now seen as just, moral, and right."[38] For, notwithstanding their vital role in conserving biodiversity, ecosystems, and even cultural resources, protected areas are not merely discursive descriptors of an area's management strategies. Nor do they simply "prescribe and proscribe" the conservation and development activities that occur within.[39] Even those that do not displace people physically or restrict their use of the area's resources unleash an array of "social, material, and symbolic effects" on their proximate and often vulnerable communities.[40] Whereas protected areas typically benefit national and international communities in an abstract sense, their costs tend to be shouldered by the local and indigenous communities who live in or around them. Even within the sites themselves, the costs and benefits are borne unequally; protected areas distribute "different types of fortune and misfortune to their neighbors and stakeholders at different spatial scales."[41] Far from simply preserving natural and human landscapes and lifestyles, the creation of protected areas accelerates processes of social change, exacerbates existing tensions, and imposes on people a new way of seeing themselves and their surroundings. Consequently, they are often "mine fields" of social and political conflict.[42] At the same time, they serve as "capital-attracting enclaves" to capture global financial "flows."[43] Thus, protected areas rarely protect the environment as much as shape it for global consumption.

BEDOUIN ABJECTION

While I lived in Homhil, I struggled to understand how a dispute over a small, abandoned goat enclosure could cause such strife. Far greater than an argument between a few individuals, this conflict pitted *all* of Homhil's inhabitants against one another, dividing not only the region along settlement lines but also each individual settlement into supporters or opponents of the Qayher men and their wives. Even families were divided, husband and wives set in opposition by their conflicting allegiances to their respective kin. And although these monsoon arrests may have been the most dramatic event in Homhil's recent history, they marked neither the beginning nor the end of the protected area's troubles. During the remainder of my fieldwork, men from Qayher were jailed repeatedly; men from Homhil and its surroundings gathered frequently at the courthouse in Hadibo to bear witness for or against each party; and both Bu Qadir and Bu Faruq spent scarce resources flying repeatedly to the mainland to contest their cave ownership in the higher courts. Meanwhile, external witnesses to this growing dispute, whether European, mainland Yemeni, or even Soqotran, were quick to attribute its acrimoniousness to the "fact" that the inhabitants of Homhil were simply "difficult," "conservative," and "extreme"—traits I had been warned of even before the start of my fieldwork there.

The Hamiliho, who were well aware of their reputation, deflected such criticisms by attributing their imputed obstinacy or ignorance to their Bedouin nature. The Soqotran pastoralists I came to know—not only in Homhil but also in other regions—often spoke of being Bedouin as a form of categorical abjection. "We are ignorant; we are Bedouin," was a common refrain. Or even, "We are goats; we are beasts." Indeed, among Soqotrans who identified as Bedouin, the terms "beasts," "goats," and "Bedouin" were often used interchangeably, as if each were a convenient shorthand to explain (or explain away) an entire social and political state of deficiency: Bedouin = illiterate = backward = powerless = speechless = goats = beasts. For example, my elderly neighbor Denowiha stopped by my house frequently to converse with me in Arabic, her second language. Nevertheless, she peppered her speech with comments like, "I can't speak like you. I don't know how to speak; we are Bedouin, humble," or "We don't know anything; we are [autochthonous] Soqotrans [*saqatira*]—Bedouin." Similarly, Denowiha's middle-aged son Bu Yunis, a herdsman who lived with his parents, told me over dinner (in the presence of his family), "I'm illiterate. I only know dates; that's my work. If I were literate, I'd work for the government! But I don't even know how to fish—I get seasick. Only dates." When I protested, he added, "We don't know anything; we are beasts. We are purely Bedouin [*badu sarih*]." And it was not only the elderly or those without formal education who referred to themselves in such abject terms. Even the young and the schooled were learning to portray themselves as dependent, wanting, and weak. "We are Bedouin. We don't know English—we are just Bedouin," blurted eight-year-old Bilqis as she skipped into my house one morning during the height of the dispute. "Well, I don't speak Soqotri," I said lamely, hoping to boost her self-confidence. "Yes, you do," Bilqis said, "You speak English and Arabic and Soqotri—all of them. We are just Bedouin."

Such comments pained me for the very reason that they seemed prompted by my presence and my reliance on Arabic, the language of the state and of northern hegemony—although, eventually, I learned that Soqotrans uttered similar statements among themselves. But they were also perplexing given the more familiar ethnographic descriptions of Bedouin honor, autonomy, and self-respect. The Bedouin one encounters in the anthropological literature are nearly always proud of their Bedouin ancestry and their collective identity, their genealogical community and their moral system. If these Bedouin reveal any vulnerability or weakness, they are said to do so modestly—for example, in the case of the Awlad 'Ali of the Egyptian Western desert, through a highly formulaic language of poetry that does not violate their personal and collective honor.[44] Strikingly, Soqotra's self-identified Bedouin did not veil their assumed deficiencies in poetic or allegorical forms. Rather, they abjected themselves in mundane conversation and, moreover, during the very years preceding and following UNESCO's recognition of their island for its "outstanding universal value"—mostly its "nature" but also (if incidentally) Soqotran stewardship practices. This was also a time when "Bedouinness" in various parts of the Arab world was (and continues to be) celebrated and commemorated as a form of cultural identity and national heritage.[45] Yet, as proud as they were of their tribal genealogy, moral community, and pastoral livelihood, Soqotran goatherds were also well aware that their particular Bedouinness marked them as doubly deficient: not Bedouin enough, in comparison to the Bedouin of the mainland (few herd camels; none, except for army recruits, live in tents; and none carry weapons), and too Bedouin (too "backward") for their own good.

What I came to realize is that my interlocutors inhabited this state of binary want—being both unduly and insufficiently Bedouin—by articulating and performing their abjection in their everyday speech. These abject articulations do several things. On the one hand, when someone like Bu Yunis referred to himself as *badu sarih*—an Arabic phrase introduced by "outsiders" to disparage Soqotrans as "*utterly* Bedouin"—his self-abjection functioned as a "dialogical invitation to at least symbolically subvert the status hierarchy that was inherent in our unequal social positions."[46] Such expressions of ignorance were invitations to substantiate *or* discredit their imputed backwardness and primitivism so that I would know that they know that I, like other foreigners, (presumably) think of them in these terms. By earnestly calling attention to their subaltern standing, Soqotran pastoralists were demonstrating themselves to be as cosmopolitan and discerning as their foreign boosters and detractors. In other instances, for example, in jokes about ignorant Bedouin or in poems about Bedouin goats, this self-abjection was deployed more ironically to "contest categories that the privileged impose"[47]—or a way of "beating the enemy to the punch line."[48] On the other hand, their appropriation of the term *badu sarih* conveyed a subtle but incisive shift from abjection to virtue, by being ignorant of and excluded from technology, politics, and all else that is ultimately corrupting. In this sense, Bu Yunis's comment—"We are pure[ly] Bedouin"—must be interpreted not just as self-denigration but also as a calculated form of self-preservation: a defense of and desire for a life that is "pure."

Contrary to my initial misgivings, these abject articulations were not a new phenomenon, nor were the stereotypes they countered. Several Soqotrans recalled that they used to disparage themselves—as goats, as stupid, as poor—even during the sultanate era. And evidence of their debasement permeates the colonial-era literature. For instance, Douglas Botting's Adeni cook shared his employer's prejudiced views, denigrating "the Bedouin" in the same manner that many Soqotran pastoralists self-denigrate today: "These people is all *alimans*," he said, "all goats. They don't know nothing."[49] Fifty years later, Soqotran pastoralists continued to suffer the precarity and confines of life in the *badiya*. But they now also found themselves increasingly emplaced within, and defined by, a "global hierarchy of value": a set of universalizing standards and conceits through which "certain places, ideas, and cultural groups appear marginal to the grand design."[50] For the very process of transforming Soqotra into a national protected area figured the pastoralists and their modernizing desires as impediments to environmental conservation.[51] This is not to say that the pastoralists were excluded from this process. To the contrary, the most significant

policy documents produced by the ICDPs depicted Soqotrans as innate, de-
liberate conservationists whose traditional custodianship of the environment
has lasted for thousands of years. Nonetheless, Soqotrans' customary rangeland management practices, albeit well documented, were never truly championed. Instead, Soqotrans living in the state-designated protected areas were
besieged with "environmental awareness campaigns" and other patronizing
"consciousness-raising projects."[52] To the extent that pastoralists were included
in the transformation of the island, they were being schooled in the "backwardness" and the "ecological alterity" of their ways.[53]

It is likely therefore that Soqotran pastoralists were becoming not only
more sensitive to their comparative abjection but also more strategic in deploy-
ing it. Calling oneself a *badu sarih*—after the concurrent arrival of international development, global environmentalism, global tourism, and the world
heritage industry—could be an ironic demonstration of one's worldliness, an
ironic contestation of one's degraded place in the world, or an expression of
virtue. It was also a ploy: We'll be the abject individuals you presume us to be
so that you provide us with aid. Or a defense: We should not be punished for
being ignorant. Moreover, the explicit positioning of oneself as Bedouin articu-
lates a Soqotran rescaling of the global hierarchy of value(s) while speaking to
a more universal grammar that alternately juxtaposes and contrasts civilization
with civility. This "Bedouin abjection" works to expose and interrogate not only
the Soqotran pastoralists' subordinate position within this global hierarchy but
also their self-described departure from their "true" (pure) Bedouin selves.[54]

During the cave fight and the various conflicts that led up to it, the inhabitants of Homhil disparaged themselves regularly as "ignorant Bedouin" or as
"goats" for the various purposes just described. However, at one point, Umm
Jum'an expressed forthrightly what lay *behind* this particular intertribal tension. In her view, the people of Riged were simply envious of those in Qayher
for benefiting more from the resources introduced by the ICDP. "They're
upset," she said, "because we have the Environment, the campground, and
Nada [Nathalie]." (At the time, I had been stringing electric wiring between
my house and those of my neighbors so that they, too, could each have one
working light bulb powered by "my" SCDP-purchased solar panels.) But, as
she also pointed out, the people of Riged profited from their connections to
PARITER (a pseudonym), a European-based development NGO. If what Umm

FIGURE 9. Inside a "Saqatri" house, Homhil, 2005.

Jum'an suggested was accurate, this dramatic contest within Homhil was rooted as much (if not more) in the foreign presence of conservation and development programs—including the anthropologist observing them—as it was in any kind of putative character flaw and the kin-based antagonisms it engendered.

MAPPING HOMHIL

Shortly after I had settled in Homhil, its adult inhabitants were invited to take part in an NGO-run course on tourism, which included a participatory mapping exercise. The course planners claim to have conscientiously "selected the main socio-economic groups" and "consider[ed] gender and age variables" to enable individuals "to express their own and their group's opinion."[55] To this end, the women of Homhil were gathered in a one-room house in Qayher, where they were grouped into craftswomen, herders, and agriculturalists. Because, in actuality, women's labor is not this differentiated—generally, women and men take care of their herds, cultivate gardens, and produce everyday material goods (handicrafts)—the Hadibo-based Soqotran facilitator told the randomly organized groups to imagine themselves in these narrow terms: "*You* will be the herders; *you* will be the agriculturalists; and *you* will be the craftswomen," she said. After she tried eliciting their expectations of tourism—which did not take long, given that the women were befuddled about why foreigners would visit their island to gape at their trees—the facilitator asked each of the "socio-economic groups" to draw a map of Homhil labeling the campground, scenic areas, agricultural plots, a potential site for a factory for the production of women's handicrafts, and other important features. One woman pointed out that they would continue to make crafts at home, which their male relatives would sell for them at the campground. None seemed to think it necessary, or even desirable, to have a designated center in which to weave the woolen rugs or plait the palm-frond mats they were accustomed to making for household use. Bemused by this idle exercise, the women departed soon after sketching their maps. I then walked to the newly established ecotourism campground, where the men had convened. They, too, had been asked to map the protected area, and they, too, had begun by drawing the mountains that edged the valley before slowly charting the structures—mosque, school, palm groves, and villages—that lay in between. As I arrived, the male facilitator, a Hadibo resident from mainland Yemen, was urging them to distinguish between settlements, grazing areas, and areas suitable for tourism. Bu Qadir insisted that the entire area was used for grazing. (Their ungulates roam free.) Like occupational groupings, land-use distinctions could not be charted. Their lands, livelihoods, and lives bore little resemblance to the map and outcomes envisioned by the NGO.

Environmental anthropologists have demonstrated that state and private efforts to delineate protected areas impose socially constructed boundaries, categories, and ideas onto both communities and landscapes. Territorial boundaries are often drawn according to externally imagined landscapes of conservation and consumption, while their target communities are expected to reflect and conform to this ecological and economic rationale. In this vein, the external actors working to actualize Soqotra's zoning plan anticipated the perimeter of the Homhil Protected Area and the boundary of the Homhil community to coincide. At the same time, these various administrators, experts, and even tourists imagined that the protected-area community should and would operate as a homogeneous, harmonious, and cooperative collective.[56] Where these actors did envision internal differentiation, they imagined it to fall sharply along tribal, gendered, and occupational lines. Scholars critical of such ideal but enduring notions of rural communities "take this process to be one of both generification, making people fit into already existing categories, and decomplexification, simplifying people's social practices and beliefs so that they fit within certain policy structures."[57] Not only do these simplifications veil other, more salient divisions within a rural community—in Homhil, distinctions between those who are salaried and those who are not; fissures between the older traditional leaders and the younger formally educated council members; inequities in access to external resources (from NGOs, migrant relatives, etc.); and disparities in access even to internal resources, such as water, come to mind—but also these simplifications, *these mappings*, exacerbate and produce the very divisions they are intended to portray.

In Soqotra, rural communities were targeted and thus simultaneously constituted through the demarcation of "community-managed" protected areas at the same time that new alliances and divisions were being forged as a result of the successive governments' changing policies regarding landownership and local authority structures. Whereas the ability to establish landownership or use rights across these shifting property regimes was challenging enough, it was further complicated by the proliferation of new party-appointed shaykhs whose political support and government stipend undermined the authority of the adjudicating tribal elders. On top of this, the rebirth and resignification of "the tribe" based on a northern Yemeni model underscored social divisions and power differentials established, in part, through landownership. Thus, at the same time that the state extended its bureaucratic control over regions like Homhil, Soqotrans from across the island frequented the state courts of Hadibo, al-Mukalla, Aden, and Sanaa to press their claims. And at the same time that the Homhil community was asked to map their (family-owned) dwellings and date groves, their (clan-owned) enclosures, and their (communally owned) rangeland on paper, its "tribes" were becoming increasingly divided over the new property lines being drawn on the ground. In this sense, it was not as much the external demarcation of the protected area that would prove problematic to the Homhil community as it was the mapping that occurred within.

The Campground

One of the first conflicts to emerge in Homhil following its protected-area designation concerned the location of its campground. Operating under the assumptions that the boundaries of the protected area and the lands owned by its inhabitants were coterminous, that the bulk of this territory was common property, and that ecotourism would financially or materially benefit the entire population, the SCDP presumed that the primary criteria for locating the community-managed campground were aesthetic and environmental. But the inhabitants in and around Homhil were less than eager to entrust their clan's lands to this new kind of common property regime. Moreover, the deceptively simple question of where to locate the campground dredged up dormant tensions regarding land use and ownership on the Homhil plateau. The resulting discord, albeit relatively minor, is emblematic of the land disputes that have plagued much of the island since the mid-1990s as changing property regimes, developing infrastructures, and environmental regulations began to collide. In recent years, these disputes have only proliferated due to the soaring costs of land: a growing population, internal migration, returning emigrants, and new incomers and investors have all placed a premium on the island's alienable territory.

Soqotra's land disputes arose initially out of the succession of government-imposed changes to landownership and the title uncertainties they caused. During the sultanate, land was owned by individual lineages/clans or by neighborhood groups who often gave one another reciprocal rights to transhumance and access to their resources (land and water) in times of scarcity. A portion of these lands was enclosed as a grazing reserve (*zeribah*), but most was treated as a controlled-access communal grazing area (*mibdihil*) open to the livestock of all who lived in the area. Whereas pasturage was thus owned and managed collectively, built structures or modified plots (such as caves) were owned and bequeathed by the families who had constructed them. Those who lived along the coasts who did not have genealogical connections to the "tribesmen" of the interior—whether they were African slaves or fishermen, Arab merchants, or even the ruling elites—did not own the land on which they lived but did own their houses and other structures. The ruling sultan was the final arbitrator in all property disputes, but even he had to negotiate usage rights to land and pasture in the interior. (The sultans owned houses outside Hadibo, but

not land—landownership, based on tribal status, being the true indicator of
Soqotran identity.) This tradition of tribal (lineage-based) landownership was
overturned in the 1970s when the socialist government confiscated land for
state use, redistributed land to the formerly dispossessed, and discouraged private ownership. With the defeat of the socialist regime following Yemen's 1994
civil war and reunification, Soqotra's clans (now resignified as tribes) tried
to reclaim their ancestral lands. But the new government's policies regarding
landownership and the legal procedures for establishing it remained unclear.
Although many continued to call on their community leaders to substantiate
their territorial claims (often by demonstrating ancestral occupation of a site),
and others dug up whatever sultanate-era documents they could find, most
Soqotrans ended up taking their disputes to Hadibo's state court. Those dis-
satisfied with these local measures traveled to the mainland to press their cases
there—if they had the means. In this way, the wealthier or well-connected
Soqotrans were able to bypass both the local state courts and the clan/tribal
elders. "What is clear," noted Miranda Morris, author of the comprehensive
Manual of Traditional Land Use Practices in the Soqotra Archipelago, in 2002,
"is that the prevailing confusion had a very deleterious effect on the fabric of
Soqotri society, with a proliferation of claims and counter claims concerning
land ownership."[58]

It was precisely during this contentious period that the SCDP tried to impose its collective management project onto these uncertain grounds. With
the aim of instituting community-based natural resource–management programs in the two pilot areas, the SCDP signed a management plan and land-
use agreement with the civil society organizations (CSOs) administering each
site. At this time, in the early 2000s, the newly established Association for the
Conservation and Development of Homhil (hereafter, Association) comprised
all the adult male residents of the Homhil Protected Area (approximately fifty)
and was administered by a five-man elected council. Chosen on the basis of
their education, their ability to participate in training courses, and equal tribal
representation, these men were not the clan elders who had previously been
in charge of all decisions regarding local resource use. The council was thus
constrained in implementing any decision but was responsible for collecting
and maintaining the Association's membership dues and other income; inter-
facing with the SCDP, the government, and NGOs; and encouraging conserva-

tion efforts within Homhil. Most important, as a legally recognized CSO, the Association was eligible to receive external funding. In early 2004, the Japanese embassy donated funds to build a campground in both pilot areas—this, despite the zoning plan decree that Soqotra's nature sanctuaries remain preserved "in as undisturbed state as possible" and free of tourism infrastructure. Eager to jump-start the development of ecotourism as an income-generating activity for the associations, SCDP staff had already visited these areas to select desirable locations for their campgrounds.

With regard to Homhil, this was not as straightforward as the SCDP might have hoped. Initially, several SCDP employees, including a random group of invited tourists, chose a bucolic spot just below Di-Zahrin, one of the area's three natural springs. Bu Qadir, in his capacity as the Association's president, approved their choice, to the ire of the Kowtir, a "tribe" living in Momi, above the Homhil plateau. Viewed through an ecological rationale, the land surrounding the spring was an integral part of the Homhil ecosystem. According to the Kowtir, this was their ancestral land to which they enjoyed exclusive use rights. The SCDP managers then selected a site farther from the spring, but an individual (who also happened to be Kowtir) claimed this land as his private property. A third attempt at site selection by the SCDP was rejected by everyone in and around Homhil, including the Kowtir, for being too close to their Friday mosque. After two years of failed negotiations, the SCDP demanded that the Association (essentially, the men of Homhil) propose a site. The Association's governing council suggested a flat, exposed piece of rangeland in the very center of the plateau. This was controlled-access common property used for grazing by the families of all four tribes residing in Homhil—the Shermat, Tahki, Sowkir, and Shedhihi—and by their Kowtir neighbors in times of need. This location had the added benefit of being distant from any settlement girdling the plateau; their inhabitants were wary of scantily clothed foreigners sauntering through their villages. But the SCDP considered this location unsuitable for tourists. The Association's governing council then proposed a verdant site near the village of Riged. This time, the families in Riged—who belong to Bu Qadir's tribe (Shermat), but not his clan, and who were themselves at odds over whether to allow tourists in their village—rejected it.

Finally, a Tahki elder offered up some of his tribal lands in return for a percentage of the campground's profits. The Association and the SCDP came to an agreement, at last. But the campground—built with foreign embassy funding and supported financially by the SCDP—operated increasingly as a private enterprise. The Tahki landowner-manager ran the "restaurant" concessions from afar, paying small irregular sums of cash to whoever worked in the kitchen (many were paid in meals, the tourists' leftovers), while giving only the lesser fees charged for lodging to the Association. Meanwhile, the SCDP's repeated efforts to increase the Association's involvement and responsibility in running the campground failed. This failure was due mainly to the complacency of the Association, which, being averse to financial risk taking, was satisfied with receiving a mere percentage of the profits. Moreover, the Association's governing council was relieved to have become exempt from actually running the camp. When it came time to renovate the campground, however, it was the Association's funds that were used.

At issue during these deliberations was not simply the pastoralists' ambivalence toward tourism. Nor was it, as some foreign project experts and tourists suggested, their Bedouin nature or "ignorance": their alleged inability to understand what tourists would find attractive. Rather, expert plans for community development based on the romanticized notion that Soqotra's novel protected areas would be managed by their inhabitants as communally owned properties—or simply, on the assumption that the boundaries of the enclaves set apart as nature sanctuaries would correspond with the collectively managed rangeland that did exist—were blind to these mounting tensions. Yet this protracted struggle over the location of the campground was a harbinger of the conflicts to come.

The Spring

It was a June morning, before my trip to Oman, when we woke up to find that the village water tank had gone dry. Word around Qayher was the Kowtir had come down from Momi and diverted the pipes that channel the spring's water to the village. The Kowtir, I was told, claimed that the land surrounding the Di-Zahrin spring belonged to them. But my neighbors claimed that their families used to live there, which makes it Shermat land. The men of Qayher assured me that the water problem would be solved after lunch. They would cross the plateau to the spring and reposition the uPVC pipes. Bu Yaqub explained that, when the Environment arrived, the Shermat of Qayher signed an agreement with the Kowtir, affirming their reciprocal rights to graze their animals in both Homhil and Momi. The Kowtir, he said, wanted to cultivate gardens near Di-Zahrin because they did not have running water in Momi. But their agreement had been "an agreement of neighborliness," Bu Yaqub insisted, not an admission that the Kowtir had ancestral rights to the spring. I asked Bu Yaqub if the Shermat had any deeds certifying their possession of the land. "Some people do; some don't," said his son.

"If you live in a place," Bu Yaqub said, "that is the deed [*wathiqa*]."

If ownership of and access to rangeland was and remains a cherished resource for pastoral Soqotrans, access to fresh water is ever more valued and safeguarded,[59] because water availability, more than pasturage alone, determines livestock's productivity and milk yield and Soqotra is an arid island, subject to a long annual dry season and prone to severe periodic droughts. Although some of its areas are rich in natural springs, streams, and groundwater aquifers, in most places islanders have had to rely on trapped rainwater for all their water needs. Rainwater—which comes "from God" and is thus "for all people"—has long been considered an open-access resource. Yaqub explained this to me once by citing a hadith accorded to the Prophet Muhammad stating that people are partners in (i.e., must share) three things: water, grasses (pasture), and fire. Therefore, naturally occurring water such as rainfall cannot be privately owned. However, *access* to regional water sources is determined by ancestral usage and geographic proximity—as is pasture. Water sources such as springs, streams, seasonal watercourses, pools, and other natural rainwater catchments are considered the common property of those with grazing rights in the area. Whereas water cannot be refused to those in need, its diversion or storage in human-made wells, irrigation channels, or rainwater catchment systems does confer private property rights to those who built or modified these systems: water collected from these wells or catchments belongs to the families or descendants of those who exerted effort and expense to construct them.

In Soqotra, as in other parts of the Arabian Peninsula, these customary regulations concerning water access and ownership have been put to the test by the relatively recent and rapid introduction of new water infrastructures and technologies.[60] Homhil has three natural springs and three seasonal riverbeds (wadis) that fill up after heavy rains. Until the 1970s, its inhabitants were largely dependent on rainwater collected in natural basins and in wadis for their and their livestock's daily needs. Additionally, each hamlet had a hand-dug well that its owners used to access groundwater for drinking and for small garden plots. The springs' water, diverted through built water channels, was used primarily for agriculture and for the communal mosque. Access to this common-property channeled water was apportioned on a rotational basis; each cultivated plot received a day (or more, depending on its size) of running water, in turn. Even tribesmen from Momi, including the Kowtir, cultivated finger millet using water from the Di-Zahrin spring. Most people had to walk some distance to fetch their daily water and their firewood, and personal water use was limited by what one could carry.

Under the socialist government, water access and availability improved. On the one hand, following the government's regular importation of rice, wheat, and sugar, crop cultivation (especially of the labor-intensive finger millet) declined. The inhabitants of Homhil began cultivating date palms instead, planting them near the wadis, where they were naturally watered. Accordingly, the need for the human-made water channels evaporated, too. On the other hand, the socialist government began constructing large, community-owned *karifs*: cement-lined holes in the ground for collecting and storing rainwater. Water was thus more easily accessible (but still rain dependent), and usage did not need to be as strictly controlled. This *karif* construction increased in the wake of Yemen's unification as imported cement and wood (for covering) became more readily available, and both emigrants and NGOs contributed to these development projects. Like the built or modified rainwater catchment systems, these new *karifs* belonged to the kin groups who constructed them. The SCDP also built *karifs* in several communities. What had an even greater impact, however, was the distribution of costly uPVC piping (by the SCDP or Gulf-based relatives), which enabled Soqotrans to divert spring water across longer distances and to reduce their dependence on rainwater. In Homhil, in 2002, PARITER provided uPVC pipes to two villages near the Di-Zahrin spring, and these villages were able to divert spring water directly to their homes. A year later, the SCDP laid pipes from the Di-Zahrin spring to Qayher, to several other villages, and to the campground. In Qayher, this water was piped directly into the community *birka*, an aboveground cement-lined holding tank. This meant that women no longer had to walk to the riverbed to fetch water. Instead, it was around the *birka* that the women gathered every morning to fill their plastic jerry cans, wash clothes and dishes, and socialize.

Because I lived in Qayher, where I shared the (new) inconvenience of the waterless *birka* over a several-month period, it was hard for me not to empathize with my hosts' version of the events. But I sympathized with "the Kowtir" version, too. According to one of the Kowtir tribesmen from Momi, Bu Qadir had wanted to use the spring water for agriculture. But the Kowtir worried that pipe irrigation would deplete "their" water supply, which they relied on for their cattle. "You can use our water—we won't deny you water for drinking, but we won't relinquish it to you," the Kowtir allegedly told Bu Qadir. One night, Bu Qadir "and his people" (his fellow Shermat from Qayher) walked to Di-Zahrin and laid pipes between the spring and his intended garden. In response, the Kowtir came down from Momi, placed the pipes on the backs of their donkeys, and hauled them up to their settlements. Bu Qadir told the police that the Kowtir had stolen their pipes. The police questioned the Kowtir, who purportedly said, "You have to go to the Environment and ask them what's going on because they know everything." The Environment (SCDP) told Bu Qadir to solve the problem since he was president of the Association. Bu Qadir went to the island's commissioner (*ma'mur*) and reported that the Kowtir had entered Qayher's homes and hit their women. The commissioner wrote a letter to the public prosecutor. The public prosecutor then called in the Kowtir tribesman who told me this story to find out what was going on. My interlocutor told the prosecutor, "We took the pipes because Bu Qadir is not solving this. Go ask the Environment. They're responsible for all of this." The prosecutor said, "You can't forbid people water." My interlocutor replied, "If they want water for drinking, they can take it. But there isn't enough water there for agriculture."

For a while, the SCDP did not intervene, despite it having provided the water-draining pipes in the first place. Eventually, Bu Qadir was asked by the Soqotra SCDP office to step down from his role as Association president because of his imperious management style. "When Bu Qadir was no longer responsible," my interlocutor said, "everything was okay—the campground worked and the water flowed." But then, about two years later, the Qayher (village)-Kowtir (tribe) conflict over the spring erupted once more. When, in the summer of 2005, the men of Qayher began constructing new walls and a foundation near the spring, the Kowtir viewed this as yet another provocation.

As a built structure, Bu Qadir's rudimentary stone wall drew a literal boundary between land (and water) claimed by the Kowtir and land (and water) claimed by one of the Shermat clans. The Kowtir responded by diverting Qayher's water pipes—hence, the empty *birka*—and by bringing their claim to the court. In this fashion, this apparently tribal conflict moved between and attached itself to a variety of topographical features: from the campground to the spring to the new garden enclosures. Moreover, this conflict that the establishment of the protected area had set in motion seemed impossible to bring to a halt. "In the past," my interlocutor lamented, "all of us worked and lived together. When there was a celebratory feast [*diyafa*], we'd all come together. When there was a death, we'd all come together. Now, it'll only get worse, and these problems will end in discord [*fitna*]."

Although my (Kowtir) interlocutor's somber prediction was not borne out, it does reveal a common concern and complaint shared by all the so-called citizens of Homhil, including their neighbors: that the Environment was "responsible for all of this." In their view, the environmental project had ignited these intertribal (Shermat-Kowtir) tensions by inscribing fixed territorial boundaries across a region previously defined by more fluid (negotiable and reciprocal) grazing rights. For the Kowtir, who lived in Momi, this meant losing "their" ancestral spring to an ecologically determined community. Meanwhile, emboldened by the SCDP's mappings, the Association's president asserted his clan's entitlement to this area's natural resources—to the frustration of the other Shermat tribesmen. Instead of dousing this fire, the uPVC pipes introduced by the SCDP and PARITER stoked tribally tinged anxieties over water scarcity and other shortcomings. Regardless of which side the people of and around Homhil took in this case, most agreed that it was these kinds of developments that were pulling at the very fabric—the *śeterhur* (Soq.: clans): literally, strips of cloth—of their community. In this fashion, the introduction of new resources did not develop or strengthen the protected-area community so much as it divided it among tribal and even intratribal (clan or residential) lines.

The Garden

A month earlier, Umm Yaqub, Umm Jum'an, and I had set out to Nur's house, where about half of the Homhil women were assembled. It was a torrid day, the kind that made some people languid but made me short-tempered and edgy, moving frenetically, as if trying to dodge the blanketing heat. Nur served us sweet milky tea while we waited for PARITER's agricultural trainers to arrive from Hadibo. They were already two hours late. Many women worried aloud whether they had left their houses, children, and chores to walk to this neighboring village under the midday sun for naught. Still waiting, they discussed the best way to cut tomatoes and joked about this being their self-provided "training." They extolled the benefits of vegetables: how vegetables make one fat (*samin*).

"Vegetables don't make you fat," I argued, unable to contain myself. "It's the tea, and rice, and bread, and ghee that make people fat." No one believed me. Their daily diet consisted of cloyingly sweet tea, buttered rice, and oily bread, but none were as "fat" as they would like to be. (I was "fat," and the women assumed that I ate my vegetables in Hadibo.)

Just as we were preparing to return home, a child alerted us to a vehicle crossing the plateau. PARITER would conduct its home-gardening workshop after all. But by the time the trainers gathered everyone together again, the women were far less interested in learning about growing vegetables than they were in voicing their objections to the project.

In addition to supporting and supervising the community campground, the SCDP (together with the Government of Yemen and various international donors and NGOs) had envisioned that sustainable development both in and outside the protected areas would be cultivated, quite literally, through a home-garden project to improve local food sources. To this end, the SCDP developed and upgraded home gardens and nurseries around the island, provided training to women in its target areas, and distributed seedlings and basic tools. In Homhil, the SCDP developed a "community garden" on Tahki lands, inadvertently benefiting the same tribe (but not the same family) that would profit the most from the campground. Still, the idea was sound. The community garden—tended by one woman (Nur), who had been trained by the SCDP—would serve as a horticultural training site and nursery for the rest of Homhil.

When, in late 2004, PARITER became responsible for the continued implementation of the SCDP's home-garden project, it selected Homhil as one of its primary targets. However, within a month's time, a dispute over the location of the new "PARITER garden" delayed the project and soon antagonized the entire community. In contrast to the recent friction over the campground's location, this dispute was waged less by the Hamiliho than it was by the foreign managers of PARITER and the SCDP. To summarize briefly: PARITER's project manager decided not to upgrade the existing garden supported by the SCDP but rather to establish a new garden closer to Di-Zahrin spring—and, incidentally, on land owned by the family of his driver, Bu Faruq. He reasoned that the initial SCDP garden suffered from water constraints. (Its water was drawn from a nearby wadi.)[61] Angered that PARITER would abandon their garden, the SCDP management insisted that PARITER work in both gardens: in the existing garden tended by Nur and in the newly selected site in Riged. Despite coming to an agreement that the primary community garden would be in Riged but that Nur's garden would continue to receive material support, PARITER and the SCDP wrangled for months over the "terms" of this support. The SCDP insisted that PARITER support both gardens more or less equally and assured the Homhil Association that this would be the case. PARITER's project manager insisted that he could fund only the garden in Riged yet would provide the SCDP garden with some training, seedlings, and tools—but not the pump, pipes, fencing, or stipends set aside for the Riged garden. These details were hashed out repeatedly at meetings in Hadibo attended by the male representatives of the SCDP, PARITER, the Ministry of Agriculture, and the (male) president of the Association. The women of Homhil, the alleged beneficiaries of and labor for this project, were never to my knowledge included in these official meetings.

In Homhil, the discord took a different turn. The Association—represented now by its new president, a relative of the (Tahki) landowners of the campground and the SCDP garden—claimed not to mind where the new community garden would be tilled, as long as the initial garden continued to receive material support. The reason is that this new garden was not considered a community garden at all but rather the good fortune (*rizq*) of the family on whose land it had materialized. In fact, the majority of Hamiliho agreed that they did not even want a single, community garden; rather, they wanted each household to receive wire fencing so that every family could protect its actual *home* gardens. Moreover, what concerned and ultimately antagonized people far more than the location of PARITER's garden was the news that the three women selected to work there would each receive a stipend of YER 5,000 (USD 25) per month. Many of my neighbors complained about the meagerness of these stipends, all the while arguing over which women should be selected and why, according to the men, men should be hired instead. (Twenty-five dollars per month was more than twice the monthly cash payment Yemen's vulnerable families received from the Social Welfare Fund.) To disperse these stipends, PARITER decided to hire one woman from each of Homhil's three major tribes, disregarding the fact that they could all still originate from the same village (as Riged is home to Shermat, Tahki, and Sowkir families). Thus, when after months of negotiations, PARITER broke ground for this garden, my neighbors in Qayher were upset only that the residents of Riged—their fellow (Shermat) tribesmen—had commandeered all of this salaried labor. Promises of training and seedlings, however enterprising, were in no way commensurate with the much-needed cash.

Furthermore, the premises underlying this project's faith in "training" were not lost on its supposed benefactors. These included assumptions that pastoral Soqotrans did not know how to productively cultivate their own land and that, if they did, they would share a dietary preference for nutritious (but not satiating) vegetables. It is thus worth recalling here that many households in Homhil had cultivated finger millet, tobacco, cotton, and several kinds of vegetables in decades past, before shifting to date palms during the socialist period. Formal agricultural instruction—which began as early as the 1940s under the "guiding hand" of the British—was also one of the interventions of the socialist government. And several men from Homhil had worked as seasonal labor in large-scale commercial farms in al-Mahra, while most households continued to tend small garden plots. If vegetable gardens were not abundant in Homhil, this was not for lack of knowledge or experience. Rather, as the unsuccessful horticultural experiments of the British officers and the socialist government showed, such gardens are regularly consumed by goats or uprooted by monsoon winds. Training was thus less beneficial than fences, and produce was less appealing than stipends. Yet, when the people of Homhil objected to this training, challenged their presumed ignorance, and asserted their actual needs, the foreign development staff dismissed them as difficult and ungracious. An overview of the home-garden workshop demonstrates how these two groups—the agricultural trainers and their beneficiaries—were thus bound to talk past one another.

At the start of her lesson, Cecilie, a young French woman who had just begun working for PARITER, explained through her assistant and translator that Nur's garden would receive seeds and technical assistance but that most of the material support would be donated to the Riged garden where future training would take place. (None of the women of Riged had come. Nur assured Cecilie that she had informed them about the meeting. But Riged was, from their perspective, far away, and in any case, the women's absence simply confirmed what everyone but PARITER had long acknowledged: Riged had its "own" garden now.) The women had been primed for this disappointment. Even before we stepped out, Umm Yaqub's husband had questioned what we had to gain from this workshop.

"What's the point of training?" Bu Yaqub asked me. "There's no benefit. They made a garden in Riged for the people who live there. There's no benefit for the rest of the inhabitants."

"But this garden is for all of you," I said.

"No, it's Nur's garden. There's no support for the rest of us."

"I think the support is supposed to be the instruction that you can then apply to your own gardens," I said.

"They gave us instruction last year, the people from the Ministry of Agriculture. Why always instruction? What's the use? And, anyway, they lie. They say they're going to help us and then they don't. They call women together for meetings. What's the point of that? Meetings and meetings, but no support. What kind of an organization is that?"

"I think they aim to give people more knowledge and training," I said.

"Training is okay, but then what? What's the point of training without support? God's poor need fences and pipes and [financial] support," Bu Yaqub said.

Emboldened perhaps by conversations like these, the women gathered in Nur's house demanded that they receive fencing materials, too. Cecilie did not quite understand them, but she heard the resentment in their voices.

"I'm worried they'll be difficult," Cecilie whispered to me in English. "They're not interested in training. They just want materials and money. I hope not, but I think so."

As she spoke, her two (mainland) Yemeni assistants unrolled their hand-drawn posters depicting the growth stages of carrots and tomatoes. But the women did not settle down. They did not want training, several insisted, unless they would receive materials or a stipend in return.

"Or at least lunch," one said, "We're hungry." (This was cheeky, and her look showed that she knew it. But Soqotrans typically remunerate communal labor or mutual assistance with generous, meat-rich meals provided by its beneficiaries.)

Other women questioned the utility of the training. One suggested that the very idea of a community garden was exploitative. "PARITER wants us to work without pay!" she said.

I told Cecilie that she had better explain to them how she thought the training would benefit them.

"Before, you just had a few days of training at the very beginning of the [SCDP] project. Now we'll give you training that continues through the agricultural season and we'll continue to monitor the garden and its progress," said Cecilie. One of Cecilie's assistants translated for her.

"Will I be paid for the use of my house?" Nur whispered to me.

I asked Cecilie. Cecilie said that Nur was being recompensed through the vegetables she grew in her garden from the seeds she had acquired from the project. Nur said that gardening was hard work for which she received no salary or income. Cecilie countered that the vegetable produce would allow Nur to decrease her overall food expenditures, explaining that Nur's family could substitute the (free) vegetables for some of their regular daily meals. "And, anyway, how can they eat rice for every meal?" Cecilie asked me.

"Will you give us money to come to training?" Umm Yaqub said loudly, punctuating our conversation.

Visibly exasperated, Cecilie leaned over to tell me how this project had been defined, from its conception, according to people's needs. In the beginning, people had been enthusiastic, the project founder had told her. But now it seemed to Cecilie that "their mentality has changed." "If they had wanted schools or something else, we would have focused on that," she told me, "but they had said they wanted vegetables."

I said that all I had ever heard people in Homhil wish for, communally, was a safer access road and more classrooms.

"Tell them, if they are not interested in our advice, then they can go home and we'll leave," said Cecilie.

"Tell her, if they don't want to help us, then thank you for your time, and good-bye!" said Umm Yaqub simultaneously, waving her hand for emphasis.

"But can't they sell the vegetables?" asked Cecilie, "To the campground? Or in Hadibo?"

I explained to her that few tourists visited Homhil and that transportation from Homhil to Hadibo was irregular.

"Tell her," Umm Yaqub interrupted, "we are not goats! We'll understand the training in one day!" (I was surprised by Umm Yaqub's statement. This was the first time I heard someone in Homhil reject their imputed ignorance. Usually, my neighbors were telling me quite the opposite: "We are Bedouin; we are goats.")

"Tell them, you can stay home if you don't want to participate," said Cecilie.

"No, we do want to!" said Umm Yaqub. "But we don't want training. We need materials and money. Otherwise, we'll stay home."

"The problem is that when we go to the houses of the shaykhs, they cause problems because they're used to eating the money of the state," said one of the assistants, a man originally from Aden, to Cecilie in English. "So, I asked them if this was the house of the shaykh and if this lady is the shaykh's wife, but she isn't." (The assumption that Umm Yaqub was strong-willed because her husband was politically connected would have struck her as amusing, had I translated this conversation. Earlier, during our walk over to Nur's house, Umm Yaqub had complained about how "useless" her husband was.)

"The problem is that they only see the money that's in their hands. They don't understand about the long-term benefits," answered Cecilie. Then, turning to me, she said, "There's no community spirit here, is there?"

I explained that a majority of the area's men had come together two days earlier to build a house, after which the laborers, including my husband, received a hearty mutton lunch for their efforts. So if a Soqotran could afford to provide his workers lunch, then it seemed strange that a European NGO could not do so.

"But that was just one day," said Cecilie. "We'll be coming here once a week, so we can't provide lunch every time. They just don't understand the value of a community garden."

All this time, the women had been talking among themselves. Again, Umm Yaqub's voice arose over the many conversations. "If there's no money, or support, or food," she said, visibly counting off each demand on her fingers, "then we're not coming back!" The women agreed.

"We're giving you our time, so we need to something in return," said Umm Jamal.

The meeting broke up without the day's scheduled lesson, but it was agreed that there would be another workshop the following week. On our walk back to Qayher I asked Umm Yaqub how she would feel if PARITER decided not to return at all.

"We want them," she replied. "We said we're going back on Saturday."

"But if they don't come back?"

"Well, then forget them. We're comfortable here. And what do we need them for if they don't bring us wells or fences or supplies?"

"We used to plant gardens long before the Environment arrived and told us to change everything," said Umm Jamal.

That evening, I ate dinner with Bu Tariq's family. Bu Tariq told me that the women had been wrong to say they were not going to return. "Training is good," he said, "knowledge is important. But what good is training if we don't have fences? The goats would eat everything! And, besides, the women know how to garden. Nur was trained by the SCDP, and she then trained all the women of Homhil in just a week. She didn't spare herself. But PARITER wants to start training us again from the beginning. And we can't plant gardens anyway without the appropriate materials." Bu Tariq told me that to upgrade his small garden, he would need three rolls of wire fencing at YER 3,000 per roll. "If I had fencing," he said, "I would leave my date trees for agriculture because date work is tiresome." The problem, he concluded, was that PARITER had not actually established a *community* garden. Riged was too far away.

Later that night, Nur's ex-husband stopped by my house. "The women were wrong to demand things," he told me; "they have no sense [*'aql*]." He went on to explain how they should have been more instrumental in their tactics: first, sitting through the training sessions and only then, once a relationship had been established, asking for material assistance.

Just before going to bed, I sat with Umm Yaqub by the light of her kerosene lantern as she applied kohl to her eyes to protect them. "Are you upset with me?" she asked. "Today, I was just joking. Next week we'll give our real response."

"No, if I was in your place, I would have said the same thing."

"You are close to my place. You are like a fellow countrywoman [*muwatina*]—

but we sat there all day without tending to our own work. And this is to continue
every week!"

As Umm Yaqub had promised, the women did show up for the workshop
the following week. Although this and subsequent workshops were not nearly
as spirited, the now communitywide dissension over the terms and benefits
of this project continued for months. In Hadibo, representatives of the SCDP,
PARITER, the Homhil Association, and even the Ministry of Agriculture
emerged from their ongoing meetings with divergent conclusions; although,
at one point, when the Ministry's representative questioned why there was an
agricultural project in a protected nature sanctuary to begin with, the SCDP
and PARITER managers colluded in essentially shutting him out of the discussion. Similarly, the Association's president's suggestion that all material support
be given to the Association for distribution was also ignored. And he was kept
unapprised of the precise terms under debate due to translations that were partially, if not directly, misleading. One person in Qayher told me that he thought
that "the people in Hadibo" (SCDP and PARITER) were deliberately obfuscat-
ing the negotiation process to benefit personally from the prolonged confusion. Meanwhile, the men in Homhil alternately demanded and rejected the
continuation of the women's training sessions. And the women continued to
pursue their own agenda, even if it meant ignoring the dictates of their husbands or fathers. That summer, Nur's entire garden and nursery were swept
away by the monsoon while the SCDP and PARITER management quibbled
over who should supply it protective fencing. By September, having given up
on receiving aid from either the SCDP or PARITER, the women of Qayher had
cleared ground for their own communal (village) garden. They were then just
awaiting seedlings—which Nur no longer had and which PARITER's garden in
Riged had yet to produce—and rain. The rains came. The community garden
was never completed.

Amid this commotion, this was clear: what had been a fairly simple plan to
improve local food production was largely thwarted by the external mapping of
the protected area as a single community that would benefit equally regardless
of the garden's location. Like the NGO that had organized the "participatory
mapping" exercise, where the SCDP and PARITER did recognize difference,
they saw it primarily in gendered and tribal form. Thus, they separated men

from women (engaging women as their "beneficiaries" and men as their interlocutors) and sought to hire women based on tribal affiliation alone. What this
did not acknowledge is that Soqotra's communities are as much geographically
localized as they are descent based, regardless of the growing influence and
idiom of "the tribe". (Thus, the benefit to the Shermat living in Riged would
not automatically translate into any benefits, real or perceived, for the Shermat living in Qayher, for example.) Moreover, it assumed that women constituted their own community—that they would naturally desire to labor together
rather than direct their efforts to their families or villages. It further assumed
that women had ample, autonomous, and free time: time during which they
could leave their children, livestock, and households to sit through trainings
they had not requested, without any direct remuneration. When women, or
men, challenged these assumptions, they were perceived to be lacking "community spirit." It having long been decided that the inhabitants of Homhil were
simply "difficult," none of the project managers seemed to think it necessary to
heed their beneficiaries' objections. Finally, what was most overlooked was that
the inhabitants of the protected area—however interrelated they are through
blood kinship, milk kinship, marriage, coresidence, and proximity—did not
conceive of themselves as a single economic unit. Certainly, reciprocity between families, tribes, and even residential communities existed and continues
to exist. Yet, for the most part, large-scale and long-term investments of land,
labor, capital, and time were waged by individual families in an entrepreneur-
ial rather than a communal fashion. Like land use, "community" could not
be charted on a map. Rather, community in this protected environment was
forged in large part by who could secure access to which natural, material, and
financial resources.

The Cave

This detour from the campground to the spring and through the garden brings
us back to the cave. While the dispute over the garden did not cause internal
social strife so much as it fomented anger toward PARITER and the SCDP,
it prepared the ground for the ensuing intratribal conflict between the Shermat of Qayher and the Shermat of Riged—much as the debate over the campground location had set the stage for the intertribal dispute between the Kowtir

and the Shermat (of Qayher). It did this, first, by generating a prolonged and explicit comparison of the material benefits that each hamlet stood to gain or lose. Although many of my neighbors in Qayher tried to curb their envy by recognizing the garden project as an instance of God's bounty (*rizq*), they were also witness to the machinations by which this *rizq* was being funneled to just one party—indeed, to the one Soqotran employed by PARITER.[62] It did this, second, by producing two political opponents, Bu Qadir (of Qayher) and Bu Faruq (of Riged), who perpetuated the conflict between the SCDP and PARITER by proxy.

Even though Bu Faruq had worked for PARITER for several years, it was with the expansion of the community garden project—especially the establishment of the Riged garden, on his father's land no less—that Bu Faruq's influence in Homhil grew. While the foreign project managers may have viewed Bu Faruq as their driver (and increasingly, their go-to guy), the inhabitants of Homhil observed Bu Faruq delivering materials, commanding workers, and building up "his" garden. To them, Bu Faruq *represented* PARITER and its resources. And to some it was precisely this connection that underlay many of the tensions in Homhil. "Before PARITER came to the island, Bu Faruq was the best of men," one of my interlocutors told me shortly after the men of Qayher had been imprisoned. "But then he turned. He uses the PARITER car, money, and influence to cause problems and to bribe the judge." I expressed surprise that the "bribe money" would come from PARITER. "Where else does he get his money from?" my interlocutor replied.

Like Bu Faruq, Bu Qadir had worked with the SCDP before through his role as the elected president of the Homhil Association. However, during the height of the SCDP's dispute with PARITER over the implementation of the garden project, its local manager single-handedly appointed Bu Qadir to a new, salaried position: "director" of the Homhil Protected Area. This was a surprising reversal from the previous SCDP manager's insistence that Bu Qadir step down from presiding over the Association because of the discord he had caused. Yet, faced with a number of small but chronic crises in the management of Homhil and a virtually powerless Association, the SCDP needed a forceful insider to act on its behalf. Thus, the SCDP invested in Bu Qadir the authority to oversee the conservation of the protected area, despite his having a (salaried) government post that required his presence in Hadibo. In this manner,

Bu Qadir was made the local representative of the Environment—and a direct rival of Bu Faruq. Accordingly, whereas some pinned the tensions on Bu Faruq, others blamed Bu Qadir. "All the problems are because of Bu Qadir. If Bu Qadir wasn't responsible, he'd be the best of men. But once he becomes responsible, he causes problems," another interlocutor told me. "The problem in Homhil is envy. Another problem is that Bu Qadir thinks he's been given the power to decide, but he doesn't consult with anyone."

The tension between Bu Qadir, local representative of conservation in Homhil, and Bu Faruq, local representative of development, reached its apogee in the dispute over the cave. Since, by this time, I had become implicated in the power struggle between Bu Qadir and Bu Faruq simply by living in Qayher, my understanding of the conflict was undoubtedly biased. Moreover, Bu Faruq and I had become locked in our own battle as well. Around the time of the garden negotiations, he had accused me publicly of causing unspecified problems, insinuated that I was a US spy, insisted on taking me to court, and threatened to have me expelled from the island. Because he refused to disclose what problems I had caused or what I had done to make him think so poorly of me, I could not defend or explain myself. This Kafkaesque situation was painful and disorienting. The growing animosity between us ended only by way of a near accident when, after I had nearly driven my vehicle and five passengers over the edge of a cliff while transporting their three tanks of propane fuel to Homhil, he was the person who reversed my car to safety. My sincere gratitude toward him seemed to have softened his anger, and, with time, I think, he also realized that I had no direct involvement in the SCDP's decisions. In fact, my neighbors tried to keep their struggles to themselves. "Do the SCDP and PARITER even realize the problems they've caused here?" I asked a friend at the time of the cave conflict.

"No," she said. "None of the men will tell them. Did they tell you?"

"No."

"And they won't tell the Environment either. It's not good to talk badly about one's brothers," she said.

What I did come to know, then, was based on the fragmentary pieces I had picked up from various Qayher-based friends. According to them, Bu Faruq wanted to expand the enclosure (*haush*) abutting one of the caves behind Qayher. This was a modified cave in which his family used to dwell during periods of seasonal transhumance. As late as the 1970s, most of the pastoral-ist families in Homhil lived with their livestock in the karstic cave settlements overlooking the plateau. (Umm Yaqub recalls that her family was living in a cave during the time of the *rubuʿ*—the "Wednesday" in 1972 when a flash flood decimated their livestock.) From there, they would transhume season-ally, moving down to the open plain during the winter when grasses were plentiful or even lower, to the coast, to seek shelter and participate in the date harvest during the monsoon. Their ascent to the caves in between these sea-sons gave the rangeland time to recover. Pastoralists moved vertically between highland and lowland pastures for other reasons, too: to escape the buildup of fleas; to be closer to a water source, a cultivated plot, or harvested plants; and to avoid the heat. These vertical movements (internal transhumance) within one's tribal/clan territory occurred regularly as a form of sustainable range-land management—in contrast to the movements outside one's tribal territory (external transhumance) necessitated by exhausted pasture, lack of water, and drought.[63]

However, by the late 1970s, more and more pastoralists had abandoned their elevated cave dwellings for circular rubble huts near the base of the pla-teau. Miranda Morris details the chronological—and spatial—progression from these rubble huts; to oblong stone houses surrounded by a walled court-yard; to, in the 1990s, enclosed family "settlements" of several one-room buildings each designated for a specific function; to, in the 2000s, rectan-gular, one-roomed houses roofed with wooden planking and rendered with cement.[64] In Homhil, families were still aspiring to build these modern, rectangular "Arab" homes. Typically, families did not tear down or renovate their houses but built new (often adjacent) ones instead. Their vacated dwell-ings were given over to livestock use—as had been the house I moved into in Qayher—or kept empty in case of future need. But even as the number of their dwellings increased, the pastoralists in Homhil and elsewhere began to move house (and transhume) less frequently. On the one hand, this is emblematic of the islandwide shift from pastoralism to other occupations. On the other hand, with their homesteads increasing in size and value and their material possessions increasing alongside them, pastoralists have become less keen to move their entire households for the sake of their livestock. "We now have too much stuff to move," Yaqub told me once, gesturing to their mattresses, blankets, clothing, and cooking pots. Instead, most (but not all) families in Homhil resided in their primary homesteads year-round and sent only their grown sons to move their cattle to suitable pastures.

But these formerly occupied cave dwellings remained useful—and cherished. Often, goatherds used these caves and their enclosures as bad-weather quarters for their goats. At least twice during my stay in Qayher, adults took the village children to the caves overnight to shelter them from torrential rains. Most important, even something as humble as a modified cave or goat byre constitutes proof of individual family (as opposed to collective) landownership: a substitute deed. Thus, during the very period that the protected areas were established, "the site of livestock quarters—goat pens, in particular—[were] selected with the aim of reinforcing an individual land claim or to make real or imagined borders between one tribe and the next, rather than because it [was] an area of good browse and graze."[65] So, when it became known that Bu Faruq intended to expand the enclosure to a cave behind Qayher, the men of Qayher interpreted this as a land grab. Claiming that their families had used the cave, too, the Qayher men told Bu Faruq that he could expand the enclosure only if he gave them permission to build a similar pen near Riged. Supposedly, Bu Faruq refused their request and destroyed one of the existent pens built by the men of Qayher and replaced it with a new wall. The Qayher men destroyed Bu Faruq's wall. Bu Faruq responded by going to the police, who then imprisoned the Qayher men. This was the situation to which I returned at the end of the monsoon season.

Bu Qadir and his brothers were held for ten days, first in Hadibo's jail and then in a police station. When I visited them, two days before their scheduled court appearance, one brother told me that he hoped the judge would have a wide heart (*qalb wasi'*) and an open mind, "especially when it comes to the Bedouin, because we don't know all the rules and regulations." This was one of the many instances during which I heard rural Soqotrans use what I call their "Bedouin abjection" as an excuse. Meanwhile, Bu Qadir's other brother had been granted leave to gather their witnesses. In the absence of ownership documents, shaykhs and elders from Homhil and Momi were ferried down to Hadibo to provide oral testimonies in support of either Bu Qadir's or Bu Faruq's claims to property rights based on usage histories. Two days later, following their court appearance, the brothers were upbeat. They had managed to gather five elders to provide supportive testimony on their behalf, whereas Bu Faruq's three witnesses provided (what they considered) conflicting accounts.

However, the judge apparently thought otherwise and did not accept their Bedouin abjection as a valid defense. Two weeks later, in mid-September, he ruled that the cave was the property of the state but that each party would be allowed to use the goat enclosure in turn. Additionally, he sentenced the Qayher men to six months of probation, ordered them to rebuild the enclosure they had destroyed, and fined them YER 20,000 (approximately USD 100) for Bu Faruq's expenses. The residents of Qayher were certain that Bu Faruq had bribed the judge with money and qat, a luxury they assumed he could afford with his PARITER salary. Convinced that the ruling had been compromised, the Qayher men decided to appeal the case in al-Mukalla, the capital of the Hadhramawt governorate and administrative seat of the Soqotra Archipelago at that time. At great cost to each party, both Bu Qadir and Bu Faruq flew repeatedly to al-Mukalla to present their case. Many observers were convinced that the parties would take the case as far as the High Court in Sanaa if no satisfactory outcome could be reached. It had become clear to all involved that this was not a mere argument over a goat enclosure, or even over land. After all, the involvement of the courts had resulted in the infelicitous outcome that neither party owned the land. (Based on the conclusion that its ownership was ambiguous, the land reverted to the state—giving the Soqotrans yet another reason to protest the mainland governments' indifference to Soqotran customary law.) It was, rather, a contest over the future leadership of the protected area, a contest instigated and financed by the arrival of the Environment and its partners in Development.

. . .

What this particular mapping exercise illustrates is how and why one of the first protected areas in Yemen became a physical site of sociopolitical conflict as well as an ideological battleground between conservation and development. We saw how the inscription of its boundaries, both external and internal, produced the very distinctions it had intended to portray. And we saw how external support to the protected area "distributed different types of fortune and misfortune" to its various inhabitants.[66] Instead of mapping onto and thus reinvigorating

Soqotrans' traditional protected areas (*zeribah* reserves and controlled-access *mibdihil*) and practices of rangeland management, the new ecologically determined and government-established protected area (*mahmiya*) cut through tribal territories and divided its residential communities. And instead of benefiting the majority of this protected area's stakeholders and inhabitants, community-based conservation and development projects disseminated new resources to a few and sowed conflict among the rest. Nor was I innocent of doing the same. Recall Umm Jum'an's facetious explanation for why the people of Riged envied the people of Qayher: "We have the Environment, the campground, and Nathalie."

One reason that so many of the conservation and development initiatives in Homhil lagged, erred, or even failed was the way in which their planners and facilitators imagined *and* viewed the protected area community. It was not just that the development experts, conservation biologists, SCDP project management, and even tourists perceived the region through their preformed environmental imaginaries or that they imagined the community to operate as a homogeneous, harmonious, and cooperative collective. Rather, the terrain itself shaped the way in which its community was literally *seen* and *not seen*. In the dry seasons, this arid terrain camouflages most of the valley's hamlets and individual homesteads—nestled as they are into rocky outcrops or mountainsides—and Homhil can seem largely vacant. In greener times, separate hamlets may appear to be one. Thus, when visiting experts did not *see* Homhil as a region occupied by several tribes across distinct settlements, they could easily envision it as a singular community that would embrace a collective project. This way of (en)visioning Homhil was incorporated into the projects planned and then held up as a standard against which to measure the peoples' community spirit (or lack thereof). The experts' sightings—which encompassed these blind spots—both conformed to and sustained their environmental imaginaries and their imaginaries of the Homhil community.

Another reason for so many of the initiatives backfiring was their administrators' blindness to their social impacts. As noted previously, protected areas have had various impacts—many of them detrimental—on the people who live in or around them. Yet in the myriad reports drafted by the SCDP and its evaluators between 2000 and 2008, the real effects of Soqotra's new protected areas were rarely assessed. Instead, results were measured according to a series of numerical and scalar objectives: the numbers of areas established, management plans instituted, campgrounds operational, trails identified, signs posted, water systems upgraded, local persons trained, and so forth. Evaluations detailing "lessons learned" or "issues to be addressed" recognized, in part, that the implementation of the protected areas had been poor. However, the reasons for this "challenge" were attributed, characteristically, to the recalcitrance of the areas' inhabitants.[67] For example, in an external evaluation report commissioned by the UNDP, the general shortcomings of the Socotra Biodiversity Project (1997–2003) were attributed less to the vision and structure of the project than to the limitations of the EPA senior management, the Government of Yemen, the local councils, community institutions, and civil society on Soqotra—that is, to the project's beneficiaries.[68] Five years later, in an evaluation commissioned by the IUCN, the primary constraints faced by the subsequent project were again attributed to its alleged beneficiaries: "Tribal diversity ensures a great range of interests which are hard to bring to a consensus and land tenure issues often hindered Socotra Conservation and Development Project [*sic*] (SCDP) activities."[69] In the view of these evaluators, it was the allegedly weak state and factious communities that were responsible for having obstructed the implementation of the multi-million-dollar project(s)—and not the maladroit and divisive implementation of the project(s) that "arrested" the community's economic development.

Finally, instead of attributing their lack of progress to "land tenure issues," global conservation and development organizations might have questioned how their interventions exacerbated these conflicts. After all, the question of land tenure was not incidental to the archipelago's transformation; it was and remains *the issue* that has defined its postsocialist era. If the power and peril of maps were not evident to the foreign experts who sought to impose them, their danger was clear to the Soqotrans abroad. While I was visiting emigrant families in the Gulf (just days before the men from Qayher were imprisoned), one man showed me a hand-drawn map of Homhil illustrated under his direction by his daughter, who had never been to Soqotra. This map of the Homhil valley indicated all the settlements, built structures, land areas, *karifs*, and springs that belonged to his tribe. Additionally, he showed me his tribe's sultanate-era land deeds and encouraged me to photograph the sultan's seal, but not the deed itself. He had removed the land deeds from Soqotra, he said, so that the other tribes in Homhil could not see how much land his tribe actually owns. This way, the documents would not *cause* internal strife but could still be referred to for the sake of resolution. "How will the next generation know what belongs to which tribe?" I asked him. He told me that, during his visits to Homhil, he asks the children as they walk along beside him: "Whose spring is this? Whose trees are these? To whom does this cave belong?" This customary mapping of Homhil occurs in a discreet, grounded, and visceral manner. In contrast, the topographical survey that renders ownership legible, comparable, authoritative, fixed, and potentially public has no place in Homhil, the area it represents. For maps, as this (former) citizen of Homhil well knew, are not merely representations. They are also provocations.

CONSERVING COMMUNITY

Although the Homhil conflicts discussed here may seem anecdotal, provincial, and even dated, they exemplify the kinds of land disputes and development frustrations that plagued—and continue to plague—much of the island. During the reign of the Environment, the people of Homhil were not the only Soqotrans taking each other to court over a cave. I heard, for instance, that some five tribes had become embroiled in a dispute over Hoq cave, which had gained a new kind of value following President Saleh's promise to hire twenty guards to protect its inscriptions. But even within families, squabbles over abandoned caves and goat byres—land tenure—were common. So common that they figured centrally in Soqotri poetry as examples of how Soqotrans have strayed. The poet Ali Abdullah al-Rigdihi decried these "ridiculous land disputes" in his poem about the loss of *baraka*. In another poem, he maintained that it was precisely these disputes that were impeding Soqotrans' advancement: "The world has become developed; people visit outer space and return. / And we're still fighting over mere goat pens and two abandoned foundations."

If land grabs were bitter then—when tribesmen wrangled against the SCDP/EPA's environmental restrictions and for external support—they became even more caustic and consequential following the collapse of the Saleh regime. On the one hand, property values had already skyrocketed following Soqotra's recognition as a World Heritage Site.[70] On the other hand, the underfunded Soqotra EPA branch was no longer able to enforce the zoning plan preventing the development or sale of Soqotra's protected regions. By the end of 2013, Soqotra's entire northern beachfront was scored by low boundary walls and stone cairns: a sign of recent land divisions and acquisitions. Soqotrans complained that a foreign buyer they called "al-Kuwaiti"—who, presumably, came from Kuwait but was working as a middleman for other Gulf-based investors— had purchased numerous coastal properties for hotel and resort development. The problem had become so acute that the government declared that it would cancel all land sales to foreign nationals. (This was before the outbreak of the war when the government still had this power; as this book goes to press, in 2018, land acquisition by foreign nationals has only increased.) When a member of the 2013 IUCN evaluation team asked some fishermen on the southern coast why people were selling their land, one replied, "Soqotrans don't know better. They're stupid—beasts."

As for Homhil, eventually, its inhabitants found a way to resolve their land and power struggles, thus avoiding the descent into social discord (*fitna*) that my hosts had feared. When I returned in the following years, I was surprised to find the women of Riged and Qayher spending their afternoons together, but perhaps I should not have been. After all, with the withdrawal of PARITER from the area and the effective collapse of the ICDPs following Soqotra's World Heritage recognition, there were fewer foreign projects and resources to divide them. Still, the NGOs that did introduce new projects continued to try to map their own vision of community onto the social and natural landscape. As a result, a highly coveted Arab-style house for the newly established women's association was constructed but never used; located on one man's property, this donor-funded house will eventually become his.[71] Similarly, another home-garden project channeled its aid to the same families who had benefited most from the campground. On the face of it, my friends appeared to take these individual gains in stride, chalking them up to their beneficiary's God-given fortune. Meanwhile, all of the villages have expanded as their youth—including Yaqub, Tariq, and Nur—married and moved into new, so-called Arab (cement) houses next to their parents' Bedouin ones. Today, each of the houses in Qayher receives piped water directly from the Di-Zahrin spring through a network of uPVC pipes cobbled together by its residents. This, perhaps more than anything, has helped these women come closer to living, as the poet Di-Girigoti had imagined, "a life of ease." Consequently, the women no longer commingle at the village tank, which has long gone dry. "The *birka* is only ornamental these days," Yaqub mused, as I noted that this former social practice had been disturbed.

It is in disturbed ground that weeds flourish.[72] I end with a tale of weeds, for it encapsulates one of the few conservation initiatives executed during the peak of Homhil's development (2004–2006) that directly (monetarily) benefited *all* of its inhabitants, despite it having been regarded as a failure by the SCDP. In Homhil, as elsewhere in Soqotra, the settlement areas and riverbeds are dappled with the bright yellow flowers of the Mexican poppy (*Argemone mexicana*) (Soq.: *miranniha*), an invasive and "alien" weed.[73] In March 2005, when the location of the community garden was being negotiated, a USAID agricultural officer and his staff visited Soqotra to explore a USD 500,000 Community-Based Livestock Development and Marketing Project to be funded by the US embassy in Sanaa. During the visit to Homhil, the agricultural officer noticed the *Argemone mexicana* thriving in the dried riverbeds and noted that these were the same weeds that disturbed his ranch in Texas—where, he said, his Mexican workers were paid to eradicate them. The agricultural officer advised the SCDP manager accompanying him to pay the children of Homhil to pull these "invasive" weeds to prohibit them from harming the native, "endemic" species: perhaps five riyals (one US penny) per weed, he suggested. The SCDP manager agreed and asked me to supervise the endeavor.

The next day, while attempting to substitute for the four out of seven teachers who were absent, I told the waiting fourth-graders to pull up the *miranniha* surrounding the school. Even with the promise of five riyals per plant, the pupils were skeptical about the value of this exercise; the stems, after all, were quite prickly. However, by the time the break ended and some hundred stems had been uprooted, every child had become a motivated gardener. Together, the teacher Hamdan and I continued counting and recording the numbers of *miranniha* removed long after the school day had ended—by the time we returned to Qayher, adults were interested in weeding, too. My neighbor Denowiha, who claimed the entire space surrounding her house, my house, and the teachers' house as hers, and shooed the children away, extracted enough weeds in that one afternoon to earn YER 2,000: the same amount as Social Welfare Fund's monthly stipend. Because this project had started at the school, which the majority of the area's children attend, each of the Homhil families knew about it and could choose whether or not to participate. All did. Men, without salaries, weeded in their young daughters' names. Others joined their wives and children, weeding as families to generate more income than they could normally earn in months. After the first three days—and approximately twenty thousand plants eradicated—the people of Homhil finally decelerated their efforts, worried that they might bankrupt the SCDP through their labor. The SCDP management, now fully aware of its (USAID's) blunder, renegotiated the terms to one riyal for "small" plants and two riyals for "large" ones. The work of measuring the dead plants, while also counting and recording them, was left to the teachers who were each promised a *futa* (a cloth wrap worn by men) for their substantial efforts. (I, too, was busy counting, but not as busy as the teachers who complained affectionately of being awoken at dawn to measure weeds.) Even with these new terms, the people of Homhil were pleased; about USD 1,000 was injected into the protected area this way—four times more than their Association had earned from the campground fees during the entire 2004–2005 tourism season. Thus, this offhand comment by a visiting USAID expert resulted in one of the most lucrative and far-reaching projects introduced to the protected area until that point.

Community development rests on the notion that the welfare of the individual (or family) is subsumed under the greater welfare of the community (or tribe). In the SCDP's efforts to develop Soqotra's protected areas, this belief manifested itself in the assumptions that an environmental ecosystem supported a single socioeconomic community; that even individually managed enterprises (i.e., the campground) could benefit everyone in this community; and that individuals would give of their time freely to invest in its potential, collective good. In this sense, the failures of these "integrated" projects stem as much from the inherent contradictions between these projects' neoliberal aims and quasi-socialist suppositions as they do from the paradoxical nature of their conservation-as-development approach. For both the SCDP and PARITER interventions—whether conceived as "conservation with capitalism as its instrument or capitalism with conservation as its instrument"[74]—anticipated the Homhil residents becoming self-reliant, market oriented, and private entrepreneurs, all the while depending on them to function as an interreliant and communally oriented cooperative. Blind to their contradictions, these projects are unlikely to have grappled with the notion that "development has never been more than a pretext for expanding the realm of the commodity."[75] Consequently, in Homhil, it was not the environment that was being conserved through the development brought to the community as much as it was the environment that was being developed—and, consequently, the *community* that required conservation. The citizens of Homhil recognized this conundrum and calculated the worth of their investments—land and time—against the value of anticipated returns. When the returns were "endemic" infighting, even those who had benefited directly from the establishment of the protected area started to question the value of its alienating effects.

FIGURE 10. Soqotra Folk Museum, Riqeleh, 2013.

CHAPTER 5

REORIENTING HERITAGE

Soqotra is an ocean jewel resembled by no other.
Her reputation throughout the world is well known.
But this trauma has been stamped upon her body.
The wound remains open and will not heal quickly.

—*Hajar al-Asas, "The Foundation Stone"*

In early 2003, several audiocassettes made their way from Oman and the UAE to Soqotra, where they were swiftly dubbed and disseminated. Captured on these cassettes was the voice of a Soqotran emigrant (then, an Omani citizen) reciting his newest poem, "The Foundation Stone" (*Hajar al-Asas*): a twenty-minute elegy about the 1974 Haybak executions of Sultan Isa's relatives and vizier. Even to my ears, an outsider with only partial understanding of the Soqotri language and historical context, the poem was—and remains—stirring. For the islanders, who had long regarded any mention of this event as an unspeakable blight on their past and an incitement to discord (*fitna*) in the present, the poem was electrifying, if not incendiary. Indeed, when the adult son of one of the "martyrs" boomed the cassette directly outside a shop owned by one of the alleged perpetrators, a street brawl ensued. Eventually, the bereaved son and his father's accused executioner were pried apart. But the poet's outcry, thirty years after Haybak, reverberated throughout the island with every cassette that exchanged hands: "Where are the avengers? / Why have you forsaken them?" Why have you forsaken *us*?

In the same years that the islanders countenanced the arrival of the conservation regime, they found themselves contending with the burgeoning influence of the diaspora in local politics. This influence was manifest materially through the emigrants' growing entanglement in land disputes and incipient investments in hotels, restaurants, and trade. It was also manifest ideologically through their various attempts to frame Soqotran identity, culture, history, and heritage *against* the formulations of international, state, and local actors. This ideological investment in Soqotran heritage acquired an acute sense of urgency in the mid-2000s, it seemed, precisely because of the island's ascendant reputation as a globally significant ecoregion and a national treasure. For at the same time that Soqotra was gaining prominence nationally and internationally, it seemed to be losing—according to its emigrants, at least—more and more of its distinctive identity, culture, and traditions. Due to Soqotra's prior protection as a restricted military site and the climate of fear precipitated by the 1974 executions, an entire generation of Soqotran emigrants—including the composer of "The Foundation Stone"—had been exiled from their homeland for a good twenty to twenty-five years. Those who returned following Yemen's unification were surprised to see just how much had changed. Bu Abbas, a Soqotran resident of Ajman (and UAE citizen), waxed nostalgic about the sultanate-era customs of conservation, cooperation, and mutual aid. "Life was orderly then," he said, detailing how all land-use and social practices had been highly regulated—before the socialists arrived and upended everything. Ahmad Sa'd, a Soqotran citizen of Oman and founder of the island's first museum, recalled his dismay when he first returned in 1991 to discover that all that he had remembered from his early youth—from camel transport to traditional apparel—seemed in danger of disappearing. As he put it, "People on the island had no interest in their past. Everything they had had was gone: the silver [jewelry] was gone—everything was gone." Like Ahmad Sa'd, Bu Abbas accused the islanders of neglecting their natural environment and their past. Nowadays, everyone wants a salary, he bemoaned; the youth flock to Hadibo, leaving the herding to old men; pastoralism will soon be abandoned; and the Soqotri language will become increasingly endangered, too. In their view, whatever customs had not been lost to socialism were being swiftly rejected by the youth, a generation in thrall to Gulf-style development.

It is now well established among scholars of critical heritage studies that heritage is not simply a set of past objects, places, or practices with inherent values to be preserved in the present. Rather, heritage—which is always a form of "heritage making"—is a present-day process of assembling certain pasts with the view to "assembling futures."[1] In this sense, heritage making is "a material-discursive process in which past and future arise out of dialogue and encounter between multiple embodied subjects in (and with) the present."[2] In the Arab Gulf States, where heritage is a booming industry, the breakneck construction of futuristic, cosmopolitan, and global cities has been scaffolded by the production of traditional, tribal, and homogenous pasts. Scholars interested in these (largely state-sponsored) heritage festivals, museums, sports, and other pageantries have rightly criticized their erasures of national socioeconomic diversity, prenational ethnic hybridity, and centuries-long cosmopolitan connectivity.[3] But such analyses tend to overlook if not erase the heterogeneity of this "material-discursive process" *as a process*. As a result, some dismiss these heritage projects as inauthentic reenactments of Orientalist fantasies: all brand and no substance; "the copy of the copy without an original."[4] Others position them as the products of encounters and partnerships between global (Western, cosmopolitan, modern, transnational) and local (Arab, national, traditional, autochtonous) discourses, experts, audiences and constituents.[5] But what of the debates, histories, and materials that disrupt these local-global distinctions—and, with them, the tired premise that only the global is cosmopolitan?[6] The following examination of the Soqotran diaspora's vital engagement in heritage-making practices in Soqotra underscores "the heterogeneity between and across these various domains of practice which undermines and complicates such simple dichotomies."[7]

In Soqotra, heritage materialized in the first decade of the twenty-first century as an effective arena for expansive modes of governance, nascent forms of political activism, and developing conceptions of sovereignty. Undoubtedly, the concept of heritage as a strategic resource gained currency largely as a result of the international investment in the Soqotra Archipelago as a World Heritage Site. This international and state focus on Soqotra's natural heritage generated a concerted interest among Soqotrans in their cultural heritage: a heritage that they could better define and control—and thus profit from. However, rather than perceive this solely as a local rejoinder to a Western and Eurocentric "authorized heritage discourse,"[8] we should comprehend the emergence of cultural heritage on Soqotra as a dialogical encounter between and among various (local) islanders, (Western and Arab) experts, and (transnational) emigrant communities—each drawing on what Margaret Litvin, in her work on the Arab reception of Shakespeare, characterizes as a "global kaleidoscope" of influences.[9] This chapter seeks to pinpoint some of these variegated influences by looking to the ways in which the Soqotran diaspora sought to reorient Soqotran heritage from nature to culture; from Soqotran autochthony to Arab descent; from Indian Ocean hybridity to genealogical purity; and from the Yemeni nation to the transnational Gulf.

SOQOTRAN IMMIGRATION TO THE ARAB GULF

In 2004, at the time of Yemen's last population census, there were approximately forty-three thousand people living on Soqotra.[10] That same year, the officially recognized shaykhs of the Soqotran emigrant communities in the UAE and in Oman estimated that roughly five thousand Soqotrans resided overseas—predominantly in the UAE but also in Oman, Bahrain, Saudi Arabia, and Qatar. If this is true, then more than one in ten Soqotrans were living in the Gulf. Even if these figures were (or have become) inaccurate, this proportion of Soqotrans in the diaspora—at least 10 percent—seems plausible. Indeed, the majority of extended households in Soqotra can point to one or more Gulf-based family members or relatives whom they continue to depend on for remittances, food shipments, and emergency assistance. Households that lack these Gulf connections often try to leverage whatever resources they have by sending their sons abroad or by marrying their daughters to Omani or Emirati citizens (preferably, but not always, of Soqotran origin). And it is precisely these—to outsiders, often invisible—networks that have prevented the islanders from being completely isolated even when the archipelago has been seasonally or militarily "closed."

Soqotrans have migrated for various reasons. Nonetheless, it is possible to identify three principal waves of this migration flow that correspond, roughly, with Soqotra's past three regimes. The first wave, which lasted until the late 1960s, can be characterized largely by the migration of young men in search of a living at sea or in the commercial port towns of the pre-oil Gulf. Of course, coastal Soqotra was itself populated by seamen, tribesmen, merchants, and slaves who had migrated there (voluntarily or involuntary) from Yemen, Oman and the Trucial States, India, and East Africa. When British political officers began regularly surveying the island during their wartime occupation of Soqotra, they noted that its population comprised several ethno-socioeconomic "classes": the ruling Mahra sultans and tribesmen; the admin-

istrative strata of sayyids from the Hadhramawt who were generally powerless
but acted as the sultans' agents; Arab merchants from Muscat, Dubai, and
Ajman, many of them "sons of dhow captains who have taken Soqotran wives";
Somali fishermen and pearl divers (expelled in 1941); Africans from Zanzibar,
Mombasa, and Nubia whose ancestors had been enslaved (including the few
who remained enslaved by the sultan and principal merchants into the 1950s);
and, finally, the "real Soqotrans" (often referred to as Bedouin), "most of whom
live[d] inland."[11] Migration to and from Soqotra was determined by the Indian
Ocean trade networks, which made the island, "in normal times . . . a centre of
the dhow traffic of the Gulf."[12] But apart from the handful of island merchants
who themselves owned dhows that they or their captains (*nakhodas*) plied between India, Oman, and Zanzibar, prior to the 1950s few Soqotrans and even
fewer so-called Bedouin proceeded overseas.

Those who did travel the seas as seasonal labor migrants in the first half of
the twentieth century worked primarily as divers, haulers, and crewmen on
Gulf-based pearling vessels. Soqotra had its own oyster beds from which its
(predominantly African) divers recovered enough pearls and mother-of-pearl
for export. These beds also attracted foreign buyers and divers from Somalia,
India, and the Trucial States. Nevertheless, so poor were the Soqotrans and "so
great [wa]s the need for labor in the Trucial pearleries" that boats "from as far
away as Socotra" sailed into the Gulf to "join the pearl fishing" there.[13] Despite
the severe pressures placed on the Gulf pearling industry by the Depression
of the 1930s and the introduction of the Japanese cultured pearl, pearling
continued as a necessary form of seasonal labor in the Trucial States—and in
Soqotra—into the 1950s.[14] In 1933, for example, the political agent in Bahrain
noted that "a number of poor men came from the Mahri coast and Socotra in
the diving season."[15] A decade later, British officers noted that "a large number
of Socotrans are engaged in the pearl fishery"—likely due to their "indebt-
edness" in an industry fueled by systemic debt.[16] While by no means large
in comparison to the Trucial States' figures, the absence of these "some 100
coolies from the seaboard" resulted in the British garrison facing a labor shortage.[17] Moreover, despite the economic disruptions caused by World War II and
the heavy taxation imposed by the newly independent Government of India
(which struck yet another blow to the Gulf pearling industry), the export of
Soqotran pearl shell remained an "important industry" into the latter half of

the 1940s.[18] British administrative records provide glimpses of the ways in which coastal Soqotrans continued to dive for and export pearl shell from the island as late as 1960.[19]

By then, however, a good portion of the Gulf's pearling labor force had been absorbed into the developing oil industry.[20] Soqotran labor migration reflected these changes. Starting in the mid-1950s, large numbers of young men traveled by dhow from Soqotra to al-Mahra to Muscat to Dubai, Doha, or Dammam to work as unskilled labor migrants in the rising petro-economies of the Gulf. And it was not merely the number of migrants that expanded; this new outflow included pastoralists from Soqotra's interior as well. Several youths from Homhil, for example, traveled to Dammam in the 1960s, where they found work in agriculture or as "houseboys." Many Soqotrans migrated cyclically, sailing annually from Soqotra to the Gulf and back; others had planned to work for several years before returning home. By 1966, enough Soqotrans were migrating for the assistant British adviser in al-Mukalla, G. H. Brown, to list "emigrant labour" as Soqotra's "most important" export—followed by dried fish and ghee. Based on his three-month survey of Soqotra's socioeconomic conditions, Brown estimated that, out of a total population of 11,220, "about 70 of the Bedu and 160 or 170 of the plainsmen are likely to be employed overseas at any one time"; elsewhere in his report he estimated that "one in every three to four ablebodied men" from among the coastal plainsmen was overseas at any given time.[21] Whether or not these figures appear significant today, it is the first record I have seen of British officials having counted "labor" among Soqotra's exports at all.[22]

If this first wave of migration was economically driven, the second wave—in the years directly following the collapse of the sultanate—was propelled by politics and fear. Between 1967, when the National Liberation Front (NLF) entered Soqotra, and 1972, when state prohibitions on foreign travel took effect, hundreds of men, women, and children (roughly three to four boatsful, one emigrant recalled) fled from Soqotra to the Gulf States each year. Ibrahim, a traditional healer (*tabib sha'bi*) whom I met in Salalah in 2005, told me the story of his departure from Soqotra in 1968. After five days at sea, the dhow (*linj*) carrying him and approximately 150 men and women reached "Muscat" (possibly Sur), where they were detained for a week by the British authorities while they investigated whether the passengers were truly Soqotran, as they had claimed, or "Adenese," as the British feared. After finally having been granted entry into Ras al-Khaimah, Ibrahim moved to Bahrain and eventually Salalah, where he fought on behalf of the sultan of Muscat and Oman *against* the Dhofar Rebellion, was awarded Omani citizenship, and settled down. Indeed, most of the Soqotrans who had managed to flee during this period became naturalized Emirati, Omani, or Saudi citizens. Unlike their island relatives, these Soqotrans and their offspring never became—and may never be—Yemeni nationals.

Archival records chronicle a similar incident of the British HMS *Zulu* intercepting an Ajman-bound dhow off Sur in June 1969.[23] Whether this was Ibrahim's *linj* (memory can be faulty) or another dhow altogether, these episodes illuminate the special status enjoyed by Soqotran—as opposed to Yemeni—migrants in the Trucial States (and later, in the UAE). When intercepted, the *nakhoda* claimed his passengers were Soqotrans, "whose ancestors had come to the island from Ajman" and "were now obliged to return to their original homeland owing to the bad conditions in Socotra."[24] This occurred just a week before the 22 June internal coup known as the "Corrective Move," marking the triumph of the leftist wing of the NLF and the transformation of South Yemen into the socialist People's Democratic Republic of Yemen. Concerned about unfettered and "illegal" immigration into the Trucial States, the British political agent in Dubai consulted with the deputy ruler of Ajman, Shaykh Humayd bin Rashid al Nu'aimi (r. 1981–present) who, "to my surprise, confirmed the story about the ancestral links between Ajman and Socotra":

> He said that at one time you could buy a bride on the island for as little as 10 or 20 Riyals, and a lot of Ajmanese had taken advantage of this situation to marry and establish families there. There was correspondence between the two places via Aden, and Humaid had heard that conditions in Socotra lately had become difficult. If this was where these people were coming from, he was quite prepared to let them in.[25]

Indeed, the rulers of Ajman, Sharjah, and Dubai all expressed their willingness to accept these—and any—Soqotrans. However, still worried that there might be some Adenese among the dhow's 145 largely undocumented passengers who had by then arrived in Ajman, the political agent detained them for questioning. Six days later, having ascertained that they were truly Soqotrans, the political agent released these undocumented immigrants who, he presumed, were "now being absorbed into the economy in the usual way, although the many fishermen and goatherds amongst them may not take kindly to the kind of casual labour which they are likely to be offered."[26] Despite a strict new immigration law having come into effect in Abu Dhabi just one month earlier (on 1 May 1969), the rulers' exception of these undocumented (and thus, by the new law, "illegal") Soqotrans was based on the widespread recognition of the historical and genealogical links that had long connected Soqotra to the Arab Gulf.[27]

However, by the mid-1970s, this corridor was essentially blocked due to the travel and trade restrictions imposed by the PDRY government. While some Soqotrans managed to journey between Soqotra and the Gulf or to send for the families they had left behind, most former labor migrants found themselves in de facto exile from their island home. This is not to say that migration in and from Soqotra ceased. Internal migration from the interior to the large coastal settlements (Hadibo and Qalansiyah) increased from the mid-1970s into the 1980s as more paid labor became available locally in the form of army, police, and government posts.[28] Others migrated to the Yemen mainland for labor or education. One of the notable accomplishments of the socialist administration in South Yemen was that it established sixteen coeducational elementary schools across Soqotra, including the boarding school for nomadic youth discussed earlier.[29] Many of these students went to Aden for their secondary schooling; a number were sent on to Moscow, Dresden, and Havana for higher education in fields such as medicine, education, mechanics, secretarial work, and factory management. Plenty of Soqotrans migrated during this period of Soqotra's closure—just not to the Gulf region, where their émigré relatives were prospering.

The third (and ongoing) phase of migration—this one, largely economic— commenced with the opening of Soqotra following Yemen's unification. In Chapter 1, I discussed that Soqotra's Gulf emigrants began visiting the island in the early 1990s, many returning to their childhood homes for the first time in twenty years. As long-separated brothers embraced one another again, as Soqotran and Emirati cousins met for the first time, as Emirati citizens procured visit and work visas for their island relatives, as aging emigrants sought "cheap" and compliant second or third wives, the historic Soqotra-Gulf connections were reawakened and mobilized. It is difficult to say how many Soqotrans have migrated to the Gulf since. What is clear is that the majority of

Soqotrans live in Bani Yas (in Abu Dhabi) or Ajman and Ras al-Khaimah (the northern emirates), where they have typically been employed by the police or military. Most received government entitlements, such as free housing and health care, as reserved for Emirati citizens. (This my emigrant friends attribute to the late Shaykh Zayed's reputed affection for Soqotrans.) And many have become naturalized Emirati citizens during the past two decades—in a country where citizenship is based on the principle of *jus sanguinis* and naturalization is exceptional. However, in the wake of the Arab uprisings and with the war in Yemen, Soqotrans' mobility has become restricted once again. This time, it is not the Yemeni state that is prohibiting their migration to the Gulf but the Gulf States that are denying nearly all Yemeni citizens visas regardless of the Soqotrans' once-special status.[30]

One aspect of Soqotran-Gulf migration that has not significantly altered or diminished over time—if anything, it has proliferated—is the unidirectional migration of Soqotran women to the Gulf. If labor was Soqotra's primary export in 1966, from circa 2006 onward it has been brides. My aim in these pages has been to show how Soqotra has been long wed to the Arab Gulf through trade, migrant labor, immigration, remittances, special dispensations, and government and private aid. Yet many of the connections undergirding these exchanges were forged precisely through marriage. Whereas the British surveyors of so-called coolie labor and the island's economic conditions tallied only the men employed abroad at any one time, it was the small but steady outflow of women—as deported witches and imported wives—that engendered the genealogical connections that sustained all of these relationships. We have seen indications of this already in the references to "Ajamese" seamen taking inexpensive Soqotran wives, whose affordability remains a major draw to this day. For example, if "at one [unspecified] time" Soqotran brides cost "as little as 10 or 20 Riyals," in 1942, they could be "purchased" for "thirty to forty [Maria Theresa] dollars" (often called riyals)—still "cheap," according to the visiting political officer who happened to note that a good date palm cost five dollars then.[31] A decade later the political officer for al-Mahra also noted that "seamen from Dhubai . . . have married there for several generations."[32] Even then, this tradition continued: that same year, the Ras al-Khaimah–born captain, Khalifa bin Mohammad al-Fuqaei, stopped in Soqotra on his return from Zanzibar to Muscat "to buy food and water and allow some of the men to marry local women."³³ Meanwhile, the alleged witches deported from the island as late as the 1960s also ended up marrying subjects (later, rent-receiving citizens) from Oman and the Trucial States. And it was their naturalization in the Gulf as a result of their banishment from Soqotra that eventually—fortuitously—enabled them to sustain their relatives back home.

If these transpelagic marriages were curtailed during the socialist decades (1970s and 1980s), they were among the first linkages revived following the opening of Soqotra in the 1990s. Visiting Soqotran emigrants (and also poorer men from the Gulf) were eager for a Soqotran wife—a girl whose bride price was relatively affordable; a woman who embodied Soqotran customs—for themselves or their Gulf-raised sons. Soqotran girls longed for a man from the Emirates who could offer them modern comforts and consumer luxuries once unimaginable on the island: running water, an air-conditioned home, a new SUV, a housemaid, more diverse food (fruits and vegetables), beautiful clothing, sumptuous gold. For their parents, these marriages were a conduit to remittances for them and Gulf citizenship for their grandchildren, if not their own emigration. In the mid-2000s, I met numerous young girls who dreamed of marrying their cousins in the Gulf. But a decade later, the marriage of young Soqotran girls to geriatric Emirati, Omani, and even mainland Yemeni men with no prior connection to the island had become a common enough occurrence to be viewed by both island and emigrant Soqotrans as a pressing social problem. Once again, Gulf men were traveling to Soqotra for the purpose of marrying local women cheaply. Islanders I know were scandalized by the stories of rich Emirati men who sent for their child-brides after having sent their new brother-in-law the latest-model SUV or by Omani men who visited Soqotra as tourists only for the sake of getting married in Hadibo's Taj Suqutra (Crown of Soqotra) hotel. (One Soqotran official told me that when he visited the Yemen consul in Dubai, a Yemeni woman working there asked him, "What's going on in Soqotra? The trade of Soqotran women?") What was especially worrisome to the Soqotrans with whom I discussed this phenomenon was not only the ages of the brides or the likelihood of them being divorced within weeks of their hotel weddings but also the rising cost of all marriages as a result. What Soqotran girl would marry a young islander without such means? Sadly, as we investigated these stories further, one of my interlocutors and I came to the conclusion that women were now among Soqotra's most viable exports—along with dragon's blood, aloe, honey, sea produce, and corals. As in 1966, it is not the number of migrants that stands out as much as the "economic value of [their] earnings."[34] When my interlocutor went to the Hadibo court to inquire into the numbers of such weddings, he was told that there had been at least twenty-five Soqotran-Gulf weddings in 2013. The court administrator wanted to know why he had asked. "Because women are our primary export!" my interlocutor said. "I completely agree," the administrator replied.

As these examples reveal, the Soqotran emigrants are thus a principal source of support and influence—as well as conflict—on the island. These exchanges, in effect, of Soqotran labor and wives for Gulf provisions, remittances, and citizenship did not begin with the opening of Soqotra in the 1990s. As noted earlier, the alleged witch I met in Abu Dhabi remitted enough money to fund the construction of a well and the first mosque in her former village in the early 1980s—and many emigrants shipped food and other goods during the socialist period. But the more that the Yemeni state encompassed Soqotra—by increasing its connectivity to the outside and extending its infrastructure within—the more the traffic and trade between Soqotra and the Gulf intensified. The bulk of Gulf support and aid for Soqotra comes from government initiatives: the UAE's Khalifa bin Zayed Al Nahyan Foundation, for example, has regularly shipped thousands of sacks of wheat, sugar, and rice to the archipelago—even before the 2015 conflict began. Yet Soqotrans continue to rely on their emigrant relatives for remittances and direct shipments (*rasa'il*) of food, cars, appliances, and building materials. In 2013, Soqotra's port director estimated that approximately half of all cargo ships received annually come from Sharjah (UAE).[35] "Everything on the island comes from the Emirates," he stressed.

This Gulf-based support, state and private, has sustained Soqotra for decades, but it has also prevented Soqotrans from truly identifying with the post-unification Yemen. Two days before I moved into the Homhil Protected Area in November 2004, Shaykh Zayed bin Sultan Al Nahyan, the revered founder and first president of the UAE, passed away. The Soqotrans I met spoke as if their own leader had died. I started to realize in those early months—when school-age children could not identify Yemen's capital but went to sleep to lullabies about "cars from Ras al-Khaimah"; or when the residents of Qayher discovered that they had broken their Ramadan fast a day earlier than the rest of the country because they had followed an Emirati broadcast rather than a Yemeni one—just how pervasive this Gulf orientation was. This is only natural, given the various personal connections that sustain the islanders. But it was also to some degree driven by the Soqotran emigrants themselves, who were vying to define Soqotran heritage, identity, and culture at a time when international, state, and local actors were advancing competing definitions. These diasporic claims to Soqotra were staked through cassette poetry, history texts, jewelry collections, and other material culture—dispatches from the Gulf that eclipse the shipments of foods and goods. Here, we turn to these "provisions" and the debates they sustained.

THE CALL OF AL-ZAHRA

In 2001, a Soqotran historian residing in the UAE, Ahmad Said Khamis al-Anbali, published and distributed a collection of historical texts whose translated title is *Soqotra, the Garments of Silk Brocade: A Commentary on the Poem of the Soqotran al-Zahra*. The nucleus of this collection, as its title suggests, is a ninth-century Arabic elegiac poem attributed to a Soqotran woman named al-Zahra.[36] In this elegy, al-Zahra beseeches Oman's then-ruling Ibadi imam, as-Salt bin Malik al-Khurusi (r. 851–886 CE), to come to the aid of the island's Muslim settlers who were besieged by its Christian population. According to the sources, al-Zahra's description of the bloody Christian rebellion against Soqotra's Ibadi regent governor was the call that launched "a hundred and one ships."[37] Imam as-Salt dispatched a fleet to retake Soqotra—the Omanis had colonized the island a century earlier[38]—but instructed his commanders to remove any Muslims who so wished, given that Soqotra was no longer hospitable to them.[39] Following this insurrection, which emboldened the imam's internal opposition, who promptly deposed him,[40] Soqotra reverted to Christian rule with ecclesiastic connections to Baghdad. Accordingly, several tenth-century Arab geographers attested to its "barbaric" majority-Christian population—as does al-Zahra herself.[41] However, exceptional as it is to recover the verses of a ninth-century female poet—especially were she truly Soqotran—this was not al-Anbali's primary motivation for resurrecting this "buried heritage."[42] More important, al-Anbali reads in this account of a millennium-old Christian aggression against Soqotrans an allegory of the near-global oppression of

Muslims today. At the same time, he hears in her call the demand for an "indigenous" response to foreign aggression and domination. Questions of historicity and credibility aside, the call of al-Zahra, al-Anbali argues, is a call that "reverberates through history, troubling generations of listeners and inciting the concerns of men."[43] It called out to al-Anbali, too.

Al-Anbali was one of those many young Soqotrans who left his pastoral home during the sultanate era to seek his livelihood abroad. Born and raised in a traditional uncoursed stone house in an isolated hamlet edging Soqotra's southern plateau, he came of age, as he describes in poetic detail in his *History of the Island of Soqotra*, herding his goats in the ravines in the late afternoons and cultivating date palms in the riverbeds.[44] This was in the time of Sultan Isa, a time of witch doctors, banished witches, drought, and hunger. But it was also the time of Soqotra's regular dhow connections to India, East Africa, and the Gulf; of British scientific expeditions to the island; of British imperial expansion into al-Mahra; of oil explorations in al-Mahra's deserts and oil rents in Sultan Isa's bank account; and of Arab nationalist currents reaching the island in gusts. In 1967, at the age of fourteen, al-Anbali departed for the Gulf. "We went, many of us, over a hundred young men," he told me when I dropped in on him during one of his return visits to this rural, childhood home. This was in 2007, precisely forty years after his initial migration. "All of them like me, maybe fourteen or fifteen years old, some older, some younger. We went. And we didn't know where we were going. We had nothing with us: no goods, no knowledge, no plan in our heads, nothing. What was important was that we went with God's blessing. And when we reached Dubai, the older ones—the ones who had traveled before us—we followed them wherever they went and went with them." Al-Anbali landed in Bahrain, where he found casual labor through the help of his cousin. Two months later, and severely homesick, he told his cousin, "That's enough; I'm going back to Soqotra." But it was then that the emigrants received word that their sultanate had been overthrown. So instead of returning home, al-Anbali moved to Saudi Arabia, where he worked various odd jobs for about a year. He then moved to Qatar, where he labored, studied (attending school for the first time), married, and had children. Eventually, he ended up in Ajman.

It was in Qatar, while browsing through volumes in the National Library in 1973, that al-Anbali happened to come across the poem of al-Zahra in the

Omani scholar al-Salimi's *Tuhfat al-a'yan bi-sirat ahl 'Uman* (A treasure of notable men from the history of the people of Oman).[45] He had heard about the Soqotran al-Zahra in his youth, he writes, but had not known that her verses had been recorded, much less where he might find them. (Later, he found and purchased a copy of al-Salimi's history in a bookstore in Oman.) Overjoyed by this discovery, al-Anbali set himself the task of collecting and reading all that had he could find on Soqotra. Noticing that the majority of European scholars and visitors writing about Soqotra "describe [its] current inhabitants according to how those who lived there ten centuries ago were described," he became convinced of the need for a history written by "one of the island's sons."[46] That is, if the call of al-Zahra did not in actuality spark an Omani naval expedition to save "Soqotran" (Ibadi) Muslims from Christian aggression, it did inspire a Soqotran emigrant in the Arab Gulf to seek to liberate Soqotran knowledge production (and knowledge about the island) from its dependence on "the books of foreigners who came as invaders of Muslim countries."[47]

Although my focus here is on the repatriation of the al-Zahra elegy and legacy from Oman to Soqotra rather than on the poem itself, it is necessary to briefly summarize its content.[48] The poet begins with the request that the "virtuous" and "noble" imam (as-Salt) be informed that the once pious, prosperous, and verdant island "has become destitute of Islam." Where sharia law, the Qur'an, and the call to prayer (*adhan*) once governed, now reigned sin, ignoble "offspring," and the sounds of wooden clappers (*nawaqis*, used by Eastern Christians instead of bells). These immoral Christians "reared by violence and plundering" rose up and killed the imam's governor of Soqotra and the island's noblemen. They even seized the island's Muslim women, who were "calling out in sorrow, wailing with grief." After describing how the "barbarians" raped the women, young virgins and widows alike, the poet decries the absence of external help: "What is in the mind of as-Salt that he can sleep the night away / while in Soqotra rape descends upon the women?" Reproaching the imam for his inaction, the poet demands that he and his men "save every Muslim woman / even if you have to crawl on your chins and knees" until Islam has been revived. Only then, continues the poet, will "the call of al-Zahra be fulfilled . . . / and the prayer for our Lord the Prophet carried out."[49]

Given the relative rarity of female poets in the early Abbasid period (750–1258 CE) and the unknown origin of al-Salimi's source(s) for the elegy and the imam's instructions to his fleet, historians have debated the historicity of the event, the identity of the poet, and the provenance of the "Christian" attackers. In his publication, al-Anbali aims to put these questions to rest. What we do know, he tells us, is that the woman referred to as al-Zahra was Fatima bint Ahmad b. Muhammad al-Jahdamiyya, the "relative" (possibly niece) of Imam as-Salt's regent governor on Soqotra, Qasim b. Muhammad al-Jahdami al-Samadi.[50] Acknowledging reasons for skepticism regarding the poet's Soqotran identity—after all, the form and elegance of this classical Arabic *ritha'* indicates that this ninth-century poet was highly educated, more literate than many Soqotrans are today—al-Anbali emphasizes that "all those who have written about her mention that she was Soqotran."[51] (In fact, he says, al-Zahra serves as a reminder that women can be fine poets, too.) Al-Anbali argues that al-Zahra composing verses in Arabic rather than Soqotri means that al-Zahra was an Arab Muslim inhabitant of Soqotra at a time *preceding* the arrival of the "Himyaritic dialect" (meaning Soqotri). In this way, al-Anbali seeks to yoke Soqotran identity to Arabs, Arabic, and Islam. This matters because he rejects the Western scholarship that depicts contemporary Soqotrans as multiracial descendants of the island's former Indian, Greek (Christian), and Arab settlers.[52] Determined to correct their "disdainful" error of attributing such false and "slanderous" genealogies to Soqotrans, al-Anbali insists that the island's "current inhabitants are Arab Muslims with none of the older races remaining."[53] Accordingly, this Soqotran-born Emirati citizen holds up al-Zahra as evidence for the Soqotrans' enduring genealogical purity, while, at the same time, implicitly rejecting Soqotri as an autochthonous or even a distinctive language.

Just as there is uncertainty about the origins of al-Zahra, there is debate about the origins of the pillaging Christians. Some scholars, as well as several Soqotrans with whom I discussed this event, confuse them with the Portuguese who occupied a fort near Suq from 1507 to 1511.[54] Others believe that Abyssinian Christians had conquered the island; indeed, Imam as-Salt's exhaustive missive to his troops instructs them to drive the invaders as far as possible, even if it meant pursuing them to the Horn of Africa (*ras al-zanj*).[55] But al-Anbali challenges these (mis)conceptions. In his view, the attackers were most likely

the Christian(ized) descendants of Greek settlers who had colonized Soqotra
during the Hellenistic period. As Christians living under Muslim rule and
protection (*dhimma*) for some decades, they would have breached or rejected
the annual peace agreement (*sulh*) contingent on a per capita tax.[56] Although
al-Anbali believes that it was these Christians who spearheaded the revolt, he
concedes that Christians from nearby Ethiopia may have come to their aid.[57]
However, what the elegy suggests—and what al-Anbali stresses—is that the violence was unleashed on Soqotra by its own progeny lacking "religion, morals
or pure lineage."[58] Significantly, for Soqotrans of al-Anbali's generation, these
were not foreigners who attacked "the best young men of Soqotra."[59] Rather, it
was the impure and ignoble "crusaders" from *within* who rose up against the
(occupying) Islamic administration.

Despite these and related questions, what matters most to al-Anbali is less
the history of the al-Zahra elegy than the legacy of her call. For "the call of
al-Zahra"—rendered by the poet in the third person—signifies not only the plea
of one Fatima bint Ahmad b. Muhammad al-Jahdamiyya but also the entreaty
of the most illustrious of Fatimas, Fatima al-Zahra the radiant: the Prophet's
youngest daughter and mother of his only grandsons. Evoking this prophetic
genealogy, this ninth-century call for help against the unbelieving aggressor becomes an allegory for all ages, reaching back to the earliest Muslim community
and forward to the inequities of the present day. Al-Anbali reminds his readers
that the Christian attack on Soqotra was not limited to the ninth century, for
the "buried Crusader hatred of Islam and Muslims" returned some six hundred
years later with the arrival of the Portuguese. Once again, "martyrs fell upon
Soqotran soil," mosques were turned into churches, and Muslim homes were
pillaged. And once again, the Arab Muslims—now under the dominion of the
Mahra sultans—rose up and "purified" the island of the Christian "menace."[60]
This threat is enduring and widespread, extending through time and across
geographies. Al-Anbali invokes this presentist, universalist reading when he
asks, "And to whom are the cries directed today? And who can help those weak
Muslims today in the eastern and western parts of the world whose sanctity is
abused in every place in clear sight and hearing of the world?"[61] The call of al-
Zahra's contemporary appeal is perhaps best demonstrated by its refashioning
as a theater piece performed in Muscat, Oman, in which the victims calling out
for help were not Soqotrans but Palestinians.[62]

Nevertheless, as al-Anbali explains, his purpose in (re)circulating "the call of al-Zahra" is neither to conjure Muslim solidarity against "crusader" occupation nor to critique the Muslim Arab leaders' somnolence. Instead, his primary motivation is more limited but concrete: to reclaim Soqotran history and heritage from Western experts. Just as the al-Zahra elegy had been unattainable to him until he had left Soqotra, much of Soqotrans' own history is obscured to them, he laments, whether because they did not record it or because the island's foreign occupants destroyed the source material. The main challenge that he and other historians face is the absence of Soqotran-authored records. And when his compatriots do write about Soqotra, he bemoans, they rely on the (mis)information culled by various Western visitors "under the guise of corporations and scientific exploration and tourism": a history "written by its colonizers."[63] During our conversation, al-Anbali recalled having encountered some of these European visitors in his youth, long before his own turn to scholarship:

> I remember when I was young. Tourists came—foreigners, be they English, German, Italian, or French, or from any other European country—they came to the island and they weren't prevented in their research, but they didn't find anyone who really understood [what they were after]. What I mean is, these researchers came and surveyed the terrain [al-'ard] and its ruins [al-athar], but they didn't benefit from [talking to] people. . . . They would come and search for shells on the coast, and we would see them and say, "Look, look at those crazy people— they are taking shells from the ground. What are they going to do with them?" They would go to the mountains and collect some rocks. *These are researchers; these are researchers.* Now, as we know, they were looking for information. But, unfortunately, when their reports were brought out or when we read some of the words they wrote, I mean, they weren't indicating the truth. There were only descriptions of what they saw of the nature of Soqotra.

It is this early and ongoing fascination with Soqotra's alien nature but Christian European past—to the exclusion of the island's present population and Arab Muslim history—that has, in his view, distorted the histories these researchers produced. What rankles al-Anbali the most is their ceaseless characterizations of Soqotrans as multiracial. Instead, he insists, over and over, that all Soqotrans are "Arabs" (with the exception of the "Africans" living in Hadibo) and that

Soqotra is "part and parcel of the Arab nation (*al-watan al-ʿarabi*), especially the Arabian Peninsula."[64]

Thus, disheartened by the speculations penned in tourists' diaries and re-cycled in Western scholarship, al-Anbali set out to write his own history of Soqotra, which he completed over a thirty-year period. Published in 2006, his Arabic-language *History of the Island of Soqotra* makes a case for Soqotra having been Arab since the dawn of time—despite including in its introduc-tion a Soqotri paragraph, transcribed using the Arabic alphabet, that delimits "authentic" knowledge of Soqotra to those who came of age as pastoralists (as did he). It does so by beginning with the ancient South Arabian kingdoms and ending with the rule of Sultan Isa. "History"—for many Soqotrans, not just al-Anbali—did not come to an end with the end of the Cold War in 1990; it ended in 1967, with the *arrival* of the socialist regime. However, this has less to do with a belief in the progression of history—or even with al-Anbali's timely departure in 1967—than it does with Soqotrans' inability to tell the history of what happened next. I asked him why this was the case. He replied:

> In my opinion, this is a difficult period to write about because there were con-troversial events during this time. Whoever writes about this period needs to have a strong character and literary courage, because blood was shed and fami-lies were violated. So, what are you going to write? These things are hard to write about and to display to the world. I would like to write about it, but I have held back and waited for another to do so.

These controversial events, like the ninth-century massacre of Muslim noble-men by the "ignoble" among them, can find expression only in elegiac poetry of the kind circulated in 2003.

Al-Anbali's slim book, *Soqotra, the Garments of Silk Brocade*, has circulated throughout the Soqotran diaspora in the UAE and Oman, as well as among the literate islanders. Additionally, multiple copies of his book were once housed in the Al-Zahra Library for Culture, the first public library on the island, opened in 2005. Located next to the hospital and near the grand state-funded mosque, both in central Hadibo, the library functioned for a few short years not only as a house of knowledge but also as a conspicuous monument to Soqotran cul-tural heritage.[65] The Soqotran "al-Zahra" had been temporarily resurrected and repatriated.

"THE FOUNDATION STONE"

If the ninth-century massacre was one of the earliest (recorded) traumas to have befallen Soqotra, the 1974 executions at Haybak may be the island's most recent (unspeakable) ordeal. Thus, these two events frame a particular narrative of Soqotran history: a history of foreign intrusions eventually vanquished by the enemy within. Notably, this narrative goes against the grain of Soqotrans' more common depiction of their island's peace and stability—especially in contrast to the profusion of weapons, kidnappings, and tribal hostilities in much of mainland Yemen, even prior to the 2015 war. When I first arrived, numerous Soqotrans extolled their island's safety: There were never troubles here, I was told; anyone can sleep outdoors without fear of disturbance; Soqotrans do not steal; they do not need weapons; there has never been a murder. When, over the course of my fieldwork, I became not only aware of but also a concerned interlocutor in conversations about break-ins, robberies, and assaults, these offenses were usually blamed on the so-called northerners or their negative influences. "Before the northerners entered, one used to be able to sleep anywhere," a young shaykh insisted, subsuming such breaches as the exception. What could not be subsumed, or comprehended, were the executions of 1974. Incompatible with the narrative of Soqotra's peace and stability, the executions have long resisted narration of any kind. The mass gravesite, located and marked a quarter century after the event, is inscribed with the spare words: "The Friday Martyrs of Soqotra, 1974." Soqotrans who may feel compelled to write about the executions, such as al-Anbali, have refrained from doing so for fear of causing further strife. The only textual references to the executions are those that have appeared obliquely in poetry.

In the months following the event now referred to as "Haybak" (after the location where the men were shot), several islanders composed poems condemning the murders. However, unlike the 2003 elegy introduced in the beginning of this chapter, the four poems that I collected from the 1970s—poems committed to memory for more than thirty years—did not reveal the perpetrators' identities. Nor were they dispatched to the island "from [across] the sea." Rather, each of these poems was addressed to the Soqotran émigrés in the Gulf, relaying both the news of the deaths and a warning against their return. Fearful for their own lives, and aware that all correspondence to and from the island was being censored, these Soqotra-based poets spoke metaphorically of the battering waves fracturing and sinking unmoored boats; of the finest livestock being swept to sea by flash floods; and of unfruitful date palms, barren in mourning. Soqotrans I met in Salalah (Oman) and Ajman (the UAE) told me that they had understood from such "epistolary" verses that prominent men had been killed.[66] But many emigrants did not know who had been executed and under what circumstances until the 1990s, following their long-deferred return to the island. Likewise, many islanders had never talked openly about this event until its early twenty-first-century recirculation through epistolary poetry by "Abu Shanab" (his nickname), a Soqotran poet living in Salalah. Abu Shanab's 2003 poem, "The Foundation Stone," subverted the narrative of peace and stability while also discounting the international and state depictions of Soqotra as a recently discovered jewel. Instead, as the epigraph to this chapter indicates, Abu Shanab chose to narrate his childhood home as he perceived it: as a body in pain from a deep-seated wound.

I met Abu Shanab in Salalah, where he had been living since the 1970s. Like al-Anbali, Abu Shanab departed Soqotra at a tender age—around eleven, he said—prior to the collapse of the sultanate. Although he had left only to ac-company an uncle seeking medical treatment in Bahrain, following his uncle's death, he ended up settling permanently on the Arabian mainland. First, Abu Shanab stayed in Bahrain, where he lived with the Saudi family who employed him. At one point, probably around 1968, he returned to Soqotra but left again shortly thereafter due to growing "problems" on the island. No longer simply an economic migrant, Abu Shanab was now among the second major wave of Soqotran emigrants fleeing the increasingly restrictive state prior to its prohibi-tion on foreign travel. Where Abu Shanab's story departs from that of many of his fellow migrants is in his attempt to unseat the NLF in Soqotra by fighting against a popular liberation front in Oman.

Abu Shanab had spent another year or two in Bahrain living with his Saudi family. It was now 1970–1971: the NLF had claimed Soqotra for South Yemen, abolishing the centuries-old Sultanate of Qishn and Soqotra; Sultan Isa and his male relatives were imprisoned in Aden; and the NLF (which had morphed into the Yemeni Socialist Party) embarked on a program of socialization, which in Soqotra amounted to the redistribution of date palms from the poor to the very poor. It was also the height of the Dhofar Rebellion (1965–1976), a guer-rilla war waged by the Popular Front for the Liberation of Oman and the Arab

Gulf (PFLOAG) to liberate the entire Gulf from imperialist powers. Opposed to the socialist regime in South Yemen (PDRY) and having been promised Omani citizenship if he fought against the insurgency in Dhofar, Abu Shanab joined an irregular counterinsurgency unit of approximately one hundred Soqotrans and fifty Mahra—this one named "the unity brigade" (*firqat al-wahda*)—to help Sultan Qaboos's armed forces defeat the PDRY-supported rebels.[67] Abu Shanab, Ibrahim, and their Soqotran peers spent months upon months on the fringes of the Empty Quarter convinced that they were battling the same revolutionary, Marxist forces that had overtaken Soqotra. "How can we return to Soqotra without putting out the fire here?" Ibrahim had asked himself then. They had also believed that once they helped defeat the Popular Front in Oman, Sultan Qaboos would liberate Soqotra from the NLF in South Yemen.

However, as early as 1972, it became clear to the Soqotran fighters that *this* Omani sultan would not dispatch a fleet to (re)take Soqotra. And by the end of 1974, most had laid down their arms. Perhaps these Soqotran counter-revolutionaries, who had by then given years of their lives to the fight against socialism, had been crushed by the rumors of executions that trickled into Salalah through poetry that year. Or perhaps they had felt defeated following PFLOAG's reorganization in July 1974 from a regional (Gulfwide) organization into two national fronts: the Popular Front in Bahrain and the Popular Front for the Liberation of Oman (PFLO). With the "Omanization" of the struggle by the PFLO, it may no longer have been so clear what the *Soqotrans* were fighting for.[68] Following the Qaboos regime's victory in 1976, approximately half of the Soqotran fighters remained in Salalah, where they received Omani citizenship for their service, and half made their way to the UAE, where they were also granted citizenship. All would have to wait until 1990, when the PDRY collapsed, to feel that it was safe for them to return to Soqotra (Yemen).

So it took them this long to discover that, on an undated Friday prior to the onset of the monsoon, Soqotran NLF members executed two of Sultan Isa's brothers, his nephew (the son of Sultan Ahmad), his vizier, a sayyid, two "Bedouin," and three noncompliant members of the NLF. Four prisoners—along with Sultan Isa, who had been imprisoned in Aden in 1967 and again in 1972–1973—narrowly escaped execution because of the eleventh-hour intervention of PDRY president Salim Rubay'a Ali, the NLF leader who had seized power during the Corrective Move of 22 June 1969. (The vizier's brother, I later heard, escaped death by rowing out to sea in a wooden dugout, where he sat out five long days, staring back at the land.) The perpetrators received life sentences in Aden, but after Rubay'a Ali was himself deposed and executed in June 1978, they were released and returned to Soqotra, where many continue to live to this day.

This was one reason for the reemergence of "Haybak poetry" three decades later and for the deferred call for justice by the Soqotrans living overseas: what the islanders had long suffered in seclusion was now circulating as news to the emigrants who had spent decades in self-exile. It was also one of the reasons that the event's early twenty-first-century recirculation through epistolary poetry alarmed the islanders. For even then, thirty years later, the islanders considered the very mention of Haybak a "raging sea" too rough to "enter." After all, the families of the so-called martyrs had lived and would continue to reside in close quarters with the executioners and their offspring. Shortly following the 1994 civil war between North and South Yemen a few of the perpetrators agreed to accompany the martyrs' relatives to the execution site to identify the mass grave. It was then that the bereaved kinsmen erected a small cemetery in the shadow of Haybak, not far from the plaque commemorating the construction of the Haybak Pass ('aqaba) by the Auxiliary Indian Pioneer Corps in 1942–1943. Despite the marked presence of this cemetery, my interlocutors continued to discuss this past event furtively, if at all. Friends became nervous whenever I tried to photograph the monument or even when I slowed while driving past it to get a better look. In fact, I first learned about Haybak from a former member of the "unity brigade" who, three months into my fieldwork, waved me into his childhood home, where he extracted a sheet of paper from his suitcase and surreptitiously proceeded to dictate to me the names of the "Friday Martyrs." At the time, I did not know why he was giving me these names or what he thought I would do with them. Repeatedly, this visiting emigrant emphasized that I should not tell other Soqotrans that I had this list, for it would mark me as an "American spy" and could lead to my deportation. But it would be acceptable, he said, if I placed the names "on the Internet" or distributed them outside Soqotra, where they would be commuted, simply, to impartial fact ('ilm).

Yet for some emigrants and some of the victims' relatives, these modest forms of expiation, commemoration, and dissemination would not be sufficient. Abu Shanab, who had fought on behalf of the Omani sultanate with the objective of restoring the Soqotran one, wanted more. It was to this end that he composed and circulated "The Foundation Stone," a poem he hoped would become the cornerstone for a concerted response. "The sultans were the base of our society," he told me after he had recited his twenty-minute elegy from memory and began to explicate its meaning: "like a house with a strong foundation, they were the cornerstone." This metaphor of the sultans as the pillar of Soqotra is not uncommon to Soqotran poetry. In 2006, I was searching for someone who had memorized the collection (*diwan*) of a deceased poet known as Karani. Upon Karani's sons' advice, I found such a person: an old gentleman walking his camel along the beach wearing Jackie O–style sunglasses. He knew just the verse I had been looking for, one composed by Karani sometime in the 1980s: "I ache for you, O ceiling beam of *talihon*, cut from the heart of the grove / Supplanted by the trunks of *i'ihahib*, all crooked and twisted. / They will not support the roof for a week before needing to be replaced." Here, the endemic *talihon* (*Zygocarpum coeruleum*), one of the hardest and finest timbers on the island, evokes the sultan who had been capable of supporting an entire house (people) on his own. His socialist successors, the twisted ceiling joists of the *i'ihahib* (*Maerua socotrana*, also endemic), are weaker and will need to be replaced again and again. In this poem, as in poems I was to hear during the Soqotra Poetry Festival in the late 2000s, memories of the sultan provoked nostalgia precisely because he was sovereign and singular. But if the sultan was the pillar of Soqotran society, as these poets suggest, what Abu Shanab laments is not simply the instability of Yemen's successive regimes. He laments also the islanders' continued inaction with regard to the Haybak executions. "Why is this shelter abandoned, and its ceiling unfinished?" he asks his listeners, suggesting that the Soqotrans have not just lost their foundation; they have abandoned it, too.

Having described his oeuvre as "action poetry" (*ash-shi'r al-fa'ili*), Abu Shanab explained that he wanted "The Foundation Stone" to be "like a toothache" that would impel Soqotrans to *do something*. Yet it is not entirely clear what kind of action Abu Shanab prescribes. On the one hand, he demands that the Soqotrans avenge these deaths, and quickly. Reminiscent of—but inversing—the call of the Soqotran al-Zahra to the sleeping imam in Oman, this Soqotran poet dispatched an elegy from Oman to Soqotra to rouse the people from their apparent indifference: "The foundation stone is calling; it cries out with the voice of the bereaved." "Do any of you disagree, or are you facing opposition?" he continues. "Have the goats [people] still not sensed the passing of the southern wind [socialist era]?" In some verses, he calls on the remaining children of the martyrs to return to the island to attend to this "open file." Advising them to withhold their mercy or even a pittance of pity, Abu Shanab appears to be advocating retributive justice: "Yesterday Haybak and today you, the wheel of history has turned./The blood of the martyrs is not lost, but still speaks to us./Where are the avengers? Why have you forsaken them?" Elsewhere, he calls on his fellow poets to metaphorically net the perpetrators, as do fishermen, with their strong lines. On the other hand, Abu Shanab insists repeatedly that the power for redress lies solely within the jurisdiction of the Yemeni state and according to sharia law. But his scattered praise of then-president Saleh as the father and leader of "the unity" comes across as strategic armor against any potential charges of sedition. After all, the most political line of the poem, according to another poet who helped me with its translation, questions whether the "wounded" Soqotra might not be better off were it separated from the paralyzed right shoulder (*al-katf al-yamin*)—that is, from Yemen (*al-yaman*).

If Abu Shanab's call for retribution raised eyebrows—fists, even—what appeared to bring my fellow listeners most discomfort was precisely his "entrance into politics" through his identification of the culprits. Again and again, I heard people say that what distinguished Abu Shanab's poem from earlier Haybak poetry was his "naming" of everyone involved. When I worked on translating "The Foundation Stone" during my stay in Qayher, my male neighbors were eager to listen along. Nevertheless, at times, they became noticeably uncomfortable—not, as I had suspected, when Abu Shanab referred directly to the "killings," which was glossed as "history," but when he began rattling off the names of former party leaders: Rubay'a, Shayi', Abd al-Fattah, and Ali 'Antar.⁶⁹ "Oh, now he is being political [*yadkhul al-siyasa*]," Bu Yaqub cautioned: "He lives in Oman and is talking about Yemeni politics."

Nathalie: Is that okay, or not?

Bu Yaqub (tentatively): It's okay.

Nathalie: But these names are all known. They are written in books.

Bu Jum'an (as if aiming to allay any tension): He's giving a history of every-
    thing; first, the sultans, but they ended. Then, the Party, and how this
    ended.

Sownhin: And down to the unity. Maybe the unity will end, too—[Sownhin
    looked as if he wished he could retract this statement]—God only knows.

"God only knows," we responded, winding down this seemingly subversive
conversation with general platitudes about how every regime has its time.

Strikingly, whereas "The Foundation Stone" does list these former (now deceased) high-ranking members of the government in South Yemen, it does not
in fact name any of the perpetrators. The poet identifies them, rather, by emphasizing their "alien" and "unknown" origins: their African roots. Again, the use
of a tree metaphor: "But stone pine [imported planking] is not genuine teak; it
is an inferior wood without value. / You know your roots and from where the
winds brought you. / We do not know your origin exactly; we are not archival
historians. / The storms could have brought you from anywhere—truly, no one
knows you." Comparing the Soqotran executioners to a tree that yields second-
rate planking and to an imported, weedy transplant, Abu Shanab insinuates that
the culprits' genealogies are inferior, degenerate, and suspect. As if this were not
enough to identify (and degrade) them, Abu Shanab drives his point home by
representing them as former slaves who have forgotten their true "work" and
station: clearing the airstrip, transporting earth and stones, with a whip at their
heels. Chastising them for not having been satisfied with their lot, Abu Shanab
denies them the political agency that they allegedly had sought by taking part in
the dissolution of the sultanate regime. He then undermines the relative financial and political successes attained by some in recent years by dehumanizing
and demeaning them as "hornless goats" (fidadi), a Soqotri slur for "Africans."

Abu Shanab does not need to name the perpetrators as he did the Yemeni
politicians because, as he says in his poem, "each one and his deeds are known."
He warns the perpetrators, moreover, that their children will inherit their
stigma: "No one doubts that you are guilty, your deeds are well known. / Your
children will be named the sons of murderers and you shall have a hard
life. / Your history resembles that of Cain and his brother Abel." Again and
again, Abu Shanab's verses work to distance the perpetrators—and, by extension, all Afro-Soqotrans—from the tribes "native" to Soqotra. Readers may be

surprised or shocked by his nativist and racist expressions. Yet his use of simile betrays this very distinction to reveal the event for what it really was (and why it was that it hit Soqotrans so hard): a *fratricide*.

"NO VEGETABLES AND SOFT DRINKS HERE"

If "The Foundation Stone" reopened a communal wound, the poet's standing as an émigré—someone who had escaped this dark period in Soqotra—rubbed salt into it. For here was an example of the relatively pampered emigrants telling the islanders how to manage their affairs. Those who were related to the martyrs seemed to appreciate this freight of verbal ammunition. I have already noted that one islander blasted the poem in the market place as a way of identifying his father's killers. Other bereaved relatives copied and disseminated the poem quietly, among allies, as if the poem itself bore witness to the executions. Two years later, one of the martyr's grandchildren demonstrated his desire for retributive action by sitting with me for hours upon hours as we tried to translate and—what was more difficult—transcribe the poem. Because Soqotri is an unwritten language without a standardized transcription system, Soqotrans themselves struggle to adequately capture and convey their language on the page. Earlier, a poet had transliterated the multilingual verses for me using, as most Soqotrans do when pressed to write their language, a modified Arabic script. But my friend Ismail, an avid collector of Soqotri poetry, had trouble reading it. I then asked a Soqotran teacher of Arabic to transcribe the poem. Ismail and other friends had trouble reading this version, too. Finally, I brought together the Soqotran poet, the martyr's grandson, and a Yemeni typist from Taiz in an effort to collaboratively transcribe and type up "Hajar al-Asas." Meeting in an empty restaurant night after night where we labored over a hushed transcription, I wondered what was more transgressive: discussing the executions or simply writing Soqotri.

Other islanders who had not been directly affected by the executions seemed more averse to supporting any action that would disturb the security they so valued. "Let God be their judge," my interlocutors would say whenever the event was discussed. One of the island's most venerated poets—an elderly man known as Di-min-Sirihan—did respond to Abu Shanab, in verse. However, in his poem, Di-min-Sirihan sidesteps the question of retribution and focuses on Abu Shanab's emigrant absence instead. Acknowledging the 1974 executions as a chronic wound for which, in Di-min-Sirihan's view, there is no "operation" or cure, the local poet admonishes the expatriate poet for criticizing his "inaction" from afar. He also rebukes Abu Shanab for his inability to speak unadulterated Soqotri. Di-min-Sirihan then seeks to end any further discussion of "the problem," which "should be left now to its owners and to God." But this was not the end of it. Shortly thereafter, Di-min-Sirihan composed a second response to Abu Shanab, which provoked yet another exchange of cassettes between Soqotra and Oman. This exchange exposed the incipient frictions between the islanders and Gulf emigrants as much as it dredged up residual resentments between the purportedly African and Arab Soqotrans. In this poem, Di-min-Sirihan chastises Abu Shanab for his purported division of the island into its eastern and western tribes. Asserting that Soqotrans are united, Di-min-Sirihan emphasizes once again that it is Abu Shanab who has forsaken the island: "You have exchanged your identity card for a new nationality." And he berates Abu Shanab for having lost sight of the island he left behind:

> Soqotra is not deserted, it is as it was before.
> There are still evil spirits lurking whose habitations are feared.
> They still have malignant power if one does not invoke God.
> Children are still raised here—how many has God created?
> Close your phone, my friend, before rumors fly.
> These words will cause problems if spread throughout Yemen.

Claiming that Soqotra has preserved its original character, heretical beliefs and all, Di-min-Sirihan indicated that the islanders have and should continue to manage their own affairs. Those who abandoned Soqotra and its customs have no right to reproach them. So the aspersions Abu Shanab had sought to cast on the "unknown" origins of the executioners served to impugn his own fidelity—and, by extension, that of the entire emigrant community.

Despite Di-min-Sirihan's pointed rebuttal, the dispute continued. A member of Soqotra's nascent Association for Heritage and History who first described this poetry cycle to me stressed just how commanding Di-min-Sirihan then was: "When Di-min-Sirihan replies to the other poets, they shut up. It's over." But Abu Shanab did not shut up. Instead, he replied—again by cassette poem—that it had not been his intention to "divide" the Soqotran people. At issue was a line from one of Abu Shanab's previous poems, in which he had stated, "The people of the east are legions [*jahafil*] and those of the west are tribesmen [*qaba'il*]." Di-min-Sirihan, who hails from the east, had interpreted this as an affront by a compatriot originating from the west: another repudiation of tribal genealogies of some Soqotrans. In his response, Abu Shanab tried to assure Di-min-Sirihan and others that he had not intended to belittle the eastern tribes; rather, he used the term *jahafil* to signify honor (*sharaf*) and strong ties. But Abu Shanab also rejected Di-min-Sirihan's depiction of his own alienation, reminding his listeners that he comes from Di-Kishin, the eponymous place-name of Soqotra's largest tribe (famous for its fine poets and its wily chieftain, Rehabhen, the leader who scared away the Franks). Conceding that only God can heal this festering wound, Abu Shanab ends his poem with an invocation of a unified Soqotra, from its eastern to its western cape.

A year or so later, in 2005, Di-min-Sirihan composed his final response to Abu Shanab. Attributing their prior misunderstanding to his own "illiteracy" in Arabic, Di-min-Sirihan accepted Abu Shanab's positive spin on the term *jahafil*. And he reaffirmed the existence of a common Soqotran identity, albeit one that is and should remain based on a "resolute localism":[70]

> We share one family, we are all offspring of Eve and Adam.
> And both of us are tribesmen, neither better than the other.
> But this new word called *jahafil*
> Should leave this week, may God protect its journey.
> It is not suited for Soqotra, there are no vegetables and soft drinks here.

As the Soqotran poet colorfully puts it, the Arabic word *jahafil* would ill survive on an island without the modern comforts of supermarket vegetables and commercial, sugar-sweetened drinks. Much like these imported products, the term is foreign to the island, as should be its implicit meaning—as understood by Di-min-Sirihan—that not all Soqotrans possess tribal genealogies of equal standing and honor. But what Di-min-Sirihan further intimates, here and in his previous poems, is that it is the emigrants who have become estranged from Soqotra's demanding nature; it is *their* alien habits and expectations that the island cannot accommodate.

Accompanied by Ismail, I went to see Di-min-Sirihan in his pastoral village in February 2006. Despite our unexpected visit, we were welcomed in traditional Soqotran fashion and each served a half head of the freshly slaughtered goat. When I asked Di-min-Sirihan about the poem cycles, he said that he had decided to give up poetry altogether—"What's the point?"—unless compelled to respond to another Abu Shanab. "We know [Haybak] is like a rough sea that we can't enter. Either you leave it alone, or you come here to do something about it," he reiterated. I asked him what he thought about the emigrant community in general. Although he had never emigrated, his children had, and he had recently spent six months in Ajman visiting them. (In fact, he was preparing for his imminent return.) Like so many other Soqotran families, Di-min-Sirihan's was stretched across the Arabian Sea. Yet he insisted the emigrants' role should be limited. "Those who have adopted a new nationality should leave Soqotra alone," he insisted, "or they should send us the good but not the bad." In this commonly shared view, the emigrants should support their relatives financially but not meddle with the past—or politics.

THE SOQOTRA FOLK MUSEUM

On the northern shore of Soqotra, an hour's drive from Hadibo and just a few kilometers shy of its easternmost cape, stands a one-room, rectangular stone building housing the island's first and only collection of material arti-

FIGURE 11. School field trip from Hadibo to the museum, 2010.

facts and culture. Visitors to this private, purpose-built museum of "Soqotran Heritage" (*al-turath al-saqatri*)—"the Soqotra Folk Museum" in English—pass through a pebbled courtyard trimmed with several transplanted endemic tree species, a dugout canoe, and a small stack of whale vertebrae. When one enters the museum, the first objects noticed are the most incongruous ones: a wooden dugout complete with sail, a female mannequin ensconced in a glass case, a crudely stuffed goat, a wall-mounted case of silver jewelry, a lifeless date palm, copious goatskins and clay pots, and a series of laminated A4 copies of photographs taken by visiting British officers in the 1950s and 1960s. A closer look reveals carefully ordered scenes depicting traditional everyday life: in the home, in the countryside, and on the coast. Other displays present cultural-religious artifacts and practices now obsolete: rituals and celebrations (amulets, a circumcision stone, wedding chests, musical instruments); religious learning (a wooden teaching tablet, ink wells, and photocopied pages from a Holy Qur'an from the late sixteenth century); and historic documents (passports issued by the sultans). And every assemblage is meticulously labeled with a list of the names (in English, Arabic, and Soqotri) and functions of each item in its range. This kind of labeling extends even to the museum's founder, whose name is cemented in stone on the museum's exterior wall. Ahmad bin Sa'd Khamis Tahki *al-Saqatri*: a man whose very name—Arabized but nevertheless emphasizing his Soqotran origins—underscores his near-lifelong displacement.

Ahmad Sa'd—known to his family as Hamad Sa'd (his Soqotri name)—was the first Soqotran emigrant I encountered. During my first weeks in Homhil, I spent many long, unstructured days helping organize the new campground. One afternoon, as I was sitting in its shelter conversing with its managers, a stranger arrived. It was clear that this man wearing a white robe, an embroidered woolen turban, and a camera slung around his neck was, as I wrote in my journal, "not from here." Nor were the two children accompanying him: a boy wearing an Omani cap (*kuma*) and a girl sporting a plastic sunhat. Yaqub, my neighbor, said that they were "from the Gulf." But in fact, Hamad Sa'd had walked over to the campground from his childhood home across the wadi. Having heard that I was a researcher living in Homhil, Hamad began lecturing my companions about the protocols of Western research: that Westerners did not conduct research for financial gain and that we fact-checked multiple times. He

then turned to instruct me, warning me that an earlier anthropologist had published several fallacies; that I would be responsible for what my readers came
to know and think about Soqotra; that I must triangulate data, avoid general-
izations, trust no one, and dig deep. "Imagine a plate of rice," he told me later;
"on the surface it's cold, while it's the food underneath that stays warm." Over
the years that I came to know Hamad better, he extended many such lessons.
He was fond of telling me that to do good research, I needed to have a wide
heart (*qalb wasi'*). It was he who first informed me about the "Friday Martyrs of
1974." And it was through him that I began to realize the magnitude of Soqotran emigration.

Like so many others of his generation, Hamad Sa'd left Soqotra as a young
teen to seek a living in the expanding economies in the Gulf. Prior to his birth,
his family had lost the majority of their herds during the 1943 drought, which
in conjunction with the regional food shortages, precipitated the islandwide
famine remembered as the "Year of the Pecking [Vultures]." Hamad Sa'd's older
brother, who migrated with him, described their family situation:

> Our life was like this. We lived [in Homhil] and moved between [our village]
> and the coast. We had a lot of animals, though—my grandfather had eleven
> hundred goats, nine hundred fifty sheep, and about one hundred cows. They
> lived here and the world was around them. Then came the drought, around the
> time of the Second World War. It was not as bad as in some places, where people
> have no food at all and have to eat other people, but we were between life and
> death. We ate fish, some dates, and it lasted for two years. All the animals died,
> all but one hundred goats, thirteen cows, and two sheep. But, two years later, life
> started again. Then, a year after the drought ended, my grandfather died—my
> mother lived for another ten years or so. I studied the Qur'an. My father taught
> me how to read, but I didn't memorize it all. I wasn't a very good student. So, at
> age eleven, I went down to the coast and started to work at sea, and at twelve, I
> first went to Saudi Arabia.

In the mid-1960s, the two brothers and another young man from Homhil journeyed thirty-two days by dhow from Soqotra to Qishn (al-Mahra), Dhofar,
Sadah, and Fujairah; overland to Dubai; and westward across the Gulf to
Dammam. There, Hamad's brother found work on one of the farms belonging
to Saud Abdullah al-Jiluwi, the governor of the Eastern Province. He returned

to Soqotra annually until 1969, when he left for good. Hamad—now Ahmad—had found work as a houseboy and stayed.

Four years later, just as Ahmad Saʿd began considering his return, a Soqotran and a Mahri visited Dammam to convince their compatriots to join their unity brigade. Ahmad Saʿd agreed. In 1971, he traveled overland from Dammam to Muscat, from where he was flown to Salalah, where he then spent another four years fighting against the rebels in the mountains and deserts of Dhofar. They lost some of their unit there. After the revolution was defeated, Ahmad Saʿd entered the Omani civil service, married, had ten children, and settled down in Salalah—now as an Omani citizen—with little hope of returning to Soqotra as long as the socialists were in power. After all, he could have been imprisoned for treason for having fought on the wrong side of the PDRY-supported war. His elder brother, who had initially traveled with him, settled in Ajman, where he eventually gained Emirati citizenship. But their third brother remained in Homhil, where there was no way for them to communicate with one another. In 1989, Ahmad Saʿd met Miranda Morris, an accomplished ethnographer and linguist studying modern South Arabian languages in Oman. He tutored her in Soqotri. She visited the island and carried with her a letter he had penned to his brother that was their first correspondence in decades.

Finally, in 1991, Ahmad Saʿd returned to his island home after some twenty-five years abroad, twenty of them in self-exile. He traveled there with Miranda Morris as an expert adviser to Douglas Botting, who was making a film about his own "return" to Soqotra. Of course, much had changed during Ahmad Saʿd's absence, but what surprised him most was the islanders' apparent disregard for past customs. He began collecting specimens of Soqotran material culture while also setting aside a few Omani riyals each month until he could build a museum to house them. Between 1991 and 2008, his collection grew as he visited the island repeatedly and worked with Miranda Morris on her manual of traditional land-use practices. Thus, despite the in situ Soqotra Folk Museum having opened officially in 2008, Ahmad Saʿd dated its establishment to 1991, when, having first viewed his island through a visitor's lens, he initiated his collection. And, as elected shaykh of the Soqotran community in Salalah, from 1993 to his death in 2010, his stature grew alongside it.

For many years, Ahmad Saʿd displayed his personal collection of Soqotran artifacts in his Salalah home, in the semipublic receiving room (*majlis*) in and around which his male constituents would gather. During my visit to Salalah in 2005, I noticed that several Soqotran homes had large murals of specific dragon's blood trees or desert roses from their home region gracing their *majlis* walls. But Ahmad Saʿd's collection—with its display cases of Soqotran jewelry, books, and documents—was distinctive in that it already resembled and functioned as a museum. Like all Omani citizens living in the time of Sultan Qaboos, Ahmad Saʿd was surrounded by—indeed, fought for—the narrative of a miraculous modernity: a "reawakening" (*nahda*) from a period of deep "political instability and poverty."[71] Moreover, Ahmad Saʿd undoubtedly witnessed the various ways in which Oman's thriving heritage industry worked to cast the nation-state as modern.[72] And surely he would have noticed that the same mundane objects that had been transformed into Oman's cultural wealth were abundant and, indeed, still in use in Soqotra—his discourse of loss notwithstanding. Then, in 2006, Ahmad Saʿd traveled to Scotland to attend the opening of the Soqotra Exhibition at the Royal Botanic Garden in Edinburgh, where he was further inspired by the musealogical model. There, as throughout the years, he received a great deal of encouragement from his researcher-friends, especially Miranda Morris, who is largely to thank for the museum's English-language documentation and collection of historic photographs. Two years later, Ahmad Saʿd's vision was realized; he opened the first museum of and on Soqotra.

In 2008, when I first visited this museum, I happened upon Ahmad Saʿd preparing for the official opening. As we talked about the project, he wrapped twine around a makeshift ball to re-create a game he used to play as a child. Minutes later, a clique of teenage girls entered the museum for the first time. The girls were fascinated with the plastic mannequin robed in a knee-length, shimmering, royal-blue dress of the kind that their mothers used to wear and draped in the silver jewelry no longer in fashion; "the new fashion" (*al-modah al-gadidah*), as the women in Homhil would say, consisted of long black abayas and gold. Even Ahmad Saʿd's middle-aged sisters, who had walked in behind the girls, were amazed by the display. "Look at that dress! Look at that silver!" they exclaimed of the styles—and quite possibly of some of the very *things*—that they used to wear before Yemen's unification, prior to their "second life" as artifacts in their brother's collection. As I sat with his sisters, Ahmad Saʿd guided the teenagers through the museum space, showing them a millstone (used daily to grind maize in their homes); a leather harness (used regularly by their menfolk to scale date palms during the pollination and harvesting seasons); goatskins (used in their own homes for churning butter and storing dates); and various products made from palm fibers (such as the mats, twine, and baskets that their mothers wove during the hot, still afternoons). For these and other "Bedouin" visitors, it must have been quite unsettling to find such an enviable concrete, modern, and "Arab" house sheltering nothing but commonplace *things*—homemade tools, implements, and materials that many would prefer to exchange for factory-made products. Yet the conversion is happening not in their homes. Rather, it is the museum that is transforming their present-day things into a past *object*, an object that suddenly appears quaint and "closed in upon itself" once it has traveled the short distance from the home to the museum.[73]

At the same time, the museum is turning past objects—the circumcision stone, the amulets, the teaching tablet, the passport issued by Sultan Isa—into *present* things: objects once discarded that are now brought near to Soqotrans' not-so-long-ago but so-distant past.[74] Having had "the ability to make things happen, to produce effects" such as protection, empowerment, and mobility, these "things" conjure a pre-1967 Soqotra that remains politically powerful today.[75] It is precisely because many of the objects exhibited remain in use that the sultanate appears to directly predate the present, eliding any references to its more proximate, socialist past. Entering into the Soqotra Folk Museum, Soqotrans are confronted with the uncanny presence of Sultan Isa in the form of a prominently placed photograph. Prior to the museum's opening, not many Soqotrans I know had seen a photograph of the last ruling sultan; when I showed my neighbors in Homhil an image I had found, they were surprised to see Sultan Isa appear less regal in the photograph than he did in their memories and imagination. (In the museum's image, Sultan Isa has been decentered by the photographer's lens trained on the African bodyguard behind him.) Exiting the museum, one cannot help noticing the more ubiquitous poster of Yemen's current president, Abdu Rabbu Mansour Hadi, affixed to the museum's door. One enters into the space of the sultanate; one exits back into the space of the republic. It is this through this "peculiar commingling of the familiar and the unfamiliar" that the Soqotra Folk Museum "disturbs any straightforward sense of what is inside and what is outside"; what is proper and what is natural; what is past and what is present; what is object and what is thing.[76]

Like the uncanny, Ahmad Sa'd's museum unsettles (itself). It is unsettling, in the most basic sense, in that it displaces the expert curation, classification, and evaluation of the archipelago with a private, lay collection situated inside a Soqotran-built house. This is certainly unsettling to experts, as I learned during a tour of the museum with Arab heritage consultants in December 2013. Having expected them to applaud Ahmad Sa'd's singular efforts to preserve his community's material culture, I was surprised by their reproof. While two of the consultants criticized the museum for being "old school"—the entire labeling system has to be redone; it needs to be reorganized; it needs proper lighting, they opined—the third criticized it for not being Soqotran enough, for being but a poor imitation of a Western model. Accordingly, the museum was neither sufficiently modern nor sufficiently traditional (indigenous) to fulfill their expert expectations. (Nor does it have a gift shop, as one of my readers pointed out.) But it is also unsettling in a more generative and transformative sense in that it represents "a sense of homeliness uprooted."[77] This is not a heritage that is local—despite the proximate source(s) of the material on display—nor is it a heritage modeled on a Western or global design, as critics of heritage projects in the Arabian Peninsula often contend. For if the Soqotra Folk Museum draws on Western models, then surely it draws on Omani examples and narratives, too. More important, the Soqotra Folk Museum tells the story not of an island that is "untouched" or "lost"—as (mainly Western) visitors repeatedly describe Soqotra in the museum's guestbook—but of a regionally interconnected society that has experienced profound transformations, much like those on the Arabian Peninsula have. It is also very much a product and project of one man's journey from Soqotra to Saudi Arabia to Oman to Scotland and back, representing the long-awaited return—through his *majlis* collection—that had been denied to Ahmad/Hamad Sa'd, *al-Saqatri*, as a young man. It represents not just a heritage crafted by the diaspora but Soqotra's history and heritage *of* diaspora.

LEGACIES

In the summer of 2006, the poet Abu Shanab passed away in Salalah, Oman. He did not live to see Soqotrans roused into action, as they would be with the start of the Arab uprisings in 2011. Prudently, Soqotrans did not heed his call to avenge the deaths at Haybak. They would, however, continue to debate—

through poetry—whether Soqotra would be better off were it to be separated
from Yemen's right shoulder (mostly in line with the Southern Separatist Movement born in 2007). Five years after his friend's death, Ahmad/Hamad Saʻd
passed away in Salalah, his Emirati brother at his side. Shortly before his death,
his Emirati nephew married Yaqub's sister, who moved to Ajman, where she
enjoys her air-conditioned house, abundant foods, and the help of an Ethiopian
domestic servant. She speaks only Arabic to their young children; she considers
it important that they learn to speak it properly. With Ahmad Saʻd's death, his
museum has died a little, too. His photograph, set atop the model pack camel
by his relatives, is now as prominently displayed as that of the late Sultan Isa.
To some, it may seem that the museum has become more like a shrine. His
relatives continue to care for the museum; over time, some objects have gone
missing; some displays have become disarranged.

But I do not wish to romanticize the museum's traditional contents or the
heritage makers themselves. Even before these losses, there was much that had
remained absent, much that had been negated. Ahmad Saʻd had not found a
way to represent Soqotra's intangible culture—the poetry performances that
occur *outside* the home and, in this region, just down the beach from where
the museum stands, at night—nor had he represented Soqotra's communities
of African descent; its "negative heritage" (the stories of male sorcerers and
banished witches); the socialist period; his own exile; or, indeed, anything post-
sultanate. Instead, Ahmad Saʻd had found another way to say what Abu Shanab
had vocalized and what al-Anbali had written: that the only (in their view)
genuine Soqotrans are those with pastoral roots and "Arab" genealogies. Islanders like Di-min-Sirihan, to their credit, have largely rejected such nativist sentiments.[78] As a result, the emigrants' calls to rise up against the perceived threats
within—crusaders, socialists, Afro-Soqotrans, Western experts, the islanders'
indifference—were largely deflected by the islanders' interrogation of the emigrants' own allegiances.

In summary, the heterogeneous, kaleidoscopic, and entangled processes
of heritage making on Soqotra in the early twenty-first century was anything
but an inauthentic reenactment of an Orientalist fantasy. It certainly was not
brand without substance. Rather, the various Gulf-to-island transmissions I
explored—of history texts, poetry, and material collections—impart a deep-
seated anguish over past political events, unrealized futures, and decades lost to

exile. They also reveal an ongoing struggle to reorient Soqotra's heritage—and future—in a variety of ways. The following chapter turns to the islanders' deployment of heritage in the face of what they considered to be *external* threats to their cultural identity and sovereignty. How did these Soqotrans come to view their heritage as a powerful mode of discourse and action during a time of political upheaval?

FIGURE 12. Festival of Soqotri Poetry 2011, panel of jurists, Hadibo (photograph taken on 2 January 2012).

CHAPTER 6

HERITAGE IN THE TIME OF REVOLUTION

Poetry was once a magnificent camel. Then, one day, it was slaughtered. So Imr'ul Qays came and took his head, 'Amr ibn Kulthum took his hump, Zuhayr the shoulders, al-A'sha and Nabigha the thighs, and Tarafa and Labid the stomach. There remained only the forearms and the offal, which we split among ourselves. The butcher then said, "Hey you, there remains only the blood and impurities. See that I get them." "They are yours," we replied. So we took the stuff, cooked it, ate it, and excreted it. Your verses are from the excrement of that butcher.

—Al-Farazdaq, eighth century, on the fate of poetry in his time[1]

29 October 2009: 3:50–4:08 a.m.

Crickets are chirping. A rooster crows. Water drips, drips. The rooster crows again. A person clears his throat. The rooster crows. The chirping loudens. In the distance, sheep are bleating. The rooster crows. Crows again. And again: *kukukuuku, kukukuuku. Kukukuuku. Kukukuuku. Kukukuuku.* Drip, drip. *Kukukuuku.* A man's voice: "Allahu akbar [Allah is the greatest]. Allahu akbar. Allahu akbar." Chirping. "Ashhadu anna la ilaha illa Allah [I profess that there is no God but Allah]. Ashhadu anna la ilaha illa Allah." A child cries. "Ashhadu anna Muhammadan rasul Ullah [I profess that Muhammad is the Messenger of Allah]." The cry grows louder. "Ashhadu anna Muhammadan rasul Ullah." A rooster crows. The child cries. "Hayya 'ala as-salah [Hasten to prayer]." *Kukukuuku.* The child cries again. Someone coughs. "Hayya 'ala as-salah." Coughing. A rooster crows. "Hayya 'ala al-falah [Hasten to success]." Coughing. "Hayya 'ala al-falah." *Kukukuuku.* "As-salatu khayrun min an-nawm [Prayer is better than sleep]." A tin thuds to the ground. "As-salatu khayrun min an-nawm. Allahu akbar." A sandgrouse sings: *Hierika faw.* "Allahu akbar." Chirping. "La ilaha illa Allah, la ilaha illa Allah." A man, yawning, wakes his son: "Ya, Abdullah; ya, Abdullah." In the distance, prayer: "Allahu akbar, Allahu akbar." A sandgrouse, again: *hierika faw.* A rooster: *Kukukuuku, kukukuuku.* Coughing. *Kukukuuku.* Water pours into a tin. A girl cries, briefly, then again. A male voice: "Bismillah, ya! [God protect you]." A woman's voice: "Howshe, Aisha, howshe [Soq.: Come, Aisha, come]." Another woman: "'Egabuh hish di'i habba [Soq.: Your grandmother wants you]." Distant sounds of prayer. The sandgrouse: *Hierika faw. Hierika faw. Hierika faw.* Pouring water. Muffled voices.

Pouring water, again. A man calls to his goats: "Woaldh! Woaldh! Ha, ha ha." Bleating goats. "Ha ha, ha ha, woaldh, woaldh, eyuh! Eyuh!" Two men's voices, calling their goats, intertwine: "Woaldh! Ha, ha ha! Woaldh! Ha, ha!"

Despite the considerable influences of the diaspora on the islandwide debates over the nature of Soqotran identity, heritage, and history, most of their commemorative projects began to bear fruit only in the early 2000s. Significantly, it was during these years that the governments and elites of the Arab Gulf States in which the Soqotran emigrants lived mounted many of their own large-scale heritage and cultural projects.[2] The turn to heritage construction in Soqotra was thus as much influenced by early twenty-first-century heritage revivalism in the boom cities of the Gulf as it was motivated by global discourses, national pressures, and dynamics internal to the island.

Nevertheless, to understand the transformative nature of heritage making in Soqotra—especially in contrast to the top-down, conservative nature of heritage construction in the Gulf—we must look precisely to the work undertaken by individual islanders. Situated at the margins of the island's conservation-focused "ecology of expertise," these Soqotrans sought to produce and position themselves within a parallel research ecology: one that contested, even as it modeled itself on, what was in Soqotra a novel "assemblage of science, administration, and foreign experts."[3] One of the ways they did so was by focusing their efforts on the cultivation of Soqotra's cultural heritage in contradistinction to the foreign experts' predominant concern for its environment (natural heritage). As a result, these lay scholars emerged as "para-experts," undertaking cultural work in simulation of and alongside the foreign experts authorized to research Soqotra's biodiversity.[4] It was through their interactions with and around these experts and the ICPD projects that these islanders learned to "enact" and communicate their own expertise and authority.[5]

SOQOTRAN PARA-EXPERTS

It all goes back to his first car. Ismail was born in the countryside (*badiya*), in a small, stone goat byre (Soq.: *terbak*). Like many children of the socialist period, he "descended" to Hadibo to attend elementary and then secondary school. And he excelled. He did so well that when he completed ninth grade in 1990, his sister sent him a 1979 Toyota Land Cruiser from Dubai. Ismail is a not a tall man; at the time, his feet could barely reach the pedals. But he loved driving. "The problem was that car," he reflected in 2012. Once he owned that car, even his aptitude for learning could not keep him in Hadibo. He stopped attending school and spent most of his time in the *badiya*. There, he drove himself into and out of mischief: offering the Bedouin rides, stealing glances from their daughters, and ingratiating himself in just about every settlement on the island. For a while, he worked as a mechanic on Soqotra's southern coast, not for wages but for gasoline to support his driving habit. In the early 1990s, all the island's cars were castoffs from the Emirates that broke down frequently. There were few mechanics then, so Ismail learned by tinkering with his own used Toyota: a car that had become what Ismail only half-jokingly refers to as his true secondary school.

In 1997, two new vehicles were offloaded at the port. These were not just new; they had come off the assembly line that year. "Everyone was talking about the importation of these cars for some new project in Soqotra. We'd heard that this environmental project had something to do with trees, birds, and plants, but not many knew what this Arabic term, *bi'a* [environment], actually meant," he said. What Ismail did know was that he wanted to drive one of these 1997 models. Against the odds, Ismail secured the last opening for a driver-mechanic. A few months later, the project hired a British Council English teacher to instruct its local staff. Drivers were not required to study English, but Ismail asked to join the class. During the week, he studied diligently, and on weekends his teacher joined him on his forays into the *badiya*. By and by, Ismail's usefulness to the project as a reliable, English-speaking driver grew. One day, Ismail was tasked with driving a photographer around, who recommended his promotion. So Ismail moved into the nascent ecotourism sector, where he helped run the short-lived Socotra Ecotourism Society: a UNDP/SCDP-funded local NGO. This was his role when I first met him: ecotourism coordinator and trainer of local guides. I often hitched rides with Ismail to Homhil, where he would teach his young Soqotran trainees about the island's various endemic plants and birds, all the while bombarding them with these species' scientific names. Over the years, Ismail guided not only tourists but also more and more of the scientific, diplomatic, and television teams who came through. He became the go-to person for all visiting documentary filmmakers—many of whom sought out Ismail precisely because of his intimate knowledge of the island. Having become indispensable to these foreign experts without having finished high school, Ismail counts the SCDP as his second, secondary school. "If not for the project, I'd still be in the *badiya* today. I would not have helped people, or my island," he said.

But for all that Ismail learned from working with the ICDPs—English included—it was not this conservation project that sparked his interest in Soqotran heritage. This goes back, again, to the car. When Ismail began cruising the countryside in the early 1990s, he also began recording Soqotri-language poetry and music. Initially, he was motivated less by the desire to preserve than by his desire to learn. He loved Soqotri poetry and music and wanted to feel comfortable hanging out with the Bedouin who composed it. Despite having been born in a goat byre in the *badiya*, Ismail felt, whenever he returned to the countryside, that he was missing something, "as if I was not a complete man." Ismail attributes this to his nine years of Arabic-language education in Hadibo and his consequent inability to herd goats, compose poetry, and follow "the traditional Soqotran path." One day, he and a similarly urbanized friend encountered a sick goat on the way to his friend's natal village. The two stopped to care for it, only to realize that they did not know how. When they reached the village, they told the inhabitants that one of their goats was ill. "What color is it?" They were asked. "What are its markings?" Ismail and his friend had not noticed; to them, a goat was a goat. To the pastoralists, a goat is like a child; it was inconceivable that they would not notice its hair color, its distinctive markings, its coat. Ismail took this as evidence that he did not really belong in the *badiya*—that he was not even "fully Soqotran." So he drove around the island recording poetry, music, stories, and sounds to learn his way to self-realization. Eventually, when Ismail started working for "the Environment," he learned that languages could become endangered, too. And it clicked: "All the problems of heritage and Soqotri language—they became my problem. I started worrying about issues of language and heritage loss. Because I have evidence, very clear evidence. For this in my self—how this language will end. I am evidence of this."

With this realization, Ismail began to seek work with television crews to "impart this message": the message that Soqotri language and cultural heritage needed protection, as well. In 2009, Ismail worked with a German film crew making a documentary for 360° GEO Reports: *Soqotra: A Treasure Island in*

Danger (*Sokotra, Schatzinsel in Gefahr*). Ismail—with his old Land Cruiser, his pastoralist friends, and his suitcase holding 350 recorded cassettes—was one of the film's main protagonists. Following its airing, members of the German Society for Endangered Languages contacted Ismail to offer their support. Faculty at the Institut für Orientalistik brought him to Vienna to lecture on the Soqotri language and its threats. The German Society gave Ismail a professional audio recorder and sent him to the Max Planck Institute for Psycholinguistics in the Netherlands for training on language documentation. Ismail had handcarried his twenty finest recordings to Europe, which his contacts uploaded into the Language Archive: their first samples of Soqotri. Sometimes, Ismail cannot believe that a high school dropout like him would play a significant role in documenting and, thus, perhaps even helping preserve his own culture. It was Ismail, not the anthropologist, who captured the sounds of his natal village waking up to the roosters, the call to worship, and bleating goats.

Yet Ismail continued to feel that he was working in a vacuum. "I returned home to see that the international organizations are still only really interested in Soqotra from an environmental point of view," he said. Although such organizations may pay lip service to cultural heritage, most work against biodiversity loss, not the loss of linguistic diversity that often accompanies it. I pointed out that Soqotrans had begun taking efforts to preserve their heritage on their own. "Yes, but this is not enough," Ismail said. "The problem now is Soqotra is very weak. The Soqotri language is disappearing—unless we write and study it." Ismail, with his practiced Soqotri and his imperfect English, did not see himself as the vehicle to make this happen.

.   .   .

The first time I met Tanuf, in March 2003, he showed me his photographs of the Brobdingnagian goats in Edinburgh. Tanuf had returned recently from his second trip to the United Kingdom, and this was the sight that had impressed him the most. Like Ismail, his junior, Tanuf was born in the small rural village. In contrast to Ismail, Tanuf had spent his entire youth there: herding his family's livestock, listening to the Il-Kishin tribe's renowned poets, and acquiring knowledge of the medicinal uses of Soqotra's flora from his father. Tanuf had not even visited Hadibo until he was around ten years old. After that, he may have descended to the coast two or three times per year—in the fall to gather dates and in the winter to work at sea. But it was only at the age of seventeen, after fulfilling his three years of compulsory military service under the socialist government, that Tanuf left the *badiya* for a sustained period of time.

After completing his service, Tanuf found periodic work at sea. He also tried opening a shop in Hadibo, without much success. Eventually, he settled for a while in his native village, where he helped his family herd their goats. In the late 1990s, Tanuf happened to meet the linguist Miranda Morris, the botanist Anthony G. Miller, and their research team. Tanuf began working with Morris, sitting with her for hours and days as they recorded the Soqotri names and traditional uses of the island's diverse flora. (This painstaking work, supported by Tanuf and many other Soqotrans, resulted in Miller and Morris's encyclopedic *Ethnoflora of the Soqotra Archipelago*.) Later, Tanuf began to assist Morris on her second, massive project, the *Manual of Traditional Land Use Practices in the Soqotra Archipelago*. Then, with funding from the American Institute for Yemeni Studies, Tanuf traveled to the United Kingdom to collaborate with Morris on a third project, their coauthored, comprehensive collection of Soqotri-language poetry. During this, his first visit to Europe, Tanuf gave a seminar on Soqotri poetry at the School of Oriental and African Studies (SOAS) in London. Not a poet himself but someone who has an excellent ear for poetry and a remarkable memory, Tanuf continued to collect traditional Soqotri poetry throughout the countryside. And again, Tanuf traveled to the United Kingdom to collaborate on this work. When I moved to Soqotra a few years later, I found that Tanuf had become famous for supposedly being "the first Soqotran invited to Europe" by a foreigner. Several times, families likened me to "Miranda" and pointedly voiced their hope that their son or daughter would become "the second Tanuf."

When the ICDPs arrived in the late 1990s, Tanuf hoped that he could put his ethnobotanical knowledge and experience to work. Despite his repeat applications, the project administrators did not see fit to hire a semiliterate pastoralist without English-language abilities or even formal education. So Tanuf marshaled his elders' teachings and the emerging interest in Soqotra's endemic flora into a newfound career in traditional medicine. Having secured a plot of land in Hadibo and a certificate from the Ministry of Health labeling him a traditional healer (*tabib sha'bi*), Tanuf opened Soqotra's first herbal pharmacy in 2005. I used to visit Tanuf regularly as he prepared his new business. Bagging ground-up, dried leaves from his perch on the floor (the table and chairs were yet to arrive), Tanuf distinguished his work from that of other herbalists and practitioners of "Arabic medicine" in town. "I am a real *tabib sha'bi*," he told me. "There is another herbalist in Hadibo, but he dabbles in magic. He is more like a soothsayer [*kahin*]; he mixes herbs and other plants from overseas together, but he is not completely straight." Unlike practitioners of Arabic medicine, Tanuf asserted a month later, "I use only plants: no Qur'an, no magic." Often, Tanuf emphasized the importance of being scientific and transparent, of not pretending to be able to treat something if one cannot. "This is the time of true information," he once said, pointing to Miller and Morris's English-language *Ethnoflora* and an Arabic-language translation of their *Plants of Dhofar* on his shelf.[6] To this end, Tanuf keeps a log of all the cases he has treated: skin diseases, rashes, primary infertility, secondary infertility, mild kidney pain, diabetes, stomachache, headaches, and joint pain. In the first month alone, he treated forty patients. He went to show me but then remembered that the goats had barged into his pharmacy and chewed the log's first pages—a common hazard that had caused me to lose field notes, too.

Tanuf's transparency, affordability, and reliance on natural products helped revive, if not produce, a local market for botanical medicines. Initially, Soqotrans like Ismail would poke fun at Tanuf's alternative treatments. Although Ismail himself had trained his guides to tell tourists how the islanders used plants such as aloes to treat burns or dragon's blood resin to stop postpartum hemorrhage, Soqotrans have long turned to biomedicine and synthetic pharmaceuticals. (Visiting British doctors in the 1950s noted Soqotrans' fervent desire for shots and pills.)[7] Initially, Tanuf's patients consisted primarily of neighborhood women who came to him for skin whiteners, beauty creams, hair treatments, and cures for infertility. Tanuf looked at me knowingly when he told me this—a year before I had my first child—promising that he would give me the fruitful herbs. (He did. I put them through a wash cycle, accidentally.) Eventually, however, Tanuf's pharmacy gained a wide and far-reaching clientele. When I visited him in 2007, he had treated eighteen patients by midmorning, many of them pastoralists who had come to Hadibo for the plant-based treatments their elders had once collected themselves. He had also employed two assistants to keep his log. Tanuf's reputation for success, particularly with regard to treating infertility, had spread not only across the island but also across the Arabian

Sea. His customers included religiously conservative men from the Hadhra-mawt purchasing herbal fertility treatments for their wives; a merchant from al-Hudaydah (Yemen) who sells Soqotra's tree resins and plant leaves in bulk to herbal stores in Dubai; and Yemeni tourists from the United Kingdom.

"This is one of the must-stops in Soqotra!" a young, Adeni woman of Kenyan-Yemeni descent exclaimed when we met at Tanuf's pharmacy in January 2012. I had been sitting inside the Pepto-Bismol-pink room chatting with Tanuf when she and her cousin entered. "We've been trying to find you for days now," she told Tanuf in Arabic. Then, turning to me, she asked if I was on vacation, too. "It's hard to find a word for how astonished I am," she said in flawless English, referring to the island's beauty. But what had really brought her to Soqotra, she explained, was the pharmacy. Her uncle had seen a documentary on Yemeni TV featuring Tanuf's herbal therapies and infertility treatments. He and his wife had been struggling for years to get pregnant and had tried all kinds of medical interventions, to no avail. (By that time, Tanuf had treated hundreds of cases of infertility, he told me, half of them successfully.) So the young Adeni had traveled to Soqotra to purchase his pulverized herbs and Soqotran honey for her hopeful relatives at home.

By this time, Tanuf and his pharmacy had appeared in several television documentaries in Yemen, France, and Japan. But Soqotra's reputation—and its herbs—continued to travel by word of mouth (and by hand). I know this because twice I delivered Tanuf's medicines to the mainland. The first time, in 2011, I delivered a plastic water bottle filled with Soqotran honey and a bag of pulverized green leaves to a young Sanaani man who had procured them for his friend in Saudi Arabia. The Saudi man, who suffered from diabetes, had read something online about Soqotran remedies; he called the Sanaani he knew (who had once lived in Dammam), who called an Adeni friend living on Soqotra, who knew Tanuf. The plants I carried would be the Saudi's second treatment; his blood sugar levels had already gone down, his friend said. The second time, a year later, I delivered a similar package to a bedraggled yet elegant Iraqi hairdresser who met me at the Sanaa airport between flights. Her friend, who had struggled for fifteen years to conceive, became pregnant after taking Tanuf's herbs. The hairdresser then spent two weeks in Soqotra being treated for infertility herself and has since gone into business with Tanuf, selling his herbal remedies to her friends farther afield. The medicines I carried were intended for an Iraqi woman in the United States, who was trying to conceive. The hairdresser, too, remained hopeful.

. . .

When Fahd was young, he considered Soqotra the world. Born in 1975 in a village in Soqotra's southern plateau, he spent his childhood on the southern coast (Noged), where his family raised goats and sheep. At that time, the other coastal villages were accessible only by boat. But even sea travel was limited. Remote as they were, Fahd's parents were "cultured" and taught their children how to read. By the time Fahd entered first grade, he had memorized the Qur'an. After he completed seventh grade, his parents sent him to Hadibo for further schooling. This was the first time Fahd had spent any time in the "city"; "I was a Bedouin, you know." A year later, he left Soqotra to attend high school in Aden. But the ship carrying the island's seventy students, in addition to Somali livestock, nearly sank. "When the ship broke down, they brought everyone up on deck, with all of the meat. There were people, goats, chicken, women, and children—as if it was Noah's Ark," Fahd laughed. The ship managed to return to Soqotra, but the students had to wait several months for another transfer. (This was just following the 1994 civil war, before there were commercial flights to Soqotra.) Fahd ended up studying at a secondary school in Lahij, north of Aden, where he excelled in the sciences. In 1997, he received a government grant to enter university, but his parents wanted their eldest son to begin working and to begin a family. He returned to Soqotra and married.

This was not the end of Fahd's education, though. Back in Hadibo, Fahd directed a local school for several years before entering university in 2001, studying first in Soqotra (through a branch of the Hadhramawt University) and later in Sanaa. When I met Fahd in the mid-2000s, he had just earned his baccalaureate degree in Arabic language. Then, and in the years thereafter, Fahd kept himself busy teaching Arabic in Hadibo's high school; working as a reporter for Saba Wire Service, Yemen's state news agency; presiding as secretary-general over the Soqotra Society for Heritage and History; writing and publishing Arabic poetry;[8] and delivering Friday sermons in a local mosque. In 2011, Fahd received a master's degree in Arabic literature from Hadhramawt University in conjunction with St. Clements University for his thesis, "The Inclination Toward the Legendary in Soqotri Literature," based, in part, on Soqotran legends he had collected through the support of a fellowship award from the American Institute for Yemeni Studies in 2005. Fahd is not the first Soqotran to have been awarded a master's degree, but he hoped to be the first Soqotran to earn a PhD, he told me in 2012 when I asked him for his life story. At least, this is what he had planned prior to his entry into national politics a year later.

At the time, Fahd ascribed his political engagement to his religious faith and to the writings of prominent Muslim intellectuals. Fahd had been influenced in particular by the vision of Islam as a comprehensive system and as a guide for how one's culture can and must shape society. As he put it, he did not wake up one day and decide to become pious; rather, "step by step, I found myself moving toward the current of moderate Islam," he said. But if the political tenets of moderate Islam have been one of Fahd's main inspirations, so has the political power of poetry. In January 2004, the German Nobel Prize–winning author Günter Grass visited Soqotra with members of the Yemeni Writer's Association and Dr. Abdul Karim al-Eryani (the adviser to President Saleh whom we met in Chapter 2). When one of the visitors asked to hear a sample of Soqotri-language poetry, it fell on Ismail to gather three of the island's best poets and on Fahd to translate their poetry into Arabic. That day, the group traveled to Homhil for a Soqotri poetry session staged by the Socotra Ecotourism Society amid the frankincense trees. The poets recited their poems in Soqotri, Fahd recited them in Arabic, and a member of the party translated them into English. The fact that a world-renowned author showed interest in these translations of translations of Soqotrans' ideas convinced Fahd that it was Soqotri-language *poetry*—not simply its environment or tourism potential—that distinguishes Soqotra. It was through this encounter that Fahd realized that Soqotrans could be worthy participants on the global stage and that poetry could be, he said, their "ambassador."

.   .   .

Although these and other Soqotran para-experts modeled their research practices on those of the foreigners with whom they had worked or on the environmental project that had excluded or marginalized them, some resented the abilities of the well-funded foreign experts to commandeer elements of their heritage and culture. Poetry that can be collected is poetry that can be taken away. People like Tanuf, Fahd, Ismail, Sughayr, al-Anbali, and Ahmad Sa'd had witnessed close-up how foreign careers—mine included—were being built on their own knowledge and generosity. Consequently, as many of my inter-locutors vied for places in this emergent Soqotra-based knowledge economy, they spoke not only of "the past" itself "as a scarce resource" but also of its documentation and dissemination as an increasingly competitive occupation.[9] Many were eager to tell me not only how other foreign researchers had failed but also how their fellow Soqotrans were erring. Interlocutor A did not trust interlocutor B or C; interlocutors B and C warned me about working with in-terlocutor A, and so forth. One friend swore me to secrecy about a cassette of X that he feared other Soqotrans would copy (conceptually or materially) and sell for themselves. Nearly everyone I knew, it had seemed, guarded his or her knowledge carefully against the predatory nature of the research market. In this environment, culture and heritage had become scarce resources, too.

"PULLING AT DIFFERENT PIECES"

In 2005, the same year that the nomination process for the archipelago's World Heritage status was initiated in earnest—the same year, moreover, that Soqotra's last openly practicing *mekoli* passed away—the Soqotra Society for Heritage and History was born. Both Fahd and Ismail attribute the establishment of this

FIGURE 13. Mawlid celebration, Hallah, 2005.

society to Günter Grass's visit the year before. According to Fahd, following the
Homhil poetry recital, one of the visitors from the Yemeni Writers' Association suggested that their hosts collect Soqotri-language poems and stories for
publication. This was a defining moment for a man who had grown up being
told that simply speaking this unwritten "dialect" was shameful. Prompted
by the outside encouragement, the UNDP SCDP site coordinator secured a
small grant (USD 4,000) from the Japanese embassy to document the Soqotri
language, monies that were ultimately expended by the Socotra Ecotourism
Society. But the idea for a Soqotran-run organization that would focus on preserving the island's cultural heritage in addition to and in tandem with its natural heritage—a territory that was increasingly mapped, defined, and directed by
external actors and organizations—had been conceived. Eventually, the SCDP
coughed up some funding for this new society: for its establishment fees and
registration; its rent of a modest, curbside office; and the publication of a small
collection of Soqotri texts. Despite Ismail's efforts to organize the island's poets,
the society's executive committee and the majority of its membership were
drawn from Hadibo's teachers and civil servants. Some members were driven as
much by their desire to tap into international funding (and salaries) earmarked
for civil society organizations as they were by any real interest in Soqotra's heritage or history. Others were convinced of the need to preserve cultural heritage,
as a way not only to legitimate positions for themselves but also to demarcate a
territory impervious to or at least shielded from outside intervention.

In its first years, the society set itself the task of salvaging Soqotri poetry
and other elements of what it classified as *turath*: material culture (pottery, bas-
ketry, weaving), customs and practices (plant harvesting, medical treatments),
and "games" (including what its members considered the traditional but erro-
neous belief in witchcraft). Initially, its vision of how to do so was modeled on
the very preservation-through-documentation practices of the ICDPs that so
many of my interlocutors had criticized. In a discussion with a visiting journalist shortly after the society's establishment, Fahd described the need to inventory Soqotra's cultural heritage in a comprehensive, projectlike fashion:

> We have not yet been able to catalogue or understand Soqotran heritage and
> culture. It is the trees, birds, mountains, et cetera, but it also consists of people
> and language. This can't be accomplished by any one person. And if we protect

the environment, but not people and language, then we have nothing. How can you preserve the hand without preserving the body? To save part without saving the rest is to let the whole body die. A realistic attempt to preserve Soqotra's heritage would have to equal the level of the ICDP [al-biʾa].

Here, Fahd's language echoed the protection discourse used by the ICDPs, that of an integrated approach to conservation and development: "environment" and "people." Yet, as Fahd implied, it was these projects that had separated nature from culture. In contrast to the conservationists' treatment of culture as an unwieldy appendage to the natural environment, Fahd and his colleagues viewed the environment as an integral part of the social body. It was not just a matter of merging nature-culture, either, for, as Fahd well knew, the significance of local culture had to be rescaled if it was to counter the increasingly dominant nature of the global environment. Thus, Fahd argued for an investment in researching and preserving Soqotra's cultural heritage at a level comparable to that which had been invested in its flora and fauna.

Given my interlocutors' evaluation of heritage as a scarce resource—a resource depleted by modernization, extracted by foreigners, and exploited by the diaspora—it is not surprising that the society also sought to stake its claim to it. However, cognizant of the damage that the already-disparate projects could inflict, Fahd argued for a more coordinated response. When I ran into him a few weeks later at the SCDP office, where he was preparing a presentation on the role of the society, he took up the metaphor of dismemberment again. This time, it was heritage itself that was being torn asunder:

Heritage is like a buried body that everyone's trying to revive, but they're all pulling at different pieces. One is pulling at the ear, saying this is the most important part; the other is pulling at the leg. What's going to happen in the end is that each person will dig up a part of the body, with a part here and another part there, but they won't be able to reassemble it.

Like al-Farazdaq's slaughtered camel, Soqotra's cadaverous heritage was being cleaved apart by the many poets and experts competing for the choicest piece. Implicit in Fahd's comments is a nostalgia for a once "magnificent" corpus and the desire for a sovereign society to reinvigorate it in full. But for all his enthusiasm for reassembling the body, there are "pieces"—"impurities"—that even the secretary-general of the Soqotra Society for Heritage and History would prefer to leave behind. The society's conception of Soqotra's heritage excluded two forms of cultural practice in particular: unorthodox beliefs and customs (consigned to the "ignorant" past) and "African" dance and music (relegated to the "ignoble" Other).

For all the talk about heritage on Soqotra, many islanders were eager to distance themselves from their unsettling and not-so-distant past, a past marked by poverty, hunger, and superstition. Several of my interlocutors were embarrassed that their grandparents' generation had banished witches or that their parents had believed in the power of witch doctors, or that they themselves had been apprenticed to these diviners. Pious Soqotrans insisted that these beliefs and practices have all but disappeared. Nevertheless, during my fieldwork, I continued to hear murmurings of female witches "eating" children. Similarly, I heard rumors about and met several men who continued to dabble in the supernatural, despite these practices having been prohibited by the socialist state and then decried as religiously forbidden (*haram*) by the Islamic proselytizers (*mutatawwi'in*) who followed. It was not just these superstitions that conservative Soqotrans rejected. Several other aspects of what Soqotrans consider their traditional cultural and religious practices—mixed-gender poetry performances, drumming, *mawlid* celebrations, the slaughtering of livestock during the (Soqotri-language) prayer for rain to *Qaninhin* (Soq.: Lord God), and women's relative independence—were discouraged by both mainland and Soqotran *mutatawwi'in*. Although many of these proscriptions were motivated by ideals of religious purification, their effects were undeniably racialized. Not only was the idiom of witchcraft more prevalent among Afro-Soqotrans, but also it was their expressive traditions that bore the brunt of this double exclusion because they were considered impious and imported.

"Lenin" is a former witch doctor who considers his divining abilities hereditary. In his late teens, as he was descending one day from his home in the Haggeher Mountains, Lenin felt something seize him from behind. He fell unconscious and awoke the next morning, screaming with pain. This happened again the next evening and continued over the course of a week. Lenin's father was not surprised, for his own father had been a *mekoli* who had worked for the sultans. "This is from your grandfather," he told Lenin. "Now you can heal people." And it was from that moment onward that Lenin was able to see devils and jinn; before this, he told me, "I was like you are now"—blind. "This is your inheritance [*wirth*]," his father told him. "If there hadn't been a healer among our ancestors, then it wouldn't have passed down to you." Like other Soqotran *mekolis*, Lenin collaborated with female jinn, but his power, he said, comes from God. "No doctor is able to do anything without the power of God," he insisted. Lenin distinguishes between doctors of "Arabic medicine," whose use of herbs, honey, and the Qur'an he considered new to the island, and "Soqotran doctors," like him, who would dig a hole, fill it with water, and submerge their heads until they (that is, the jinn) had seen who had caused the condition or illness (the witch).[10] Like this, he boasted, he succeeded in healing a woman whom the then recently-deceased Qalansiyah-based *mekoli,* the most powerful of them all, had not been able to cure. "But now people have repented," he said, "and all [*mekolis*] have died. It's all finished. There are the proselytizers [*mutatawwi'in*]. No one works in this [field]. Maybe there are a few who work secretly, but no one hears about them." Despite Lenin's professional solitude, he was certain that his inheritance would be passed down, if not to his son, then to his grandson. "Perhaps it will appear to him in a period when it is not forbidden," Lenin said—his socialist-era nickname and his inheritance a relic of another time.

Dawud is one of the island's best drummers. He is also a practicing Muslim of African descent who lives in Masaqabihin, a suburb of Hadibo, where Afro-Soqotran musicians perform regularly. In the early 2000s, some neighborly proselytizers offered to buy Dawud a new house if he ceased drumming. Dawud told them he would have to think about it. In the early to mid-1990s, before the post-unification religious zeal eventually subsided, many musicians had discontinued their practice. Drumming was considered particularly problematic for it encouraged mixed-sex dancing and distracted others from their prayers. One Soqotran, who had studied in Cuba during the socialist period, returned home in 1995 at the same time that *mutatawwi'in* from Sanaa and al-Hudaydah were traveling around the island calling people to God (*da'wa*). Joining them, he traveled from mosque to mosque, reading from the Qur'an and learning about Islam. He realized, he said, just how brainwashed he had been in Cuba, where he danced, drank, and cavorted with Christian girls. Now this congenial man who works in tourism (because he cannot use his degree in quality control on Soqotra) considers drumming the devil's work. It was one of the practices he and his traveling companions had tried to curtail. Dawud's neighbors were people like the former "Cuban": fellow Soqotrans who wanted to revive Islam in their own communities after two decades of socialist pressure against it. But when Dawud reached his current home that day, he heard the sounds of the *tabla* (a percussion instrument) all around him. Soqotra has two official dance groups that have been performing at weddings, during holidays, and at cultural celebrations since the early 1970s. The tradition of Thursday-evening drumming-and-dancing parties goes back even further. Dawud realized it would be unthinkable for him to give this up. He told the *mutatawwi'in,* "I am sorry; I can't stop drumming. Drumming was passed down from my parents to me and from their parents to them." So he did not receive the new house, but he still drums.

The idea of a Soqotran heritage woven out of these examples of individual inheritance troubled the members of the society, who considered both divining and drumming *haram.* Fahd suggested that they might preserve the story of the *mekolis* (for instance, in a museum), but not their practices. Nor did the society's leadership consider the Afro-Soqotran music to be an expression of Soqotran heritage: at least, not its authentic/pure heritage (*turath asli*). Yet, what seemed to have vexed them the most—as it did some of my other interlocutors—was that it was precisely these African dance groups and impious diviners who had begun to represent Soqotra on the global stage. As the international film crews who promoted the island in the mid- to late 2000s sought footage of Soqotra's exotic landscapes and cultures, they began "pulling at [these] different pieces," too. More cinematogenic than oral poets, it was the dance groups who were paid to perform for tourists and featured prominently on television. Even the shunned *mekolis*—or, in some cases, pastoralists pretending to be *mekolis*—had managed to conjure a new role for themselves as actors in documentary films. (The German documentary curated by Ismail depicts a *mekoli* communing with jinn as if the film crew just happened to have stumbled on an ancient and ongoing healing ritual in the middle of the night.)

In all societies, people struggle with questions of how to engage or endure their "negative heritage."[11] Should we commemorate traditions or past actions even if they make us uncomfortable—*because* they make us uncomfortable—or is the memorialization itself a form of injustice? Whose inheritance is marginalized in the assemblage of a group or a nation's heritage? How are these decisions made? What interests me here is not the obvious point that Soqotra's heritage was political and contested—as scholars have demonstrated, all heritage is a political *act* of consolidating or claiming forms of power—but rather how the one autochthonous civil society organization tasked with heritage assemblage on the island thought to put this "body" together.

For Fahd, if not for others, the answer was clear. Not to be distracted by its pieces, the Soqotra Society for Heritage and History would focus on the dying torso of Soqotra's culture and identity: its poetry and, above all, its language. As people like Fahd and Ismail have experienced in their own lifetimes, their oral language has been losing ground to the Arabic spoken in school, the mosque, public office, the marketplace—even at home. Many Soqotran youth, especially along the coast, are unable to speak unadulterated Soqotri, and most second-generation Soqotrans raised in the Gulf cannot speak their parents' language at all. With the loss of specific terminology (regarding livestock, for example), traditional ecological knowledge has been forgotten, while new concepts—like the "environment" and, indeed, "heritage"—have been introduced through Arabic terms.

"The Soqotri language is like this lantern in the light of electricity," Fahd reflected, as I turned on my porch light after it had become too dark to continue note taking by my kerosene lamp. "Does anyone ever work by this lantern?" He persisted. "No, they work by electricity. In the future, the Soqotri language will disappear, like the lantern."

In an earlier meeting with the poets interested in establishing a poetry society (before the heritage society was formed in its place), Ismail expressed a similar concern: "[in Arabic] Many people don't know why it matters if we lose the Soqotri language. But if we lose our language, we lose ourselves. [in English] We lose our passport, our nationality. . . . I need some help. After fifty years, how will my grandson stay Soqotran? And my great-grandson! After fifty, one hundred years—how will he be Soqotran?" It is specifically the language loss that Fahd had in mind when he told me, in 2005, "In twenty-five years, people will say, 'we *used* to have heritage.'"

THE "FIFTY'S POET"

Soqotrans concerned about language loss are not alone; language endangerment and extinction are, like biological extinction, occurring at unprecedented rates. Indeed, languages are disappearing even more rapidly than are biotic species.[12] If today's rates prevail—and if biologists and linguists are correct—up to 50 percent of the world's species and up to 90 percent of the world's seven thousand known languages will be "committed to extinction" by 2100.[13] Given Soqotri's classification as an "endangered" language, Ismail's fear that his great-grandchildren's generation will no longer speak Soqotri in 2100 is well justified. It is quite likely that this oral vernacular spoken by fewer than seventy-five thousand persons will be moribund even by 2050—when Ismail's grandchildren are in their prime. (As may be Soqotra's flagship *Dracaena cinnabari*.)[14]

Ironically, Soqotrans anxious about losing their oral vernacular to their national language share a concern with Gulf nationals anxious about losing Arabic to the globally dominant English. In the UAE, for example, where nearly 90 percent of the population consists of migrants, the Emirati government and its citizens consider Arabic to be a threatened "heritage language." The UAE's government-owned newspapers regularly feature articles (both in Arabic and English) bemoaning the marginalization of Arabic and its declining use among students in particular. Concerned about their nationals losing their Arabic and, with it, their Emirati identity and culture, the UAE's Federal National Council promoted legislation to protect the Arabic language. Each of the seven Emirates has also invested in a variety of projects to safeguard its people's intangible cultural heritage (including Arabic language and poetry), in addition to archaeological, cultural, and historic sites. In 2005, the same year that a group of Soqotrans established their Society for Heritage and History, the Emirate of Abu Dhabi established the Abu Dhabi Authority for Culture and Heritage (ADACH) to maintain its cultural heritage. Clearly, their mandates, purview, and resources differed enormously, but their missions did not. Fahd's society was not "just" some nostalgic guild; it was, in its vision and timing, as forward-thinking (and, arguably, as economically motivated) as that of its most developed and cosmopolitan neighbors.

ADACH executed several high-profile projects before its merger into the Abu Dhabi Tourism and Culture Authority in 2012. One of its most popular initiatives, still running today, is *Million's Poet* (*sha'ir al-milyun*), a poetry competition launched in 2006.[15] Applauded during its inaugural season as "one of the most successful cultural media projects in the Middle East,"[16] *Million's Poet* attracted international press in 2010 when the female Saudi poet Hissa Hilal won third place based, in part, on her poem condemning intolerant fatwas.[17]

English-language journalists regularly described the competition, shown on Abu Dhabi TV and a dedicated *Million's Poet* channel, as an Arab version of *American Idol*. In this competition, however, forty-eight poet contestants selected from thousands of international applicants compete by reciting Nabati (Bedouin, vernacular) poetry on live TV. Challenged with composing poetry on a select topic, the poets are judged by a jury of leading critics, the live audience, and the viewing public. The top five poets earn cash prizes from one to five million dirham (USD 270,000 to 1.3 million)—hence the title, which the champion also takes home—and the rest receive consolation prizes. But the true success of *Million's Poet* lies not in its flashy and climactic entertainment value. The show has helped revitalize Nabati poetry, a centuries-old vernacular art form rooted in popular expression and Bedouin tradition.[18] In addition to popularizing this oral tradition among its millions of young viewers, the show's success prompted the opening of a Nabati poetry academy in Abu Dhabi, a Nabati Poetry Center in Sharjah, several published anthologies, and even a Nabati Twitter competition. It also inspired Soqotra's own vernacular poetry competition, which in turn gave new direction to the rudderless and underfunded Soqotra Society for Heritage and History.

When a young Gulf-based Soqotran visiting the island in 2006–2007 suggested that the heritage society stage a similar contest there, Fahd considered the idea crazy. How could something so glitzy and grand—and competitive—be organized without institutional or governmental backing? But Fahd's experience of state-supported heritage preservation had not been encouraging either. By that time, the society had been working together with a Darwin Initiative (UK-government funded) project to develop relevant environmental education materials to be integrated into the school curriculum.[19] From late 2005 through early 2007, the society (in actuality, Fahd) identified local teachers to test the materials in select schools and help in the training workshops. However, after an auspicious start, the project was stalled for bureaucratic reasons—the minister of education insisted that all materials be approved formally by the national curriculum committee—only to lose its key support when the SCDP collapsed in 2008.[20] (At this time, the society lost its minimal funding and rent-paid office.) What bothered my Soqotran interlocutors more was that the initial idea to include several Soqotri-language phrases in the textbook was outright rejected by the Yemeni Ministry. Based on this experience, Fahd concluded that

Soqotrans could not count on state-led programs to revive their culture and language. Instead, they would have to make the people themselves care about their heritage. A grassroots poetry contest began to seem like just the solution.

In December 2008, the heritage society organized Soqotra's first *Million's Poet*-inspired "Competition of the Soqotran Poet." This "metacultural" performance of Soqotra's intangible heritage—staged just five months after UNESCO inscribed the archipelago as a natural World Heritage Site—was, like its model, a runaway success.[21] So much so that the Soqotra Society organized an annual competition five years running. Despite their modest budget and limited institutional support, the society tried as well as they could to replicate the reality TV show format on a local stage: through a geographically diverse body of contestants, an expert jury, a live audience, and a grand prize. Of course, there were differences in scope and scale. Instead of holding auditions, the society selected—and to some extent, had to cajole into participating—nine poets each year. The competition—in 2011, its name was changed to "The Festival of Soqotri Poetry" to soften its competitive edge—was held over four consecutive evenings in the courtyard of a Hadibo school. During each of the first three evenings, three poets took turns reciting two original Soqotri-language poems (Soq.: *tentiru/tenowtir*), after which the jury evaluated each poem's strengths and weaknesses. On the last evening, the three finalists competed against one another. The all-male audience did not have voting capabilities, but many of the youth held up their new smart phones to record, photograph, and take videos of their favorite poets. In 2008, the winning poet took home YER 50,000 (USD 250) and a glass trophy with the title "Soqotran Poet of the Year 2008"; in 2009, with financial support from Gulf Soqotrans having risen from USD 1,500 to 4,000, the first prize increased to YER 100,000, and each participant received YER 20,000 and a cell phone compliments of a local poet-sponsor.

"In the Gulf, they call it the *Million's Poet*. Here, we call it the *Fifty's Poet*," scoffed Qayuf, when I asked him what he thought of the contest. For years, I had thought of Qayuf as "the jewelry man," as I often encountered him in the market hawking Maria Theresa dollar silver bracelets to foreigners. (In the eyes of the women of Homhil, the island's *real* jewelry salesmen were those who traveled the interior biannually pushing the latest gold fashions from Dubai.) Like his cousin Tanuf, Qayuf loved and memorized poetry. So I was surprised to hear him say, in 2009, that the competition was "useless." It was useless, he thought, not just because it did not—could not—measure up to its Emirati model: a disparity captured in his quip about the grand prize of *fifty* thousand riyals in contrast to the UAE's five *million* dirham. It was useless, Qayuf went on to explain, because the contestants recited only "new poetry."

"Poetry like, 'Oh my eyes, stop your crying' [Soq.: *bas esh diho 'ayn min bowshi*]," Qayuf said, pointedly reciting the first line of "my" poem. This was a poem that the teacher Hamdan had "given" me shortly after my arrival. It was the poem I recited feebly whenever Soqotrans questioned my credentials. Usually, friends and strangers delighted in hearing my Soqotri poem; it is why Qayuf remembered it. But as he intimated, this poem, like most new poetry, was infused with Arabic.

"And we even gave [the society] the old *tenowtir* and *temowtil*," Qayuf said, referring to different forms of classic Soqotri poetry.

At the heart of Qayuf's critique, I suspected, was a resentment that it was the young, urbanized members of the society who were in charge of the competition, not the island's venerable pastoralist poets, like Qayuf himself. Despite his disdain for the predominantly bilingual poetry composed today, the competition actually forced Soqotran poets to limit their use of Arabic. In this and in other regards, the "Fifty's Poet" was not just a poor imitation of the *Million's Poet*. It differed in some essential ways.

First, whereas the *Million's Poet* championed its modern spin on a traditional practice, the Soqotra competition demanded a pivot from the present toward the "premodern." For ADACH, the *Million's Poet* constituted "a way of uniting modernization with tradition," the performance of Arab tradition a demonstration of Emirati modernity.[22] Indeed, many commentators seemed captivated precisely by the spectacle's "hybridity," relishing, for example, the use of "tribal" poetry to describe glittering shopping malls.[23] In Soqotra, however, the very parameters of the competition encouraged the fresh production of traditional Soqotri *tenowtir*. The jury evaluated the poets' compositions first and foremost according to their linguistic integrity. But after the past forty-some years of increasing Arabization and integration within the Yemeni nation-state, the present is infused with and defined largely by Arabic terms: *the state, the environment*, and *employment* have no Soqotri analogues. Thus, poems about Palestinian suffering as well as panegyrics to Yemen's then-president Saleh lost out—in 2008 and 2009—to poems about the sultanate period.

"Shall I tell you, or not, what Soqotra once was?" So began Uthman Abdullah Uthman Baidobah's—the Soqotra Poet of the Year 2008—winning poem. The past, Baidobah went on to describe, was a period of want and generosity. This was a past when there were no roads or schools; when Soqotrans had no rice or canned foods, like tomato paste; when there were no radios or tape recorders, no electricity or airplanes; when Soqotrans depended solely on their livestock and the fruits of the sea; when they slept on goatskins and ate from rudimentary clay vessels and stones; when they had to rely on cauterization or herbs in place of pharmaceuticals. Yet this was a time, Baidobah declared, when God acted on the people; when the Soqotrans would pull each other into their houses insistent on slaughtering their best goats for one another. It was a time, moreover, when there was only one leader, who had the last word, rather than the current climate of corruption. True "Soqotranness," his audience was reminded then, and during the festivals that followed, is determined if not bound by this past temporality and singular sovereignty. "If we could beckon for that past to return," Abdullah Said Sulayman Batimhi, the twenty-five-year-old Soqotra Poet of the Year of 2009, concluded, "I would know how to greet it respectfully. I love and cherish it. / For I was not created for civilization, I am a Bedouin from Soqotra."

Second, whereas the *Million's Poet* celebrates a regional, transnational Arab heritage even as it promotes national pride, the Soqotra competition was framed deliberately as a subset of Yemeni heritage divorced of its Arab Gulf connections. In the case of the *Million's Poet*, this transnationalism displaces the impact of political or religious critique; for example, Hissa Hilal's 2010 poem, "The Chaos of Fatwas," was interpreted both narrowly as a criticism of an individual Saudi cleric and broadly as a critique of hard-liner clerics throughout the Muslim world. In Soqotra—where the event was in fact a transnational production encouraged and funded by Soqotran citizens of the UAE and Oman—the society sought to diffuse any government censure by locating this heritage geographically (if not temporally) within the space of the nation. With the government fighting an insurrection in the north and a growing secessionist movement in the south—and with the majority of the Soqotri-language poetry exalting a preunity past—the society members worried that the contest might be deemed contentious. Moreover, during its first year, several *mutatawwi'in* had denounced the competition for being un-Islamic. Thus, when in the days prior to the 2009 competition, a Soqotran government official condemned it as an antistate event, the society responded by affixing printed slogans around the schoolyard venue affirming its significance. But they were also careful to proclaim: "The preservation of Soqotran heritage and its revival exalts the qualities of belonging to the great Yemeni nation" and "Soqotran heritage is pure Yemeni heritage." What these posters revealed was that whatever the society identified as "Soqotran heritage"—if it was to be performed and celebrated in the late 2000s—could be neither transnational nor antinational.

However, for the Yemeni mainlanders living on the island, the competition was largely unintelligible and thus irrelevant. "Just noise," a friend from Taiz said, when I asked him what he thought about this celebration of Yemeni heritage. If this so-called Fifty's Poet with its meager resources, nostalgic focus, and nationalist framing appears any less significant than its Abu Dhabi prototype, then this may be so because for us, too, it would be largely unintelligible. Indeed, unlike the *Million's Poet*, or any of the other heritage festivals so prevalent in the Arab Gulf, this Soqotri-language event was intended strictly for its indigenous population. It was exclusive in other ways, too: women poets, who are abundant, were not invited to participate (nor were there any Soqotran women in the audience); other forms of Soqotri linguistic heritage (stories, legends, ritual prayers) were precluded; and its organizers were not interested in featuring Afro-Soqotran performers and musicians. But the conservatism in which the competition was cloaked barely concealed the fact that this grassroots endeavor organized by para-experts outside the official heritage regime was already political enough.

For, within its "noise," a shift had occurred. Unlike traditional Soqotri-language poetry in which nostalgia for the sultanate is obscured by metaphor, the competition gave a platform to the Soqotrans' *sovereign nostalgia*: the nostalgia for a past governed by unconditional hospitality and by a singular, decisive sovereign; the "sole architect," personified and indivisible.[24] This was not the shared sovereignty deployed in enclaves—like World Heritage Sites—through which states temporarily relinquish some control to multilateral agencies to attract international investment and expertise.[25] This was the sovereignty embodied in the autonomous host: the Soqotran who is sovereign in his own home. And this sovereign nostalgia, expressed not only in Baidobah's poem but also in several other poems presented during the 2008–2010 contests, was not just past-oriented. Rather, it articulated less the longing to return to Soqotra's era of despotism and deprivation than the desire for a decisive, pastoral state in the present. This sovereign nostalgia was a rejection by the Soqotrans of the shared sovereignty that diluted the state's accountability and obscured their access to it, while maximizing international involvement in their affairs. In this noise, then, a sovereign past *and future* were recalled, imagined, and committed to smart phone memory cards.

"FROM SOQOTRA TO 'AMRAN"

In January 2011, I watched coverage of the Tunisian protests and the ouster of longtime president Ben Ali in Hadibo's juice shops, where many male pastoralists—people like Sughayr, Sownhin, and Yaqub—catch up on world events whenever they come down to the coast. When I visited Homhil during those fateful weeks, however, the talk was not about Tunisia's revolution but about the impending installation of the Soqotra "Authority" (*hai'a*) that had been mandated back in 2008. This special "independent" Authority was meant to work in tandem with the latest UNDP-GEF-government project, the Socotra Governance and Biodiversity Project, to uphold the government's administrative and financial decentralization policies. But my interlocutors questioned whether this "local" Authority was not an extension of the kind of "transnational governmentality" they had experienced in 2001–2008, when the SCDP had appeared as the de facto government on Soqotra.[26] What would this Authority do? Would the *hai'a* be an expansion of the *bi'a*? ("The Environment" was fine—a man from Homhil hastened to assure me—albeit "a little lacking" in its development outcomes.) Who would own the Authority? Would it be dominated by one person or tribe? Who would select the five-member governing body? And why couldn't the archipelago be designated a conventional Yemeni governorate (*muhafaza*) instead? As the Tunisian revolution began to ignite uprisings elsewhere, including in Yemen, my interlocutors were arguing that the archipelago should become more integrated into the mainland's administrative structure, not less.

One reason that my interlocutors were animated about the development of the Authority in January 2011—but not in February 2008 when the Authority was decreed, or even in January 2010, when I had last visited—had much to do with the SGBP's own delay. Although this project was approved in June 2008 and officially commenced its work a year later, it had had virtually no presence on the island until the spring of 2010. Nor had it run the planned workshops to solicit community involvement and support. If it had, its employees might have explained to Soqotrans how, from an ecodevelopment perspective, the proposed Authority made good sense. Tasked with liaising with the central government and international donors directly, the Authority was authorized to bypass the regional governorate-level administration, which mediates between the central government and Yemen's 333 local districts. This would relieve Soqotra's two local districts from having to vie with the twenty-eight other districts in the Hadhramawt (the largest of Yemen's twenty-one governorates) for services and support. Moreover, modeled after Jordan's Aqaba Special Economic Zone Authority, the Soqotra Authority would work to capture global capital within Soqotra's boundaries and Yemen's state territory.

From my interlocutors' perspectives, the proposed Authority represented a step away from strong, centralized rule. What they wanted was for the archipelago to be redistricted as Yemen's twenty-second governorate—to be elevated, not excepted—so that all its allocated state and donor funds would reach its elected councils directly. Notably, this streamlining was one of the rationales for the proposed Authority. Still, for Soqotrans eager for government employment and services, the Authority seemed like one more project standing between themselves and the central state. Several of my interlocutors expressed concern that, under this Authority, the monies allocated to Soqotra would be "eaten" along the way—as they suspected the governorate-level bureaucrats and ICDP administrators of doing already. Then, before the SGBP managed to assuage these fears, the UNDP suspended it and other pending projects in Yemen, Bahrain, and Syria.[27] By April 2011, with the Yemeni Revolution having spilled out into the streets of Hadibo, the SGBP's expatriate staff had been evacuated.

Nevertheless, these very questions took on new urgency and meaning in the context of the Arab uprisings. Incidentally, it was also in 2011 that the island gained increased (DSL) Internet access. Not only were Soqotrans able to follow the events in Tunisia, Egypt, Libya, Bahrain, Syria, and mainland Yemen on television, but now they were also following them online and through social media. Hadibo-based youth took to Facebook like their parents took to the street. Facebook became the preferred medium for communicating with Soqotrans living or studying abroad, replacing in one short decade the cassette tapes that had networked these "virtual" communities before. Online, in person, and—still—through poetry, Soqotrans debated how the archipelago should be governed. But instead of arguing only for or against the merits of the proposed Authority, Soqotrans began envisioning a range of political and administrative alternatives, including their island becoming a governorate (*muhafaza*); a self-administering region (*wikala*); a province (*iqlim*) within a federal Yemen; part of a new South Yemen; or even an independent state. What was novel at this time was not just the array of no-longer-implausible options for their political future but also the boldness with which Soqotrans defended their positions. My biggest surprise, when I returned in December 2011, was to find that the days of caution before "entering politics" had disappeared. Now, even people I had just met shared their political views freely or, grabbing my arm, pulled me into their demonstrations.

These variously imagined futures correlated, to a certain degree, with the different coalitions that emerged in Soqotra (and nationally) to cut across political parties or opposition groups. In May 2011, a group of Soqotran "youth" (aged forty and younger) established a nonpartisan coalition of all ages interested in shifting the focus from toppling the Saleh regime to advocating for the island's special status. This so-called national council (*al-majlis al-watani*) presented itself as a counter to the "failed system" (*al-nizam al-fashil*) represented by the local councils (*al-majlis al-mahalli*) and their presidents, the district directors of Soqotra.[28] If its members shared one goal, it was for the Soqotra Archipelago to become an autonomous province (*iqlim*) within Yemen, similar to Iraqi Kurdistan. Describing Soqotra as a ball that had been tossed around from governorate (Aden) to governorate (Hadhramawt), the national council's president, Fahmi Ali Ibrahim, advocated tirelessly for its autonomy (*khususiya*) under the central government.

"Don't we have political aspirations?" Fahmi asked rhetorically, when we met again in December 2011. "Don't we want to have the same thing that the people in the Arab world want? The people in the Arab world are making their demands. They have desires—and we don't?"

A high school teacher, travel agent, and herbal doctor—and, for a while, my Soqotri-language tutor in Hadibo—Fahmi is perhaps best known as the grandson of Sultan Isa's vizier Ibrahim Khalid Ali al-Nubi al-Takali, one of the men martyred at Haybak in 1974. It may be for this reason that his detractors accused him of wanting to reestablish an independent sultanate, a charge Fahmi rejects. (As he points out, his uncle, the vizier's own son, was the local president of al-Islah, the Islamist "reform" party that had been calling for Soqotra to become Yemen's twenty-second governorate; genealogy does not determine political orientation.) Following a successful visit to al-Mahra with several Soqotran delegates in fall 2011, Fahmi and his colleagues began to explore possibilities for renewed cooperation between these historically linked territories. Eventually, in July 2012, the national councils of Soqotra and al-Mahra merged into the General Council of the Sons of Soqotra and al-Mahra, united under the leadership of "Sultan" Abdullah Isa bin 'Afrar, Sultan Isa's son. Like the national council that preceded it, the general council lobbied for Soqotra to become an autonomous region within a federal Yemen, but now as an entity joined with al-Mahra under the presidency of Sultan Abdullah. Sultan Abdullah, who grew up primarily in Saudi Arabia but lives currently in Oman, visited Soqotra in February 2013, his first public return. Whether the crowds he drew were political supporters or just curious, Soqotrans gathered in the thousands to meet— and lay eyes on—"our sultan."

Around this period, shortly after the establishment of the national council, Fahd had formed a people's council (*al-majlis al-ahli*) to advocate for the archipelago's elevation to governorate. Supporters of the national council charged that the people's council was simply an arm of al-Islah. Fahd argued otherwise, telling me in January 2012 that he had modeled the people's council on people's councils established on the mainland. The difference, he stressed, was that the Soqotran council was not under the authority of its namesake in the Hadhramawt. It also focused on local matters, acting as "link between the authorities and the people regarding common issues such as food and fuel prices" and developing ideas for a less bureaucratic administration of the islands, but not autonomy. Fahd would like the archipelago to achieve independence, he offered, but he considered this a decades-long project. In his view, Soqotrans were just not ready yet.

The authorities in Soqotra were barraged not only with these opinions, and others; they were also forced to respond to popular initiatives.[29] As early as March 2011, Hadibo demonstrators and the "revolutionary youth" (as they called themselves) mobilized in unprecedented ways. In addition to demanding President Saleh's resignation—something my Homhil friends would not have dreamed of asserting or even hearing publicly three years earlier—Hadibo's revolutionaries forced the resignations of several local leaders whom they considered ineffective or corrupt.

"Now the reins of power are in the hands of the people," Yahya gushed while apprising me in January 2012 of the revolutionaries' recent efforts to "purify" the local government. "We'll go after any sign of corruption, any director who doesn't work out, who creates problems with his workers, whose work isn't excellent. . . . And then, that's it. He leaves, he leaves [*yirhal*]." An Afro-Soqotran whom I had known for years, Yahya had often moved me to fits of laughter with his irreverent jokes about "the northerners." Now he was telling me how the lessons of Sanaa had moved him: "We have benefited from this Arab spring: *irhal* [leave], *isqat an-nizam* [bring down the regime]. These are new words we didn't know before. The revolutions brought this talk and, thank God, Soqotran society is beginning to understand, to acquire civilization, to change by itself."[30] Later, Yahya articulated what these successes had meant for him personally: "Now, thank God, I feel as if I'm a free citizen. I feel inside that I am a citizen who is free. Noble! I don't feel afraid like I did before. I speak from strength, and I'll press my demands until they are realized."

With this newfound sense of empowerment, Soqotrans also stepped in to fill the void left by the withdrawal of international NGOs and the suspension of aid. This political subjectivity—what Benoît Challand identified as an emergent "presentism" in the Arab-majority states affected by the uprisings—was manifested not only in calls for the end of the regime but also through the beginning of individuals embracing immediate, even if seemingly nonpolitical, causes. Challand's argument draws on Hamad Dabashi's claim that the widespread call for the "fall of the regime" referred both to the end of political regimes and the end of the regime of knowledge—the end of external expertise, foreign aid, and organization by NGOs. Despite the uprisings' many failings and disappointments, through them, "the people had "regained [their] capacity to decide what should be done here and now."[31] In Hadibo, as in Sanaa and Cairo, individuals took to the streets not only to protest the governing regime but also to clean the streets literally and metaphorically. In doing so, Soqotran "youth" demonstrated to their anemic administration—and themselves—that they could self-manage both their immediate environment and the Environment long managed by foreigner experts.

For instance, one of the most gainful initiatives during these heady days of revolution was the creation of special price-watch committees to control against commodity hoarding and price gouging by unscrupulous merchants. During the 2011 monsoon season, when the price of gasoline rose from YER 75 per liter to YER 125, the "revolutionaries" padlocked the door to the Hadibo gas station. Eventually, with the support of the island's general director and police force, these committees managed to control the prices of cement, sugar, wheat, and other imports by confiscating any hoarded goods and selling them at standard costs. Buoyed by these successes, in October 2011, supporters of the national council and other nonaffiliated revolutionaries took it upon themselves to pick up the garbage layering the streets of Hadibo—accomplishing in one day, one of the organizers pointed out, what the Environment had failed to do in a decade.[32] Shortly thereafter, the national council evicted the qat sellers from Hadibo and Qalansiyah. Tempting as it may be to interpret the banishment of qat—and the plastic bags it comes in—as a symbolic purge of northern influence, the national council framed its action as one of self- and environmental care: "Do not spoil Soqotra" (*la takhrab suqutra*) was the rallying call. Reflecting back on these actions two years later, the secretary of the Soqotra Society for Heritage and History told my summer research assistant (a student from NYUAD): "People's attitudes changed. Their love for the homeland began to revive, whereas before it didn't exist—negligence, the discarding of trash. But now people began to realize that this is our country and that we must take care of it. And so, this love for the homeland motivated people to go out into the street, pick up a broom, and sweep."

This was the inspired climate during which the 2011 Festival of Soqotri Poetry occurred. Initially, the society questioned whether it would be appropriate to organize another festival in the midst of the revolution. They worried about security and were preoccupied with current events, while also attending or following the near-daily demonstrations organized, alternately, by the national council, the people's council, the southern movement, and al-Islah—such as the protests against the cessation of Yemenia's Soqotra routes, described in the Introduction. Moreover, the society had even less external funding this year, so the festival would have to be cobbled together by volunteers. But under the "revolutionary tent" erected near Hadibo's central soccer pitch—an area that Soqotrans, inspired by their mainland counterparts, had begun to call

Change Square—Soqotri poetry accompanied the pan-Arab slogans. And it was revolutionary youth who loaned their equipment and labor to the festival. "This was the proof that most people were with the revolution—and most of them supported our heritage," the secretary of the Soqotra Society for Heritage and History said.

On January 3, 2012, the penultimate day of the 2011 festival, a pink-hued procession snaked its way from Change Square through Hadibo's central market, pulling in vegetable vendors, children, an elderly man riding a donkey, and a lone woman, who grabbed my arm. Pink was the color donned by protesters across Yemen to signal their peaceful, "Jasmine" revolution. Taking cues from an al-Islah Party member atop a slowly moving Land Cruiser, the demonstrators chanted various slogans. One they returned to over and over: "Revolution, revolution in all of Yemen, from Soqotra to 'Amran!"[33] In Hadibo, so removed from Yemen in so many ways—yet increasingly beset with factions of its own—this vow of unity was electrifying.

POETIC JUSTICE

"We in Soqotra have suffered for forty years before reaching this place, this gathering," Fahd said to the large, all-male crowd seated cross-legged on the pebbly ground (or, if they were esteemed elders, on chairs to the side) of the school's inner courtyard. Dressed in an oversized leather jacket with a wool scarf cinched around his neck, Fahd was seated at the jury table onstage in front of a large banner proclaiming, "The Festival of Soqotri Poetry 2011." The wind whipped at the microphone.

"I say on this day with complete awareness, believing that as you have gathered here today, you are not divided by partisanship; you are not divided by regionalism; you are not divided according to the political power and its opposition; and you are not divided by personal interests. What unites you? Your rights, first, to Soqotra and your mutual rights over each other," Fahd continued, trying to unite the audience as he had rallied the poets that morning. "With this celebration, we are not simply celebrating a person, listening to some poems, and then going home. There is a great deal of work in front of us. There is a great future ahead of us," he said, his brow raised. Although still seated, Fahd's voice and energy rose.

"Soqotra needs us in the cultural sphere," Fahd said, jabbing his left index finger into the air. "It needs us in the economic sphere; it needs us in the political sphere; it needs us in the social sphere. It needs us to build these together. Building them begins now—it begins from this place." Speaking without notes, Fahd looked directly at the audience below him, the majority school-age boys. "We have lived through many periods and many circumstances," he said, still jabbing at the air with every phrase. "And many authorities, regrettably, were able to place in our souls the notion that our past is shameful; that our language is shameful; that our customs are shameful; that our traditions are shameful. And it was forbidden to speak Soqotri inside official buildings."

"You're speaking Soqotri? Shame on you! Speak Arabic!" Fahd impersonated in an officious tone. "That's what they said to you," he reminded his listeners in his perfect, eloquent Arabic (*fusha*). "Why? Is our language shameful? Are our customs shameful? Are our traditions shameful? Is our heritage shameful? Today we hold our celebration. We have been able to reach the point where it is our right to celebrate the values of Soqotra itself, without denying those of others. We hope to God that we will be able to celebrate when the Soqotri language and customs have a place in the school curriculum, a place in the university curriculum, a place in all the foundations that deal with preserving Soqotran heritage."

The audience applauded.

"The Society will take up the issue of Soqotri language, culture, and customs having their place, one day, in the school and university curriculums and in cultural institutions. And that we have a clear call for the rights to our culture, the rights to our history, the rights to our identity—for all our rights, without exception," Fahd promised. "I hope that all of these good faces of the young people attending here will have the ability to shape the future by recognizing the importance of the beautiful past. With the permission of God, great and powerful, we will reach the goal we desire. We will reach an end favored by God. Peace be upon you, and the mercy and blessings of God," he concluded, to more applause.

Fahd's address was flanked by several opening acts. Before he spoke, a young teen recited a verse from the Qur'an and six of the island's renowned poets (including the winners of 2008, 2009, and 2010) chanted verses of the singsong "hedon" poetry (named for its refrain: *hedon hedon*). Following Fahd's address, Baidobah, the winner in 2008, returned to the stage to recite a new poem, another nostalgic ode to the premodern past. Next, a tin whistler played a melody evoking the impression of a lone Soqotran entertaining his goats. Finally, the jury was seated; Fahd returned to the stage with two of the island's great poets, Ali Abdullah al-Rigdihi and Muhammad Amr Di-Girigoti, and the competition began. One by one, the evening's three contestants were called up to recite their first poem. Following each hesitant, staccato delivery, the jury took turns evaluating the Soqotri-language poem's content and merits—all in Arabic. Then, during an entr'acte, several senior poets recited their own compositions prior to the commencement of the contestants' second round.

In this first evening's first round, the contestants stuck to trusted subjects: Soqotra's past generosity/hospitality (*karam*), the Islamic path to salvation, and the competition itself. However, by the second round—and with each evening that followed—more and more of the contestants and entr'acte wordsmiths zeroed in on the Arab uprisings, other present-day social disorders, and the future of Soqotra. And their critiques were not timid. Arab leaders were condemned for the deaths of protesters and portrayed, by one poet, as being worse than "Benjamin" (Netanyahu), who "kills only in small amounts." President Saleh and his supporters were likened to a countrywide infestation of fleas requiring extermination; to travelers on a ship at port, which, when it finally departs, will sink under the weight of its stolen cargo; and to a lumbering camel that has irritated otherwise harmless bees, causing them to swarm and attack. Several poets bemoaned the marriage of Soqotran girls to Gulf State citizens (a week earlier, an Omani man had married a young Soqotran with one million riyals in bridewealth, approximately USD 5,000); the negative effects of qat; alcoholic tourists; and intertribal skirmishes over land. But most wrestled over the future of Soqotra, with some calling for a return to South Yemen (through secession with the southern governorates) and others calling for complete independence. A few presented practical problems of secession. Others argued for or against the former socialist regime and Yemen's 1990 unification. Many poets decried the factionalism brewing in Soqotra. One warned evocatively that, in such a climate, not even swollen riverbeds yield pasture—albeit the streets were not yet stained with the "colors" (blood) of Tunisia or Libya. Another argued against the proposed Soqotra Authority. Even the few verses about the sultanate were juxtaposed to the "fires" or "dark rain clouds" of the present.[34]

"The Soqotran winter has been affected by the Arab Spring," said Ismail, noting that the competition had taken a 180-degree turn this year: from expressions of (what I call) sovereign nostalgia to expressions of sovereign anticipation. For the festival's organizers, the promotion of Soqotran cultural heritage (in particular, Soqotri-language poetry) was still its essential function. For Fahd, who had spent three mornings that week leading demonstrations arguing for national services and Soqotrans' "rights" *as* Yemeni citizens—protesters in front of the Yemenia office waved national flags and signs proclaiming, "Yemeni Soqotra is in need of the return of Yemenia Airlines"—the festival facilitated two things.

It encouraged the production and advancement of Soqotri-language poetry. "As it is now, it is a poetry without rules or defined standards," Fahd explained in the week following the competition; "like *jahili* poetry two thousand years ago, there is no criticism; there are no defined standards." In Fahd's view, it was the jury's commentary in particular that has challenged poets artistically. "I think in the future we are going to see a transformation of [Soqotri] poetry, in structure and form." In this sense, again, what Tanuf's cousin called "the Fifty's Poet" was not just a poor replica of its upscale Emirati model. It encouraged fresh production, too.

And it helped to instill in Soqotrans not only a love for their heritage but also the popular consciousness that Fahd knew to be the prerequisite for any large-scale social change. Of course, as Fahd conceded, the society was limited by the island's (and their own) economic reality:

> What's the problem? Funding. First of all, the people are poor, and second, they don't believe in supporting heritage [for its own sake]. That someone would take from his pocket—would sell a goat, maybe—so that he or someone else could recite a poem? This, no. This is hard. We have to give someone money for him to come and recite a poem. Until now, we buy heritage. *We buy it.* We've begun to convince people of the importance of heritage, but we haven't gotten to the point yet of convincing people to give something for the sake of their heritage, without compensation.

Despite these limitations, during the festival's third evening, Fahd had returned to his vision of the transformative nature of heritage. Noting that all the "texts" to date had been redolent with the discontent of the Arab uprisings, Fahd stressed to his captivated audience, "I hope that the revolution here is also a cultural one and includes literature, poetry, and stories and produces new values alongside a rejection of the old ones. This is a worthy project."

But a difficult one. Midway through each evening's program, a large portion of the youth ducked out to catch the Arabic-dubbed Turkish television serial *Valley of the Wolves* on Abu Dhabi TV—a striking portent of the Soqotri tongue's chances to survive against the global media onslaught and in the face of Arabic and English linguistic hegemony. Indeed, the audience was well aware of the irony of the jury members evaluating the linguistic achievements of the poets through their Arabic-language commentary. Someone in Ismail's village quipped that they should bring the revolutionary youth to the competition to demonstrate against the use of Arabic—as much a critique of the ubiquity of demonstrations during this period as a critique of the use of Arabic itself. But when, in response to these criticisms, a jury member tried evaluating a Soqotri-language poem in Soqotri, the audience snickered. In Soqotra, Arabic is the language of education and analysis; Soqotri is the voice of illiteracy. It may explain why Fahd, one of the most vocal supporters of the Soqotri language, never speaks Soqotri in public. These and other challenges facing Soqotra were evoked in the final composition presented by Sulayman Saʿd Ahmad, the winning poet of 2011: "We have been struck by powerful storms and we have only wooden log-boats [*hawari*]."

A few days later, I met one of the festival's participants in the lobby of Hadibo's relatively fancy Summer Land Hotel. A supporter of the national council, Zayd had recited a poem warning against the creation of the UNDP-envisioned Authority proposed long before the uprisings began. Surprised to hear that Soqotrans were still debating this particular form of administration, I asked him why he was so opposed to this idea.

"The Authority is like a pregnant woman; you don't know if you'll end up with a boy or a girl," Zayd said. He went on to explain that the real problem was that they would not know what would happen to landownership, one of the major sources of friction on the island. Would they still be able to appeal to Yemeni law to settle property cases? Would the state finally relinquish state-owned land, annexed under the socialists, to the tribes? What Zayd wanted was total separation from Yemen, from the north and the south. "I want Soqotra to be autonomous," he said. "Soqotra used to be its own state [*dawla*]. But then the [National Liberation] Front came and asked the sultan what he ruled over. He said al-Mahra, so they took that. And then they took Soqotra, too." Zayd pointed out how far Soqotra lies from Yemen. "We are in the midst of the Indian Ocean, three hundred kilometers from Hadhramawt. We wouldn't have become part of Yemen at all had the Front not arrived and taken us."

As Zayd spoke, I noticed Usama, the "northern" hotel manager from Taiz shaking his head in disbelief. As I discussed in Chapter 1, Usama is one of the many young men from the mainland who migrated to Soqotra and struggled to make a living there. Later, I asked him what he thought of the Soqotrans' call for independence. Usama shook his head again.

"What can they do?" he said. "Not a single Soqotran has ever reached a position higher than that of a schoolteacher. None have become doctors or scientists or engineers. How will they run a country?"

. . .

A challenging pregnancy prevented me from returning to Soqotra until late 2013. Through Facebook posts, phone calls, and the help of my exceptional student research assistant, I followed the revolution's progress from a distance. In February 2012, Yemenia resumed one of its weekly flights between Sanaa and Hadibo. That same month, demonstrators began calling for the resignation of the archipelago's new district director. Demonstrations against the regime continued, as did the voluntary acts of self-government and the popular "enactments of expertise."[35] For example, when the poaching of Soqotra's nesting sea turtles rose to disturbing levels in 2012—the SCDP had supported a community's turtle monitoring program, which stopped when its funding ceased in 2007—the nearby residents created check points to control road access to the two beaches where the turtles lay their eggs. In a similar vein, several youth groups formed to continue to foster this spirit of volunteerism and to fill the void left by the cessation of NGO projects and the withdrawal of development aid. These included two Facebook groups focused on raising environmental awareness and the al-Mahabba Association, a group started by a Hadibo schoolteacher and his friends that initiated several cleanups and environmental awareness campaigns in the spring of 2013. These local initiatives were pegged to international events, such as World Wetlands Day and World Environment Day, to signal the Soqotran youth's (desired) connection to the international community and commitment to environmental protection. In the absence of the Environment and other international projects, Soqotran youth found an opening to care for their environmental heritage.

In March 2013, just a month after Sultan Abdullah Isa's historic visit drew tremendous crowds, three Soqotran delegates went to Sanaa to participate in the transitional National Dialogue Conference (NDC). This representative forum, stipulated by the Gulf Cooperation Council Initiative brokered in November 2011, was tasked with resolving Yemen's political problems and with formulating the basis for a new constitution.[36] One of these delegates was Fahd, rapporteur for the "Independence of Special Entities" (istiqlaliyat al-hai'at) working group, which focused on developing ways to protect the rights of Yemen's vulnerable populations.[37] As elsewhere in Yemen, Soqotran supporters of the Southern Movement (al-hirak) denounced the NDC as a Sanaa-controlled proceeding that had rejected their calls for secession or even a bipartite federal state (along the lines of the former North and South Yemen). Meanwhile, supporters of Soqotra's General Council for the Sons of Soqotra and al-Mahra rejected the NDC for not including a delegate who represented their vision for a joint, autonomous province. When in May 2013 an NDC committee, which included Fahd, visited Soqotra to discuss their progress, protesters from both groups blockaded them and the accompanying TV crew in the Summer Land. Unable to pursue dialogue, the committee members were evacuated from Soqotra by military plane. That summer, my NYUAD student research assistant captured the frustration of several youth who were "fed up with these dependencies"—to Aden, to Hadhramawt, and even, potentially, al-Mahra—and just wanted Soqotra to have some form of independence.[38]

"I'm not interested in these designations and names," said the secretary of the Society for Heritage and History, dismissing the distinctions fought between governorate, province, authority, and so forth. "Even if Soqotra were designated a nightclub—but with autonomy—I wouldn't have a problem with that. What's important is that we have some autonomy in decreeing some laws—environmental laws, heritage and cultural laws—specific to our traditions. Our language is beginning to go extinct. Some words have been lost already. We're afraid it might perish."

Then, just a few months later, Soqotrans' shared goal for some form of independence was in fact achieved. On 14 October, Yemen's transitional president,

Abdu Rabbu Mansour Hadi, performed Eid al-Adha prayers in Hadibo—on the fiftieth anniversary of the beginning of the 1963 revolution against the British, no less—and announced that the Soqotra Archipelago would become an independent governorate. Fahd had petitioned for this outcome, after having gained the support of 80 percent of the NDC's delegates.[39] And in December 2013, the government issued Law No. 31 establishing its twenty-second governorate. For the first time in six years, the society did not organize the annual poetry festival. Was this because "heritage" had lost its purchase? Was it because the festival, like so many forms of heritage engineering, exhibited its own exclusions? Or was it because the society's members were preoccupied, once again, with the near-daily demonstrations organized by al-Islah and al-Hirak in turn? When I ran into Fahd in the Summer Land lobby, I asked him why the festival was off. Clearly preoccupied with other matters—Soqotra's new governorate status, his NDC work (which continued until February 2014), and the latest rumors that the United States was looking to move its Yemeni Guantanamo Bay prisoners to Soqotra—Fahd suggested that the so-called Fifty's Poet had fulfilled its aims.

"Now the whole world knows that Soqotra has poets," Fahd said.

As for Soqotrans not being able to "run a country," my northern Yemeni friend was wrong. He was not only factually incorrect; Soqotrans have reached positions "higher than schoolteachers": Ba Haqiba, Soqotra's member of Parliament and first "native" commissioner, being a case in point. He was also mistaken in his assessment of the new, post-unity generation's—"the youth"—capabilities and progress. For the Soqotran and Mahra NDC delegates managed to work into Article 3 of the "draft constitution for the new Yemen" (released in January 2015) what only three other Arab-majority states have enacted to date: the constitutional recognition of a non-Arabic language.[40] If this new Yemen were ever able to stitch itself back together after its current complex war, it would find in its draft constitution—between "Islam is the religion of the State, and Arabic its official language" (Article 2) and "Islamic Sharia is the source of legislation" (Article 4)—the following commitment: "The State shall pay special attention to both the Mehri and Soqotri languages."[41] Although the outcomes produced by the NDC with regard to these languages went further than the wording that eventually made it into this draft, this was still a soaring recognition for two groups of language speakers that make up less than

0.01 percent of Yemen's total population.[42] And at least one of the catalysts for this recognition was a speech given (in Arabic) during the second plenary session of the NDC by Fahd Saleem Kafayan, a man who had grown up hearing that his language was shameful. (A second speech, on the status of Mehri, was given by one of the Mahra delegates, Badr Salim Kalshat, who did deliver it in Mehri.) Fahd had launched his cultural revolution—or, at least, he lit the torch—and he got there not through the ballot box, as he had recognized he would not, but through a sort of poetry. A poetry—he realized, in the wake of his Günter Grass encounter—that was worthy enough to be Soqotrans' ambassador on the international stage. In November 2014, Fahd, this one-time Bedouin—for whom, as a child, Soqotra had been the entire world—was appointed minister of the Republic of Yemen's Ministry of Fish Wealth under President Hadi's exiled regime: the first Soqotran to make it to the cabinet level.[43]

HERITAGE TRANSFORMED

In Soqotra, at a time when the archipelago was inscribed as a natural World Heritage Site for its biological diversity and threatened species, individual Soqotrans took to salvaging, performing, and promoting what they considered to be a threatened cultural heritage. This was a heritage that enabled them to position themselves within a parallel ecology of expertise—one that contested even as it modeled itself on the regime of foreign expertise, international aid, and government by NGOs. It was in this context, in December 2008, that the Soqotra Society for Heritage and History staged its first grassroots Soqotri-language poetry contest modeled on a government initiative to preserve vernacular Arabic poetry in the Gulf. In this first, tentative year, the contest's organizers sought to frame their cultural heritage as a necessary ingredient of the nation-state deserving of national recognition—in contrast to the foreign experts' framing of Soqotra's environmental heritage as being so unique that it needed international protection. However, by the end of 2011, the event had become a platform for demonstrating Soqotra's cultural sovereignty as a legitimizing discourse for Soqotrans' contending visions of—and verses on—the prospects for their island's political sovereignty. But was this turn to (cultural) heritage in Soqotra just a small-scale version of heritage engineering happening elsewhere, particular in the Gulf? Likewise, is this chapter's discussion of

Soqotrans' call for revolution simply a micro-history of a minute fragment of the Arab uprisings told from a peripheral part of the Arab world?

While it is questionable whether Soqotrans would have become as politically emboldened as they have, and as quickly, had it not been for the momentous uprisings happening on the mainland, their grassroots engineering of a creative, activist heritage preceded the events of 2011 and provided the scaffolding from which the Soqotran demonstrations could be launched. To see this mobilization of heritage for its full "revolutionary" potential, I will step back for a moment—both away from the region and back in time—to compare the cultivation of cultural heritage in Soqotra in the first decade of the new millennium to what cultural historian Joep Leerssen describes as the "cultivation of culture" in nineteenth-century Europe. (This is not to suggest that Europe is the measure of all things but rather simply to show that the example of Soqotra is less "peripheral" than one might think.) If we consider Soqotrans' cultural preoccupations not just as a nostalgic form of "heritage revival" but as a form of cultural nationalism—whether or not Soqotra ever becomes an independent nation—then we can evaluate them within a framework that connects preservation to transformation.

As scholars of European nationalism well know, nationalism is not the invention but the inventor of the nation.[44] According to Miroslav Hroch's influential chronology of the development of nationalist movements, it is the raising of cultural consciousness (Phase A) that precedes social demands (Phase B) and, ultimately, political/separatist movements (Phase C).[45] As Leerssen puts it, Hroch's model shows "that the schoolmasters and poets who collect proverbs and folktales are the unwitting avant-garde for the social and political activists."[46] However, the problem with this A-B-C model is that if one studies Phase A nationalism as a mere teleological prelude to the resultant Phases B and C, one loses sight of all the "failed nationalisms" that did not develop beyond this cultural phase.[47] (Another problem is that this model suggests that cultural concerns cease if and when people take up social and political demands, which has not been the case.) Therefore, Leerssen proposes that scholars study this early Phase A cultural nationalism according to its own (nonteleological) aims. What are these aims? For Leerssen, the "underlying, unifying concern of early cultural nationalism and romantic historicism [in Europe] lies in the *cultivation of culture*": "the new interest in demotic, vernacular, non-classical culture . . . as something which represents the very identity of the nation, its specificity amidst other nations."[48] Heuristically, he divides this culture into four broad fields: language, literature and discourse, material culture, and the performance of immaterial culture. These fields of culture are "cultivated" through three types of endeavors: inventory and salvage, fresh cultural productivity, and propagandist proclamation in the public sphere. For example, after those "schoolmasters" have captured their threatened vernacular language in dictionaries and grammars (inventory and salvage), they may turn to its standardization and maintenance (fresh cultural productivity), and, finally, to teaching it in schools (propagandist proclamation). All of these activities, across all fields of culture, may be facilitated through the "bottom-up" establishment of associations and clubs by the urban professional and middle classes and/or through the "top-down" management of state-controlled institutions, such as national academies or universities.[49] Of course, Leerssen's model is both more complicated and illuminating than described here, but even this brief overview should suffice for illustrating similar endeavors in Soqotra.

In Soqotra, in the wake of the island's opening in the mid-1990s, islanders with varying degrees of education began to view their culture (language, literature, material culture, and performances) as having become increasingly threatened by a host of outside forces: for example, modernization, development, religious piety, environmental governance, and the infusion of Arabic. These islanders included schoolteachers like Fahd, who received a master's degree through studying Soqotri literature, but also school dropouts and poets, like Ismail and Tanuf, who took it upon themselves to collect and inventory vernacular poetry, folk tales, oral histories, and traditional ecological knowledge. As in nineteenth-century Europe, these "early cultural nationalists and intellectuals [have been] work[ing] in dense patterns of mutual influence and exchange," many of them external to the archipelago itself.[50] As we have seen, Soqotran cultivators of culture were influenced by—and included—Soqotrans living in the Gulf who were also engaged in salvage, fresh productivity, and propagation activities. Not only were these emigrants influenced by the cultural and political nationalism of their host states, but so were the islanders influenced by the intellectual and ideological climate of the Arabian Peninsula and beyond. Notably, Tanuf was moved to revive Soqotra's traditional herbal medicine following his work with a British ethnobotanist and his visits to apothecaries in the United Kingdom.

Ismail's recordings of Soqotri poetry, which began as a personal project, turned into a salvage operation following his interactions with heritage experts on the island and with linguists in Europe. And Fahd drew inspiration from the local *daʿwa* (piety) movement and his meeting with Günter Grass. Animated by these international intellectual exchanges and supported by a network of actors, Soqotran laymen established an association to collect Soqotran heritage (inventory and salvage). Soon thereafter, inspired by events elsewhere, this society organized a festival to encourage the production of Soqotri-language poetry and literary criticism (fresh cultural production). And again, inspired by international events, its members used this platform to "suffuse the public sphere with a sense of collective national identity" and to launch their language activism (propagandist proclamation).[51]

This "cultivation of culture"—what Soqotrans call "heritage"—was not provincial, insular, or conservative, even if it was small-scale. Indeed, there may be only two things that distinguish Soqotrans' preoccupation with cultural heritage today from the nineteenth-century European cultural nationalism that, in some cases, led to full-scale political movements. First, Soqotrans have ignited their cultural revolution outside the framework of any institutional infrastructure. Unlike in the Gulf, where both heritage engineering and the cultivation of culture are primarily state-managed operations, all of the Soqotrans' activities to date—even the establishment of the museum—have been grassroots pursuits. Second, Soqotrans' nostalgia is not simply structural, in the sense of being a "rhetoric of change and decay" replicated across the generations.[52] It is also symptomatic of a distinctly twenty-first-century preoccupation: the growing awareness that vernacular languages and endemic species are on the verge of extinction. In this sense, Soqotrans are showing us what cultural nationalism may look like in the Anthropocene. In contexts like these, heritage from below is not only a worthy—and potentially revolutionary—project, but it is likely to matter all the more.

FIGURE 14. "We want back our country," Hadibo, 2013.

CONCLUSION

In December 2016, a cargo vessel en route from al-Mukalla to Soqotra capsized about twenty-six nautical miles northwest of the island. Nearly two-thirds of its sixty-four passengers and crew members drowned. Most of the passengers were Soqotrans who had resorted to traveling by overloaded cargo ships to and from the mainland because there were no dependable, commercial flights. Several of the drowned passengers were children, including a young boy named Khalid Ahmad. Soqotrans expressing their despair and outrage online denounced the air blockade that had suspended regular air travel to and from the island since the start of the Saudi-led intervention in Yemen in March 2015. In addition to demanding the reinstallation of weekly flights, they urged their Facebook friends to show their solidarity by alerting "the world" that Soqotrans were drowning due to the aerial "siege." One widely shared meme juxtaposed a photograph of a crowd of Soqotrans at the harbor waiting for the bodies of the deceased next to the iconic photograph of the drowned Syrian toddler, Alan Kurdi, whose beached body has come to stand for the global migration crisis. This meme was disseminated under the hashtags (in Arabic): #Soqotra calls for help, #we are all Khalid Ahmad, #we demand the return of flights to Soqotra, and #break the siege on Soqotra.

At the time of writing (April 2018), the Soqotra Archipelago has been effectively disconnected from the Arabian Peninsula for much of the past three years. Although Soqotrans have thus been subjected to a new "regime of artificial isolation,"¹ this current-day embargo has nevertheless "safeguarded" the island from the fighting that has spread throughout the rest of Yemen's governorates. During a phone conversation in May 2015, shortly after the initial bombing campaign, Operation Decisive Storm, had come to an end, one friend quipped that he hoped the monsoon would arrive soon so as to fully quarantine Soqotra before "the criminals" (the Houthis, ISIS members, and the like) could reach the island. But after three months of complete isolation, the islanders were short on baby formula, foods, cooking gas, and medicines. Moreover, dozens required urgent medical care, such as dialysis, which they could receive only in mainland hospitals. By September 2015, Soqotrans were once again demonstrating in the streets of Hadibo for their "right" to regular flights—as they had in December 2011—while others posted "distress calls" on Facebook to elicit international support (also under the hashtag #Soqotra calls for help). In the year that followed, Soqotrans became even more dependent on their relatives in and connections to the Arab Gulf States. Between September 2015 and April 2016, for instance, the UAE's Khalifa bin Zayed Al Nahyan Foundation delivered several hundred tons of food supplies and other relief aid to the island by air.² Eventually, in the summer of 2016, Yemen's national airline, Yemenia, reinstated bimonthly flights between Soqotra and Sayun (the Hadhramawt), but flights were often canceled and islanders ended up stranded on the mainland for weeks. Meanwhile, Gulf-based investors began arriving on the island in droves—by private plane or charter flights—to buy up more property and to export Soqotra's fish to markets at home. When I spoke with that same friend on the day after the boat capsized, he was less flippant about the island's confinement. "Everything is upside down now," he said. "I mean, the fish are flying in the air, while the people are drowning in the sea."

Since I began researching and writing this book, the world has been effectively "turned upside down" for many, if not most, of the inhabitants of Yemen. In early 2018, reports estimated that 17.8 million people (60 percent of Yemen's population) were food insecure; that 22.2 million people (75 percent of the population) required humanitarian or protection assistance; and that more than 3 million people—over 10 percent of the population—had been internally displaced. Meanwhile, more than 9,000 Yemenis have died due to the conflict, more than 52,000 have been injured, and more than 190,000 Yemeni citizens and foreign nationals have fled the country since March 2015.³ With Yemen's northern border sealed, the majority of these refugees have had nowhere to go but south, by cargo ship or cattle boat to Somalia or Djibouti—to the very famine-prone region that many of them or their parents had already fled. While scores of refugees and migrants have drowned trying to cross the aptly named Strait of Despair (Bab al Mandeb), the "fortunate" ones are languishing in the Markazi refugee camp in Djibouti, where they feel that they are dying, too—just slowly. An elderly man from Aden whom I met in the camp in December 2016 walked me through an outdoor "museum" he created through a series of displays curated from the various objects discarded in the surrounding desert by a people on the move. Three small adjacent plots, outlined by conch shells, form the crux of this refugee museum/museum refuge. In their middle, a rusted sewing machine, an old radio, a kerosene lantern, a coffee pot, a Yemeni shisha pipe (mada'a), and scale weights represent the remnants of "civilization"; to the left, a miniature graveyard of bullets, casings, animal bones, and a decapitated doll depict the results of "the war"; to the right, a sun-bleached plastic baby walker, a teddy bear, and blue-eyed dolls expose the hopes pinned to future "life." In the tangle of dried branches that form the museum's exterior walls, its creator had affixed a water faucet pointing skyward. "It's upside down," he told me, "like everything in Yemen."

In light of these tragedies, and the humanitarian crisis in Yemen and the Horn of Africa that is still unfolding, what is there to say about heritage? What futures are there for Soqotrans' linguistic, cultural, and political expression when the future of Yemen is so alarming and uncertain? And, given the lack of protections afforded Soqotra's environment since the start of the war and the signs of its current and increasing exploitation for external markets, has this book not been too critical of the state's conservation efforts and the ICDP projects that did exist? After all, in this era of increasing assaults on our planet's biocultural diversity of all kinds, it is noteworthy that the ailing Republic of Yemen had incorporated environmental protections and responsibilities into its national constitution. It is remarkable, moreover, that this distant and once-marginalized archipelago was transformed into an internationally recognized protected area at all.

This book has examined the ways in which "the Environment" (al-bi'a) and heritage (al-turath)—as discursive practices, governing regimes, and material things—were introduced to a people at the geographic and cultural margins of the so-called Arab world. For nearly a decade, I witnessed Soqotrans engaging these "protection regimes" in three principal ways. First, the pastoralists among whom I lived accommodated and sustained the ICDPs as a de facto transitory state. In doing so, the island's settled Bedouin positioned themselves as sovereign hosts to the ICDPs and the Yemeni state: a reversal of the common metaphor of states offering hospitality to mobile guests—migrants, asylum seekers, and refugees—that has animated much of the literature on hospitality and sovereignty, as well as immigration debates in Western countries. These accommodations were not a form of acquiescence as much as they were pragmatic responses in an environment that is besieged, time and again, by regimes and ideologies "from [across] the sea."

Second, Soqotrans responded to the World Heritage Convention's nature-culture divide and what had effectively become the commandeering of their environment as a global commons by appropriating the language of heritage to claim a place for themselves and their culture that could withstand external control. For Soqotran pastoralists, there is no environment without culture, or culture without nature. Recall the Homhil shaykhs' bewilderment at the thought of someone willy-nilly cutting down trees—or traveling across the world just to see their trees. "We love our trees—they are *our* trees! They are our children! They are our wives!" Bu Qadir responded, using a kinship metaphor to convey what scholars in the environmental humanities now refer to as "multi-species entanglements."[4] Having seen how the ICDPs paid lip service to people's "traditional environmental knowledge" and "culture" while promoting only "science-based" (and secular) natural resource management strategies, I have grown suspicious of the academic discourse around bridging or transcending the nature-culture divide. Certainly, this dualistic thinking is a product of Western "rationality." Yet, in the face of powerful states and transnational organizations exerting pressure on indigenous populations in the name of environmental conservation, the ability to maintain the nature-culture distinction—to maintain a form of sovereignty, however limited, *through* one's culture—may be another necessary accommodation.

Thus, and finally, the Soqotrans' mobilization of cultural heritage has evolved into a key way to preserve their property, as well as (parts of) their identity. This has not been a straightforward process. As discussed earlier, the majority of the island's Muslim population considers certain practices—among them forms of witchcraft that survived until the middle of last century, if not longer—deviant or ignorant, despite their influential role in shoring up transnational networks. Moreover, many of my interlocutors were all too willing to disregard the Afro-Soqotrans' religious, cultural, and expressive traditions—a blind spot that has made its way into this book, too. (One potential avenue for further research would be an ethnographic collaboration with the coastal communities of African descent on their histories and heritage futures.) Still, for many Hadibo-based Soqotrans of various backgrounds, this mobilization of cultural heritage dovetailed with and lent weight to their calls for political and cultural revolution. Through all three approaches—accommodation, appropriation, and mobilization—Soqotrans developed techniques to embrace parts of the *conservation-as-heritage-as-development* regime as a way of defending and promoting their cultural and, through it, their political sovereignty.

This book shows, then, how a small group of Soqotrans with varying degrees of formal education embarked on what Tizini called *al-thawra al-turathiyya*. Translated awkwardly as a "heritagial revolution," Boullata took this to mean "not only a revolution in the cognitive understanding of heritage but also a revolution grounded in the progressive elements of heritage."[5] Following Soqotrans' public recognition of the *right* to use, celebrate, and transmit to future generations their formerly ostracized language through the annual Soqotri poetry festivals—which were modeled after similar (but institutional) endeavors to shore up the use of Arabic among English-inundated youth in the Arab Gulf—Soqotran (and Mahra) delegates to the National Dialogue Conference in Sanaa were sufficiently emboldened to insist on inscribing constitutional protections for their endangered languages. Although it is unclear whether this draft constitution will ever again see the light of day following Yemen's current war, it is clear that these attempts, however small, to readjust the political imbalances in Yemen were "grounded" in some of the most "progressive elements of heritage": protections for "endemic" languages that teeter, together with species, on the "dull edge of extinction."[6]

In recent years, as the future of Yemen—and with it, that of Soqotra—has become ever more tenuous and uncertain, my interlocutors have lost much of the optimism they experienced in the heady days of the revolution. Moreover, threats to the archipelago's extraordinary environment have only increased since its recognition as a UNESCO World Heritage Site in 2008. Road con-

struction intensified and was then abandoned. More and more coral and charcoal were harvested and collected for export to the Gulf. More and more trees
were chopped down as islanders were forced to rely on wood fires because of
shortages of cooking gas. The beaches have been sold to foreign investors for
hotel and resort development. And the local EPA no longer has the funding to
monitor these threats, much less the power to enforce the environmental regulations ratified through the Conservation Zoning Plan. On top of all this, while
Soqotra may have been isolated from the fighting on the mainland, it is no
longer protected from international investments or exploitation. So intensified
has been the Emirati presence on the island that some Soqotrans may begin to
believe the rumors that their island will become the UAE's eighth emirate. The
inauguration in the spring of 2017 of direct, biweekly charter flights between
Hadibo and Abu Dhabi portends even greater Gulf-Soqotran connections and
commerce in future years. Whether these developments will be mindful of conservation—and whether the islanders will in turn be granted visas to visit their
relatives in the Gulf—remains to be seen.

In concert with the UAE's military presence, infrastructural development,
and humanitarian work on Soqotra, the UAE has taken an active role in promoting Soqotran cultural heritage. In January 2018, the Khalifa bin Zayed Al
Nahyan Foundation sponsored a week-long Festival of Soqotran Poetry that
elaborated on the poetry festivals of years past. On a stage flanked by the Emirati and Yemeni flags and murals of the presidents of the UAE and Yemen, the
island's governor presided over televised camel races, sword dances, and musical performances, in addition to the high-stakes contest between poets.[7] (This
year's winning poet was awarded YER 13 million.) The merging of flags and
traditions—with many events more reminiscent of Emirati heritage festivals
than of practices performed on the island—implied the affinity of Soqotran
and Emirati culture. The top-down, state-funded, and nationalistic nature of
this extensive heritage production/appropriation stands in stark contrast to the
islanders' earlier achievements and aspirations described in this book.

At the same time, another large-scale, GEF-funded conservation-and-
development project has been launched. This USD 5 million "support" project
seeks "to prevent the irreversible loss" of the archipelago's unique natural resources by "sustainably strengthen[ing] governmental and non-governmental
capacities to manage and protect" this World Heritage Site.[8] Even though this

project aims to build on past achievements and to learn from past challenges—and takes note of Soqotra's unique cultural heritage (e.g., Soqotri language and customary resource-management practices) and its connection with Soqotra's natural (biological) heritage—its focus is still primarily environmental. Its main objectives are to improve biodiversity conservation and protected-area management; to control against invasive alien species; to support sustainable land-management strategies as a defense against land degradation; and to foster an "enabling environment" that will strengthen local institutions and capacities and secure continuing funding. Notably, this project attributes today's overgrazing-induced land degradation not to pastoralism per se but rather to the loss of traditional land-management practices, including transhumance. It thus aims to develop a community-based sustainable land-management strategy and action plan that is "documented and clearly articulated in the indigenous Soqotri language."[9] This embrace of the Soqotri language alone—in this and in other project outcomes—is itself a major advance.

Ideally, both of these new yet potentially competing visions will foster an "enabling environment" for the islanders, too. Enabling (by conserving) the environment requires enabling peoples and their cultures. Committed Soqotrans like Ismail, Fahd, Tanuf, and others should be assisted in their efforts to document and revitalize their language, over and above the utilitarian translation needs of any project. And just as future projects are likely to have more traction among their local "stakeholders" if they employ the Soqotri language to help revitalize Soqotrans' traditional land-management practices, they are also more likely to succeed if they do not shirk from drawing on Islamic precepts relevant to natural resource conservation. Finally, these and other future interventions, be they UN implemented or UAE sponsored, will gain more willing collaborators by supporting and promoting *Soqotrans'* expressions of heritage, however the islanders define this. Material and financial support for museums, festivals, workshops, and exhibits—if these are developed by the islanders themselves—should enable Soqotrans to assemble their own heritage(s) in anticipation of their island's future.

I would like to end with a few of the many lessons I have learned *from* my Soqotran friends, not about them. Tanuf told me long ago that "true knowledge" comes from "research that is done on foot. . . . Truth comes from old poetry, from tiredness, from sun, and from walking." I don't know if I have fulfilled his definition of true research, but I do feel that I have been wading through this book's material for a long, long time. I hope that he will recognize some truth in what I have written here. Many of the Soqotrans I have met would agree with the sentiment that their seas, pastures, and livestock are less productive today because of their own selfishness and greed. Whether one attributes today's diminishing natural resources to anthropogenic climate change or to the loss of God's *baraka*, we would be wise to acknowledge how our own selfish actions are endangering our individual and collective resources. Finally, true generosity and hospitality toward others do not detract from our cultural identity or material possibilities; rather, generosity may be the most important way toward recognizing and restoring our more entangled "naturecultures"[10]— just as opening our homes and nations to strangers may be the foremost way to enact our sovereignty. The anthropologist Mary Douglas once wrote that "anthropology suggests, not a solution to a problem, but new problems with more hope of solution."[11] Although my friends in Soqotra have been short on hope in recent years, their deep love for their island despite the problems it has faced continues to fill me with hopefulness for them, and for Yemen.

APPENDIX

The House of ʿAfrar

The House of ʿAfrar. Printed with permission from ʿAbdullah ʿIsa bin ʿAfrar.

THE HOUSE of 'AFRĀR, RULERS of QISHN and SOQOTRA (early 16th c.–1967)

Treaty sultans identified by capital letters; order of succession by numbers

Twentieth-century line of succession moves between paternal cousins of the Sa'd branch

Birth order of male sons (in known cases) is indicated from left to right

Boldface names appear in the text; (*) = executed at Haybak (1974)

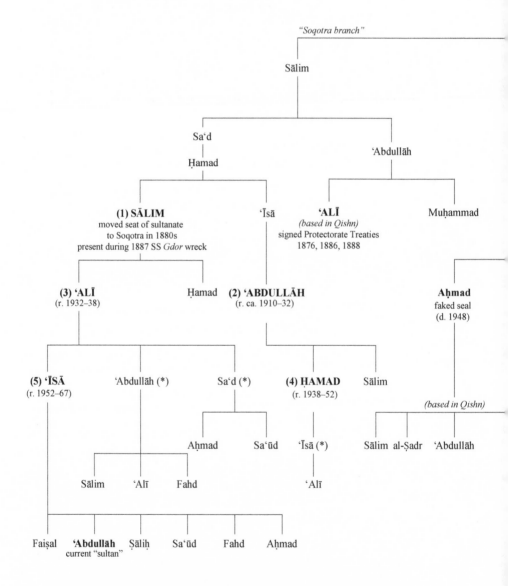

This genealogy is based on a combination of British archival sources and al-'Afrār oral history; the precise kinship connections prior to (1) Sālim Ḥamad Sa'd's generation are uncertain

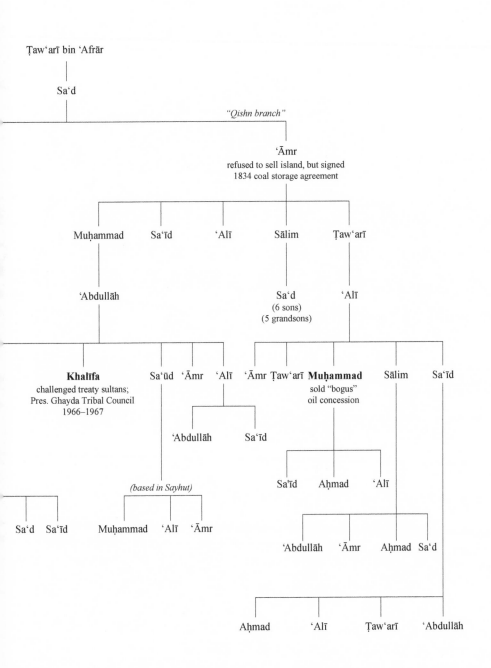

Ṭawʿarī bin ʿAfrār

Saʿd

"Qishn branch"

ʿĀmr
refused to sell island, but signed
1834 coal storage agreement

Muḥammad   Saʿīd   ʿAlī   Sālim   Ṭawʿarī

ʿAbdullāh   Saʿd   ʿAlī
                                        (6 sons)
                                        (5 grandsons)

Khalīfa   Saʿūd ʿĀmr ʿAlī   ʿĀmr Ṭawʿarī **Muḥammad**   Sālim   Saʿīd
challenged treaty sultans;   sold "bogus"
Pres. Ghayda Tribal Council   oil concession
1966–1967

                              ʿAbdullāh Saʿīd

                    (based in Sayhut)   Saʿīd   Aḥmad   ʿAlī

Saʿd Saʿīd   Muḥammad ʿAlī ʿĀmr   ʿAbdullāh ʿĀmr   Aḥmad Saʿd

                                        Aḥmad   ʿAlī   Ṭawʿarī   ʿAbdullāh

NOTES

NOTES TO FRONT MATTER

1. IOR R/20/C/1345: "Witch Trials in Soqotra, November 1955," Ian E. Snell, Assistant Adviser Mahra, 26.11.1955.

2. Simeone-Senelle 2004.

3. A few scripts may be gaining traction, including the modified Arabic scripts devised by Naumkin and Kogan (2015) and by the Modern South Arabian Language documentation project (see http://www.leeds.ac.uk/arts/homepage/462/modern_south_arabian_languages, accessed 30 November 2017).

NOTES TO INTRODUCTION

A portion of the Introduction was published in "Heritage in (the) Ruins," *International Journal of Middle East Studies* 49, no. 4 (2017): 721–728.

1. WFP 2014.

2. Yemen's average annual rainfall varies from 50 to 100 mm in its hyperarid coastal areas to 400 to 1,000 mm in the semiarid highlands (Almas and Scholz 2006). In Soqotra, the average annual rainfall (between 2002 and 2006) was 216 mm (Scholte and De Geest 2010). Yemen's mainland suffers from a growing water deficit due mainly to agriculture, which uses more than 90 percent of Yemen's water supply (Ward 2015: 81).

3. Khalidi 2017. On the conservation of old Sanaa, see Lamprakos 2015.

4. UNESCO 2017.

5. For critiques of "culture," see Abu Lughod 1991; and Brumann 1999. For the military's turn to culture, see K. Brown 2008; Gusterson 2010; and R. Ferguson 2013.

6. See Descola 2013.

7. Harrison 2015: 38.

8. See, for example, Harrison 2013: 228–229; D. Harvey 2001; Holtorf and Högsberg 2013; and Meskell 2012: 2.

9. See Bsheer 2017.

10. See Peutz 2017 and the collection of essays in this roundtable.

11. This was not the first time that Arab intellectuals conceived of Arab-Islamic heritage as a filter against the influences of a seemingly superior Western modernity (*hadatha*). The relationship between *turath* and *hadatha* had been a central question of the nineteenth-century Arab renaissance. What distinguishes the intellectuals' preoccupation with the "problematic of *al-turath*" in the 1970s and 1980s is their reconceptualization of heritage in dynamic, progressive terms rather than mere passive, imitative traditions (*taqalid*) (Wardeh 2008: 13; see also Boullatta 1990; and Salvatore 1995).

12. Wardeh 2008: 63.

13. Boullatta 1990: 34, citing Tizini 1978: 271.

14. Culture Resource, European Cultural Foundation, and Boekmanstudies 2010.

15. See Cooke 2014; Exell 2016; Exell and Rico 2014; Khalaf 2000, 2002; and Limbert 2010.

16. International concern for cultural heritage protections goes back well over a century to a series of treaties that prohibit the pillaging of historical monuments. But the 1954 Convention for the Protection of Cultural Heritage in the Event of Armed Conflict was the first treaty to equate "damage to cultural property belonging to any people whatsoever" with "damage to the cultural heritage of all mankind," thereby laying the groundwork for the idea of world heritage (UNESCO 1954; see Toman 1996: 3–36).

17. UNESCO 1972.

18. In 1985, the World Heritage Committee created new guidelines to accommodate "mixed" properties that contain elements of cultural and natural significance; in 1992, in response to further criticism, it adopted the concept of a "cultural landscape" to recognize "the combined works of nature and humankind." Nevertheless, properties remain classified as "cultural" or "natural"—or "mixed," if they fulfill both sets of criteria—but cannot fall in between, or bridge, this elemental divide (Harrison 2013: 125).

19. In 1994, the committee promoted its global strategy to encourage nominations from underrepresented regions and to consider a more inclusive (less European, Christian, historical, and "monumental") view of cultural heritage.

20. T. Schmitt 2008; and Nas 2002.

21. When the 2003 convention came into force in 2006, the Masterpieces program was discontinued and its list of ninety masterpieces, including Jemaa el Fna, was incorporated into and superseded by two new lists: the Representative List of the Intangible Cultural Heritage of Humanity and the List of Intangible Cultural Heritage in Need of Urgent Safeguarding.

22. In her influential book *Uses of Heritage*, archaeologist Laurajane Smith maintains that UNESCO and its advisory bodies have institutionalized a Eurocentric "authorized heritage discourse" (2006: 11–12), which constructs heritage through expert pronouncements that define what is innately valuable, privileges elite social values, and excludes competing (non-expert) discourses.

23. In this view, heritage is not just one of the many "things" that are governed; rather, heritage—concerned as it is with what Foucault calls the "right disposition of things," including "men in their relation to that other kind of things, customs, habits, ways of acting, thinking, etc." (1991: 93)—is especially suited as a technology of governing. See Bendix, Eggert, and Peselmann 2012; Coombe 2012; Coombe and Weiss 2015; and De Cesari 2010.

24. Rose 2006: 155.

25. Ibid., 159.

26. Ibid.

27. De Cesari 2010: 627; see also De Cesari 2017.

28. In light of the material and ontological turns in the social sciences, several scholars argue that the linguistic/social constructivist approaches mentioned previously obscure the "vital materiality" of heritage: its constituent things and the capacity of these things "to act as quasi agents or forces with trajectories, propensities, or tendencies of their own" (J. Bennett 2010: viii; see also Pétursdóttir 2013). Likewise, recent scholarship on heritage endeavors to underscore the agency of nonhuman others (animals, nature) in a renewed effort to bridge the culture-nature and human-animal-thing divides (see Byrne and Ween 2015; Fredengren 2015; and Harrison 2015).

29. Miller and Morris 2004: 8. Soqotra (area: 3,796 km²), the largest and most populated of this eponymous archipelago, has an estimated population of 60,000 (45,000 according to the 2004 census). The archipelago's other islands are Abd al-Kuri (area: 133km²; est. population: 400); Samha (area: 41 km²; est. population: 150) and Darsa (area 5.41 km²; unpopulated), known as "the brothers"; and the two rock outcrops, Sabuniyah and Ka'l Fir'awn.

30. Molecular genetic studies and recent archaeological findings provide evidence of much earlier human and ancient hominid settlements on Soqotra (Černý et al. 2009; Zhukov 2014).

31. Roe (1926) 1990: 23.

32. See Boxhall 1967: 549.

33. Casson 1989: 67–69 (*Periplus* § 27, 30–31). For discussion, see Bukharin (2012), who sug-

gests that Diodorus's description of Hiera (meaning "Sacred") and Philostratus's description of the "sacred island" of Selera may have actually referred to Soqotra and its "sacred," embargoed nature.

34. Wilkinson 1981: 280.

35. G. Smith 1985: 86. As Roxani Margariti brilliantly posits, "Religious polemics and literary roots aside, Ibn al-Mujāwir's motif of the disappearing island hints at Socotra's disconnection from Yemen, and thereby at the fact that Socotra formed part of different networks at different times in its history . . . : an insular form both connected and separated from the rest of the region by the Indian Ocean" (2013: 218).

36. Albuquerque 2010: 1:45.

37. *Socotra: The Hidden Land* is the title of a 2015 Spanish documentary. The phrase "archipelago of enclaves" comes from Ong 2006: 104.

38. These adjectives come from the titles used in the following media coverage: Mel White, "Socotra: Yemen's Legendary Island (tagline: Where the Weird Things Are)," *National Geographic Magazine*, June 2012; Catherine Monnet, "Océan indien: L'Île mystérieuse de Socotra," *GEO* (France), 24 May 2012; Elizabeth Eaves, "Strange, Strange Socotra," *Islands*, January/February 2005; and Mike Carter, "The Land That Time Forgot," *The Observer: The Observer Escape*, 16 April 2006. Even the renowned US urban theorist and political scholar Mike Davis (2004) has drawn inspiration from the island's legendary nature, making it the setting of the second volume of his young adult trilogy, *Islands Mysterious: Where Science Rediscovers Nature*.

39. See "Ex-Yemen President" 2016. Many Soqotrans who are aware of the history of outside powers envisioning their island as a prison or base believed these rumors.

40. Margariti 2013: 200.

41. On the paradox of visitors flocking to "remote areas," see Ardener 1987.

42. Mackintosh-Smith 2000: 206.

43. See Naumkin and Kogan 2015: 234–239. Naumkin and Kogan confirm that this is a "true story"—"as far as our informants are concerned" (6).

44. Between October 2004 and December 2005, I spent approximately two-thirds of the time in Homhil and the rest in Hadibo. I also traveled throughout the island, traveled with Soqotran friends to Sanaa, and interviewed Soqotrans living in Oman and the UAE. I then returned to Soqotra for follow-up visits nearly annually through 2013: in February 2006; summer 2007; December–January 2009–2010, 2010–2011, 2011–2012; and in December 2013. The renewed seclusion of Soqotra since March 2015 has prevented me from visiting since.

45. Anthropologists have written influential monographs on the social and political importance of poetry in Yemen (see Caton 1990, 2005; Miller 2007; and Taminian 2000). Although I had known how central poetry was to all sorts of communication, I did not anticipate that I would have to seek out poetry until realizing that certain topics would remain elusive unless I did. For the uses of poetry on Soqotra, see Morris 2011, 2013.

46. On "collaboration," see Marcus 2007; on "engagement," see Low and Merry 2010.

47. See Peutz 2013.

48. This drone strike was the first (known) US attack in Yemen; extrajudicial targeted assassinations (drone strikes) on al-Qaeda on the Arabian Peninsula began in December 2009 and numbered more than one hundred by 2013 (HRW 2013).

49. For more on this "empty" time before oil in Oman, see Limbert 2010; in the UAE, see Bristol-Rhys 2010.

50. Sahlins 1985.

51. For another take on insularity—as "the essential quality of worlds both connected and isolated to varying degrees by that which surrounds them—sea, land or both," see Margariti 2013: 209.

NOTES TO CHAPTER 1

Portions of this chapter appeared in "Bedouin 'Abjection': World Heritage, Worldliness, and Worthiness at the Margins of Arabia," *American Ethnologist* 38, no. 2 (2011): 338–360.

1. In Arabic, *miskin* means "poor," "miserable," or "humble." In Soqotri, *miskin* is used in

praise of people (and milch animals) who are complaisant or good-natured. Although Umm Yaqub was speaking Arabic, these two connotations are often conflated, a sense I try to relay with the translation "poor fellow" (or poor soul).

2. Although the Salafi movement is best described as a "radical reformist movement whose aim is to reinstate an authentic practice of Islam" (Bonnefoy 2011: 5), it encompasses a diversity of actors, interpretations, and aims.

3. Prohibitions against smoking, music, and distraction by worldly affairs are common among pietist Salafis, who reject innovation, any form of mediation between God and believers, and direct forms of political involvement (ibid.: 50).

4. Sayf was drawing on the principle of *al-wala' wa-l-bara'* (loyalty and disavowal) guiding Muslims to associate with fellow Muslims and disavow non-Muslims, a doctrine that is emphasized more strongly in some branches of Islam than in others.

5. In many traditional societies hospitality has been considered a male virtue, enabled by the backstage labor of marginalized women and achieved at their expense, if not sacrifice (see McNulty 2007: xxvii; and Diprose 2009). On this day, and on others, it was women who offered me *karam* supported by men's labor backstage.

6. My use of to "*give place* to" draws on Derrida (2000: 25). Dikeç, Clark, and Barnett extend Derrida's analysis to point out that every act of hospitality is a gift of both space and time: in their words, hospitality is "not just an act that takes place *in* time, but one that actually generates or *gives* time (2009: 11). In analogous fashion, "if we think of space not only in terms of positioning or movement, but as the relations that give us our bearings, our grounding, our self-identity, then there is indeed a terrain *which is given*" (ibid.: 12).

7. Herzfeld 1991: 81, 84.

8. Whereas this particular "crisis of hospitality" has been kindled by the recent influx of migrants and refugees in Europe, it has its contemporary roots in the *sans-papiers* affair and immigration debates of the 1990s (Rosello 2001: 165). Other scholars interpret the "crisis of hospitality" more broadly as being constitutive of the "crisis of modernity" (see McNulty 2007: xlvii).

9. Herzfeld 1997: 109.

10. Shryock 2004.

11. Although Herzfeld (1997: 115) and others have demonstrated that there is nothing apolitical or even static about the *uses* of nostalgia, nostalgia is often pathologized in popular and academic discourse as "merely" sentimental yearnings toward an imagined pristine past. However, as Özyürek (2006) demonstrates, today's nostalgia is uniquely connected to the neoliberal modernity in which it flourishes; moreover, it has been spreading globally, particularly in postsocialist countries such as the former South Yemen.

12. When the protected area was established (2000), Homhil was home to 156 different plant species, 86 of which are endemic to Soqotra. It was also home to around 20 bird species, 4 of which are endemic to the island.

13. On hearing that the "resident Governor of Soqotra" (Sultan Salim) had sold the ship's wreckage to Indian merchants, the political resident (PR) in Aden insisted that the governor cede the wreck to the German consul but agreed to give him one-third of its value and cargo in compensation for having had his men guard the wrecked vessel (IOR R/20/A/4554: "Report," Assistant PR Aden, 04.10.1887). It is quite possible that this shipping log was part of this compensation. Ten years later, the British archaeologist J. Theodore Bent was shown "several fragments of German print, which [the Bedouin] had treasured up [from the wreck], and which they deemed of fabulous value" (Bent 1897: 990).

14. This is not a new phenomenon. A British linguist for the Middle East Command's 1967 Soqotra expedition noted that his camel man had memorized the Latin names of all the plants documented by the team's botanist (Tomkinson 1967).

15. In the mid-2000s, families received annual allowances of cooking oil, flour, and wheat (from United States Agency for International Development [USAID], the French embassy, and the World Food Programme [WFP]) for each of their daughters attending school.

16. Pitt-Rivers 1968: 19.

17. Shryock 2009: 47.

18. Shryock and Howell 2001: 266.

19. See Meneley 1996.

20. The use of turmeric paste as a skin lightener is not only common across southern Yemen but also dates back at least a century in Soqotra (see Bent 1897: 986). In recent years, women in Homhil have supplanted the turmeric with commercial bleaching creams such as Fair and Lovely, which they were able to purchase with the cash they received selling dragon's blood resin as a "natural" cosmetic to European tourists.

21. Derrida 2000: 75–83.

22. McNulty 2007: xx.

23. Shryock 2004: 36.

24. Al-Rigdihi had composed this "modern" poem for the anthology *Island Voices: The Oral Art of Soqotra*, by Miranda Morris and Tanuf Nuh Salim Di-Kishin (forthcoming). I am grateful to Miranda Morris for this translation.

25. Sughayr's poem draws attention to the temporality and seasonality of hospitality. In Soqotra, the main seasons are *horf* (June to September), the southwest summer monsoon when scorching winds effectively close the island but dates are harvested; *serebhen* (September), the transitional post-monsoon period when wind directions shift; *serb* (October to February), the northeast monsoon when winter rains bring green pasture; *qeyat* (late February to March), the hot summer season when dates are pollinated; and *doti* (mid-April to June), the transitional pre-monsoon when summer rains fall, before *horf* begins. (The *sudhayten* refers to the period of two stars, *ber sud* and *sud*, that appear just before the southwest monsoon.) See Miller and Morris 2004: 14–16; and Serjeant 1992: 172–173.

26. The Kuwaiti *'iqal* is the black cord used by men to keep their white headdress in place.

27. Limbert 2010.

28. During the socialist period, the only flights to and from Soqotra were military flights. In the early 1990s, air travel was provided by the Republic of Yemen's air force (Cheung and DeVantier 2006: 260).

29. One of my interlocutors suggested that this "competition" augured the end of times, citing a prophetic tradition that states (in his words), "Among the signs of the end of the hour is a profusion of mosques," and the Hadith of Gabriel, according to which the Prophet Muhammad had warned of the following signs: "that you will see the barefooted, naked, destitute herdsmen competing in constructing lofty buildings."

30. Saba Mahmood (2005) describes *da'wa* (calling to God) as a piety movement that enjoins others to do right. While this pedagogical *da'wa* is widespread on Soqotra, it is precisely the island's geographic distance that lends the practitioners of *da'wa* (m. pl.: *du'at*) their "missionary" character. Nevertheless, Soqotrans tend to use the term *da'wa* (more accurately, *da'waa*) to refer to lawsuits over land, water, and usufruct rights (M. Morris, pers. comm., November 2017). They thus refer to these practitioners as *mutatawwi'in* (volunteers), which carries connotations of being religiously conservative.

31. Art. 3 of the Constitution of the Republic of Yemen, as amended on 29 September 1994 (emphasis added). Prior to Yemen's 1994 civil war and northern victory, sharia had been affirmed as "the main source of legislation" (Art. 2 of the 1991 Constitution) but not the only one. See Badran 1998; and Molyneux 1995.

32. See Elie 2004.

33. Soqotrans adopted the term *dahabisha* (pl.) from southern Yemenis, who were the first to associate the northern tribesmen with the television character named Daḥbāsh (Dresch 2000: 190). Qat (*Catha edulis*), is a leafy shrub grown in mainland Yemen and chewed frequently by the majority of Yemeni men and women. It does not grow on Soqotra, where its use has been restricted to the coastal areas around Hadibo, to which it was flown in weekly (see Elie 2014).

34. Herzfeld 2001: 75.

35. According to the tourist police who registered the daily arrivals of foreign researchers, tourists, and workers at the airport, tourists in Soqotra increased from 193 in 2000 to 3,874 in 2010 (peaking at 4,150 in 2008): a twentyfold increase in a decade.

36. Some say these *ifrang* were the British, who first scouted the island in the mid-nineteenth century; others are certain that they were the Portuguese, who occupied Soqotra in the early sixteenth century. In most versions, the *ifrang* fled the island; in one version, they moved to Suq, the erstwhile Portuguese capital. See Naumkin 1993: 389; 2015: 94–96.

37. IOR R/20/C/727: "Movement Order 1/39," Air HQ, Aden, 13.12.1939. Three years later, a British political officer (PO) stationed in Sootra during the war tried to refute similar rumors: "There is no evidence to justify the belief held in British mercantile circles that the inhabitants of Socotra were cannibalistic until quite recently" (IOR R/20/B/1640: "Report on Socotra," PO Soqotra [Tudor-Pole], May 1943).

38. The three versions I recorded in the mid-2000s all stress that the Portuguese slaughtered the Soqotrans' livestock. In contrast, the version that Naumkin recorded in the 1980s states only that the Europeans (*ifrang*) settled on Soqotra but makes no mention of animal theft (Naumkin and Kogan 2015: 94–96).

39. See, for example, Bourdieu 1965; Herzfeld 1987; Pitt-Rivers 1968; Meneley 1996; and Shryock 2009.

40. McNulty 2007: xlii.

41. Li 2007: 1–4.

42. See, respectively, West 2006; Walley 2004; and Heatherington 2010.

43. Heatherington 2010: 192; Herzfeld 1987: 77; and Shryock 2004: 58.

44. Shryock 2004: 36.

45. See ibid.; and El-Barghuthi 1924: 195n1.

46. Bourdieu 1965: 197–198.

47. McNulty 2007: viii; Dikeç, Clark, and Barnett 2009: 2; and Shryock 2009: 33.

48. See Shryock 2004: 60.

NOTES TO CHAPTER 2

1. Ferguson and Gupta 2002: 987. In contrast to those who take state-centered or objectivist approaches that view the state as a distinct and autonomous entity, anthropologists tend to view the state as an idea (Abrams 1988), a cultural form (Steinmetz 1999), or a fetish (Taussig 1992) that exists not above or outside society but coterminous with it (Mitchell 1999; Navaro-Yashin 2002). Throughout this book, I use the term "the state" as a metonymy for the various offices, persons, practices, and effects of this "disaggregated and multilayered institution" (Gupta 1995: 391) as it is imagined, embodied, and encountered in Soqotra.

2. See Gupta 1995.

3. Shryock and Howell 2001: 254.

4. I am grateful to Miranda Morris for this formulation.

5. Bayart 1993: 235, 241, 269.

6. The Mahra sought in Soqotra a retreat from their rivals, the Kathiri sultans of Shihr (Hadhramawt). According to Ibn Majid, writing circa 1490, Soqotra was initially jointly ruled by the Banu 'Afrar and the Banu Sulaimani al-Himyari, both from al-Mahra. Prior to this, the islanders had killed their Mahra ruler, Ahmad Muhammad al-'Afrar, giving rise to the saying that Soqotrans "would bring bad luck to anyone who reigned over them" (al-Najdi 1971: 223–224). It is unclear if Ibn Majid ever visited Soqotra, but he claimed to have known the murdered ruler's father, who sought his advice regarding their rivalry with the Kathiris (see also Serjeant 1974: 157–158). Following the Portuguese "occupation" of Soqotra—their takeover of this Mahra fort from 1507 to 1511—the Mahra resettled the island and even allied themselves with the Portuguese. Motivated by their common resistance to Ottoman expansion in the region, the Portuguese sent a fleet from Goa to help the Mahra liberate their port of Qishn, which had been captured by the Ottoman-allied Kathiris in 1546 (Biedermann 2010). It was as a result of this counterattack led by Said Abdullah

al-'Afrar (a Mahra chieftain who had escaped to Soqotra) that the 'Afrar family established its exclusive sovereignty over Soqotra (Dostal 1989).

7. Haines 1845: 108. (He did grant them permission for coal storage in 1834.)

8. Other attempts to acquire Soqotra during this period were made by a French company in 1859 (Ingrams and Ingrams 1993: 3:565–569); Archduke Maximilian of Austria-Este in 1857, who wanted to use it a trading post (Dostal 1998; IOR Mss Eur F231/30); the Italian government in 1871, for use as a penal colony; and the Egyptian khedive in the 1870s (Ingrams and Ingrams 1993: 4:160–162).

9. For the 1876, 1886, and 1888 protectorate treaties, see Ingrams and Ingrams 1993: 4:181–184. For the 1834 agreement for coal storage on the island, see ibid.: 1:593. For the 1954 Advisory Treaty, see ibid.: 12:595.

10. Their full names are "Sayyid" Salim Hamad Sa'd (d. ca. 1910); Sayyid Salim's nephew, Abdullah Isa Hamad (d. 1932); "Sultan" Abdullah's paternal first cousin, Ali Salim Hamad (d. 1938); Sultan Ali's first cousin once removed, Hamad Abdullah Isa (d. 1952); and Sultan Hamad's first cousin, Isa Ali Salim (d. 1976). ("Hamad" is what the Soqotrans call their penultimate sultan, who in his correspondence Arabized his name to Ahmad.) See Appendix for an approximate, partial genealogy.

11. G. Brown 1966: sec. 1, 1.

12. Alpers 2009: 36.

13. Botting 1958a: 213. Similar assumptions of Soqotrans' utter ignorance and isolation are still found in travelers' descriptions today. See, for example, Burdick 2007.

14. Botting 1958a: 65–69.

15. G. Brown 1966; and Serjeant 1992.

16. Geertz 1983: 138; see also Chatty 2009.

17. Al-Anbali 2006: 105. *Msilhim* is a term specific to the eastern half of the island; the more general term was *etihi* (M. Morris, pers. comm., November 2017).

18. IOR R/20/C/2060: "Patrol Report by Captain F. J. O. Spender, Aden Protectorate Levies, on the Haggier Mountains, Socotra Island, January 29–March 3, 1944."

19. Agamben 1998: 10. During his 1956 visit, Douglas Botting heard that 160 Bedouin, 40 from each principal tribe, had recently been selected at random and deported en masse as punishment for livestock thefts (1958a: 67).

20. Morris 2003: 322.

21. Accused witches used to be thrown off a cliff (Haybak) into the sea before the sultans turned to banishment. As late as 1944, a British captain of the Aden Protectorate Levies reported that his guide listed all the livestock he would receive if he cut the throat of a middle-aged "witch" living near his home. The captain asked whether he needed the sultan's permission, and his guide said no. IOR R/20/C/2060: "Patrol Report," Captain Spender, March 1944.

22. Until the early 1960s, the only school on Soqotra had been a Qur'an school accommodating roughly thirty pupils. In 1954, six pupils were enrolled in the Bedouin Boys School in al-Mukalla—a boarding school set up by Harold Ingrams in 1944 as a "famine relief scheme" and a funnel into the Hadhrami Bedouin Legion (Ingrams 1966: 360)—and two were trained as health assistants (IOR R/20/B/2564: "Report on Socotra Island," PO Snell, 11.03.1954). In 1958, an additional three boys attended the Bedouin Boys School in al-Mukalla (IOR R/20/C/1346: Sultan to Resident Adviser in al-Mukalla [RA Mukalla], 20.03.1958), and by 1963 at least five Soqotrans were studying in Kuwait (IOR R/20/C/1350: Protectorate Education Adviser to RA Mukalla, 22.06.1963).

23. Morris 2002: 17.

24. Ibid.: 150.

25. See ibid.: 510–512, for the various strategies used by pastoralists to survive drought.

26. Al-Anbali 2006: 108; and Chatty 2009: 52.

27. Al-Anbali 2006: 109.

28. Low (1877) 1992: 76.

29. IOR L/P&S/10/215: PR Aden (J. A. Bell) to Secretary to Govt. of Bombay, 24.02.1912.

30. IOR R/20/A/1316: J. A. Bell to Secretary to Govt. of Bombay, 10.01.1914.

31. IOR R/15/2/531: Chief Commissioner Aden to PR in Persian Gulf, Bushire, 04.02.1933.

32. IOR R/20/C/728: "Report on Socotra Visit," Assistant RA Mukalla (Figgis), 28.12.1939; see also Ingrams and Ingrams 1993: 9:706–728. Sultan Ahmad asked twice for the Mahra ban to be lifted (in December 1939 and in February 1940). The ban was lifted finally in August 1940, not because the sultan had consented to the military base but because the Qu'aytis were losing money because of it (IOR R/20/C/1667: "The Mahra Ban," note 8 in Minutes).

33. IOR R/20/C/727: Naval Officer-in-Charge to Governor of Aden, 20.10.1939.

34. IOR R/20/C/728: "Destruction of Tamrida Landing Ground," Lt. Commander, H.M.S. *Shoreham*, 10.07.1940.

35. IOR R/20/C/1666: "An Account of a Visit to Sokotra," Agricultural Officer (B. J. Hartley), June 1941.

36. Ibid.; IOR R/20/C/1666: Sultan Ahmad to Resident Adviser (RA) Mukalla (G. A. Joy), 01.02.1941.

37. Sultan Ahmad's election was challenged by "Sultans" Khalifa Abdullah Muhammad and Ahmad Abdullah Muhammad, his distant (Qishn-based) cousins. In the 1940s, Sultan Ahmad of Qishn tried to pass himself off as *the sultan* by using a "false" seal that exploited their shared first and fathers' names (IOR R/20/B/1635: "Report on Socotra," PO Aden [P. D. Fletcher], 04.05.1942). Sultan Ahmad Abdullah *Isa* was descended from the Sa'd branch of the 'Afrar family (who had the traditional right to the sultanate), whereas the brothers Khalifa and Ahmad Abdullah *Muhammad* were descended from the 'Amr branch of the 'Afrar family (who had the right to be appointed the sultan's viceroys in Qishn). But the British were often confused about whom they should be dealing with; not only did the two Ahmads share the same patronym (Abdullah), but every male member of the 'Afrar family called himself "sultan." Sultan Ahmad of Soqotra traveled to Qishn in the fall of 1941 to confront his relatives; he then replaced Ahmad with Khalifa (as his viceroy on the mainland), but this opposition would continue.

38. IOR R/20/B/2087: "Soqotra Diary," PO Aden (Fletcher), 26.02.1942.

39. IOR R/20/B/2087: Governor of Aden (J. Hathorn Hall) to Sultan of Soqotra, 09.04.1942; see also PRO CAB/84/45: "Indian Ocean–Strategy in Certain Eventualities," War Cabinet, May 1942.

40. IOR R/20/B/1639: "Political Report November," Assistant PO (A/PO) Soqotra (Tudor-Pole), 26.11.1942.

41. IOR R/20/C/2061: "Submarine Attack on Dhows," A/PO Soqotra (Tudor-Pole) to Chief Secretary Aden, 14.02.1944.

42. IOR R/20/B/2088: HQBF Aden to A/Governor (R. S. Champion), 30.12.1942; IOR R/20/B/2089: "Instructions for Security and Maintenance of the R.A.F. Airfield at Socotra," HQBF Aden, 30.09.1944; PRO WO 208/5278: "Report of the RAF Army Expedition to Socotra, Dec. 1964–Feb. 1965," para. 182.

43. IOR R/20/C/1666: "An Account of a Visit to Sokotra," Ag. Officer (B. J. Hartley), June 1941; see also IOR R/20/C/728: "Report on Socotra Visit," A/RA Mukalla (Figgis), 28.12.1939.

44. IOR R/20/B/2087: "Soqotra Diary," PO Aden (Fletcher), 26.02.1942; "February 29, 1942," RA Mukalla (G. A. Joy); "Payments to the Wazir of Soqotra," PO Aden (Fletcher), 01.04.1942; for population estimate, see IOR R/20/C/1404: "Report on Soqotra Island," A/PO Soqotra (Spencer-Cooke), 29.07.1943.

45. IOR R/20/B/1639: "Report on Labour Supply in Socotra," A/PO Soqotra (Tudor-Pole), 26.11.1942.

46. IOR R/20/B/2088: Chief Secretary Aden to RA Mukalla (W. H. Ingrams), 09.06.1942; RA Mukalla to Chief Secretary, 08.07.1942.

47. IOR R/20/B/2087: "Soqotra Diary," PO Aden (Fletcher), April 1942; IOR R/20/B/2088: "Report for July–August," A/PO Soqotra (Goodall), 26.09.1942.

48. IOR R/20/B/2088: "Report for July–August," A/PO Soqotra (Goodall), 26.09.1942.

49. IOR R/20/B/1639: Shaykh Qablan and his brothers to Governor of Aden, 02.12.1942. Importantly, and as yet unrealized by the British, the sultans did not have exclusive rights over land

in Soqotra; in fact, they owned just a few parcels in Hadibo and Goʻo. As the headmen of Qadhub wrote: "All the people of Socotra are masters of their belongings, and the said Sultan is only our Ruler and we submit to him and render him homage, but we do not agree to give him or anyone else our possessions" (ibid., Aden Government translation).

50. IOR R/20/B/1639: A/PO Soqotra (Tudor-Pole) to Chief Secretary Aden, 14.02.1943.

51. IOR R/20/B/1639: Chief Secretary Aden (R. S. Champion) to HQBF Aden, 19.02.1943.

52. Ibid. By this time, Sultan Ahmad had "complete control" over "coolie labor" and received about a quarter of all their wages. IOR R/20/B/1639: "Report on Labour Supply in Socotra," A/PO Soqotra (Tudor-Pole), 26.11.1942; see also IOR R/20/C/1666: A/PO Soqotra (Tudor-Pole) to Chief Secretary Aden, 07.03.1943).

53. IOR R/20/B/1639: "Report on Labour Supply," A/PO Soqotra (Tudor-Pole), 26.11.1942.

54. IOR R/20/B/1635: "Report on Socotra," PO Aden (Fletcher), 04.05.1942; see also "Food Situation on the Island," A/PO Soqotra (Goodall), 04.06.1942.

55. IOR R/20/B/2088: Sultan Ahmad to Governor of Aden, 18.04.1942.

56. IOR R/20/C/1404: "Report on Socotra Island," A/PO Soqotra (Spencer-Cooke), 29.07.1943.

57. IOR R/20/C/1666: Sultan Ahmad to Governor of Aden, 12.04.1943; A/PO Soqotra (Spencer-Cooke) to Chief Secretary Aden (Inge), 05.05.1943; IOR R/20/C/2061: A/PO Soqotra to Chief Secretary, 08.07.1943; Sultan Ahmad to Governor of Aden, 13.6.1943; OC Troops Soqotra to Chief Secretary, 17.06.1943.

58. IOR R/20/B/1639: "Political Report August," A/PO Soqotra (Spencer-Cooke), 01.09.1943.

59. IOR R/20/B/1639: "Malnutrition on Socotra," Squadron Leader BF to Chief Secretary Aden, 18.09.1943.

60. IOR R/20/C/1404: "Bulletin, November & December," A/PO Soqotra (Tudor-Pole), 13.01.1944.

61. IOR R/20/C/2061: Chief Secretary Aden to PO Soqotra, 16.09.1943; "Political Report October," A/PO Soqotra (Spencer-Cooke), 01.11.1943; IOR R/20/C/1404: "Bulletin, January & February 1944," A/PO Soqotra (Tudor-Pole), n.d. At least one hundred dhows en route from the Persian Gulf to East Africa stopped in Qalansiyah between December 1943 and February 1944. Three were attacked by Axis submarines off Soqotra in February ("Submarine Attack on Dhows," A/PO Soqotra to Chief Secretary Aden, 14.02.1944).

62. IOR R/20/C/2060: A/PO Soqotra (Tudor-Pole) to Chief Secretary Aden, 01.01.1944.

63. "Extract from Memorandum by Secretary of State for India" (Leo Amery), 31.07.1943 (in Ingrams and Ingrams 1993: 9:742).

64. IOR R/20/C/1404: A/PO Soqotra (Spencer-Cooke) to Chief Secretary Aden, 01.10.1943.

65. IOR R/20/C/1404: "Bulletin, November & December," A/PO Soqotra (Tudor-Pole), 13.01.1944.

66. IOR R/20/C/2061: A/PO Soqotra (Allen) to HQBF Aden, 19.08.1944; A/PO to Chief Secretary Aden,o 3.09.1944.

67. The "free issue" grain was never actually free, as Aden recovered its expenditures by proportionally raising the price of grain issued to the sultan, who passed on his "expenses" to his subjects. IOR R/20/C/2061: Chief Secretary to A/PO, 19.10.1944.

68. IOR R/20/C/2061: A/PO Soqotra (Maddi) to A/PO (Allen), 29.09.1944.

69. IOR R/20/C/2061: Sultan Ahmad to His People, n.d.; Sultan to PO Soqotra (Stonebanks), 19.12.1944.

70. IOR R/20/C/2062: O. C. Troops Soqotra to Sultan Ahmad, 13.04.1945; Sultan to O .C. Troops, 15.05.1945; Sultan to O. C. Troops, 17.05.1945; IOR R/20/C/2063; PO Soqotra (Butters) to Sultan, 19.05.1945; Sultan to Butters, 30.05.1945; Butters to Sultan, 31.05.1945; Sultan to PO Soqotra (Forbes), 19.06.1945; Forbes to Sultan, 21.06.1945.

71. IOR R/20/B/1640: PO Soqotra (Hargreaves) to Chief Secretary Aden, 17.10.1945.

72. A decade later, a visiting health adviser noted "a white half-cast, not albino, in Qathub

[Qadhub] of the highly significant age of 14." IOR R/20/C/1345: "Notes on a Visit to Socotra," Corkill, 15.04.1956.

73. PRO WO 208/5278: "Report of the RAF Army Expedition to Socotra," para. 52.

74. IOR R/20/B/1640: "Political Report September," A/PO Soqotra (Spencer-Cooke), 01.10.1943.

75. IOR R/20/B/1640: "Report on Socotra," PO Soqotra (Tudor-Pole), May 1943; see also IOR R/20/C/2060: "Patrol Report," Captain Spender, March 1944.

76. IOR R/20/B/2089: Air Vice Marshall (McNamara) to A/Governor of Aden (R. S. Champion), 26.08.1944.

77. IOR R/20/C/2061: Chief Secretary Aden to A/PO Soqotra (Allen), 05.10.1944.

78. IOR R/20/B/1639: A/PO Soqotra (Tudor-Pole) to Chief Secretary Aden, 18.04.43.

79. IOR R/20/B/1639: "Political Report August," A/PO Soqotra (Spencer-Cooke), 01.09.1943.

80. IOR R/20/B/2451: "Intelligence Report," RA Mukalla to Chief Secretary Aden, 19.02.1957.

81. See IOR R/20/B/3089: RA Mukalla to Chief Secretary Aden, 22.03.1961; IOR R/20/C/1822: RA Mukalla to Sultan Isa, 27.09.1963; IOR R/20/D/54: Extract from Winsum, 28.09.1963.

82. Ducker 2006: 137. For the first Mahra penetration plan, see file IOR R/20/B/2657; for the Pan American agreement, see CO 1015/2191; on Operation Gunboat, see IOR R/20/C/1822; on the Mahra Tribal Council, see IOR R/20/C/1665 and IOR R/20/D/266.

83. IOR R/20/C/1932: RA Mukalla to Deputy High Commissioner Aden, 21.05.1967.

84. PRO POWE 33/2519: Secretary of State for the Colonies to High Commissioner (HiCom) Aden (Turnbull), 29.04.1966.

85. IOR R/20/D/266: J. Weakley to Deputy HiCom Aden (Oates), 04.05.1966.

86. IOR R/20/D/266: A/RA Mukalla (Ellis) to Deputy HiCom Aden (Oates), 10.10.1966.

87. IOR R/20/C/1953: AAM Ghaydhah to RA Mukalla, 01.03.1967.

88. IOR R/20/C/1953: "Report on Operation 'Snaffle,' Socotra Island," 08.03.1967. Operation Snaffle was the first of two military operations (the second was Operation Waffle) planned in 1967 to uphold this nascent Mahra Tribal Council and to "make Mahra look more like a state." IOR R/20/C/1932: RA Mukalla (Ellis) to Commander-in-Chief, HQMEC Aden, 22.04.1967.

89. Bin Bukhayt was one of the few pupils sent to Kuwait at the behest of the British adviser, where he was schooled in Arab nationalism and anti-imperialist thought. IOR R/20/C/1953: "Operation Snaffle," A/RA Mukalla to Deputy HiCom Aden, 12.03.1967.

90. During his conversation with the high commissioner of Aden in 1965, Sultan Isa reportedly said, "The Mahra and Soqotrans are not yet fit for independence," and "I wish to keep the ties with [the] British Government to protect my people." PRO CO 1055/239: "Meeting in Guest House, Hadibo," 19.10.1965.

91. IOR R/20/C/1953: RA Mukalla to Sultan Isa, 12.03.1967.

92. IOR R/20/C/1953: A. J. Wilton to RA Mukalla (Ellis), 26.03.1967.

93. Ismael and Ismael 1986: 110–111.

94. Ibid.: 81–107.

95. The first Soqotran to hold a comparable office was Said Salim Sa'd Ba Haqiba, general director of the Soqotra Archipelago from 1991 to 1994 and governor from 2014 to 2015.

96. Morris 2002: 259.

97. Ismael and Ismael 1986: 128.

98. Ibid.: 113–114.

99. Religious worship was not expressly forbidden, but it was not encouraged. Practicing Muslims were critical of the Family Law of 1974, which prohibited their Islamic right to polygamy (see Molyneux 1982: 9), even though the majority of Soqotrans were and still are monogamous. The State Security Law of 1975 made it "an offense for a Yemeni to speak with a non-Yemeni without official approval" (Halliday 1990: 228).

100. These interests extend back at least as far as 1963, when the wireless operators of the Hadhrami Bedouin Legion in Soqotra reported sighting several Russian ships anchored off the

eastern end of the island. IOR R/20/D/54: Extract from Winsum, 14.08.1963; IOR R/20/C/1352: RA Mukalla to CIO Aden, 10.06.1964; RA Mukalla to HiCom Aden, 04.08.1964.

101. Halliday 1990: 203. For video of a 1980 drill, see https://www.youtube.com/watch?v=kab GaoQeFRk. I am grateful to V. Agafonov for this link and history.

102. Phillips 2008: 4; and Dresch and Haykal 1995.

103. See Dresch 2000; and Day 2012: 56–85.

104. Colton 2007.

105. Fergany 2007; and Whitaker 2005.

106. Al-Iryani, de Janvry, and Sadoulet 2015.

107. RoY 2007: 62 (emphasis in original).

108. Ibid.: 25–31; and Fergany 2007.

109. Phillips 2008: 106.

110. Elie 2007: 126–127; and Phillips 2008: 104–107.

111. Elie 2007: 125–128.

112. In some cases, informal elections were held to determine the actual shaykh, thus allowing for new leaders to emerge. In one village, a nineteen-year old man was elected shaykh after having resolved a dispute during which the former (appointed) shaykh had been considered too partial.

113. Wedeen 2003: 684.

114. See Carapico 1998: 140–151.

115. Elie 2007: 129.

116. P. Harvey 2005; and Scott 1998.

117. EPC 2000: sec. 15, 14.

118. Christie 2005; Van Damme and Banfield 2011; Van Damme and De Geest 2006; and Zandri 2006.

119. See NCEA 2009.

120. In 2008, the government placed restrictions on road construction in Soqotra and commissioned a strategic environmental assessment for an updated road plan (Cabinet Decree No. 49, 2008). By then, however, most of the ring road had been completed (NCEA 2009).

121. See Limbert 2014.

122. See Peutz 2011.

123. See Phillips 2008: 103–111.

124. P. Harvey 2005: 129; see also Taussig 2004: 134.

125. Taussig 2004: 134.

126. P. Harvey 2005: 128.

127. Wedeen 2003: 682.

128. Das and Poole 2004: 30.

129. Several Soqotri poems engage this theme of the "poor" and "inferior" goat encountering his seemingly more "well-off" and "civilized"—but ultimately ignorant—urban counterpart as a commentary on the degenerate temptations of urban modern life (Morris 2005).

130. WFP 2014: 22.

131. Harrigan 2014: 215–217.

132. WFP 2014: 23; "Yemen Fuel Subsidy" 2014.

133. Droughts under socialist rule were mitigated by the government's stockpiling of staple foods prior to the monsoon season, but Soqotrans still faced food and water shortages in the years in which poor winter rains were followed by poor pre-monsoon rains (Morris 2002: 512).

134. Ibid.: 512–514.

135. Gardner 1999.

136. Morris 2002: 514.

137. UNEP 2005; see also Fritz and Okal 2008.

138. "Yemen: People Struggling" 2007.

139. As Jacques Derrida contends, hospitality is contingent on these substitutions: "It is indeed the master, the one who invites, the inviting host, who becomes the hostage—and who really

always has been. And the guest, the invited hostage, becomes the one who invites the one who invites, the master of the host. The guest becomes the host's host. The guest (*hôte*) becomes the host (*hôte*) of the host (*hôte*). These substitutions make everyone into everyone else's hostage. Such are the laws of hospitality" (2000: 125).

140. Christie 2005.

141. Fabian 1983: 37–69.

142. Gupta and Sharma 2006: 291.

NOTES TO CHAPTER 3

1. Scientific names of the plants listed (all endemic), respectively: *Commiphora ornifolia, Aloe perryi, Croton Soqotranus, Euphorbia arbuscula, Dracaena cinnabari, Dendrosicyos socotrana, Punica protopunica,* and *Boswellia socotrana.*

2. RoY 2000a: 16; Cheung and DeVantier 2006: 270; see also RoY 2006: 36, 70; the term "global ecocrats" comes from Sachs 1993: 18.

3. West 2006: xii.

4. D. Davis 2011a: 3.

5. Sawyer and Agrawal 2000.

6. D. Davis 2011a; Burke 2009b.

7. See Chatty 2003; D. Davis 2011a.

8. D. Davis 2011b: 62–63. Not all non-Western environments were considered alien or abject. Diana Davis argues that, in contrast to the British experience of the "foreign" nature of landscapes in India and the Arabian Peninsula, the French viewed North Africa as "a landscape of Gallo-Roman 'self' ": a ruined variant of its imagined Roman past (ibid.).

9. PRO CO 1055/239: Colonial Office (C. S. Roberts) to HiCom Aden (Richard Turnbull), 01.12.1965.

10. PRO CO 1055/239: HiCom to Colonial Office, 19.12.1965 (emphasis added).

11. Grove 1995: 349.

12. Crone 1987: 27. Diodorus Siculus (first century BCE) described the island of Hiera, commonly understood to be Soqotra, as producing "frankincense in such abundance as to suffice for the honours paid to the gods throughout the entire inhabited world" (Diodorus of Sicily 1939: 3:213 [book 5, chap. 41, sec. 4]).

13. Strauch 2012a: 541–543.

14. Crone 1987: 21–29; and Freedman 2008: 80–81.

15. Soqotrans may have converted to Christianity following contact with Theophilos the Indian, an island envoy sent by Constantius II (r. 337–361 CE) on an apostolic mission to South Arabia circa 350 CE. Bukharin (2012) argues that Theophilos may have even originated from Soqotra; for an alternative view, see Müller (2001).

16. Cosmas (1897) 2010: 119.

17. Crone 1987: 28.

18. Al-Sirafi 2014: 123.

19. See al-Mas'udi 1948: 20; al-Idrisi 1990: 49–50; Yaqut 1906: 5:93–94. Contemporary scholars conclude that the first Greek colonists arrived closer to the end of the Ptolemaic period (first century BCE). See Bukharin 2012: 504; Crone 1987: 35; and Ubaydli 1989.

20. Despite the rumors of Soqotrans being, in the words of Marco Polo, "the best enchanters of the world" ([1903] 1993: 2:406–407), they were not powerful enough, evidently, to resist foreign rule. In 1507, some twenty-five years after the Mahra settled Soqotra, the Portuguese captured their fort. They failed, however, to capture the support of the "St. Thomas Christians" whom they had ostensibly come to liberate from the "Moors"—even though Albuquerque's men gave the Mahra's palm groves to these "native Christians" (Albuquerque [1875] 2010: 1:55). Instead, the isolated Portuguese garrison endured severe famine and disease. In 1511, after what had been a hostile, four-year standoff between the Portuguese and the surviving Mahra and rebellious "natives," Al-

buquerque (now viceroy of Portuguese India) sent forces to dismantle the fort and transfer its occupants to Goa (see ibid.: 4:3–4; Beckingham 1983; and Biedermann 2006, 2010).

21. Casson 1989: 69 [*Periplus* § 30].

22. G. Smith 1985: 85–86.

23. Al-Najdi 1971: 223.

24. Portuguese missionaries visited Soqotra in 1542, 1549, 1562–1563, and 1603 (Biedermann 2010: 19; Brásio 1943).

25. Xavier 1921: 1:117. A similar claim about Soqotrans' degraded Christianity had been made in 1514 by Duarte Barbosa, brother-in-law of Ferdinand Magellan and officer in Portuguese India (Barbosa 1970: 29–30). In contrast, João de Castro, who spent two weeks anchored off Soqotra in 1541, described the Soqotrans as "very devoted to the Crosse" and, while wanting in religious instruction, "very desirous of it" (Purchas 1905: 7:239, 238).

26. Xavier 1921: 2:77–78.

27. Ibid.: 88. This was not the first time that Soqotra's "barren" nature was ascribed to its degraded religious state; in Chapter 5, I discuss an elegy decrying the loss of verdancy following the so-called Christian uprising against Soqotra's ninth-century Omani rulers.

28. Merchant Finch 1608 (in Purchas 1905: 4:18); Captain Jourdain 1609 (in Jourdain 1905: 109).

29. One exception was the two ships of the Third Voyage, which in 1608 spent six and twelve weeks, respectively, weathering the monsoon in Di-Lishah bay. But there is no indication that their men ventured inland (see Geddes 1964).

30. Jourdain 1905: 54; and Captain Downton 1610 (in Purchas 1905: 3:208).

31. Finch 1608 (in Purchas 1905: 4:16).

32. Downton 1610 (in Purchas 1905: 3:207); Captain Saris 1611 (in Purchas 1905: 3:371). In contrast, a decade later, the Dutch captain Van den Broecke had no trouble purchasing "a good amount of aloes" in "the famous island of Soccotora," which he found "very fertile" (Beckingham 1951b: 173–174).

33. Geddes 1964: 71.

34. As late as 1659, the Surat presidency suggested drawing up a contract with the sultan of Soqotra for an annual supply of Socotrine aloes (Foster 1921: 206).

35. Beckingham 1951a, 1951b, 1983; La Rogue 1732: 23–25; and Serjeant 1992: 162.

36. Barendse 2009: 73–74.

37. Recently discovered coastal inscriptions point to the presence of Gujarati sailors and merchants on Soqotra into the 1720s, and possibly much later (Shelat 2012; Strauch 2012b: 390).

38. Bent 1897: 992.

39. See Low (1877) 1992: 73; Haines 1845; and Wellsted 1835.

40. As the Scottish botanist I. B. Balfour would put it: "Thus it happens that at present in this island, over which Great Britain has now openly declared a protectorate, and within but three weeks' journey from England, there dwells a people whose origin is still involved in myth, and of whose speech the true relations are undetermined, who, according to received records, having attained to some degree of civilization and embraced Christianity, have gone back from their advanced position to the lower stage in which we now find them, and thus present to us a feature of exceptional interest in the history of mankind" (1888: xviii).

41. Van Rampelbergh et al. 2013.

42. Kipling (1902) 2015: 23.

43. Robinson 1878: 48.

44. In 1881, the German naturalists Emil Riebeck and George Schweinfurth spent six weeks on Soqotra studying its languages and people, and flora and fauna, respectively (Schweinfurth 1884). In 1896–1897, the British archaeologists Theodore and Mabel Bent spent two months investigating Himyaritic and Christian remains (Bent 1897); they were accompanied by Ernest N. Bennett (1897), who collected arthropods. In February–March 1897, the Imperial Academy of Sciences of Vienna sent Swedish orientalist Carlo Landberg and English adventurer G. W. Bury for philo-

logical investigations (Macro 1990). In December 1898, another Imperial Academy expedition, led
by linguist D. H. Müller but joined again by Landberg and others, spent a month on Soqotra and
Samha studying Soqotri language, pre-Islamic inscriptions, and archaeological ruins and collecting
insects, reptiles, and flora (Macro 1990). And in 1898–1889, overlapping with the Austrian team,
W. R. Olgivie-Grant, ornithologist at the British Museum, and Henry O. Forbes (1903), director of
the Liverpool Museums, led a three-month zoological expedition to Soqotra and Abd al-Kuri, collecting hundreds of specimens of birds and Lepidoptera, among others. For an account of Balfour's
expedition, see Balfour (1881).

45. See Miller and Bazara'a 1998; Mies and Beyl 1998; and Wranik 1998.

46. Grove 1995; and Tilley 2011.

47. D. Davis 2011a; and Sawyer and Agrawal 2000.

48. Burke 2009a.

49. Wellsted 1835: 160.

50. Wellsted describes the aloes, dragon's blood trees, and olibanum (frankincense) before
noting: "Sketches and descriptions were taken of the other varieties of trees on the island, but as
they are not suitable for building or any useful purpose, and are *merely remarkable for being indigenous to the island*, it does not seem necessary to swell this paper with more than a few general
remarks respecting them" (1835: 198; emphasis added). Yet Wellsted was interested in the "indigenous" human population; his writings focus largely on his encounters with the "savage" but "pure"
and hospitable Bedouin whom he contrasted favorably to the "mongrel" and "zealous" Arabs of the
coast (ibid.: 206–219; 1840: 301–333). Subsequent visitors recycled these stereotypes (see Ravenstein 1876: 122; Balfour 1881: 491–492; E. Bennett 1897: 410; and Bent 1897: 979).

51. Wellsted 1835: 194 (emphasis added). In a later, abridged publication, Wellsted or his editor tempered this statement to this: "and the scenery in *some* places *little inferior* to that of our own
country" (1837: 141).

52. Wellsted 1840: 281.

53. IOR R/20/A/530: Balfour to A/PR Aden (Goodfellow), 16.02.1880. Balfour's expedition,
just four years after the British had secured their first Soqotra treaty, was facilitated and duly recompensed by the annual presents of arms and ammunitions to the sultan: "gifts" that shored up the
power of the 'Afrar in Soqotra, while providing the British a secure entry for their ongoing explorations. See IOR R/20/A/530: PR Aden (Loch) to Sultan Salim of Soqotra, 29.04.1880.

54. Bent 1897: 981.

55. Ibid.; E. Bennett 1897: 412.

56. Bent 1897: 981; Forbes 1903: xli.

57. Moser had accompanied Aden's PR James Bell to Soqotra—the same Bell who returned
from his 1912 looting investigation convinced that "there must be some lucrative asset in the
island."

58. Moser 1918: 271–274.

59. Wellsted 1835: 201.

60. Balfour 1881: 494.

61. Schweinfurth 1881 (in Ingrams and Ingrams 1993, 4:197). Less optimistic about Soqotra's
agricultural prospects, Schweinfurth opined that, if only the world's physicians prescribed aloes
again, Soqotrans could earn their living through aloe cultivation, as they had in the time of Alexander the Great (1884: 19).

62. E. Bennett 1897: 412.

63. For example, in 1910, an English financial syndicate sought to acquire "the territorial and
sovereign rights of the island of Socotra with a view to the development of cotton growing." And in
1912, a Bombay merchant requested a letter for the sultan "as a sort of passport" authorizing him to
purchase pearls there. The Bombay government rejected these and other requests on the grounds
that it did not want to divest the sultan of his sovereignty or "encourage the exploitation of Socotra
by private enterprise" (IOR R/20/A/2828: H. Noar to India Office, 24.06.1910; H. Pack to Assistant
Resident Aden, 13.02.1912, minutes). Even Bell's repeated exhortations to return to Soqotra with a

survey party to ascertain whether Soqotra contained lucrative mineral resources such as diamonds or gold were deferred.

64. IOR R/20/A/3520: Chief Commissioner Aden (Reilly) to Secretary of State for the Colonies, 27.03.1933; IOR/L/P&S/12/1466: Reilly to Secretary of State, 27.03.1933.

65. "Visits to Abd el Kuri and Socotra," A. R. Farquhar, Commander-in-Chief (Ingrams and Ingrams 1993: 9:15).

66. IOR R/20/B/552: J. Hughes (Manchester) to British Resident (BR) Aden, 30.03.1937; IOR R/20/C/1279: T. Sharp to Secretariat Aden, 07.07.1937; Secretariat to RA Mukalla (Ingrams), 29.11.1937; T. Wikeley to Secretariat Aden, 01.02.1938; IOR R/20/C/244: F. Howard to Governor of Aden, 05.11.1938.

67. IOR R/20/C/1279: Sultan Ali to Governor of Aden, 19.12.1937 (16 Shawwal 1356).

68. IOR R/20/C/633: Colonial Office (Shuckburgh) to Governor of Aden (Reilly), 23.03.1939; Shuckburgh to Reilly, 13.04.1939. A year earlier, Ernest Bennett concluded an article on his trip to Soqotra with the question: "What adventurous souls—Jew or Gentile—will undertake the development of this delectable island, and bring back its former prosperity and the significance of its old-time name, 'the island of the abode of bliss'?" (1938: 539).

69. "Extract" (Leo Amery), 31.07.1943 (in Ingrams and Ingrams 1993: 9:742).

70. IOR R/20/C/633: RA Mukalla (Ingrams) to Governor Reilly, 15.04.1939.

71. IOR R/20/C/633: Reilly to Shuckburgh, 25.04.1939.

72. IOR R/20/B/2087: "Soqotra Diary," PO Aden (Fletcher), 14.03.1942.

73. IOR R/20/C/2061: Sultan Ahmad to Governor of Aden, 13.06.1943; IOR R/20/B/1639: "Political Report August," A/PO Soqotra (Spencer-Cooke), 01.09.1943.

74. IOR R/20/C/2060: "Agricultural Development in Socotra," Ag. Officer Aden (Hartley), April 1944.

75. IOR R/20/C/2060: A/PO Soqotra (Tudor-Pole) to Ag. Officer (Hartley), 30.05.1944.

76. IOR R/20/C/2060: "Vegetable Production-Socotra," A/PO Soqotra (Tudor-Pole), 08.05.1944.

77. IOR R/20/C/1530: RA Mukalla to Sultan Isa (Soqotra), 17.01.1953; RA Mukalla to Sultan Isa, 03.03.1953.

78. IOR R/20/C/1530: Sultan Khalifa (al-Mahra) to RA Mukalla, 09.07.1949.

79. IOR R/20/B/2654: Bedouin Affairs Assistant to RA Mukalla, 24.05.1953.

80. IOR R/20/B/2654: "Treaty between HMG in the UK and the Sultan of Qishn and Socotra," 11.04.1954; IOR R/20/B/2657: "Chronological Notes on the Expansion into Mahra with Particular Reference to the Question of the Appointment of a Naib for Mahra," 31.12.1954; PRO CO 1055/239: "Meeting in Guest House," 19.10.1965.

81. IOR R/20/C/1345: "Witch Trials in Soqotra, November 1955," I. E. Snell, AA Mahra, 26.11.1955.

82. See, for example, the rationale for refusing access to an Italian journalist in IOR R/20/B/2451: "Visit of Italian Journalist," 23.01.56.

83. PRO CO 1015/975: "Qishn & Socotra," Governor of Aden (Hickinbotham) to Secretary of State for the Colonies (Lennox-Boyd), 16.04.1956; "Relations with the Sultan of Qishn and Socotra," Memorandum by Secretary of State for the Colonies, 23.05.1956.

84. Botting 1958b: 201.

85. Botting 1958a: 93.

86. Botting 1957: 288; 1958a: 51.

87. Botting 1958a: 95, 210, 218.

88. PRO CO 1015/1733: J. C. Morgan (Colonial Office) to W. L. Gorell Barnes, 13.02.1959.

89. During these same years, a group of Mahra tried to separate the al-Mahra territory from Soqotra. Rejecting Sultan Isa's sovereignty over al-Mahra and his right to profit from its potential oil, a Qishn-based distant relative of Isa—"Sultan" Muhammad—managed to sell a "bogus" oil concession to the fictitious "Kingdom of Afrar" (al-Mahra) to two US wildcatters consecutively: Forest Oil in 1955 and Hunt Oil in 1958 (IOR R/20/C/1984: S. S. Ansari to Forest Oil Corporation,

15.12.1955; IOR R/20/B/3107: "Memorandum of Agreement between N. B. Hunt and Sh. Ham-dan," 10.01.1958). Despite Britain's rebuttals, these US companies (and, for a while, their State Department backers) believed "Sultan" Muhammad's claims that Sultan Isa was a "pretender" who had usurped the legitimate power of the true sultan of al-Mahra and ruler of the "Himyarite Kingdom of Afrar" (thus invalidating the PCL concession to the same territory). These compet-ing claims to the Mahra concession, which PCL ultimately won, turned a dynastic skirmish over local sovereignty into a near-international skirmish between the nascent US empire and the fading British one. Not ones to give up, the Mahri "sultan" and his Bombay lawyers appealed to the gover-nor of Aden, the Indian minister of commerce and industries, and US president John F. Kennedy for their help in establishing an independent Mahra state separated from the island of Soqotra. In 1962, "Sultan" Muhammad even offered the British government territory for military bases in his "kingdom" in exchange for direct aid (IOR/R/20/B/3089: Sh. Hamdan Salim bin Ali al-Mahri, Hyderabad to Governor of Aden, 23.04.1959; IOR R/20/B/3107: Sh. Hamdan to Minister of Com-merce and Industries India, n.d.; J. A. Brown, Rep. of Sultan Muhammad Ali to President of USA, 20.09.1962; Brown to the Earl of Home, Secretary of State for Foreign Affairs, 28.08.1962).

90. PRO CO 1015/1733: "Socotra," Central African and Aden Department, 28.01.1965; Gorell Barnes to J. Amery, 28.01.1965; Amery to Gorell Barnes, 30.01.1965.

91. PRO CO 1015/1733: Governor of Aden (W. H. Luce) to Colonial Office (J. C. Morgan), 18.03.1959.

92. IOR R/20/C/1351: RA Mukalla (T. Eyre) to Sultan Isa, 09.02.1964.

93. At this point, the person calling for the separation of Soqotra was none other than Prime Minister Harold MacMillan (Mawby 2005: 73), Julian Amery's father-in-law.

94. Forbes-Watson 1964: 7. Despite referencing the sultan's oil profits, talk of Soqotra becom-ing a British base, and the landing on Soqotra of Arab "refugees" from Zanzibar, Forbes-Watson concluded; "Perhaps nowhere else in the world is there such peace . . . and it would be a shame if the twentieth century arrived to spoil it all" (ibid).

95. PRO WO 208/5278: "Report of the RAF/Army Expedition to Socotra," para. 260. Boxhall had been stationed there in 1958 to guard a political prisoner deported from Aden, during which time he and his officers were tasked with collecting specimens of aloe and mangrove shoots (IOR R/20/C/1346: Boxhall to BA Mukalla, 26.05.1958; BA Mukalla to APL HQ Aden, 14.06.1958; Es-cort Soqotra to BA Mukalla, 10.08.1965; see also PRO CO 1015/1887, on the imprisonment of Abdullah al-Jifri).

96. PRO CO 1055/239: Ministry of Defense (D. M. Dell) to Colonial Office (J. D. Higham), 24.02.1965. Julian Amery had even planned to visit Soqotra during the RAF/Army expedition, but his trip was canceled at the eleventh hour (IOR R/20/C/1353: RA Mukalla to Wazir Ibrahim of Socotra, 18.01.1965; PRO WO 208/5278: "Report of the RAF/Army Expedition," para. 206).

97. G. Brown 1966: sec. 1, 5.

98. IOR R/20/G/152: "Confidential Addendum to Report on Conditions and Development in Socotra," G. H. Brown 16.07.1966 (4). Describing Sultan Isa as "sluggish, unintelligent, timid, shifty and avaricious" (1), Brown asserted that it was the monopolies that shored up the ruling elites' authority. What Brown neglected to see or describe was the degree to which these monopolies had been reinforced by the British occupation of the island.

99. G. Brown 1966: sec. 5, 11.

100. Doe 1992: 7.

101. Tomkinson 1967: 318.

102. G. Brown 1966: sec. 1, 1.

103. Popov 1957: 716.

104. As summarized in Miller and Morris 2004: 5.

105. Lucas and Synge 1978: 181; Koopowitz and Kaye 1983: 63, cited in Miller and Bazara'a 1998.

106. See Chatty 2003.

107. In 1974, the Russian-Arabist ethnographer Vitaly Naumkin and his team were the first

"Soviet citizens to visit Socotra" (Naumkin 1993: ix). Naumkin returned as part of a joint Soviet-Yemeni scientific expedition that conducted archaeological, ethnographic, and linguistic research in Hadhramawt, al-Mahra, and Soqotra between 1983 and 1987. During these years, Lothar and Heidi Stein also visited the island to conduct ethnographic research and collect material for the Museum of Ethnography in Leipzig (Stein 1986).

108. The Cambridge University botanist Quentin Cronk disputed this assumption following his brief visit to Soqotra in 1985, but it took the botanical explorations of the 1990s to lay it to rest (Miller and Morris 2004: 5.)

109. Miller and Bazara'a 1998: 15.

110. Miller and Morris 2004: 8.

111. Ibid.

112. Van Damme and Banfield 2011.

113. RoY 2005; Varisco 1995, 2003; Ward 2015; see also Haq 2007: 125; and Foltz, Denny, and Baharuddin 2003.

114. Morris 2002; Pietsch and Morris 2010.

115. Cheung and DeVantier 2006.

116. RoY 2004.

117. World Bank 2000.

118. Article 35 of the Constitution of the Republic of Yemen, 1994, states, "Environmental protection is the collective responsibility of the state and the community at large. Each individual shall have a religious and national duty to protect the environment."

119. In 2002, in a move that reflected its increasing political commitment to resource conservation and management, the government reorganized its Ministry of Tourism and Environment (established in 2001) and Ministry of Water and Electricity into a Ministry of Water and Environment (that oversees the EPA), a Ministry of Tourism and Culture, and a Ministry of Electricity and Energy.

120. RoY 2005.

121. UNDP-GEF 1997: 6. Three years earlier, following Yemen's signing of the Convention on Biological Diversity, the EPC had sent a thirteen-member international fact-finding mission to Soqotra to determine whether Soqotra could qualify as a UNESCO "Man and the Biosphere" reserve.

122. See Meskell 2012.

123. At the time of writing (spring 2018), the "Arab States" have successively nominated 74 cultural sites (9 percent of the world's total of 832); 6 natural sites, including Oman's delisted site (3 percent of the world's 206); and 3 mixed (natural and cultural) sites (9 percent of the world's total of 35) to the World Heritage List. At present, 22 of these sites are considered "in danger" (compared to 54 sites worldwide).

124. Wedeen 2008.

125. UNDP-GEF 2008: 7.

126. UNDP-GEF 1997: 14. Officially named "Conservation and Sustainable Use of Biodiversity of Socotra Archipelago," this USD 5 million project was funded by the GEF, implemented by Yemen's Environment Protection Council, executed by the United Nations Office for Project Services, and supervised by the UNDP. It leveraged an additional USD 5 million in parallel financing on top of the government's allocation of circa USD 2 million for transport infrastructure (road, seaport, and airport construction).

127. Elie 2007: 278.

128. See RoY 2000a.

129. Zandri 2003: 32.

130. RoY 2000a.

131. Elie 2007: 284.

132. RoY 2000b: xxxi.

133. Elie 2007: 283–284.

134. See, for example, UNDP-GEF 2003: 6–7.

135. Borgerhoff Mulder and Coppolillo 2005: 248.

136. Zandri 2003: 31; Ceballos-Lascuráin 1999.

137. RoY 2000b: sec. 17, 1.

138. Officially named "Conservation and Sustainable Use of the Biodiversity of Socotra Archipelago (Continuation Phase)," the SCDP received USD 1.5 million in bridge funding from the UNDP and the Netherlands (UNDP-GEF 2001).

139. Infield and Al Deen 2003: 22. Officially named "The Environment, Natural Resources and Poverty Alleviation for the Populations of Socotra Island, Yemen" (YEM/00/001/01/31), this project was financed by the UNDP and the governments of Italy and Poland.

140. Ibid.: 35.

141. Officially named "Sustainable Development and Biodiversity Conservation for the People of Socotra Islands, Yemen—Socotra Sustainable Development," the SCDP-2 received USD 5.3 million from the UNDP, Italy, and Yemen. In addition, approximately USD 3.5 million of foreign aid (from governments or NGOs in France, Japan, Italy, the United States, United Kingdom, and Czech Republic) supported smaller, ancillary projects during this period (UNDP-GEF 2003).

142. Ibid.: 83. Additionally, in 2008, the Government of Yemen allocated USD 171,000 to Soqotra's EPA office—up from USD 360 in 1997 (UNEP-WCMC 2008: 9).

143. One of these, the Rosh Protected Area Community, was one of twenty-five Equator Prize winners in 2010, a UNDP prize awarded in recognition of community efforts "to reduce poverty through the conservation and sustainable use of biodiversity" ("Equator Initiative," accessed 15 June 2017, http://www.equatorinitiative.org/).

144. UNDP-GEF 2003: 6.

145. In 1996, the government decreed the formation of the High Committee for the Development of Soqotra to oversee the development and environmental management of the archipelago. But this interministerial committee never materialized, nor was the SCDP Coordination Unit (established in phase two to oversee the implementation of the zoning and master plans) ever invested with "real authority, capacity and political strength to coordinate investment" there (Infield and Al Deen 2003: 15). It was the Soqotra Authority that was to assume this role.

146. Officially named "Strengthening Socotra's Policy and Regulatory Framework for Mainstreaming Biodiversity," the SGBP received USD 3.14 million from the UNDP, GEF, and the Government of Yemen (UNDP-GEF 2008).

147. Ibid.: 10, 13.

148. Zandri 2003: 32.

149. Constitution of 1994, Art. 35.

150. Tsing 1993; J. Ferguson 2006: 22.

151. Abulhawa and Abdulhalim 2013: 26.

152. Ibid.: 19–20.

153. This 2011 initiative, adopted by the IUCN and supported regionally by the Arab Regional Center for World Heritage in Bahrain (established in 2011), seeks to guide state parties through the nomination and conservation processes.

154. Abulhawa et al. 2014.

NOTES TO CHAPTER 4

Portions of this chapter appeared in "Bedouin 'Abjection': World Heritage, Worldliness, and Worthiness at the Margins of Arabia," *American Ethnologist* 38, no. 2 (2011): 338–360.

1. Muhammad Di-Girigoti is a prominent Soqotran poet. I thank Miranda Morris for this poem and its translation.

2. UNDP-GEF 2003: 47.

3. "Yemen, West Asia," Protected Planet, accessed 22 May 2018, https://www.protectedplanet.net/country/YE.

4. Zandri 2003: 33.

5. Ong 2006: 103.

6. Brockington, Duffy, and Igoe 2008: 18.

7. See Büscher et al. 2012.

8. Rist 1996: 201.

9. Meskell 2012; and Brockington, Duffy, and Igoe 2008.

10. Borgerhoff Mulder and Coppolillo 2005: 28.

11. The IUPN changed its name to International Union for the Conservation of Nature and Natural Resources (IUCN) in 1956; from 1990 to 2008, it went by the name World Conservation Union (still IUCN).

12. Oates 1999: 46.

13. Borgerhoff Mulder and Coppolillo 2005: 37–39.

14. Rist 1996: 141.

15. UNESCO 1972: 2; on "outstanding universal value," see Titchen 1996; for an extraordinary ethnography of heritage as a moralizing promise of "redemption," see Collins 2015.

16. Orlove and Brush 1996: 331.

17. Rist 1996: 1970.

18. Oates 1999: 50.

19. IUCN, UNEP, and WWF 1980.

20. Wells, Brandon, and Hannah 1992: 2.

21. WCED 1988: 8, cited in Rist 1996: 181.

22. Borgerhoff Mulder and Coppolillo 2005: 41.

23. Sachs 1993; Oates 1999.

24. Oates 1999: 52–53.

25. UN 1992: art. 8.

26. Zimmerer 2006: 5–7; West, Igoe, and Brockington 2006.

27. McNeely, Harrison, and Dingwall 1994: 81–85. Historically, the MENA region has had the lowest average proportion of each country set aside for protected areas among all world regions (Brockington, Duffy, and Igoe 2008: 31).

28. See Wells, Brandon, and Hannah 1992; and West 2006.

29. Brosius, Tsing, and Zerner 1998.

30. West 2006: 35 (emphasis added).

31. Ibid.: 184; see also Rist 1996: 218.

32. Zimmerer 2006: 9.

33. Hames 2007; Redford 1991.

34. Chatty 2003.

35. Agrawal and Gibson 1999: 633, 634, 635.

36. Anderson 1983.

37. Moore 1998: 400.

38. West, Igoe, and Brockington 2006: 255.

39. Ibid.: 255.

40. Ibid.: 252.

41. Brockington, Duffy, and Igoe 2008: 63.

42. Borgerhoff Mulder and Coppolillo 2005: 32.

43. J. Ferguson 2006: 40.

44. Abu-Lughod 1986.

45. See Chatty 2014; Cole 2003; Cooke 2014; Eickelman 1998; Khalaf 2000, 2002; and Prager 2014.

46. De Genova 2005: 49.

47. Fernandez and Huber 2001: 13.

48. Taylor 2001: 185.

49. Botting 1958a: 130.

50. Herzfeld 2004: 4.

51. See Heatherington 2010: 137–138.

52. Abu-Lughod 2004: 109.

53. Heatherington 2010: 23, 130–134.

54. In an earlier article (Peutz 2011), I argue that the specter of abjection haunts not only the socially marginalized, politically excluded, and geographically displaced but also those who are now icons of national heritage.

55. Ucodep y Movimondo 2005: 50. This "course" was part of a study on the impacts of rural tourism and sustainable development on poverty reduction in four countries. Thus, it was not strictly a course, but this is how it was represented to and understood by the local community.

56. See Agrawal and Gibson 1999.

57. West, Igoe, and Brockington 2006: 261.

58. Morris 2002: 427.

59. See ibid.: 33–53.

60. Limbert 2010; Ward 2015; and Jones 2010.

61. In addition to seasonal constraints, customary law delimits the use of wadis for agricultural irrigation. Because water flowing through a wadi is considered common property, it is prohibited for anyone to take more than she can by hand (through pumps or machinery)—even if it is for a community garden.

62. PARITER employed Soqotran guards and office staff, but Bu Faruq, their driver, was the only Soqotran to work in the field (outside Hadibo).

63. Morris 2002: 471–478.

64. Ibid.: 233.

65. Ibid.: 247.

66. Brockington, Duffy, and Igoe 2008: 63.

67. West, Igoe, and Brockington 2006: 261.

68. Infield and Al Deen 2003.

69. Shadie and Epps 2008: 23. Of course, the legislative uncertainty regarding land tenure rights did negatively impact these projects and will continue to frustrate any future projects, foreign or local, until it is resolved. I thank Miranda Morris for this point.

70. The rising cost of land was a concern of Soqotrans and northern Yemenis alike. In 2000, a man from Taiz had considered buying a 14 × 10-meter plot for YER 400,000 on which to build a store; in 2008, the same piece of land sold for YER 11 million to a woman from "the north." Prices have increased even more since the start of the war: in 2016, a 10 × 10-meter plot sold for YER 30 million.

71. See Peutz 2013.

72. For a discussion of the actual and allegorical disturbances caused by weeds, foreign flora, and alien species (including "alien" migrants), see Comaroff and Comaroff 2005; and Tsing 2005.

73. Cheung and DeVantier 2006: 325. Botanists have debated whether or not the *Argemone mexicana* (originally from South America) is truly invasive; regardless, this species has existed on Soqotra at least since the 1880s when I. B. Balfour noted its presence (Balfour 1888: 3).

74. Brockington, Duffy, and Igoe 2008: 6.

75. Rist 1996: 227.

NOTES TO CHAPTER 5

An earlier version of this chapter was published in "Reorienting Heritage: Poetic Exchanges between Suqutra and the Gulf," *Revue des mondes musulmans et de la Méditerranée* 121–122 (2008): 163–182.

1. Harrison 2015: 28.

2. Ibid.: 27.

3. See Vora 2013; and Cooke 2014.

4. Cooke 2014: 122.

5. See Khalaf 2002; Fox, Mourtada-Sabbah, and al-Mutawa 2006; and Wakefield 2014.

6. See Fibiger 2011; Exell and Rico 2013.

7. Harrison 2015: 28.

8. L. Smith 2006: 11.

9. Litvin 2011: 6.

10. Yemen's new "Population, Housing and Establishment" census planned for 2014 was deferred due to its financial and political difficulties.

11. IOR R/20/B/1635: "Report on Socotra," PO Aden (Fletcher), 04.05.1942.

12. IOR R/20/B/1640: "Report on Socotra," PO Soqotra (Tudor-Pole), May 1943.

13. Bowen 1951: 169. See also Dostal (1998: 268) on Soqotrans hired to work the guano depots in the Kuria Muria islands in the 1850s.

14. Carter 2005.

15. IOR R/15/2/531: "Bushire Printed Letter 160-S," 17.02.1933. This information was elicited in the context of the Aden Residency seeking to ban all Mahra and Soqotrans from the ports of al-Mukalla, Dhofar, Muscat, and Bahrain after the Mahra authorities at Qishn had opposed the construction of a British landing ground there.

16. IOR R/20/C/2060: "Socotra Island Fisheries," Ag. Officer (Hartley), April 1944; see also Hightower 2013.

17. IOR R/20/B/1639: "Report on Labour Supply," A/PO Soqotra (Tudor-Pole), 26.11.1942.

18. IOR R/20/C/1343: "Report on a Visit to Socotra," Boustead, 24.10.1949.

19. In 1954, when Assistant RA Mukalla traveled to Soqotra to coerce Sultan Isa into signing the more-binding Advisory Treaty, he found that all but one of the sultan's advisers "were away at Ras Mumin [Momi] buying pearls" (IOR R/20/B/2654: "Report on the Signing of the Advisory Treaty," I. E. Snell, 13.04.1954); in 1959, the crew of a Spanish dhow stopping at Soqotra purchased pearls at a cost of USD 100 and paid with an American Express traveler's check (IOR R/20/C/1348: W/OP Soqotra to BA Mukalla, 18.04.59); and in 1960, when Snell returned to Soqotra to convince Sultan Isa to visit his al-Mahra territories, he discovered an extant market for exported pearl shell, albeit at reduced rates (IOR R/20/B/3089: "Report by CO HBL on Visit to Socotra," Snell, 10.02.1960).

20. Bowen 1951: 180.

21. G. Brown 1966: sec. 1, 1; sec. 4, 10.

22. British lists of Soqotran exports in the 1940s and 1950s typically include ghee, woolen rugs, skins, dried fish, salt, civet, pearls, dragon's blood, and ambergris.

23. See also Abdulrahman 2014: 34–38.

24. PRO FCO 8/1272: "Socotri Immigration into the Trucial States," Political Agency Dubai, 16.06.1969. I thank Diana Gluck for this reference.

25. Ibid.

26. Ibid.

27. Gluck 2016: 138–147.

28. Naumkin 1989: 137.

29. Stein and Stein 1999: 215; see also Noman 1995.

30. Although Soqotrans continue to face difficulties acquiring entry visas through their Yemeni passports, they are currently receiving (in spring 2018) special identity cards that may enable them to enter the UAE more easily: a resurrection of their once-special status. Since 2016, hundreds of Soqotrans have been flown to the UAE for medical care, education, and training.

31. IOR R/20/B/1635: "Report on Socotra," PO Aden (Fletcher), 04.05.1942. In 1835, Wellsted heard that "Arabs" journeyed to Soqotra to marry a bride for 8–10 dollars (1840: 211).

32. IOR R/20/C/1344: "Report on Socotra Island," PO Mahra (Snell), 11.03.1954.

33. Abdulrahman 2014: 39. After setting sail from Soqotra, Al Fuqaei's dhow and its accompanying fleet were caught in a storm; Al Fuqaei's dhow returned to Soqotra and made it ashore; the seven other ships sank—brides and all.

34. L. Brown 1966: sec. 1, 2.

35. The port director estimated that, each year, Soqotra's Haulaf port receives ninety-five (six hundred– to seven hundred–ton) "Indian dhows" from Yemen, Oman, and elsewhere; ten (fifteen hundred–ton) tankers from Yemen (carrying diesel, petrol, and gas); and forty to fifty (six hundred– to seven hundred–ton) ships from Sharjah. He further estimated that approximately 60

percent of the cargo from Sharjah is imported by merchants, while the rest consists of goods sent by individuals (the emigrants).

36. For more on this *ritha'*-style poetry (mournful incitements to vengeance composed by freeborn women following the death of their kinsmen), see Stetevych 1993.

37. Al-Salimi 1931: 139; see also Serjeant 1992: 139.

38. Circa 752 CE, Soqotra was captured by Oman's first Ibadi imam (Julanda bin Masud, r. 750–752) as a strategic base for Oman's East African slave trade. Soqotra's Christians were given protected (*dhimmi*) status in exchange for concluding an annual peace agreement (*sulh*) and submitting to a per capita tax (Wilkinson 1981: 280–281; 1987: 47).

39. Al-Salimi 1931: 151.

40. Al-Rawas 1990: 274.

41. See al-Hamdani 1968: 53; al-Sirafi 2014: 123; and al-Mas'udi 1948: 20. However, according to al-Hamdani (CE 893–945), it was the fanatical Ibadi warriors (*al-shurat*), not the Christians, who killed the other Muslims living there (see Wilkinson 1987: 184–185).

42. Al-Anbali 2001: 7.

43. Ibid.: 8.

44. Al-Anbali 2006: 11.

45. Al-Anbali 2001: 77.

46. Ibid.: 73, 75.

47. Ibid.: 73.

48. Al-Ain, the UAE city in which al-Anbali resided in 2001, was historically a part of the Buraimi Oasis (in today's Oman), which was under Ibadi rule in the ninth century; it is in this sense that the elegy can be said to have been repatriated from "Oman" to Soqotra. The texts that round out al-Anbali's collection are his commentary on the poem, Imam as-Salt's instructions to his fleet, and a history of the Christian presence on Soqotra.

49. For a partial translation of additional verses, see Serjeant 1992: 138–139.

50. Al-Anbali 2001: 11, 51.

51. Ibid.: 11.

52. Ibid.: 73.

53. Ibid.: 74, 45.

54. See al-Zirikli 1989: 209.

55. Al-Salimi 1931: 152; al-Rawas 1990: 273–274.

56. See Wilkinson 1981: 280–281; 1987: 47.

57. Al-Anbali 2001: 63. Recent scholarship casts doubt on this Abyssinian connection, noting Soqotra's connections to the Nestorian Church of Persia, most likely through missionaries and merchants by way of the sixth-century CE Sassanid province in southern Arabia (Dhofar). These ecclesiastic connections preceded the (first) Ibadi colonization of Soqotra circa 750–886 CE and continued through the thirteenth century, if not longer (see Biedermann 2010; and Müller 2001).

58. Al-Anbali 2001: 50.

59. Ibid.: 51.

60. Ibid.: 70–72.

61. Ibid.: 10.

62. François Burgat, pers. comm., February 2006.

63. Al-Anbali 2001: 73.

64. Ibid.: 65

65. Established by Miranda Morris and Friends of Soqotra (FoS), with funding from various institutions and private donors, the well-stocked library was initially well received. Nevertheless, the elected local Library Committee did little to keep it operational; in 2010, it was officially closed because of administrative neglect. See *Tayf: The Soqotra Newsletter* 7 (2010): 9, http://www.friendsofsoqotra.org/Activities/pdfs/Tayf%207%20English%20FINAL.pdf.

66. Miller 2002: 39.

67. Remarkably, this brigade fought in opposition to the Mahra, who supported PFLOAG

and permitted it to run a "supply, military and educational centre" out of Hauf, in Mahra territory (Takriti 2013: 78); see also Ladwig 2008.

68. Takriti 2013: 300.

69. (Salim) Rubay'a (Ali "Salmayn") was head of state of the PDRY from 1969 until his deposition and execution by Ali Nasir Muhammad in 1978; Abd al-Fattah (Ismail) was the de facto leader of South Yemen from 1969 to 1980; (Ali) Shayi' and Ali (Ahmad Nasir) 'Antar were politburo members who, along with Abd al-Fattah, were killed by Ali Nasir's men during a suspected coup attempt in 1986.

70. Ho 2006: 68.

71. Limbert 2010: 3.

72. See Dirks 1990.

73. Ingold 2012: 436.

74. Heidegger 1971.

75. J. Bennett 2010: 5.

76. Royle 2003: 1–2.

77. Ibid.

78. This is not to say that Haybak has been forgotten; in 2013, a Facebook post calling for vengeance generated another impassioned transnational debate, and then, silence; before I could read it, the thread had been removed.

NOTES TO CHAPTER 6

Portions of this chapter appeared in "Revolution in Socotra: A Perspective from Yemen's Periphery," *Middle East Report* 263 (2012): 14–20.

1. Cited in Irwin 2000: 50.

2. See Lawson and al-Naboodah 2008; and Exell and Rico 2013.

3. Ong 2005: 341.

4. These individuals may be considered "para-experts" in the same way that some anthropologists consider their interlocutors to be "para-ethnographers" (Holmes and Marcus 2008). Para-ethnographers are the collaborators who work alongside ethnographers—not in a subservient but in an auxiliary sense—and thus contribute to the anthropological project while destabilizing the anthropologist's expertise (Kirksey, Schuetze, and Helmreich 2014: 10). I call these Soqotrans para-experts, however, and not para-ethnographers (although they are that, too) because of their initial position vis-à-vis the project experts.

5. Carr 2010: 19.

6. Miller and Morris 1988, 2004.

7. IOR R/20/C/1345: "Health Advisor's Notes on a Visit to Socotra," Corkill, 15.04.1956. According to Corkill, Soqotrans were "clamour[ing]" for a "health injection" of penicillin, which he attributed to the wartime popularity of arsphenamine "606" injections as a reputed aphrodisiac. (There were cases of syphilis on the island in the 1940s, so this 606 compound may have been introduced for this reason.) But Soqotrans were said to have been "clamouring for . . . *dowa Inglizi* [English medicine]" as early as the 1890s, when British visitors distributed their pills (E. Bennett 1897: 411).

8. Al-Shizabi 2006.

9. Appadurai 1981.

10. Cheung and DeVantier 2006: 236–237.

11. Meskell 2002.

12. Sutherland 2003.

13. Urban 2015; Austin and Sallabank 2011. These projections are problematic because models used to predict extinction rates vary substantially and because the majority of species and many languages remain unknown. However, most projections remain conservative (Ceballos, Ehrlich, and Dirzo 2017).

14. See Attorre et al. 2007.

15. Langham and Barker 2014; Cooke 2014: 130–137.

16. *Million's Poet*, accessed 26 January 2012, http://www.adach.ae/en/portal/poet.ofthemillion. aspx [site discontinued].

17. Wright 2011: 160–168.

18. Holes and Abu Athera 2011.

19. See "Environmental Educational Programme," n.d.

20. Eventually, with the help of another local partner, Development for Isolated Peoples (an Australian NGO), the project published and distributed ten thousand copies of a general resource text, *Soqotra—Heritage and Future* (in English and in Arabic), to each household throughout the island in 2011 (see Christie and Dutton 2009).

21. Kirschenblatt-Gimblett 2006.

22. *Million's Poet.*

23. Cooke 2014; and Langham and Barker 2014.

24. C. Schmitt (1922) 1985: 47.

25. Ong 2006: 78.

26. Ferguson and Gupta 2002.

27. "UNDP Defers Programmes" 2011.

28. Its official name was the National Council of Soqotra Archipelago Youth in the Republic of Yemen.

29. Other opposition groups active in Soqotra included the Southern Separatist Movement, the Joint Meeting Parties (a coalition advocating for general reform), and several voluntary associations formed during the revolution.

30. Yahya was invoking a political slogan that emerged in Tunisia in 2011 and was used by protesters throughout the Arab world during the Arab uprisings: *ash-sha'b yurid isqat an-nizam* (the people want to bring down the regime). See Dabashi 2012; and Harb Michel 2013.

31. Challand 2013: 178; see also Dabashi 2012: 40–48.

32. The SCDP did support a trash removal project in the mid-2000s and encouraged several Hadibo cleanup events; however, these were deemed less successful as few people outside the project staff or army pitched in.

33. 'Amran is the (small) capital of the 'Amran governorate, north of Sanaa. In addition to its internal rhyme (*thawra thawra fi kul-l-yaman, min suqutra ila 'amran*), this particular slogan emphasizes the extent of the revolution, from Yemen's southernmost island to its (nearly) northernmost governorate. For some, the reference to 'Amran may have also underscored their call for Soqotra to become a governorate.

34. By my estimate, of the seventy-nine poems recited in 2011, more than a third focused explicitly on current political events (see Peutz 2012).

35. Carr 2010.

36. Schmitz 2014.

37. Soqotra fielded 3 of the NDC's 595 delegates: Fahd Saleem Kafayan; Said Salim Sa'd Ba Haqiba (GPC representative and member of Parliament; first Soqotran commissioner of Soqotra from 1991 to 1994); and Afrah Said Ahmad Said (an independent "youth" representative). Al-Mahra fielded 15 delegates (Liebhaber 2015).

38. Fahdl al-Eryani, a student at the time at NYU Abu Dhabi, spent three weeks on the island in June 2013 expertly interviewing key persons on my behalf.

39. Abulohoom 2013.

40. Liebhaber 2015. These states are Algeria, Iraq, and Morocco.

41. ConstitutionNet, "Yemen: Draft Constitution of 2015," accessed 30 June 2017, http://www .constitutionnet.org/vl/item/yemen-draft-constitution-2015.

42. Liebhaber 2015.

43. Prior to this, Fahd Saleem had served as the representative of the Governorate of Soqotra.

44. Gellner 1983.

45. Hroch 1985.

46. Leerssen 2006: 562.
47. Ibid.: 564.
48. Ibid.: 568.
49. Ibid.: 572.
50. Ibid.: 565.
51. Ibid.: 571.
52. Herzfeld 1997: 111–112.

NOTES TO CONCLUSION

1. Bukharin 2012: 517.

2. By April 2016, the UAE's Khalifa Foundation had dispatched twenty-nine relief planes to Soqotra, along with several shipments of food and other emergency supplies. More relief planes followed. See "Khalifa Foundation" 2016.

3. Estimates are from OCHA (Office for the Coordination of Humanitarian Affairs; http://www.unocha.org/yemen) and UNCHR (United Nations High Commission for Refugees; http://www.unhcr.org/yemen-emergency.html) data (both accessed 23 March 2018). See also Sharp 2018.

4. Kirksey, Schuetze, and Helmreich 2014: 14; Van Dooren 2016: 46, 57; see also Haraway 2016.

5. Boullata 1990: 34.

6. Van Dooren 2016: 58.

7. Broadcast on the satellite channel *al-ghad al-mushriq* (the Bright Future), videos of the festival are available on YouTube: https://www.youtube.com/watch?v=p7HoYqfLI14, and https://www.youtube.com/watch?v=m9njRftXmjY.

8. UNEP-GEF 2013: 2. Officially named "Support to the Integrated Program for the Conservation and Sustainable Development of the Socotra Archipelago," this four-year project is being funded by the GEF (USD 4.8 million), implemented by the UNEP, and executed by Yemen's Ministry of Water and Environment and EPA in collaboration with the Senckenberg Society for Nature Research. Cofinancing by the project partners for concurrent conservation and development interventions is estimated to reach USD 15 million.

9. UNEP-GEF 2013: 61.

10. Haraway 2014: 242.

11. Douglas 1999: 313.

REFERENCES

ARCHIVAL SOURCES

India Office Records, British Library, London, UK (IOR)

Political and Secret Department Records (L/P&S)
Robert Vernon Smith, Papers (Mss Eur F231/30)
Records of the British Residency and Agencies in the Persian Gulf (R/15)
Records of the British Administration in Aden (R/20)

National Archives, London (Kew), UK (PRO)

Records of the Cabinet (CAB)
Records of the Colonial Office (CO)
Records of the Foreign and Commonwealth Office (FCO)
Ministry of Power (POWE)
Records of the War Office (WO)

PUBLICATIONS

Abdulrahman, Abdullah. 2014. *Between Sips of Coffee: Oral Narratives from the United Arab Emirates*. Edited and translated by K. Al-Masri. Abu Dhabi: Abu Dhabi Authority for Tourism and Culture.

Abrams, Philip. 1988. "Notes on the Difficulty of Studying the State." *Journal of Historical Sociology* 1 (1): 58–89.

Abulhawa, Tarek, and Haifaa Abdulhalim. 2013. *Report on the IUCN Mission to Socotra Archipelago (Yemen)*. http://whc.unesco.org/en/documents/123001/.

Abulhawa, Tarek, Haifaa Abdulhalim, Elena Osipova, and Tricia Cummings. 2014. *TABE'A II Report: Enhancing Regional Capacities for World Heritage*. Amman: IUCN. doi:10.2305/IUCN/CH.2015.04.en.

Abulohoom, Ali. 2013. "Independent Socotra Governorate: Paving the Way for a Federal Yemen or a Hint at Separation?" *Yemen Times*,29 October. http://archive.li/xzQ5P.

Abu-Lughod, Lila. 2004. *Dramas of Nationhood: The Politics of Television in Egypt*. Chicago: University of Chicago Press.

———. 1991. "Writing against Culture." In *Recapturing Anthropology: Working in the Present*, edited by R. Fox, 137–162. Santa Fe, NM: School of American Research Press.

———. 1986. *Veiled Sentiments: Honor and Poetry in a Bedouin Society*. Berkeley: University of California Press.

Agamben, Georgio. 1998. *Homo Sacer: Sovereign Power and Bare Life*. Translated by D. Heller-Roazen. Stanford, CA: Stanford University Press.

Agrawal, Arun, and Clark C. Gibson. 1999. "Enchantment and Disenchantment: The Role of Community in Natural Resource Conservation." *World Development* 27 (4): 629–649.

Albuquerque, Alfonso de. 2010. *The Commentaries of the Great Afonso Dalboquerque*. Translated from the Portuguese edition of 1774 by Walter de Gray Birch, 4 vols. Cambridge: Cambridge University Press.

Almas, Ahmed A. M., and Miklas Scholz. 2006. "Agriculture and Water Resources Crisis in Yemen: Need for Sustainable Agriculture." *Journal of Sustainable Agriculture* 28 (3): 55–75.

Alpers, Edward A. 2009. *East Africa and the Indian Ocean*. Princeton, NJ: Markus Wiener.

Al-Anbali, Ahmad Said Khamis. 2006. *Tārīkh Jazīrat Suquṭrā*. Al-Ain, UAE: Matba'at al-sahaba.

———. 2001. *Suquṭrā, al-Ḥulal al-Sundusīya: Sharḥ qaṣīdat al-Zahrā' al-Suquṭrīya*. Cairo: Dar Umm al-Qura.

Anderson, Benedict. 1983. *Imagined Communities: Reflections on the Origin and Spread of Nationalism*. London: Verso.

Appadurai, Arjun. 1981. "The Past as a Scarce Resource." *Man* 16 (2): 201–219.

Ardener, Edwin. 1987. "'Remote Areas': Some Theoretical Considerations." In *Anthropology at Home*, edited by A. Jackson, 38–54. New York: Tavistock.

Attorre, Fabio, Fabio Francesconi, Nadim Taleb, Paul Scholte, Ahmed Saed, Maro Alfo, and Franco Bruno. 2007. "Will Dragonblood Survive the Next Period of Climate Change? Current and Future Potential Distribution of *Dracaena cinnabari* (Socotra, Yemen)." *Biological Conservation* 138:430–439.

Austin, Peter K., and Julia Sallabank, eds. 2011. *Cambridge Handbook of Endangered Languages*. Cambridge: Cambridge University Press.

Badran, Margot. 1998. "Unifying Women: Feminist Pasts and Presents in Yemen." *Gender & History* 10 (3): 498–518.

Balfour, Isaac Bayley. 1888. *Botany of Socotra*. Edinburgh: Robert Grant and Son.

———. 1881. "On the Island of Socotra." *Report of the Meeting of the British Association for the Advancement of Science* 51:482–494.

Barbosa, Duarte. 1970. *A Description of the Coasts of East Africa and Malabar in the Beginning of the Sixteenth Century by Duarte Barbosa*. Translated by H. E. J. Stanley. London: Hakluyt Society.

Barendse, R. J. 2009. *Arabian Seas 1700–1763*. Vol. 1, *The Western Indian Ocean in the Eighteenth Century*. Leiden, Netherlands: Brill.

El-Barghuthi, 'Omar Salih. 1924. "Rules of Hospitality." *Journal of the Palestine Oriental Society* 4:175–203.

Bayart, Jean-François. 1993. *The State in Africa: The Politics of the Belly*. New York: Longman.

Beckingham, C. F. 1983. "Some Notes on the History of Socotra." In *Arabian and Islamic Studies: Articles Presented to R. B. Serjeant on the Occasion of His Retirement from the Sir Thomas Adam's Chair of Arabic at the University of Cambridge*, edited by R. L. Bidwell and G. R. Smith, 172–181. New York: Longman.

———. 1951a. "Dutch Travellers in Arabia in the Seventeenth Century. Part I." *Journal of the Royal Asiatic Society of Great Britain and Ireland* 1/2 (April): 64–81.

———. 1951b. "Dutch Travellers in Arabia in the Seventeenth Century. Part II." *Journal of the Royal Asiatic Society of Great Britain and Ireland* 3/4 (October): 170–181.

———. 1949. "Some Early Travels in Arabia." *Journal of the Royal Asiatic Society of Great Britain and Ireland* 3/4 (October):155–176.

Bendix, Regina F., Aditya Eggert, and Arnika Peselmann, eds. 2012. *Heritage Regimes and the State*. Göttingen, Germany: Universitätsverlag Göttingen.

Bennett, Ernest. 1938. "The Isle of Bliss." *Living Age* 24 (August): 536–539.

———. 1897. "Two Months in Sokotra." *Longman's Magazine* 30 (179): 405–413.

Bennett, Jane. 2010. *Vibrant Matter: A Political Ecology of Things*. Durham, NC: Duke University Press.

Bent, J. Theodore. 1897. "The Island of Socotra." *Nineteenth Century* 244:975–992.

Biedermann, Zoltán. 2010. "An Island under the Influence: Soqotra at the Crossroads of Egypt, Persia and India from Antiquity to the Early Modern Ages." In *The Silk Route of the Seas: From the Persian Gulf to the China Seas*, edited by A. Schottenhammer and R. Kauz, 9–24. Wiesbaden, Germany: Harrassowitz Verlag.

———. 2006. *Soqotra: Geschichte einer christlichen Insel im Indischen Ozean vom Altertum bis zur frühen Neuzeit.* Wiesbaden, Germany: Harrassowitz Verlag.

Bonnefoy, Laurent. 2011. *Salafism in Yemen: Transnationalism and Religious Identity.* London: Hurst.

Borgerhoff Mulder, Monique, and Peter Coppolillo. 2005. *Conservation: Linking Ecology, Economics, and Culture.* Princeton, NJ: Princeton University Press.

Botting, Douglas. 1958a. *Island of the Dragon's Blood.* London: Hodder and Stoughton.

———. 1958b. "The Oxford University Expedition to Socotra." *Geographical Journal* 124 (2): 200–207.

———. 1957. "Socotra: Island of the Dragon's Blood." *Geographical Magazine* 30 (8): 183–193.

Boullata, Issa. 1990. *Trends and Issues in Contemporary Arab Thought.* Albany: State University of New York Press.

Bourdieu, Pierre. 1965. "The Sentiment of Honour in Kabyle Society." In *Honour and Shame: The Values of Mediterranean Society,* edited by J. G. Peristiany, 191–242. London: Weidenfeld and Nicolson.

Bowen, Richard LeBaron. 1951. "The Pearl Fisheries of the Persian Gulf." *Middle East Journal* 5 (2): 161–180.

Boxhall, Peter G. 1967. "Tribesmen of Socotra." *Geographical Magazine* 40 (7): 548–555.

Brásio, António. 1943. *Missões portuguesas de Socotorá.* Colecção Pelo Império, No. 93. Lisbon: República Portugeusa Ministério das Colónias.

Bristol-Rhys, Jane. 2010. *Emirati Women: Generations of Change.* New York: Columbia University Press.

Brockington, Dan, Rosaleen Duffy, and Jim Igoe. 2008. *Nature Unbound: Conservation, Capitalism and the Future of Protected Areas.* London: Earthscan.

Brosius, Peter, Anna Tsing, and Charles Zerner. 1998. "Representing Communities: Histories and Politics of Community-Based Natural Resource Management." *Society and Natural Resources* 11 (2): 157–168.

Brown, G. H. H. 1966. *Social and Economic Conditions and Possible Development in Socotra.* Mukalla, Aden: Federal Government.

Brown, Keith. 2008. "'All They Understand Is Force': Debating Culture in Operation Iraqi Freedom." *American Anthropologist* 110 (4): 443–453.

Brumann, Christoph. 1999. "Writing for Culture: Why a Successful Concept Should Not Be Discarded." *Current Anthropology* 40 (S1): 1–27.

Bsheer, Rosie. 2017. "Heritage as War." *International Journal of Middle East Studies* 49 (4): 729–734.

Bukharin, Mikhail D. 2012. "The Mediterranean World and Socotra." In *Foreign Sailors on Socotra: The Inscriptions and Drawing from the Cave Hoq,* edited by I. Strauch, 494–539. Berlin: Hempen Verlag.

Burdick, Alan. 2007. "The Wonder Land of Socotra, Yemen." *New York Times Style Magazine,* March 25. http://www.nytimes.com/2007/03/25/travel/tmagazine/03well.socotra.t.html.

Burke, Edmund, III. 2009a. "The Big Story: Human History, Energy Regimes, and the Environment." In *The Environment and World History,* edited by E. Burke III and K. Pomeranz, 33–53. Berkeley: University of California Press.

———. 2009b. "The Transformation of the Middle Eastern Environment, 1500 BCE–2000 CE." In *The Environment and World History,* edited by E. Burke III and K. Pomeranz, 81–117. Berkeley: University of California Press.

Büscher, Bram, Sian Sullivan, Katja Neves, Jim Igoe, and Dan Brockington. 2012. "Toward a Synthesized Critique of Neoliberal Conservation." *Capitalism, Nature, Socialism* 23 (2): 4–30.

Byrne, Denis, and Gro Birgit Ween. 2015. "Bridging Cultural and Natural Heritage." In *Global Heritage: A Reader,* edited by L. Meskell, 94–111. Malden, MA: Wiley Blackwell.

Carapico, Sheila. 1998. *Civil Society in Yemen: The Political Economy of Activism in Modern Arabia.* Cambridge: Cambridge University Press.

Carr, E. Summerson. 2010. "Enactments of Expertise." *Annual Review of Anthropology* 39:17–32.

Carter, Robert. 2005. "The History and Prehistory of Pearling in the Persian Gulf." *Journal of the Economic and Social History of the Orient* 48 (2): 139–209.

Casson, Lionel. 1989. *The Periplus Maris Erythraei: Text with Introduction, Translation, and Commentary.* Princeton, NJ: Princeton University Press.

Caton, Steven C. 2005. *Yemen Chronicle: An Anthropology of War and Mediation.* New York: Hill and Wang.

———. 1990. *"Peaks of Yemen I Summon": Poetry as Cultural Practice in a North Yemeni Tribe.* Berkeley: University of California Press.

Ceballos, Gerardo, Paul R. Ehrlich, and Rodolfo Dirzo. 2017. "Biological Annihilation via the Ongoing Sixth Mass Extinction Signaled by Vertebrate Population Losses and Declines." *Proceedings of the National Academy of Sciences of the United States of America* (PNAS) 114 (30): E6089–E6096.

Ceballos-Lascuráin, Héctor. 1999. *Ecotourism Development Plan for Socotra Archipelago, Yemen (Phase II). Final Report.* Mexico D.F.: Programme of International Consultancy on Ecotourism.

Černý, Viktor, Luísa Pereira, Martina Kujanová, Alžběta Vašíková, Martin Hájek, Miranda Morris, and Connie J. Mulligan. 2009. "Out of Arabia—the Settlement of Island Socotra as Revealed by Mitochondrial and Y Chromosome Genetic Diversity." *American Journal of Physical Anthropology* 138 (4): 439–447.

Challand, Benoît. 2013. "Citizenship against the Grain: Locating the Spirit of the Arab Uprisings in Times of Counterrevolution." *Constellations* 20 (2): 169–187.

Chatty, Dawn. 2014. "The Persistence of Bedouin Identity and Increasing Political Self-Representation in Lebanon and Syria." *Nomadic Peoples* 18 (2): 16–33.

———. 2009. "Rituals of Royalty and the Elaboration of Ceremony in Oman: View from the Edge." *International Journal of Middle East Studies* 41 (1): 39–58.

———. 2003. "Environmentalism in the Syrian Badia: The Assumptions of Degradation, Protection and Bedouin Misuse." In *Ethnographies of Conservation: Environmentalism and the Distribution of Privilege*, edited by D. G. Anderson and E. Berglund, 87–99. New York: Berghahn Books.

Cheung, Catherine and Lyndon DeVantier, with science editor Kay Van Damme. 2006. *Socotra: A Natural History of the Islands and Their People.* Hong Kong: Odyssey Books and Guides.

Christie, Sue, and Roderic Dutton. 2009. *Soqotra: Heritage and Future.* St. Ives, Cambridgeshire, UK: CLE Print.

Christie, Susan J. 2005. "Socotra's Road to Ruin." *Geographical* 77 (5): 60–64.

Cole, Donald. 2003. "Where Have All the Bedouin Gone?" *Anthropological Quarterly* 76 (2): 235–267.

Collins, John F. 2015. *Revolt of the Saints: Memory and Redemption in the Twilight of Brazilian Racial Democracy.* Durham, NC: Duke University Press.

Colton, Nora Ann. 2007. "Political and Economic Realities of Labour Migration in Yemen." In *Yemen into the Twenty-First Century: Continuity and Change*, edited by K. A. Mahdi, A. Würth, and H. Lackner, 53–96. Reading, UK: Ithaca Press.

Comaroff, Jean, and John L. Comaroff. 2005. "Naturing the Nation: Aliens, Apocalypse, and the Postcolonial State." In *Sovereign Bodies: Citizens, Migrants, and States in the Postcolonial World*, edited by T. Blom Hansen and F. Stepputat, 120–147. Princeton, NJ: Princeton University Press.

Cooke, Miriam. 2014. *Tribal Modern: Branding New Nations in the Arab Gulf.* Berkeley: University of California Press.

Coombe, Rosemary J. 2012. "Managing Cultural Heritage as Neoliberal Governmentality." In *Heritage Regimes and the State*, edited by R. F. Bendix, A. Eggert, and A. Peselmann, 375–388. Göttingen, Germany: Universitätsverlag Göttingen.

Coombe, Rosemary J., and Lindsay M. Weiss. 2015. "Neoliberalism, Heritage Regimes, and Cultural Rights." In *Global Heritage: A Reader*, edited by L. Meskell, 43–69. Malden, MA: Wiley Blackwell.

Cosmas. (1897) 2010. *The Christian Topography of Cosmas, an Egyptian Monk.* Edited by John W. McCrindle. Reprint, London: Hakluyt Society.

Crone, Patricia. 1987. *Meccan Trade and the Rise of Islam*. Princeton, NJ: Princeton University Press.

Culture Resource, European Cultural Foundation, and Boekmanstudies. 2010. *Cultural Policies in Algeria, Egypt, Jordan, Lebanon, Morocco, Palestine, Syria and Tunisia: An Introduction*. Amsterdam: Boekman Foundation.

Dabashi, Hamad. 2012. *The Arab Spring: The End of Postcolonialism*. London: Zed Books.

Das, Veena, and Deborah Poole, eds. 2004. *Anthropology in the Margins of the State*. Santa Fe, NM: School of American Research Press.

Davis, Diana K. 2011a. "Introduction: Imperialism, Orientalism, and the Environment in the Middle East." In *Environmental Imaginaries of the Middle East and North Africa*, edited by D. K. Davis and E. Burke III, 1–22. Athens: Ohio University Press.

———. 2011b. "Restoring Roman Nature: French Identity and North African Environmental History." In *Environmental Imaginaries of the Middle East and North Africa*, edited by D. K. Davis and E. Burke III, 60–86. Athens: Ohio University Press.

Davis, Mike. 2004. *Pirates, Bats and Dragons: A Science Adventure*. Santa Monica, CA: Perceval Press.

Day, Stephen W. 2012. *Regionalism and Rebellion in Yemen: A Troubled National Union*. Cambridge: Cambridge University Press.

De Cesari, Chiara. 2017. "Heritage between Resistance and Government in Palestine." *International Journal of Middle East Studies* 49 (4): 747–751.

———. 2010. "Creative Heritage: Palestinian Heritage NGOs and Defiant Arts of Government." *American Anthropologist* 112 (4): 625–637.

De Genova, Nicholas. 2005. *Working the Boundaries: Race, Space, and "Illegality" in Mexican Chicago*. Durham, NC: Duke University Press.

Derrida, Jacques. 2000. *Of Hospitality: Anne Dufourmantelle Invites Jacques Derrida to Respond*. Translated by R. Bowlby. Stanford, CA: Stanford University Press.

Descola, Philipe. 2013. *Beyond Nature and Culture*. Chicago: University of Chicago Press.

Dikeç, Mustafa, Nigel Clark, and Clive Barnett. 2009. "Extending Hospitality: Giving Space, Taking Time." *Paragraph* 32 (1): 1–14.

Diodorus of Sicily. 1939. *The Library of History of Diodorus of Sicily*. Vol. 3. Translated by C. H. Oldfather. Cambridge, MA: Harvard University Press.

Diprose, Rosalyn. 2009. "Women's Bodies: Giving Time for Hospitality." *Hypatia: A Journal of Feminist Philosophy* 24 (2): 142–163.

Dirks, Nicholas B. 1990. "History as a Sign of the Modern." *Public Culture* 2 (2): 25–32.

Doe, Brian. 1992. *Socotra: Island of Tranquility*. London: Immel.

Dostal, Walter. 1998. "Some Visions on the Political and Economic Situation in Soqotra in the 19th Century from Reports of the Austrian Marine Archive." In *Proceedings of the First International Symposium on Soqotra Island: Present and Future*, vol. 1, edited by H. J. Dumont, 265–269. New York: United Nations Publications.

———. 1989. "Mahra and Arabs in South Arabia: A Study in Inter-ethnical Relations." In *Arabian Studies in Honour of Mahmoud Ghul: Symposium at Yarmouk University December 8-11 1984*, edited by M. Ibrahim, 27–36. Wiesbaden, Germany: Harrasowitz Verlag.

Douglas, Mary. 1999. *Implicit Meanings: Selected Essays in Anthropology*. New York: Routledge.

Dresch, Paul. 2000. *A History of Modern Yemen*. Cambridge: Cambridge University Press.

Dresch, Paul, and Bernard Haykal. 1995. "Stereotypes and Political Styles: Islamists and Tribesfolk in Yemen." *International Journal of Middle East Studies* 27 (4): 405–431.

Ducker, John T. 2006. "The Eastern Aden Protectorate (EAP)." In *Without Glory in Arabia: The British Retreat from Aden*, edited by P. Hinchcliffe, J. T. Ducker, and M. Holt, 108–148. New York: I. B. Tauris.

Eickelman, Dale F. 1998. "Being Bedouin: Nomads and Tribes in the Arab Social Imagination." In *Changing Nomads in a Changing World*, edited by J. Ginat and A. Khazanov, 38–49. Portland, OR: Sussex Academic Press.

Elie, Serge D. 2014. "*Qāt* Consumption in Soqotra: Diaspora Formation and Cultural Conversion." *Northeast African Studies* 14 (1): 1–41.

———. 2007. "The Waning of a Pastoralist Community: An Ethnographic Exploration of Soqotra as a Transitional Social Formation." PhD diss., University of Sussex.

———. 2004. "Hadiboh: From Peripheral Village to Emerging City." *Chroniques yéménites* 12:53–80.

"Environmental Educational Programme Promoting Biodiversity Conservation on Socotra, Yemen." n.d. Darwin Initiative. Accessed 30 September 2017. http://www.darwininitiative.org.uk/project/14002/.

EPC (Environment Protection Council). 2000. *Socotra Archipelago Master Plan*. Project YEM/B7-3000/IB/97/0787, April. Commission of the European Communities–Republic of Yemen. Surrey, UK: W. S. Atkins International.

Exell, Karen. 2016. *Modernity and the Museum in the Arabian Peninsula*. New York: Routledge.

Exell, Karen, and Trinidad Rico, eds. 2014. *Cultural Heritage in the Arabian Peninsula: Debates, Discourses and Practices*. Burlington, VT: Ashgate.

———. 2013. "'There Is No Heritage in Qatar': Orientalism, Colonialism and Other Problematic Histories." *World Archaeology* 45 (4): 670–685.

"Ex-Yemen President Hires Out Socotra Isle to UAE for 99 Years." 2016. Press TV, 13 February. http://www.presstv.com/Detail/2016/02/13/450057/Yemen-Socotra-UAE-Abd-Rabbuh-Mansur-Hadi/.

Fabian, Johannes. 1983. *Time and the Other: How Anthropology Makes Its Object*. New York: Columbia University Press.

Fergany, Nader. 2007. "Structural Adjustment versus Human Development in Yemen." In *Yemen into the Twenty-First Century: Continuity and Change*, edited by K. A. Mahdi, A. Würth, and H. Lackner, 3–29. Reading, UK: Ithaca Press.

Ferguson, James. 2006. *Global Shadows: Africa in the Neoliberal World Order*. Durham, NC: Duke University Press.

Ferguson, James, and Akhil Gupta. 2002. "Spatializing States: Toward an Ethnography of Neoliberal Governmentality." *American Ethnologist* 29 (4): 981–1002.

Ferguson, R. Brian. 2013. "Full Spectrum: The Military Invasion of Anthropology." In *Virtual War and Magical Death: Technologies and Imaginaries of Terror and Killing*, edited by N. L. Whitehead and S. Finnström, 85–110. Durham, NC: Duke University Press.

Fernandez, James W., and Mary Taylor Huber. 2001. "Introduction: The Anthropology of Irony." In *Irony in Action: Anthropology, Practice, and the Moral Imagination*, edited by J. W. Fernandez and M. T. Huber, 1–37. Chicago: University of Chicago Press.

Fibiger, Thomas. 2011. "Global Display—Local Dismay. Debating 'Globalized Heritage' in Bahrain." *History and Anthropology* 22 (2): 187–202.

Foltz, Richard, Frederick Denny, and Azizan Baharuddin. 2003. *Islam and Ecology: A Bestowed Trust*. Cambridge, MA: Harvard University Press.

Forbes, Henry O., ed. 1903. *The Natural History of Sokotra and Abd-el-Kuri*. London: R. H. Porter.

Forbes-Watson, Alec. 1964. "A Step Backwards into Biblical Days." *East African Standard*, 24 July, 7, 11.

Foster, William, ed. 1921. *The English Factories in India 1655–1660: A Calendar of Documents in the India Office, British Museum and the Public Record Office*. Vol. 10. Oxford: Clarendon Press.

Foucault, Michel. 1991. "Governmentality." In *The Foucault Effect: Studies in Governmentality*, edited by G. Burchell, C. Gordon, and P. Miller, 87–104. Chicago: University of Chicago Press.

Fox, John W., Nada Mourtada-Sabbah, and Mohammed al-Mutawa. 2006. "Heritage Revivalism in Sharjah." In *Globalization and the Gulf*, edited by J. W. Fox, N. Mourtada-Sabbah, and M. al-Mutawa, 266–287. London: Routledge.

Fredengren, Christina. 2015. "Nature:Cultures: Heritage, Sustainability and Feminist Posthumanism." *Current Swedish Archaeology* 23:109–130.

Freedman, Paul. 2008. *Out of the East: Spices and the Medieval Imagination*. New Haven, CT: Yale University Press.

Fritz, Hermann M., and Emile A. Okal. 2008. "Socotra Island, Yemen: Field Survey of the 2004 Indian Ocean Tsunami." *Natural Hazards* 46 (1): 107–117.

Gardner, Frank. 1999. "Socotra Celebrates End of Drought," *BBC News*, 11 October. http://news
.bbc.co.uk/2/hi/middle_east/471772.stm.

Geddes, Charles L. 1964. "An Account of Socotra in the Early 17th Century." *University of Colorado
Studies in History* 3:70–77.

Geertz, Clifford. 1983. *Local Knowledge: Further Essays in Interpretive Anthropology*. New York:
Basic Books.

Gellner, Ernest. 1983. *Nations and Nationalisms*. Oxford: Blackwell.

Gluck, Diana. 2016. "Britain's 'Pantomime Horse' Sets the Pace: Mobility in the Trucial States,
1950–1970." Bachelor's thesis, New York University Abu Dhabi.

Grove, Richard H. 1995. *Green Imperialism: Colonial Expansion, Tropical Island Edens and the Origins of Environmentalism, 1600–1860*. Cambridge: Cambridge University Press.

Gupta, Akhil. 1995. "Blurred Boundaries: The Discourse of Corruption, the Culture of Politics, and
the Imagined State." *American Ethnologist* 22:375–402.

Gupta, Akhil, and Aradhana Sharma. 2006. "Globalization and Postcolonial States." *Current Anthropology* 47 (2): 277–307.

Gusterson, Hugh. 2010. "The Cultural Turn in the War on Terror." In *Anthropology and Global
Counterinsurgency*, edited by J. D. Kelly, B. Jauregui, S. T. Mitchell, and J. Walton, 279–295.
Chicago: University of Chicago Press.

Haines, Stafford Bettesworth. 1845. "Memoir of the South and East Coasts of Arabia, Part II." *Journal of the Royal Geographical Society of London* 15:104–160.

Halliday, Fred. 1990. *Revolution and Foreign Policy: The Case of South Yemen 1967–1987*. New York:
Cambridge University Press.

Al-Hamdani, al-Hasan ibn Ahmad. 1968. *Geographie der Arabischen Halbinsel*. Edited and translated by D. H. Müller. Amsterdam: Oriental Press.

Hames, Raymond. 2007. "The Ecologically Noble Savage Debate." *Annual Review of Anthropology*
36:177–190.

Haq, S. Nomanul 2007. "Islam." In *A Companion Guide to Environmental Philosophy*, edited by D.
Jamieson, 111–129. Malden, MA: Blackwell Publishers.

Haraway, Donna J. 2016. *Staying with the Trouble: Making Kin in the Chthulucene*. Durham, NC:
Duke University Press.

———. 2014. "Speculative Fabulations for Technoculture's Generations: Taking Care of Unexpected
Country." In *The Multispecies Salon*, edited by E. Kirksey, 242–261. Durham, NC: Duke University Press.

Harb Michel, Nazir N. 2013. " 'IrHal!': The Role of Language in the Arab Spring." Master's thesis,
Georgetown University.

Harrigan, Jane. 2014. *The Political Economy of Arab Food Sovereignty*. New York: Palgrave
Macmillan.

Harrison, Rodney. 2015. "Beyond 'Natural' and 'Cultural' Heritage: Toward an Ontological Politics
of Heritage in the Age of the Anthropocene." *Heritage and Society* 18 (1): 24–42.

———. 2013. *Heritage: Critical Approaches*. New York: Routledge.

Harvey, David C. 2001. "Heritage Pasts and Heritage Presents: Temporality, Meaning and the Scope
of Heritage Studies." *International Journal of Heritage Studies* 7 (4): 319–338.

Harvey, Penelope. 2005. "The Materiality of State-Effects: An Ethnography of a Road in the Peru-
vian Andes." In *State Formation: Anthropological Perspectives*, edited by C. Krohn-Hansen and
K. G. Nustad, 123–141. Ann Arbor, MI: Pluto Press.

Heatherington, Tracey. 2010. *Wild Sardinia: Indigeneity and the Global Dreamtimes of Environmentalism*. Seattle: University of Washington Press.

Heidegger, Martin. 1971. *Poetry, Language, Thought*. Translated by A. Hofstadter. New York:
Harper and Row.

Herzfeld, Michael. 2004. *The Body Impolitic: Artisans and Artifice in the Global Hierarchy of Value*.
Chicago: University of Chicago Press.

———. 2001. "Irony and Power: Toward a Politics of Mockery in Greece." In *Irony in Action: An-*

thropology, Practice, and the Moral Imagination, edited by J. W. Fernandez and M. T. Huber, 63–83. Chicago: University of Chicago Press.

———. 1997. *Cultural Intimacy: Social Poetics in the Nation-State.* New York: Routledge.

———. 1991. *A Place in History: Social and Monumental Time in a Cretan Town.* Princeton, NJ: Princeton University Press.

———. 1987. "'As in Your Own House': Hospitality, Ethnography, and the Stereotype of Mediterranean Society." In *Honor and Shame and the Unity of the Mediterranean*, edited by D. D. Gilmore, 75–89. Arlington, VA: American Anthropological Association.

Hightower, Victoria Penziner. 2013. "Pearling and Political Power in the Trucial States, 1850–1930: Debts, Taxes, and Politics." *Journal of Arabian Studies* 3 (2): 215–231.

Ho, Engseng. 2006. *The Graves of Tarim: Genealogy and Mobility across the Indian Ocean.* Berkeley: University of California Press.

Holes, Clive, and Said Salman Abu Athera. 2011. *The Nabati Poetry of the United Arab Emirates: Selected Poems, Annotated and Translated into English.* Reading, UK: Ithaca Press.

Holmes, Douglas R., and George E. Marcus. 2008. "Cultures of Expertise and the Management of Globalization: Toward the Refunctioning of Ethnography." In *Global Assemblages: Technology, Politics and Ethics as Anthropological Problems*, edited by A. Ong and S. Collier, 235–252. Malden, MA: Blackwell.

Holtorf, Cornelius, and Anders Högsberg. 2013. "Heritage Futures and the Future of Heritage." In *Counterpoint: Essays in Archaeology and Heritage Studies in Honour of Professor Kristian Kristiansen*, edited by S. Bergerbrant and S. Sabatini, 739–746. Oxford: Archaeopress.

Hroch, Miroslav. 1985. *Social Preconditions of National Revival in Europe: A Comparative Analysis of the Social Composition of Patriotic Groups among the Smaller European Nations.* Translated by B. Fowkes. Cambridge: Cambridge University Press.

HRW (Human Rights Watch). 2013. "'Between a Drone and Al-Qaeda': The Civilian Cost of US Targeted Killings in Yemen." October. https://www.hrw.org/sites/default/files/report_pdf/yemen1013web.pdf.

Al-Idrisi, Muhammad. 1990. *Kitāb nuzhat al-mushtāq fī ikhtirāq al-āfāq.* Vol. 1. Cairo: Maktabat al-thaqafa al-diniya.

Infield, Mark, and Ibrahim Sharaf Al Deen. 2003. *Conservation and Sustainable Use of Biodiversity of Socotra Archipelago, YEM/96/G32/B/1G/31 (Phase 1) and YEM/01/003/01/B (Continuation Phase): Report of the Terminal Evaluation Mission.* August. https://erc.undp.org/evaluation/documents/download/656.

Ingold, Tim. 2012. "Toward an Ecology of Materials." *Annual Review of Anthropology* 41:427–442.

Ingrams, Doreen, and Leila Ingrams, eds. 1993. *Records of Yemen 1798–1960.* Archive Editions, vols. 1–16. Chippenham, UK: Antony Rowe.

Ingrams, Harold. 1966. *Arabia and the Isles.* Vol. 1. London: Routledge.

Irwin, Robert, ed. 2002. *Night & Horses & the Desert: An Anthology of Classical Arabic Literature.* Woodstock, NY: Overlook Press.

Al-Iryani, Lamis, Alain de Janvry, and Elisabeth Sadoulet. 2015. "The Yemen Social Fund for Development: An Effective Community-Based Approach amid Political Instability." *International Peacekeeping* 22 (4): 321–333.

Ismael, Tareq, and Jacqueline Ismael. 1986. *The People's Democratic Republic of Yemen: Politics, Economics and Society.* Boulder, CO: Lynne Rienner.

IUCN, UNEP, and WWF. 1980. *World Conservation Strategy: Living Resource Conservation for Sustainable Development.* Gland, Switzerland: International Union for Conservation of Nature and Natural Resources.

Jones, Toby. 2010. *Desert Kingdom: How Oil and Water Forged Modern Saudi Arabia.* Cambridge, MA: Harvard University Press.

Jourdain, John. 1905. *The Journal of John Jourdain, 1608–1617: Describing His Experiences in Arabia, India, and the Malay Archipelago.* Edited by W. Foster. Cambridge, UK: Hakluyt Society.

Khalaf, Sulayman. 2002. "Globalization and Heritage Revival in the Gulf: An Anthropological Look at Dubai Heritage Village." *Journal of Social Affairs* 19 (75): 13–42.

———. 2000. "Poetics and Politics of Newly Invented Traditions in the Gulf: Camel Racing in the United Arab Emirates." *Ethnology* 39 (3): 243–261.

Khalidi, Lamya. 2017. "The Destruction of Yemen and Its Cultural Heritage." *International Journal of Middle East Studies* 49 (4): 735–738.

"Khalifa Foundation Sends Relief Plane to Socotra Island." *The National*, April 18, 2016. https://www .thenational.ae/uae/government/khalifa-fund-sends-relief-plane-to-socotra-island-1.136937

Kipling, Rudyard. (1902) 2015. *Just So Stories*. Reprint, London: MacMillan Children's Books.

Kirksey, Eben, Craig Schuetze, and Stefan Helmreich. 2014. "Introduction: Tactics of Multispecies Ethnography." In *The Multispecies Salon*, edited by E. Kirksey, 1–24. Durham, NC: Duke University Press.

Kirschenblatt-Gimblett, Barbara. 2006. "World Heritage and Cultural Economics." In *Museum Frictions: Public Cultures/Global Transformations*, edited by I. Karp, C. Kratz, L. Szwaja, and T. Ybarro-Frausto, 161–202. Durham, NC: Duke University Press.

Koopowitz, Harold, and Hilary Kaye. 1983. *Plant Extinction: A Global Crisis*. Washington, DC: Stone Wall Press.

Ladwig, Walter C., III 2008. "Supporting Allies in Counterinsurgency: Britain and the Dhofar Rebellion." *Small Wars & Insurgencies* 19 (1): 62–88.

Lamprakos, Michelle. 2015. *Building a World Heritage City: Sanaa, Yemen*. Burlington, VT: Ashgate.

Langham, Eric, and Darren Barker. 2014. "Spectacle and Participation: A New Heritage Model from the UAE." In *Cultural Heritage in the Arabian Peninsula: Debates, Discourses and Practices*, edited by K. Exell and T. Rico, 85–98. Burlington, VT: Ashgate.

Lawson, Fred, and Hasan M. al-Naboodah. 2008. "Heritage and Cultural Nationalism in the United Arab Emirates." In *Popular Culture and Political Identity in the Arab Gulf States*, edited by A. Alsharekh and R. Springborg, 15–29. London: Saqi.

Leerssen, Joep. 2006. "Nationalism and the Cultivation of Culture." *Nations and Nationalism* 12 (4): 559–578.

Li, Tania Murray. 2007. *The Will to Improve: Governmentality, Development, and the Practice of Politics*. Durham, NC: Duke University Press.

Liebhaber, Samuel. 2015. "Section 1, Article 3 of the Yemeni Constitution: A New Era for Language Diversity in Yemen?" Paper presented at the Middle East Studies Association annual meeting, Denver, Colorado, 11 November.

Limbert, Mandana. 2014. "Caste, Ethnicity, and the Politics of Arabness in Southern Arabia." *Comparative Studies of South Asia, Africa, and the Middle East* 34 (4): 590–598.

———. 2010. *In the Time of Oil: Piety, Memory and Social Life in an Omani Town*. Stanford, CA: Stanford University Press.

Litvin, Margaret. 2011. *Hamlet's Arab Journey: Shakespeare's Prince and Nasser's Ghost*. Princeton, NJ: Princeton University Press.

Low, Charles Rathbone. (1877) 1992. *History of the Indian Navy 1613–1863*. Vol. 2. London: Richard Bentley and Son.

Low, Setha M., and Sally Engle Merry. 2010. "Engaged Anthropology: Diversity and Dilemmas." *Current Anthropology* 51 (2): S203–S226.

Lucas, Gren, and Hugh Synge. 1978. *The IUCN Plant Red Data Book*. Morges, Switzerland: IUCN.

Mackintosh-Smith, Timothy. 2000. *Yemen: The Unknown Arabia*. New York: Overlook Press.

Macro, Eric. 1990. "The Austrians in South West Arabia, 1897–1900." *Proceedings of the Seminar for Arabian Studies* 20:101–109.

Mahmood, Saba. 2005. *Politics of Piety: The Islamic Revival and the Feminist Subject*. Princeton, NJ: Princeton University Press.

Marcus, George E. 2007. "Collaborative Imaginaries." *Taiwan Journal of Anthropology* 5 (1): 1–17.

Margariti, Roxani. 2013. "An Ocean of Islands: Islands, Insularity, and Historiography in the Indian

Ocean." In *The Sea: Thalassography and Historiography*, edited by P. Miller, 198–229. Ann Arbor: University of Michigan Press.

Al-Masʿudi. 1948. *Murūj al-dhahab wa maʿādin al-jawhar*. Vol. 2. Beirut: Dar al-maʿarifa.

Mawby, Spencer. 2005. *British Policy in Aden and the Protectorates, 1955–67: Last Outpost of a Middle Eastern Empire*. London: Routledge.

McNeely, Jeffrey A., J. Harrison, and P. Dingwall. 1994. *Protecting Nature: Regional Reviews of Protected Areas*. Gland, Switzerland: IUCN.

McNulty, Tracy. 2007. *The Hostess: Hospitality, Femininity, and the Expropriation of Identity*. Minneapolis: University of Minnesota Press.

Meneley, Anne. 1996. *Tournaments of Value: Sociability and Hierarchy in a Yemeni Town*. Toronto: University of Toronto Press.

Meskell, Lynn. 2012. *The Nature of Heritage: The New South Africa*. New York: Wiley-Blackwell.

———. 2002. "Negative Heritage and Past Mastering." *Anthropological Quarterly* 75 (3): 557–574.

Mies, Bruno A., and Friedrich E. Beyl. 1998. "The Vegetation Ecology of Soqotra." In *Proceedings of the First International Symposium on Soqotra Island: Present and Future*, vol. 1, edited by H. J. Dumont, 35–82. New York: United Nations Publications.

Miller, Anthony G., and M. Bazaraʿa. 1998. "The Conservation Status of the Flora of the Soqotran Archipelago." In *Proceedings of the First International Symposium on Soqotra Island: Present and Future*, vol. 1, edited by H. J. Dumont, 15–34. New York: United Nations Publications.

Miller, Anthony G., and Miranda Morris. 2004. *Ethnoflora of the Soqotra Archipelago*. Edinburgh: Royal Botanic Garden.

———. 1988. *Plants of Dhofar, the Southern Region of Oman: Traditional, Economic, and Medicinal Uses*. Muscat, Oman: Office of the Advisor for Conservation of the Environment, Diwan of the Royal Court, Sultanate of Oman.

Miller, Flagg. 2007. *The Moral Resonance of Arab Media: Audiocassette Poetry and Culture in Yemen*. Cambridge, MA: Harvard University Press.

———. 2002. "Metaphors of Commerce: Trans-valuing Tribalism in Yemeni Audiocassette Poetry." *International Journal of Middle East Studies* 34:29–57.

Mitchell, Timothy. 1999. "Society, Economy, and the State Effect." In *State/Culture: State Formation after the Cultural Turn*, edited by G. Steinmetz, 76–97. Ithaca, NY: Cornell University Press.

Molyneux, Maxine. 1995. "Women's Rights and Political Contingency: The Case of Yemen, 1990–1994." *Middle East Journal* 49 (3): 418–431.

———. 1982. *State Policies and the Position of Women Workers in the People's Democratic Republic of Yemen, 1967–77*. Geneva: International Labour Office.

Moore, Donald S. 1998. "Clear Waters and Muddied Histories: Environmental History and the Politics of Community in Zimbabwe's Eastern Highlands." *Journal of Southern African Studies* 24 (2): 377–403.

Morris, Miranda. 2013. "The Use of 'Veiled Language' in Soqotri Poetry." *Proceedings of the Seminar for Arabian Studies* 43:239–244.

———. 2011. "The Songs and Poems of Soqotra." *Wasafiri* 26 (2): 51–58.

———. 2005. "Soqotra: The Poem of Abduh and Hammudi by Ali Abdullah al-Rigdihi." In *Arabia Vitalis: Arabskii Vostok, islam, Drevniaia Araviia*, edited by A. V. Sedov and I. M. Smilianskaia, 354–370. Moscow: Institut stran Azii i Afriki pri MGU (Moskovskom gosudarstvennom universitete).

———. 2003. "The Soqotra Archipelago: Concepts of Good Health and Everyday Remedies or Illness." *Proceedings of the Seminar for Arabian Studies* 33:319–341.

———. 2002. *Manual of Traditional Land Use Practices in the Soqotra Archipelago*. Report for the UNDP/GEF Project YEM/96/G32. Edinburgh: Royal Botanic Garden.

Moser, Charles K. 1918. "The Isle of Frankincense." *National Geographic Magazine* 33:267–278.

Müller, Walter W. 2001. "Antike und mittelalterliche Quellen als Zeugnisse über Soqotra, eine einstmals christliche Insel." *Oriens Christianus: Hefte für die Kunde des christlichen Orients* 85:131–161.

al-Najdi, Ahmad b. Majid. 1971. *Arab Navigation in the Indian Ocean before the Coming of the Portuguese*. Translated by G. R. Tibbetts. London: Royal Asiatic Society of Great Britain and Ireland.

Nas, Peter J. M. 2002. "Masterpieces of Oral and Intangible Culture: Reflections on the UNESCO World Heritage List." *Current Anthropology* 43 (1): 139–148.

Naumkin, Vitaly. 1993. *Island of the Phoenix: An Ethnographic Study of the People of Socotra*. Reading, UK: Ithaca Press.

———. 1989. "Fieldwork in Socotra." *British Society for Middle Eastern Studies* 16 (2): 133–142.

Naumkin, Vitaly, and Leonid E. Kogan, eds. 2015. *Corpus of Soqotri Oral Literature*. Vol. 1. Leiden, Netherlands: Brill.

Navaro-Yashin, Yael. 2002. *Faces of the State: Secularism and Public Life in Turkey*. Princeton, NJ: Princeton University Press.

NCEA (Netherlands Commission for Environmental Assessment). 2009. *Advice on Terms of Reference for an SEA for a Road Master Plan, Socotra-Yemen*. 9 July. Utrecht, Netherlands: NCEA. http://api.commissiemer.nl/docs/os/i00/i0084/os25-084_advice_on_tor-_sea_road_master_plan _socotra_.pdf.

Noman, Laila. 1995. "Education of Girls in the Yemen." *British-Yemeni Society Journal*, November. http://al-bab.com/albab-orig/albab/bys/articles/noman95.htm.

Oates, John F. 1999. *Myth and Reality in the Rain Forest: How Conservation Strategies Are Failing in West Africa*. Berkeley: University of California Press.

Ong, Aihwa. 2006. *Neoliberalism as Exception: Mutations in Citizenship and Sovereignty*. Durham, NC: Duke University Press.

———. 2005. "Ecologies of Expertise: Assembling Flows, Managing Citizenship." In *Global Assemblages: Technology, Politics and Ethics as Anthropological Problems*, edited by A. Ong and S. Collier, 337–353. Malden, MA: Blackwell.

Orlove, Benjamin S., and Stephen B. Brush. 1996. "Anthropology and the Conservation of Biodiversity." *Annual Review of Anthropology* 25:329–352.

Özyürek, Esra. 2006. *Nostalgia for the Modern: State Secularism and Everyday Politics in Turkey*. Durham, NC: Duke University Press.

Pétursdóttir, Þóra. 2013. "Concrete Matters: Ruins of Modernity and the Things Called Heritage." *Journal of Social Archaeology* 13 (1): 31–53.

Peutz, Nathalie. 2017. "Heritage in (the) Ruins." *International Journal of Middle East Studies* 49 (4): 721–728.

———. 2013. "Targeted Women and Barred Development in Soqotra, Yemen." *Arabian Humanities: International Journal of Archaeology and Social Sciences in the Arabian Peninsula* 1. http:// cy.revues.org/1991.

———. 2012. "Revolution in Socotra: A Perspective from Yemen's Periphery." *Middle East Report* 263:14–20.

———. 2011. "Bedouin 'Abjection': World Heritage, Worldliness, and Worthiness at the Margins of Arabia." *American Ethnologist* 38 (2): 338–360.

———. 2008. "Reorienting Heritage: Poetic Exchanges between Suqutra and the Gulf." *Revue des mondes musulmans et de la Méditerranée* 121–122:163–182.

Phillips, Sarah. 2008. *Yemen's Democracy Experiment in Regional Perspective: Patronage and Pluralized Authoritarianism*. New York: Palgrave Macmillan.

Pietsch, Dana, and Miranda Morris. 2010. "Modern and Ancient Knowledge of Conserving Soils in Socotra Island, Yemen." In *Land Degradation and Desertification: Assessment, Mitigation and Remediation*, edited by P. Zdruli, M. Pagliai, S. Kapur, and A. Faz Cano, 375–386. New York: Springer Books.

Pitt-Rivers, Julian. 1968. "The Stranger, the Guest and the Hostile Host: Introduction to the Laws of Hospitality." In *Contributions to Mediterranean Sociology*, edited by J. G. Peristiany, 13–30. Paris: Mouton.

Polo, Marco. (1903) 1993. *The Travels of Marco Polo: The Complete Yule-Cordier Edition*. Vol. 2. Reprint, New York: Dover.

Popov, G. B. 1957. "The Vegetation of Socotra." *Journal of the Linnean Society of Botany* 55:706–720.
Prager, Laila. 2014. "Bedouinity on Stage: The Rise of the Bedouin Soap Opera "(Musalsal Badawi)" in Arab Television." *Nomadic Peoples* 18 (2): 53–77.
Purchas, Samuel. 1905. *Hakluytus Posthumus or Purchas His Pilgrimes. Contayning a History of the World in Sea Voyages and Land Travells by Englishmen and Others.* Vols. 2–4, 7. Glasgow: James MacLehose and Sons.
Ravenstein, Ernest Georg. 1876. "Sokotra." *Geographical Magazine* 3 (May): 119–124.
Al-Rawas, Isam Ali Ahmad. 1990. "Early Islamic Oman (ca. 622/280–893): A Political History." PhD diss., Durham University.
Redford, Kent. 1991. "The Ecologically Noble Savage." *Orion* 9:24–29.
Rist, Gilbert. 1996. *The History of Development: From Western Origins to Global Faith.* Translated by P. Camiller. New York: Zed Books.
Robinson, Phil. 1878. *Cyprus and Sokotra: 'The New Colony,' and 'The New Field for Missionary Enterprise'; Their Physical, Commercial, Economic, Historical, and Social Aspects.* London: William Clowes and Sons.
Roe, Sir Thomas. (1926) 1990. *The Embassy of Sir Thomas Roe to India 1615–19: As Narrated in His Journal and Correspondence.* Edited by W. Foster. Reprint, New Delhi: Munshiram Manoharlal.
La Rogue, Jean de. 1732. *A Voyage to Arabia Felix through the Eastern Ocean and the Streights of the Red-Sea, Being the First Made by the French in the Years 1708, 1709 and, 1710.* London: E. Symon.
Rose, Nikolas. 2006. "Governing 'Advanced' Liberal Democracies." In *The Anthropology of the State: A Reader*, edited by A. Sharma and A. Gupta, 144–162. Malden, MA: Blackwell.
Rosello, Mireille. 2001. *Postcolonial Hospitality: The Immigrant as Guest.* Stanford, CA: Stanford University Press.
RoY (Republic of Yemen). 2007. *Yemen Poverty Assessment Report 2007.* Vol. 1, *Main Report (November).* World Bank and the United Nations Development Program. http://www.ye.undp.org/content/yemen/en/home/library/poverty/yemen-poverty-assessment-report-2007.html.
———. 2006. *Socotra Archipelago: Proposal for Inclusion in the World Heritage List.* Prepared by Mario Caruso, January. https://whc.unesco.org/uploads/nominations/1263.pdf.
———. 2005. *National Biodiversity Strategy and Action Plan.* UNDP/GEF/IUCN YEM/96/G31. Sanaa: Ministry of Water and Environment, the Environment Protection Authority, January. https://www.cbd.int/doc/world/ye/ye-nbsap-01-en.pdf.
———. 2004. *Yemen First National Report to the Convention on Biodiversity.* Sanaa: Ministry of Water and Environment, the Environment Protection Authority, October. https://www.cbd.int/doc/world/ye/ye-nr-01-en.pdf.
———. 2000a. *Conservation Zoning Plan of Socotra Islands: Presidential Decree No. 275 of the Year 2000.* Prepared by the UNDP-GEF Soqotra Biodiversity Project YEM/96/G32. Sanaa: Environment Protection Council.
http://www.friendsofsoqotra.org/Bibliography/pdfs/Zoning%20plan%202000.pdf.
———. 2000b. *Socotra Archipelago Master Plan.* YEM/B7/3000/IB/97/0787. Financed by the Commission of the European Communities and prepared by W. S. Atkins International, April. Sanaa: Environment Protection Council.
Royle, Nicholas. 2003. *The Uncanny.* Manchester, UK: Manchester University Press.
Sachs, Wolfgang. 1993. "Global Ecology and the Shadow of Development." In *Global Ecology: A New Arena of Political Conflict*, edited by W. Sachs, 3–20. London: Zed Books.
Sahlins, Marshall. 1985. *Islands of History.* Chicago: University of Chicago Press.
Al-Salimi, Abdullah ibn Humayyid. 1931. *Tuḥfat al-a'yān bi-sīrat ahl 'Umān.* Vol 1. Cairo: Matba'at al-shabab.
Salvatore, Armando. 1995. "The Rational Authentication of *Turāth* in Contemporary Arab Thought: Muḥammad al-Jābirī and Ḥasan Ḥanafī." *Muslim World* 85 (3/4): 191–214.
Sawyer, Suzana, and Arun Agrawal. 2000. "Environmental Orientalisms." *Cultural Critique* 45 (Spring): 71–108.

Schmitt, Carl. (1922) 1985. *Political Theology: Four Chapters on the Concept of Sovereignty*. Translated by G. Schwab. Reprint, Chicago: University of Chicago Press.

Schmitt, Thomas M. 2008. "The UNESCO Concept of Safeguarding Intangible Cultural Heritage: Its Background and *Marrakchi* Roots." *International Journal of Heritage Studies* 14 (2): 95–111.

Schmitz, Charles. 2014. "Yemen's National Dialogue." Middle East Institute Policy Paper 2014-1, February. http://www.mei.edu/content/yemens-national-dialogue.

Scholte, Paul, and Peter De Geest. 2010. "The Climate of Socotra Island (Yemen): A First-Time Assessment of the Timing of the Monsoon Wind Reversal and Its Influence on Precipitation and Vegetation Patterns." *Journal of Arid Environments* 30:1–9.

Schweinfurth, George. 1884. *Ein Besuch auf Socotra mit der Riebeck'schen Expedition. Vortrag in der Zweiten Offtenlichen Sitzung der 56. Versammlung Deutscher Naturforscher und Aertze zu Freiburg I.B. 1883*. Freiburg: C. A. Wagner.

Scott, James. 1998. *Seeing like a State: How Certain Schemes to Improve the Human Condition Have Failed*. New Haven, CT: Yale University Press.

Serjeant, Robert B. 1992. "The Coastal Population of Socotra." In *Socotra: Island of Tranquility*, edited by B. Doe, 133–180. London: Immel.

———. 1974. *The Portuguese off the South Arabian Coast: Ḥaḍramī Chronicles*. Beirut: Librairie du Liban.

Shadie, Peter, and Minna Epps, eds. 2008. *Securing Protected Areas in the Face of Global Change: Key Lessons Learned from Case Studies and Field Learning Sites in Protected Areas*. Bangkok: IUCN Asia Regional Office.

Sharp, Jeremy M. 2018. *Yemen: Civil War and Regional Intervention*. Congressional Research Service Report R43960, April 12. https://fas.org/sgp/crs/mideast/R43960.pdf.

Shelat, Bharati. 2012. "The Gujarati Stone Inscriptions from Rās Ḥowlef (Socotra)." In *Foreign Sailors on Socotra: The Inscriptions and Drawing from the Cave Hoq*, edited by I. Strauch, 407–432. Berlin: Hempen Verlag.

Al-Shizabi, Fahd Saleem Kafayan. 2006. *Mukhtārāt min al-ādab al-suquṭrī*. Sanaa: Socotra Conservation Fund.

Shryock, Andrew. 2009. "Hospitality Lessons: Learning the Shared Language of Derrida and the Balga Bedouin." *Paragraph* 32 (1): 32–50.

———. 2004. "The New Jordanian Hospitality: House, Host and Guest in the Culture of Public Display." *Comparative Studies in Society and History* 46 (1): 35–62.

Shryock, Andrew, and Sally Howell. 2001. " 'Ever a Guest in Our House': The Emir Abdullah, Shaykh Majid al-Adwan, and the Practice of Jordanian House Politics, as Remembered by Umm Sultan, the Widow of Majid." *International Journal of Middle East Studies* 33 (2): 247–269.

Simeone-Senelle, Marie-Claude. 2004. "Soqotra Dialectology and the Evaluation of the Language Endangerment." In *The Developing Strategy of Soqotra Archipelago and the Other Yemeni Islands" 14–16 December 2003*, 1–13. Aden, Yemen: University of Aden. https://halshs.archives-ouvertes.fr/halshs-00338711.

Al-Sirafi, Abu Zayd. 2014. "Accounts of China and India." In *Two Arabic Travel Books*, edited and translated by T. Mackintosh-Smith, 22–161. New York: New York University Press.

Smith, G. Rex. 1985. "Ibn al-Mujāwir on Dhofar and Socotra." *Proceedings of the Seminar for Arabian Studies* 15:79–92.

Smith, Laurajane. 2006. *Uses of Heritage*. New York: Routledge.

Stein, Lothar. 1986. "Feldforshung auf Sokotra." *Mitteilungen aus dem Museum für Völkerkunde zu Leipzig* 51:2–7.

Stein, Lothar, and Heidi Stein. 1999. "Die Bewohner der Insel Sokotra." In *Sokotra: Mensch und Natur*, edited by W. Wranik, 195–226. Wiesbaden, Germany: Dr. Ludwig Reichert Verlag.

Steinmetz, George. 1999. "Introduction: Culture and the State." In *State/Culture: State Formation after the Cultural Turn*, edited by G. Steinmetz, 1–50. Ithaca, NY: Cornell University Press.

Stetevych, Suzanne. 1993. *The Mute Immortals Speak: Pre-Islamic Poetry and the Poetics of Ritual*. Ithaca, NY: Cornell University Press.

Strauch, Ingo. 2012a. "The Discoveries in the Cave Hoq: A Short Evaluation of Their Historical Meaning." In *Foreign Sailors on Socotra: The Inscriptions and Drawing from the Cave Hoq*, edited by I. Strauch, 540–544. Berlin: Hempen Verlag.

———. 2012b. "India and Socotra." In *Foreign Sailors on Socotra: The Inscriptions and Drawing from the Cave Hoq*, edited by I. Strauch, 254–406. Berlin: Hempen Verlag.

Sutherland, William J. 2003. "Parallel Extinction Risk and Global Distribution of Languages and Species." *Nature* 423 (May): 276–279.

Takriti, Abdel Razzaq. 2013. *Monsoon Revolution: Republicans, Sultans, and Empires in Oman, 1965–1976*. Oxford: Oxford University Press.

Taminian, Lucine. 2000. "Playing with Words: The Ethnography of Poetic Genres in Yemen." PhD diss., University of Michigan.

Taussig, Michael. 2004. *My Cocaine Museum*. Chicago: University of Chicago Press.

———. 1992. *The Nervous System*. New York: Routledge.

Taylor, Lawrence J. 2001. "'Paddy's Pig': Irony and Self-Irony in Irish Culture." In *Irony in Action: Anthropology, Practice, and the Moral Imagination*, edited by J. W. Fernandez and M. T. Huber, 172–187. Chicago: University of Chicago Press.

Tilley, Helen. 2011. *Africa as a Living Laboratory: Empire, Development, and the Problem of Scientific Knowledge, 1870–1950*. Chicago: University of Chicago Press.

Titchen, Sarah M. 1996. "On the Construction of 'Outstanding Universal Value': Some Comments on the Implementation of the 1972 UNESCO World Heritage Convention." *Conservation and Management of Archaeological Sites* 1 (4): 235–242.

Tizini, Tayyib. 1978. *Min al-turāth ilā al-thawra: Ḥawl naẓariyya muqtaraḥa fi qaḍiyyat al-turāth al-ʿarabī*. Beirut: Dar Ibn Khaldun.

Toman, Jiří. 1996. *The Protection of Cultural Property in the Event of Armed Conflict*. Brookfield, VT: Dartmouth.

Tomkinson, Michael. 1967. "Teach Yourself Socotran." *Punch*, 30 August, 318–321.

Tsing, Anna Lowenhaupt. 2005. *Friction: An Ethnography of Global Connection*. Princeton, NJ: Princeton University Press.

———. 1993. *In the Realm of the Diamond Queen: Marginality in an Out-of-the-Way Place*. Princeton, NJ: Princeton University Press.

Ubaydli, Ahmad. 1989. "The Population of Sūquṭrā in the Early Arabic Sources." *Proceedings of the Seminar for Arabian Studies* 19:137–154.

Ucodep y Movimondo. 2005. *Rural Tourism and Sustainable Development: Notes*. Project Promoting Small and Micro Rural Enterprise through Pro-Poor Ecotourism Policies in Developing Countries.http://www.ibrarian.net/navon/paper/RURALTOURISM_AND_SUSTAINABLE_DEVELOPMENT_NOTES.pdf?paperid=10202114.

UN (United Nations). 1992. *Convention on Biological Diversity*. Treaty Series No. 30619. Rio de Janeiro. https://www.cbd.int/doc/legal/cbd-en.pdf.

"UNDP Defers Programmes for Yemen, Bahrain and Syria." 2011. UNDP, 30 April. http://www.undp.org/content/undp/en/home/presscenter/articles/2011/04/30/undp-defers-upcoming-five-year-programme-for-syria.html.

UNDP-GEF (United Nations Development Programme–Global Environment Facility). 2008. *Strengthening Socotra's Policy and Regulatory Framework for Mainstreaming Biodiversity*. Project Document. Atlas Award #00049646. https://info.undp.org/docs/pdc/Documents/YEM/socotra%20project%20document%20Yemen.pdf.

———. 2003. *Sustainable Development and Biodiversity Conservation for the People of Socotra Islands, Yemen*. Project Document. YEM/03/004/A/01/99. Unpublished manuscript in author's possession.

———. 2001. *Conservation and Sustainable Use of the Biodiversity of Socotra Archipelago (Continuation Phase)*. Project Document. YEM/01/003/01/B. Unpublished manuscript in author's possession.

REFERENCES 331

———. 1997. *Conservation and Sustainable Use of the Biodiversity of Socotra Archipelago*. Project Document. YEM/96/G32/B/1G/31. Unpublished manuscript in author's possession.

UNEP (United Nations Environment Programme). 2005. *After the Tsunami: Rapid Environmental Assessment*. Nairobi: UNEP Division of Communication and Public Information.

UNEP-GEF (United Nations Environment Programme–Global Environment Facility). 2013. *Support to the Integrated Program for the Conservation and Sustainable Development of the Socotra Archipelago*. Project Document. Full-Size Project #5347. https://www.thegef.org/sites/default/files/documents/12-01-14_Project_Document_PAD.pdf.

UNEP-WCMC (United Nations Environment Programme and World Conservation Monitoring Centre). 2008. "Socotra Archipelago, Yemen." UNESCO Fact Sheet. World Heritage Sites–Protected Areas and World Heritage. Unpublished document in author's possession.

UNESCO (United Nations Educational, Scientific and Cultural Organization). 2017. "Cultural Heritage Must Be Saved from New '21st Century Wars.'" http://www.unesco.org/new/en/media-services/in-focus-articles/cultural-heritage-must-be-saved-from-new-21st-century-wars/.

———. 1972. *Convention Concerning the Protection of the World Cultural and Natural Heritage*. Paris, 16 November. http://whc.unesco.org/archive/convention-en.pdf.

———. 1954. *Convention for the Protection of Cultural Property in the Event of Armed Conflict with Regulations for the Execution of the Convention*. http://portal.unesco.org/en/ev.php-URL_ID=13637&URL_DO=DO_TOPIC&URL_SECTION=201.html.

Urban, Mark C. 2015. "Accelerating Extinction Risk from Climate Change." *Science* 348 (6234): 571–573.

Van Damme, Kay, and Lisa Banfield. 2011. "Past and Present Human Impacts on the Biodiversity of Socotra Island (Yemen): Implications for Future Conservation." *Zoology in the Middle East* 3:31–88.

Van Damme, Kay, and Peter De Geest. 2006. "Case Study 2: Diksam Road and Eriosh's Unique Archaeology and Biology." In *Socotra: A Natural History of the Islands and Their People*, edited by C. Cheung and L. DeVantier, 350. Hong Kong: Odyssey Books and Guides.

Van Dooren, Thom. 2016. *Flight Ways: Life and Loss at the Edge of Extinction*. New York: Columbia University Press.

Van Rampelbergh, Maïté, Dominik Fleitmann, Sophie Verheyden, Hai Cheng, Lawrence Edwards, Peter De Geest, David De Vleeschouwer, Stephen J. Burns, Albert Matter, Philippe Claeys, and Eddy Keppens. 2013. "Mid- to Late Holocene Indian Ocean Monsoon Variability Recorded in Four Speleothems from Socotra Island, Yemen." *Quaternary Science Reviews* 65: 129–142.

Varisco, Daniel Martin. 2003. "Indigenous Knowledge and Traditional Yemeni Irrigation." In *Indigenous Knowledge and Sustainable Agriculture in Yemen*, edited by A. al-Hakimi and F. Pelat, 115–120. Sanaa: Centre Français d'Archéologie et de Sciences Sociales de Sanaa.

———. 1995. "Indigenous Plant Protection Methods in Yemen." *GeoJournal* 37 (1): 27–38.

Vora, Neha. 2013. *Impossible Citizens: Dubai's Indian Diaspora*. Durham, NC: Duke University Press.

Wakefield, Sarina. 2014. "Heritage, Cosmopolitanism and Identity in Abu Dhabi." In *Cultural Heritage in the Arabian Peninsula: Debates, Discourses and Practices*, edited by K. Exell and T. Rico, 99–115. Burlington, VT: Ashgate.

Walley, Christine J. 2004. *Rough Waters: Nature and Development in an East African Marine Park*. Princeton, NJ: Princeton University Press.

Ward, Christopher. 2015. *The Water Crisis in Yemen: Managing Extreme Water Scarcity in the Middle East*. London: I. B. Tauris.

Wardeh, Nadia. 2008. "The Problematic of *Turāth* in Contemporary Arab Thought: A Study of Adonis and Ḥasan Ḥanafī." PhD diss., McGill University.

WECD (World Commission on Environment and Development). 1988. *Our Common Future*. Introduction by Gro Harlem Brundtland. London: Fontana Books.

Wedeen, Lisa. 2008. *Peripheral Visions: Publics, Power, and Performance in Yemen*. Chicago: University of Chicago Press.

———. 2003. "Seeing like a Citizen, Acting like a State: Exemplary Events in Unified Yemen." *Comparative Studies in Society and History* 45 (4): 680–713.

Wells, Michael, Katrina Brandon, and Lee Hannah. 1992. *People and Parks: Linking Protected Area Management with Local Communities*. Washington, DC: International Bank for Reconstruction and Development/World Bank.

Wellsted, James Raymond. 1840. *Travels to the City of the Caliphs, along the Shores of the Persian Gulf and the Mediterranean*. Vol. 2. London: Henry Colburn.

———. 1837. "Travels in Arabia." *Journal of the Royal Geographic Society of London* 7:400–403.

———. 1835. "Memoir on the Island of Socotra." *Journal of the Royal Geographical Society of London* 5:129–229.

West, Paige. 2006. *Conservation Is Our Government Now: The Politics of Ecology in Papua New Guinea*. Durham, NC: Duke University Press.

West, Paige, James Igoe, and Dan Brockington. 2006. "Parks and Peoples: The Social Impacts of Protected Areas." *Annual Review of Anthropology* 35:251–277.

WFP (World Food Program). 2014. *Yemen: Comprehensive Food Security Survey [CFSS], November 2014*. Sanaa: World Food Program. https://www.wfp.org/content/yemen-comprehensive-food-security-survey-november-2014.

Whitaker, Brian. 2005. "Thirty-Six Die in Riots after Yemen Fuel Price Hikes," *The Guardian*, 23 July. https://www.theguardian.com/world/2005/jul/23/yemen.brianwhitaker.

Wilkinson, John C. 1987. *The Imamate Tradition of Oman*. Cambridge: Cambridge University Press.

———. 1981. "Oman and East Africa: New Light on Early Kilwan History from the Omani Sources." *International Journal of African Historical Studies* 14 (2): 272–305.

World Bank. 2000. *The Republic of Yemen: Comprehensive Development Review—Environment. Middle East and North Africa Region: Rural Development, Water, and Environment Department*. 21 January. https://openknowledge.worldbank.org/bitstream/handle/10986/15277/multiopage.pdf?sequence=1&isAllowed=y.

Wranik, Wolfgang. 1998. "Faunistic Notes on Soqotra Island." In *Proceedings of the First International Symposium on Soqotra Island: Present and Future*, vol. 1, edited by H. J. Dumont, 135–198. New York: United Nations Publications.

Wright, Robin. 2011. *Rock the Casbah: Rage and Rebellion across the Islamic World*. New York: Simon and Schuster.

Xavier, St. Francis. 1921. *The Life and Letters of St. Francis Xavier*. 2 vols. Edited by H. J. Coleridge. London: Burns, Oates and Washbourne.

Yaqut. 1906. *Mu'jam al-buldān*. Vol. 5. Cairo: Matba'at al-sa'ada.

"Yemen Fuel Subsidy Cuts Hit Poor Hardest." 2014. *IRIN News*, 25 August. http://www.irinnews.org/analysis/2014/08/25/yemen-fuel-subsidy-cuts-hit-poor-hardest.

"Yemen: People Struggling with Drought on Socotra island." 2007. *IRIN News*, 25 September. http://www.irinnews.org/news/2007/09/25/people-struggling-drought-socotra-island.

Zandri, Eduardo. 2006. "Case Study 1: Hadiboh-Qalansiyah Road and Ditwah Lagoon." In *Socotra: A Natural History of the Islands and Their People*, edited by C. Cheung and L. DeVantier, 348–349. Hong Kong: Odyssey Books and Guides.

———. 2003. *Saving Socotra: The Treasure Island of Yemen*. Rome: Darwin S.C. a. r.l.

Zhukov, Valery A. 2014. *Rezul'taty issledovanii pamiatnikov kamennogo veka ostrova Sokotra (Yemen) v 2008–2012*. Moscow: Triada.

Zimmerer, Karl S. 2006. "Geographical Perspectives on Globalization and Environmental Issues: The Inner-Connections of Conservation, Agriculture, and Livelihoods." In *Globalization & New Geographies of Conservation*, edited by K. Zimmerer, 1–43. Chicago: University of Chicago Press.

Al-Zirikli, Khayr al-Din. 1989. *Al-A'lām*. Vol. 3. Beirut: Dar al-'ilm li-l-malayin.

INDEX

Abdullah, Sultan, 67, 75–76

Abdullah Isa bin 'Afrar, 263

Abu Dhabi: flights to Soqotra, 284; Soqotran migrants, ix, 206, 209. See also United Arab Emirates

Abu Dhabi Authority for Culture and Heritage (ADACH), 254–55, 257

Abu Dhabi Tourism and Culture Authority (from 2017, Department of Culture and Tourism), 254

Abu Shanab: in counterinsurgency unit, 219, 221; death, 233; emigration, 218; "The Foundation Stone," 199, 218, 221–25; poetry exchanged with Di-min-Sirihan, 225–27

ADACH, see Abu Dhabi Authority for Culture and Heritage

Aden: flights to Soqotra, 49; migrants to Soqotra, 52; migrant workers in, 52; schools, 245; USS Cole bombing, 19

Aden Protectorate: administrators, 67, 77–78, 85, 120–22; British withdrawal, 112, 123, 125–26; as Crown Colony, 121; establishment, 14, 77; food shipments, 82–83; opposition to British rule, 77; policies toward Soqotra, 14, 112–13, 120–23, 124–28; political officers, 79, 80, 82, 83, 84–85, 122, 202–3; relations with sultans, 67, 78, 80–81, 85, 86–87; road construction, 84–85; soldiers sent to Soqotra, 79; trade embargo, 77–78, 81

'Afrar family, 12, 14, 66, 78, 288–89, 296–97n6, 298n37, 304n53, 305–6n89. See also Sultanate of Qishn and Socotra

Afro-Soqotrans: coastal communities, 13; marginalization of cultural heritage, 250, 251–53, 259, 283; musicians, 251–52; participation in Haybak executions, 223–24;

political involvement, 264; slaves, 74; on social change, 47–48; tensions with other Soqotrans, 223, 225, 234; witchcraft beliefs, 250

Agriculture: commercial, 179; crops, 179; foreign development proposals, 121, 122–23, 127; gardens, 89, 122–23, 175, 176–86; irrigation, 174, 175; migrant labor, 45–47, 179, 204; potential in Soqotra, 120; under socialist government, 89, 129; training, 179–84. See also Date palms; Food

Ahmad, Sulayman Sa'd, 270

Air Felix, 49

Airlines, see Airport; Yemenia Airlines

Air Ministry Works Directorate (AMWD), Britain, 79, 81, 84–85

Airport, 12, 48–49, 95–96, 103, 147, 284, 296n35. See also Royal Air Force

Ajman: ancestral links to Soqotra, 205; maritime trade, 68, 203, 205; Soqotran migrants, 50, 71, 200, 218, 227, 230, 234

Alexander the Great, 114

Algerian cultural heritage, 6, 9

Ali, Sultan, 67, 78

Aloes: exports, 67, 116, 120, 303n34; foreign interest in, 12, 114, 115, 116, 121, 304n61; harvesting, 32

Amazigh (Berber) language, 9

American Institute for Yemeni Studies, 242, 246

Amery, Julian, 126, 306n93, 306n96

Amery, Leopold, 121–22

AMWD, see Air Ministry Works Directorate

Al-Anbali, Ahmad Said Khamis, 70, 76, 210–12, 213–16, 312n48

Anderson, Benedict, 160

Anthropology: fictive kin relationships, 18, 19, 20–21; heritage study and, 5–6; para-eth-

funding, 171, 172; local employees, 26, 28, 58; location, 169, 171–72; management, 18, 172; meals served, 26, 58, 104, 105, 172

Cannibalism stories, 55–56, 296n37

Capitalism, conservation and, 156–57, 161, 196–97

CBD, see Convention on Biological Diversity

CBNRM, see Community-based natural resource management

Ceballos-Lascuráin, Hector, 134

Cell phones, 32, 49–50

Challand, Benoît, 264

Chatty, Dawn, 160

Christians in Soqotra: Abyssinians, 213, 214; Catholic missionaries, 115, 117, 303n24; conversions, 302n15; foreign rulers and, 13; Greek colonists, 12, 113–14, 117, 213–14, 302n19; Nestorians, 12, 312n57; origins, 213–14; Portuguese, 13–14, 115, 213, 214, 296n36, 296–97n6, 302–3n20, 303nn24–25; protection by Arab rulers, 312n38; rebellion, 210–15; scholarly interest in, 117, 213, 215; "St. Thomas," 12, 115, 302–3n20

Civil society organizations (CSOs), 89–90, 135, 170. See also Association for the Conservation and Development of Homhil; Soqotra Society for Heritage and History

Climate: droughts, 73, 82, 102–3, 116, 173, 229, 301n133; monsoon season, 12, 33–34, 46, 63, 65, 72, 184, 295n25; rainfall, 173–74, 291n2 (Intro); seasons, 46–47, 295n25; storms and floods, 33–34, 73, 103, 150, 188

Communities: in Homhil, 185; imagined, 160–61; outside perceptions, 191

Community-Based Livestock Development and Marketing Project, 195

Community-based natural resource management (CBNRM) program: assumptions, 159–60; critiques, 160–61; in future, 285; in Homhil, 156, 168, 170–71, 172

Conservation: economic development links, 110–11, 156–57, 158–59, 160; history, 157–60; Islamic principles, 139, 140, 146–47, 285; traditional practices, 110, 111–12. See also Environmental management; Integrated conservation and development projects; Natural resources

Conservation International, 15

Conservation Zoning Plan of Socotra Islands: contents, 133, 141, 167; criticism of, 133; effects, 136; failure, 133–34, 141, 193–94, 284; local awareness and involvement, 133, 145, 146; violations, 96, 171

Convention on Biological Diversity (CBD), 159

Cosmas Indicopleustes, 113–14

Crime, 217

Critical heritage studies, 5–6, 200–201

Cronk, Quentin, 307n108

CSOs, see Civil society organizations

Cultural heritage: Afro-Soqotran, 250, 251–53, 259, 283; Arab-Islamic, 6–7, 213, 215–16, 234; dance groups, 252; European, 275–76, 277; external threats, 249, 270, 276; focus on, 4–5, 201–2, 274–75; foreign funding, 284; of Gulf states, 254; international treaties, 292n16; inventories, 248–49, 276–77, 283; library, 216, 312n65; mawlid celebrations, 38, 247 (fig.), 250; music, 251–52; natural heritage and, 201, 282, 285; performances for tourists, 252; preservation efforts and identity, 200, 215, 240, 241, 253, 277, 282–83; as scarce resource, 247, 249; unorthodox beliefs excluded, 51, 249–53, 282–83. See also Heritage; Soqotra Society for Heritage and History; Soqotri language; World Heritage Sites

Cultural nationalism, 275–76, 277, 284

Cyclones, 73, 150

Dabashi, Hamid, 264

Darwin Initiative, 255

Date palms: as food source, 67, 72, 73; as imports, 68, 82; plantations, 30, 31, 42, 174, 179, 183, 218; trees cut for road construction, 84–85

De Cesari, Chiara, 10

Declaration of the Human Environment, 158

Derrida, Jacques, 41, 294n6, 301–2n139

Dhofar Liberation Front, 87

Dhofar Rebellion, 218–19, 230, 312–13n67

Diaspora, see Soqotran diaspora

Di-Girigoti, Muhammad Amr, 153, 194, 268

Di-Kishin, 55, 226. See also Kishin tribe

Diksam, 40, 55, 97, 98, 105

Di-min-Sirihan, 224–27, 234

Diodorus Siculus, 302n12

Djibouti: Markazi refugee camp, 281; US Marine Corps base, 20

Soqotra, 13, 51–53, 271; from Soqotra to
Yemen, 32, 45–47, 206
Miller, Anthony G., 242, 243
Million's Poet, 254–55, 257, 258, 259
Ministry of Agriculture, 178, 180, 184
Ministry of Education, 148, 255–56
Ministry of Fish Wealth, 274
Ministry of Health, 242
Ministry of Water and Environment, 131, 141,
307n119, 315n8
Monsoon season, 12, 33–34, 46, 63, 65, 72,
184, 295n25
Moroccan cultural heritage, 6, 8, 9
Morris, Miranda, 72, 103, 170, 188, 230, 231,
242, 243, 312n65
Moser, Charles, 119, 304n57
Mosques, ix, 30, 49, 72, 95–96, 209, 295n29.
See also Islam
Mouri: Royal Air Force base, 80, 84; Salimin
School for Nomadic Bedouin, 90
Al-Mukalla: Bedouin Boys School, 85, 297n22;
British in, 77–78, 121–22, 124, 127, 204;
courts, 168, 190; schools, 72
Museum, see Soqotra Folk Museum
Music, drummers, 38, 51, 247 (fig.), 251–52

Nabati poetry, 255
National Biodiversity Strategy and Action Plan
(NBSAP), 131
National Dialogue Conference (NDC), 9, 272,
273–74, 283, 314n37
National Environmental Action Plan (NEAP),
131
Nationalism: Arab, 6; cultural, 275–76, 277,
284; European, 275; heritage and, 2;
Yemeni, 259
National Liberation Front (NLF): Haybak
executions (1974), 93, 199, 217–18, 219–
25, 262; insurgency, 87, 205; in Soqotra,
87–88, 204, 218–19, 270–71
Natural heritage: cultural heritage and, 201,
282, 285; World Heritage Sites, 4, 132,
292n18, 307n123
Natural resources: centralized management,
130; common ownership, 173–74; community-based management programs, 156,
159–61, 168, 170–71, 172; degradation,
112–13, 128; exploitation efforts, 118, 120,
121, 304–5n63; exports, 67, 113, 114, 115,
209, 284, 311n22; oil, 85–86, 123–24, 126,
204, 305–6n89; sustainable management,
129, 130, 131, 143, 158–59, 284–85. See

also Biological diversity; Environmental
management; Fisheries; Plants
Nature sanctuaries, 31, 133, 141, 156, 171. See
also Protected areas
Naumkin, Vitaly, 56, 306–7n107
NBSAP, see National Biodiversity Strategy and
Action Plan
NDC, see National Dialogue Conference
NEAP, see National Environmental Action Plan
NGOs, see Nongovernmental organizations
NLF, see National Liberation Front
Nongovernmental organizations (NGOs): in
Homhil, 165–67, 194; local, 134–35, 239;
local employees, 186–88, 189–90, 310n62;
vegetable gardens project, 177–86; water
projects, 174
North Africa, see Middle East and North
Africa
Northern Yemenis, 13, 20, 51–53, 56–58, 168,
295n33
Nostalgia: cultural, 277; of emigrants, 200;
global spread, 294n11; poetry expressing,
66, 221, 258, 259–60; for socialist era, 48,
88, 92, 101–2, 104; for social relations, 29,
42–45, 47–48, 55, 200; for sultanate, 66,
221, 259–60

Officials, see Government officials
Oil industry, 85–86, 123–24, 126, 204,
305–6n89
Oman: cultural heritage, 8–9; Dhofar
Liberation Front, 87; Dhofar Rebellion,
205, 218–19, 230, 312n67; heritage indus-
try, 231; historical control of Soqotra,
12, 13, 312–13n38; Ibadi imams, 13,
210, 312n38, 312n41, 312n57; Soqotran
migrants, 37, 200, 202, 205, 218–19,
230–31; trade, 68
Opening period (al-infitah), 12, 29, 48–49,
93–105, 118
Operation Decisive Storm, 280
Operation Gunboat, 86
Operation Snaffle, 87, 300n88
Operation Waffle, 300n88
Orientalism, 111, 118, 201

Palestinian cultural heritage, 10
Pan American Oil Company, 85–86, 126, 128
Para-ethnographers, 313n4
Para-experts, 238–47, 259, 274
PCL, see Petroleum Concessions Ltd